COMPUTING IN PSYCHOLOGY

An Introduction to Programming Methods and Concepts

James H. Reynolds

Colgate University

PRENTICE-HALL, INC. ENGLEWOOD CLIFFS, NEW JERSEY 07632

Library of Congress Cataloging-in-Publication Data

Reynolds, James H.
   Computing in psychology.

   Bibliography: p. 343
   Includes index.
   1. Psychology—Data processing.   2. Programming
(Electronic computers)   I. Title.
BF39.5.R49   1987   150'.28'5526   86-593
ISBN 0-13-165812-3

Editorial/production supervision and
   interior design: Debbie Ford
Cover design: Lundgren Graphics, Ltd.
Manufacturing buyer: Barbara Kittle

ISBN 0-13-165812-3 01

Prentice-Hall International (UK) Limited, *London*
Prentice-Hall of Australia Pty. Limited, *Sydney*
Prentice-Hall Canada Inc., *Toronto*
Prentice-Hall Hispanoamericana, S.A., *Mexico*
Prentice-Hall of India Private Limited, *New Delhi*
Prentice-Hall of Japan, Inc., *Tokyo*
Prentice-Hall of Southeast Asia Pte. Ltd., *Singapore*
Editora Prentice-Hall do Brasil, Ltda., *Rio de Janeiro*

Dedicated to
Shirl
and Jim, Jeff, and Leslie

Contents

Part IV: Computer Modeling Using LISP

viii   Contents

Preface

Anyone familiar with the field of psychology is well aware of the recent and substantial growth of computer usage in virtually every arena of the psychological domain, including the construction of computer models of numerous psychological processes, the use of the computer in real-time control of laboratory experiments, its use in clinical and educational assessment, as well as its use as a tool for statistical analysis. Most students who go beyond the introductory level of psychology now become familiar with the latter usage when they take courses in statistics and research design. They are much less likely, however, to study or develop programming skills in the other important types of computer usage. The aim of this text is to introduce to upper-level undergraduate and beginning graduate students in psychology the computing skills and concepts that will allow them to understand and write these several kinds of advanced computer programs. It assumes the student has already completed one semester of computer programming using Pascal, BASIC, or FORTRAN at either the high school or college level. Its emphasis is upon the development and use of intermediate programming skills using the Pascal language, and upon providing an introduction to the LISP language, which has become so important in modeling human psychological functions.

The text is divided into four major parts. Part I (Chapters 1 and 2) provides a perspective of the ways in which psychology and computing interact, how the advent of computing and information-processing has influenced psychological theory and methodology, and also reviews the basic principles of structured programming. Since Chapters 2 through 8 use the Pascal language, students whose prior programming experience has been with BASIC or FORTRAN should also read Appendix A while working through Part I. This appendix shows programmers who are unfamiliar with Pascal the similarities between Pascal and other languages. It then introduces the unique features of Pascal that will be needed when reading Parts I, II, and III of this text. Appendix A may also be useful for students who have studied Pascal but wish to review it before going on to Part II of the text. (The appendix is *not* intended, however, to be used as a substitute for a beginning course in computing; it is a review for those already familiar with basic programming concepts and skills, and students with no previous programming experience should first study one of the many introductory texts in Pascal before attempting to use this book.)

Part II presents, both by descriptions and through examples, the basic principles and objectives of computer modeling of psychological processes. It distinguishes between a computer model, which is viewed as a formal theoretical statement, and computer simulation, which in this text is taken to be that aspect of a computer program which applies the theoretical model to some behavioral situation. The limitations of computer modeling, as well as its benefits, are presented in detail over the several chapters in this part.

The chapters in Part II present, in turn, a basic model of a perceptual process, a simple model of memory, and one of the first computer models of a personality process. All programs in this part are written in Pascal. The emphasis, as in all of the chapters in the text, is upon programming; but each chapter begins with a summary description of the psychological background for the model, giving a quick review of psychological terms, definitions, and experimental findings related to the topic. Following this psychological introduction, the typical chapter will present various segments of a program that models the theory or process reviewed, introducing programming methods and explanations of concepts as needed.

Since the main intent is the development of skills and concepts for students whose previous programming experience has been only at the introductory level, all of the programs presented are introductory to intermediate in difficulty, and no attempt is made to present program analyses or listings of any of the advanced models that are found in the current research literature. Students wishing to learn more about either advanced computer modeling or the general topic being covered will find additional information in materials recommended in the Suggested Readings section at the end of each chapter. After reading each chapter the student should then write the program(s) described, including additional elaborations or variations as suggested in the exercises found at the end of the chapter.

Part III consists of two chapters that introduce the reader to other ways that psychologists make use of computers; particularly microcomputers. The programming language used for illustration in each of these chapters is Pascal. Chapter 7 describes the various ways that clinical, social/ personality, and educational psychologists make use of computers to score various types of personality or other tests and questionaires, to draw test profiles, and conduct automated interviews. Chapter 8 then describes elementary programming techniques used in real-time control of laboratory experiments. Each of these topics can, of course, quickly become very technical. The intent of the chapters is not to introduce all of the technicalities needed for writing professional programs in these areas, but rather to inform the reader about the possibilities of such usages, about some of the problems that are inevitably encountered, and also to provide some basic programming examples that will get the student started. Advanced texts and articles are then recommended for those who wish to pursue these fascinating and useful topics further.

Part IV, consisting of Chapters 9 through 13, introduces the programming language LISP and shows how it can be used to model various components of such higher mental processes as concept formation, language analysis, and problem solving. A working knowledge of LISP has become increasingly important to psychologists because, as anyone who has had any contact with computer models in cognitive psychology or artificial intelligence knows, most of the sophisticated models involving higher mental processes and the use of natural language are programmed in LISP. The intent of this last part of the text is to introduce the psychology student to this important language in an illustrative and non-technical way that shows both its similarities and its differences relative to the language or languages most students learn first. The limited introduction given here will not make anyone an expert, but if the examples are studied and the exercises completed, the reader will be in a good position to understand existing models written in LISP and also to continue building his or her LISP programming competency independently.

The book can be used in any of several ways depending upon the intent of the course and the programming sophistication of the readers. Students who are already good programmers and have some background in psychology can easily complete the text in one semester. For psychology students whose programming skills are not yet strong, the first three to four weeks of a semester can be used to review a good text that is simply intended to teach Pascal, and then use the Pascal chapters 1 through 8 of this text to provide an introduction to psychological uses of computers. Finally, for those interested primarily or only in psychological theory and computer modeling, Chapters 1 through 6 followed by Chapters 9 through 13 will give a comprehensive introduction.

I want to express thanks to a number of people for their help and guidance in the construction of this text. Students in several of the courses I have given on this topic have used various chapters in manuscript form, and have offered many helpful reviews and suggestions. The entire manuscript and most of the programs were written, tested, and printed on the computing facilities at the Colgate Computer Center, and I give sincere thanks to the Center's staff—and particularly Jeanne Kellogg—for their help, advice, and patience. Finally, thanks are due to a number of anonymous reviewers and to my production editor, Debbie Ford, for her cooperation and constructive comments.

James H. Reynolds

1

Interactions Between Psychology and Computer Science: An Overview

Computer science has had a major influence upon the older discipline of psychology in two significant contexts—its *theory* and its scientific *methodology*. The impact upon psychological theory is apparent in the phrase *information-processing psychology,* which can be found nowadays in virtually any psychological text and which, indeed, is considered by many psychologists to be synonymous with *cognitive psychology,* the term given to the most influential type of current psychological theorizing. The second influence, upon methods, relates to the substantial and seemingly ever-increasing use of the computer by psychologists as a tool for such psychological chores as data handling, test scoring, statistical analysis, interviewing, and running or controlling experiments in the psychology laboratory.

This text examines in some detail both of these impacts. In the first two chapters we will review both the historical development of the interaction between computing and psychology and also the general principles of structured programming with Pascal.* Beginning with Chapter 3, the general strategy will be first to describe a given psychology topic or problem, then analyze it from an information-processing viewpoint and write one or

---

*If you wish to review the details of the Pascal language that are necessary for understanding the Pascal problems presented in this text, see Appendix A.

more computer programs that enhance, clarify, or solve the questions asked. Our purposes are twofold: (1) to give the reader insight into the types of aids and enrichments that computing is bringing to psychologists, and (2) to develop your programming skills to the point where you can write and understand programs and program types that are meaningful and important to the discipline of psychology.

We begin by taking a brief look at the historical development of the interaction between computing and psychological theorizing.

THE THEORETICAL INFLUENCE

Theoretical Trends in Psychology: A Brief History

Like most other disciplines, and particularly scientific disciplines, psychology has experienced a number of major theoretical changes as it has grown and developed. Until the late nineteenth century there was really not a separate discipline that could be formally called "psychology" in its modern, scientific sense. Several other disciplines had worried about the topic, of course—physiology, medicine, philosophy, for example. But around 1879 the first psychological laboratory designed strictly for the investigation of psychological functions was established by Wilhelm Wundt at the University at Leipzig, Germany. Most psychologists consider this date to mark the beginning of an independent discipline devoted specifically to the scientific study of the mind and behavior of humans and other animals.

Since 1879, the field of psychology has entertained a variety of viewpoints about how best to conceptualize human behavior and mental processes, some of which have lasted while others have not. One major viewpoint, familiar to most educated people, has been Freud's psychoanalytic orientation. He proposed that we can look upon and understand behavior as being driven by basic motives which act as energies that continually build in strength and must be released in the form of behavior. Freud's theory attempts to describe in detail these energies, how they are controlled and directed, and their behavioral consequences. This viewpoint is, of course, a long-standing one that maintains a powerful influence on psychology today.

Although it is not our purpose to explore Freudian theory in detail, it is important to analyze briefly some of the terminology of the preceding paragraph in order to clarify certain rather complex concepts that will be needed later. First, one should distinguish between "viewpoint," as used above, and "theory." Freud's *theory* consists of a detailed set of constructs and a set of postulates stating how these constructs interact with each other to determine the way a person will behave at any given moment. But more about that in a minute. For now, simply contrast the details of such a theory with Freud's *pretheoretical view* of looking at a person generally as an energy (he called it "psychic energy") system. The philosopher of science Thomas Kuhn (1970) has referred to these pretheoretical viewpoints upon which theories eventually get built as *paradigms*. Thus using the terms of modern philosophy of science, we can say that the Freudian paradigm (viewing humans as a psychic energy system whose actions depend upon how basic energies are controlled and directed) is one influential paradigm in psychology today and it has been the basis for a number of particular theories, including those of Freud, Jung, and others.

Having gotten a feel for what paradigm means, look for a moment at the term *theory*. Different theories can vary dramatically from each other, of course; but when one must evaluate or compare them there are a few major features that appear quite generally among nearly all of them, and these commonalities can serve as focal points for analyzing and comparing theories. Probably the two most common components (mentioned above) are *constructs* and *postulates*. A construct identifies an assumed structure that the theorist uses to help explain the phenomenon in question. Most often the construct is an abstraction—that is, it is not a real or physical "thing" that can be pointed at, or felt or touched, but rather is a hypothetical construction proposed by the theorist as having explanatory importance. Freud's constructs of ego, id, and superego are good examples. He did not pretend that they were physical entities; instead, he defined them as hypothetical psychic systems, each of which has certain assumed properties and characteristics.

Sometimes constructs that have no physical identity at one time become identifiable at a later time. For example, the electron was first proposed as an explanatory construct, and only later was the technology developed that permitted physicists to identify electrons physically. But physical verification is not a necessity for a construct to be of value; "quarks" in physics, "voter appeal" in political science, and "beauty" in the arts all help us to understand some very complex phenomena, regardless of whether they may become physically identifiable at some future time. As we shall see, many of the constructs proposed by psychological theorists are of a type that will never be identified as physical entities; nevertheless, they can have powerful explanatory capabilities.

The other major component common to nearly all psychological theories, and of interest to us at the moment, is the *postulate*. A postulate is a kind of working assumption, often given without proof, which presents a description or a proposal (usually verbal) about some aspect of the theory. Postulates may refer to a number of different components of a theory. They might state how the proposed constructs interact with each other, or what the properties and processes of a construct are, or what is assumed to be the effect of nature upon a system, and so on. For example, Freud postulated that the id stores the energy of the psychic system, and that the ego and superego control and direct how the energy is used in overt behavior.

This brief discussion of paradigms and theories is, of course, grossly incomplete. The terms reviewed are themselves controversial and refer to only a small part of what philosophers of science have to say about the nature of theories and theory building. But they will suffice for the moment as an aid in putting into perspective three other paradigms that are of particular interest to us—*behaviorism, neo-behaviorism,* and *information-processing.*

In the early 1900s a group of psychologists became disenchanted with contemporary attempts to propose and validate constructs describing the structure and content of the mind. Led by the American psychologist John B. Watson, these theorists claimed that, because "mind" is itself a construct and thus not knowable as a physical entity, it is not possible to describe and explore it scientifically.

They advocated that the discipline of psychology should ignore mentalism and concentrate only upon the study of those phenomena and events that are observable, measurable, and capable of being examined empirically. For psychology, such aspects are limited to (1) the surrounding environment present at the time an organism does something (that is, the *stimulus*), and (2) how the organism behaves in, or as a consequence of, that environment (that is, the *response*). This paradigm, which became known as *behaviorism* or stimulus-response (S-R) psychology, arrived at a time when many American psychologists were looking for something new and it quickly caught on and became a dominant psychological viewpoint. In essence, behaviorism insisted that there should be no mentalistic constructs proposing how the "mind" might be structured or what its processes might be. It has at times been referred to as a "black box" paradigm, signifying the attitude that we can never come to know the workings of that mysterious box referred to as mind.

In place of mentalistic constructs, behaviorism simply postulated *conditioning* as the theory explaining how and why people behave in the ways they do. The principles of conditioning were assumed to be part of the laws of nature. These principles are known by every student who has finished an introductory psychology course and they need not be reviewed here. But it is worthwhile simply to point out that the behavioristic paradigm did indeed propose a strong and concise theory, and for a number of years it produced significant research that has led to our understanding of basic learning processes in both humans and lower animals.

Despite remarkable early gains made by advocates of the strictly antimentalistic behaviorist paradigm, many psychologists eventually became concerned with the limitations of a paradigm that permits no theoretical constructs. Although they still agreed with the basic behavioristic doctrine that the only psychological phenomena ultimately available for scientific study are physically observable stimuli and responses, these pyschologists proposed that inferences could be made in a scientific manner about possible unobservable events or states presumed to intervene between the observable stimulus and response. This emerging *neo-behavioristic* paradigm thus permitted the reinstatement of certain hypothetical constructs as explanations of behavior, provided they were defined in such a way that they could ultimately be measured in terms of stimulus-response relationships. The arguments and justifications for this emergent paradigm were complex and took place over a number of years from the early 1940s onward—often amidst a great deal of emotion and perhaps a bit of illogic—among well-meaning theorists who wanted to preserve their scientific orientation while expanding their spheres of operation beyond the limits of strictly empirical (that is, observable) data. So the black box was opened, albeit a tiny bit, to permit certain formally defined constructs—such as intelligence, drive level, habit strength, and a few selected others—into scientific psychology.

Historically, neo-behaviorism has been a very powerful and important paradigm, and it remains so today. However, although it permitted a liberalization of the use of hypothetical constructs as explanatory theoretical mechanisms, it retained another major component of the older "pure" behaviorism out of which it grew. That component was a pretheoretical assumption that the behavior of the living animal organism can always be traced back to mechanistic processes determined by natural laws; for example, classical and instrumental conditioning. Taken to its logical conclusion, this assumption predicates that the human is a *passive system* that does not act in any way to determine its next response but instead responds as a mechanism conditioned to behave in certain ways in the presence of certain stimulus situations. Experimental psychologists adhering to the neo-behavioristic paradigm had difficulty justifying, and proving experimentally, that such complex behaviors as reasoning, problem solving, and the use of language are explainable strictly within the rules of conditioning. Thus the stage gradually was set for a willingness among pyschologists to shift to a paradigm other than behaviorism; namely one that would allow for explanations of complex psychological functions yet still ensure a continuation of a scientific, experimental approach to the study of psychological phenomena.

The Shift to the Information-Processing Paradigm

A. Multiple pressures lead to a shift.   The theoretical orientations of many experimental psychologists changed over the decade of the 1960s from a predominantly behavioristic paradigm to the *information-processing* paradigm. The impetus for the shift came from several sources. One, of course, was the general and increasing disenchantment with behaviorism described above. However, theoretical views tend to remain, despite their inappropriateness or inadequacy or incompleteness, until better or more fruitful directions come along. Other sources pushing toward a change in the direction of information-processing included research in verbal learning, linguistics, human engineering, and information theory. Results obtained in all of these research areas pointed away from the passive-mechanistic view of human behavior toward the more realistic proposal that human beings—and indeed lower animal organisms as well—*actively reorganize* or *process* the stimuli impinging upon them from the outside world, and that their responses are based upon this active processing rather than, or in addition to, their history of prior conditioning.

Each of these influences has its own detailed history, which, because of the specificity of our main topic, need not be reviewed here. More pertinent for us is the fact that this theoretical unrest with behaviorism was occurring at about the same time that the development of the modern digital computer and the corresponding development of the discipline of computer science were taking place. While these latter events cannot be considered the sole basis for the resulting change in theoretical psychology, they certainly played a major role in provoking a shift away from behaviorism to a new paradigm. The basic assumption of that new paradigm is that humans are not passive mechanisms who make conditioned responses to stimuli. Rather, they are symbol-manipulating systems that can receive information and actively process and reorganize it, and use that information as a basis for their behavior.

What really was at the core of the problem and what was the proposed solution? Consider for a moment the (relatively) simple behavior of picking up a fork when one sits down at the dinner table. The strict behaviorist would explain this behavior solely in terms of conditioning; for example, the organism has been conditioned to respond to the stimuli present (the plate, table, fork-on-table, internal sensations of hunger, and so forth) with movements that result in grasping the fork in a certain way. This learned response, argues the behaviorist, results from a past history in which conditioning processes reinforced grasping the fork and extinguished alternative (incorrect or undesirable) responses. The result of this history is that the organism's present response is now highly predictable and automatic; furthermore, it is explainable in terms of the natural laws of conditioning. Thus, there is no reason to invoke mentalistic processes to account for the behavior.

Conversely, the information-processing view would include in the account of this simple behavior the proposal that the fork and plate are symbols that evoke in the organism the retrieval of memories that include such information as what these objects are called, their purpose, and the conditions under which they are used. Further, according to this theoretical viewpoint, these symbolic activities may in turn lead to an active search to determine if all of the latter conditions have been met, and perhaps to a decision by the organism (based upon the information processed) to pick up the fork. Clearly major differences exist between these two theoretical explanations, even when they attempt to describe such a simple behavior as lifting a fork. Explanations of more complex behaviors provoke even wider explanatory differences.

B. The subtle influence of the Turing machine.   Some of the important seeds for the change to the information-processing view were planted back in 1936 by the British mathematician Alan Turing. He was interested in trying to find an effective procedure that would solve logical problems automatically. As a solution, Turing defined an abstract device that has since become known familiarly as the "Turing machine." This apparatus could perform only a few basic operations, yet in theory it was able to solve a wide range of mathematical and logical problems. Of interest to us is the fact that Turing's argument for the machine begins with an analysis of how a human "computes," or solves, a problem; and it ends with a definition of a machine that, given a very limited set of processes, will replicate the human solution.

The following quote by Turing contains his analysis of how a person "computes." (Note that when Turing uses the word "computer" in the following he means the *person* doing the computing. Turing also uses the word "tape" to stand for the paper from which the person reads—or to which the person writes—symbols related to the problem. It is assumed that this tape is divided into squares. Figure 1–1 provides a simple illustration of the system, in which the "computer" represents a Turing machine, be it a person or what we currently think of as a computer.)

> The behaviour of the computer at any moment is determined by the symbols which he is observing, and his "state of mind" at that moment. We may suppose that there is a bound B to the number of symbols or squares which the computer can observe at one moment. If he wishes to observe more, he must use successive observations. We will suppose that the number of states of mind which need be taken into account is finite. . . .
> Let us imagine the number of operations performed by the computer to be split up into "simple operations" that are so elementary that it is not easy to imagine them further divided. Every such operation consists of some change

FIGURE 1–1. A Turing Machine, consisting of a "computer" and its tape. The tape may contain symbols in each square. The "computer" can read or write symbols via its tapehead.

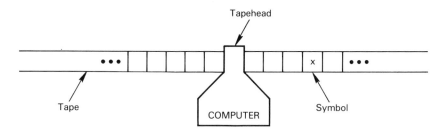

of the physical system consisting of the computer and his tape. We know the state of the system if we know the sequence of symbols on the tape, which of these are observed by the computer (possibly with a special order), and the state of mind of the computer. . . .

After clarifying certain details in this statement, Turing listed the "simple operations" that he proposed were necessary and sufficient to compute most problems:

The simple operations must therefore include:
(a) Changes of the symbol on one of the observed squares.
(b) Changes of one of the squares observed to another square within L squares of the previously observed squares.
It may be that some of these changes necessarily involve a change of state of mind. The most general single operation must therefore be taken to be one of the following:
(A) A possible change (a) of symbol together with a possible change of state of mind.
(B) A possible change (b) of observed squares, together with a possible change of state of mind.
(Turing, 1936, section 9; taken from Minsky, 1967, pp. 109–110.)

Turing went on to conclude that a machine which could read a symbol, write a symbol and attend to a given new symbol as a result of observing the previous symbol would be able to solve most solvable problems. Although the simplicity of this conclusion seems suspect, it has been reached independently by other theorists and, even after more than 40 years of testing, has not been refuted. One product of its implications has been the development of the digital computer—which is, in essence, a Turing machine.

The theoretical import of the mathematical, logical, and computing developments that took place from the time of Turing's theory up to the 1950's was that symbols, and the processing of symbols, changed from being viewed as mentalistic abstractions to being recognized as tangible objects and events that could be observed, measured, and studied scientifically. By the late 1950's, scientists from several disciplines— psychology, computer science, linguistics, biology—were becoming comfortable with the view that strictly mechanistic symbol-manipulating machines could exhibit complex intelligent behaviors comparable to those previously shown only by human beings. Interest within the broader arena of scientific psychology mounted as these early representatives of the new view showed increasingly impressive results obtained from adopting this orientation: results demonstrable in the form of computer programs that could learn, solve problems, form concepts, recognize and respond intelligently to objects in the real world, and to a considerable degree handle natural language. Operations and behaviors previously considered "mentalistic," and therefore not addressable from the standpoint of the scientific method, were being investigated and manipulated in a scientifically acceptable manner.

It is neither possible nor desirable to name a specific date when this developing orientation acquired sufficient momentum and support to be considered a new paradigm within psychology. Some of the influential landmarks were computer simulations of psychological phenomena, which we shall study in some detail later. A major impact was the formal theory presented in 1972 by Newell and Simon, which is based upon the assumption that the mind can be construed and defined as a symbol-manipulating system. Significant contributions by the psychologists Miller, Galanter, and Pribram (1960), Neisser (1967), and Lachman, Lachman, and Butterfield (1979) were milestones in defining the new pretheoretical view, which, by considering the human as an active manipulator and processor of information, has allowed psychology to return to examination of mental processes while maintaining—perhaps even enhancing—its scientific credibility.

C. Newell and Simon's IPS: An example.   Thus far our discussion of the information-processing paradigm has been general and historical, and it is now time to become more specific. How might the concept of a human information-processing system be characterized, and what might be its components? We shall see in future chapters that there are at present several potentially valid answers to this question, no one of which is accepted in all of its details by all information-processing psychologists. Even so, the several existent versions are substantially similar, so that it is possible to single out one as an example without doing an injustice to theorists who propose alternatives. We use here as a prototype example Newell and Simon's theoretical system, which they call, quite simply, the *Information-Processing System* (IPS). Figure 1–2 illustrates the structure of IPS. Note that, in contrast with a "black box" approach to psychological phenomena, IPS assumes a *processor* and a *memory* as mental constructs, which interact with the outside world via the body's receptors and effectors—the sensory-motor system of the organism.

To complete their formal statement of IPS, Newell and Simon present the set of definitions and postulates shown in Table 1–1. These statements describe the proposed contents and components of the processor and the memory, and they introduce certain other terms that are critical to the theoretical system; for example, "symbol," "symbol structure," "program," and "elementary information processes" (eip's). In their book, Newell and Simon describe and illustrate the system in considerable detail, and they then apply it to such complex problem-solving situations as solving cryptarithmetic puzzles and playing chess. They show that a

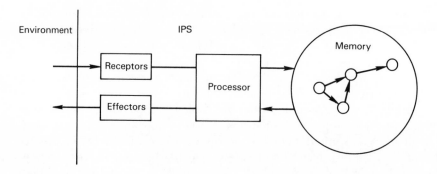

FIGURE 1–2. The general structure of Newell and Simon's Information-Processing System (IPS). *(A. Newell and H.A. Simon, Human Problem Solving, 1972, p. 20. Reprinted by permission of Prentice-Hall.)*

symbol-processing system as defined in Figure 1–2 and Table 1–1 can behave in these complex situations in ways that closely match the intellectual performances of humans in the same circumstances. Such demonstrations provide convincing evidence that their theory is at least a possible explanation of human intellectual behavior.

The IPS system is examined in more detail in Chapter 13, where we shall develop a program that matches one of Newell and Simon's problem-

TABLE 1–1   Definitions and Postulates for Newell and Simon's IPS*

1. There is a set of elements, called *symbols.*
2. A *symbol structure* consists of a set of *tokens* (equivalently, *instances* or *occurrences*) of symbols connected by a set of *relations.*
3. A *memory* is a component of an IPS capable of storing and retaining symbol structures.
4. An *information process* is a process that has symbol structures for (some of) its inputs or outputs.
5. A *processor* is a component of an IPS consisting of:
   (a) a (fixed) set of *elementary information processes* (eip's);
   (b) a *short-term memory* (STM) that holds the input and output symbol structures of the eip's;
   (c) an *interpreter* that determines the sequence of eip's to be executed by the IPS as a function of the symbol structures in STM.
6. A symbol structure *designates* (equivalently, *references* or *points to*) an object if there exist information processes that admit the symbol structure as input and either:
   (a) affect the object; or
   (b) produce, as output, symbol structures that depend on the object.
7. A symbol structure is a *program* if (a) the object it designates is an information process and (b) the interpreter, if given the program, can execute the designated process. (Literally this should read, "if given an input that designates the program.")
8. A symbol is *primitive* if its designation (or its creation) is fixed by the elementary information processes or by the external environment of the IPS.

*(A. Newell and H. A. Simon, *Human Problem Solving*, 1972, pp. 20–21. Reprinted by permission of Prentice-Hall.)

olving illustrations. For the present, let us simply capture some of the flavor of the IPS approach by considering how it might explain a deceptively simple process such as recognizing the word BAT. Using the definitions in Table 1–1, we conclude that BAT is a symbol structure, made up of the symbols B, A, and T. Furthermore, in this particular experience of BAT each symbol is a *token*, or *instance*, of these letters. (Presumably representations of the letters are also stored in memory; Newell and Simon refer to the latter as *types*, to distinguish them from the tokens.) When the receptors relay the symbol structure to the processor's short-term memory (STM) the interpreter determines a sequence of eip's that search memory for a match between the tokens presently in STM and the symbols (types) that have been stored in memory as a result of preceding experience. When the match is found, the system has "recognized" the input. Of course, the question of exactly *what* types are stored in memory or *how* they got stored there are further theoretical problems that would need to be addressed in a more detailed analysis (for example, the fact that we recognize the word as BAT rather than TAB suggests that the memory match in this case is at the level of the entire symbol structure rather than being a simple match of three separate symbols). We shall have more to say and do with memory and matching later; for now, this simple example will serve as a preview of the information-processing approach to explaining psychological phenomena. Perhaps, too, it will give a hint of the real complexities and problems involved in psychological explanation.

Computer Simulation, Programs, and Psychological Theory

One important aspect of the paradigm shift outlined above, and in fact one reason for the shift, is that psychologists receptive to the information-processing view have available to them a mechanism that simultaneously serves (1) as a *model* of the pretheoretical assumptions of the paradigm, and (2) as a *tool* that can be used to build and test theoretical postulates, or less formal hunches, or even wild speculations, about mental structures and processes. The combination model-and-tool mechanism is, of course, the computer. The model aspect of the computer stems from the types of capabilities it has as a symbol processor. Everyone who has written a program knows that a computer's vast capabilities are built upon just a few simple processes; for example, reading (input), writing (output), storage and retrieval of information in a memory (akin to reading and writing, but internally rather than externally), comparing symbols, replacing symbols, and making decisions about next steps depending upon present information. Clearly these are the "simple operations" proposed by Turing, albeit slightly reworded and embellished. Thus the symbol-manipulating features of the digital computer are analogous to the elementary operations assumed by the information-processing psychologist to be necessary and sufficient for describing human cognitive processes. This analogy allows us to say that the computer as a machine "models," or "is a model of," the paradigm. (Note that, because the paradigm is limited to intellectual processes, the model has the corresponding limitation. That is, we are not saying anything such as "the human being is a computer" or "computers are human," but rather that certain operations of the computer are analogous to a point of view concerning intelligent action.)

The importance of the computer as a tool for theory building stems from the additional fact that, via computer programming, the psychologist can put together a sequence of elementary processes and test out—at a physical and empirical level rather than simply rationally or logically—the behavioral outcome of proposed mental structures and processes. This procedure has come to be known as *computer simulation*. Computer simulation is a technique used nowadays in many fields other than psychology, so when we use the phrase here we must take it to mean simulation of *psychological processes*. Moreover, it is useful to distinguish computer simulation of psychological processes from the somewhat overlapping but technically different phrase *artificial intelligence* (AI). The latter term refers to the task of making machines behave intelligently, regardless of whether in doing so they mimic human psychological processes. Conversely, computer simulation as employed by information-processing psychologists has as its objectives the statement and testing of hypotheses about how human intellectual processes operate; thus it is not primarily concerned about whether a machine (be it a computer, a robot, or an artillery gun) can or does perform some type of intelligent behavior. Workers in AI and psychological simulation may arrive at the same result, but their objectives—and in many cases their modes of operation—often differ. When the information-processing paradigm first emerged, this distinction between AI and psychological simulation corresponded closely to the different objectives of the disciplines of computer science and psychology. As time goes on, however, the distinction is becoming more blurred. (Indeed, by 1981 an interdisciplinary melding of these approaches had been achieved, with the formation of the new field called *cognitive science*. More about that later.)

If a psychologist writes a program that effectively simulates some complex psychological process—such as solving a problem, playing a sophisticated game, or interacting socially with a human being—what really is the theoretical import of the program and the simulation? This is a question that at present does not have a definite answer, but it is a subject of considerable debate among psychologists, computer scientists, and philosophers of science. Some of those receptive to the information-processing paradigm consider that the program that successfully demonstrates a psychological process is itself a formal theoretical statement that is written in a rigorous and unambiguous language. They argue that this kind of rigor is what psychology lacks and needs, and that for the first time it is possible to state psychological theory in a manner that is precise, testable, and unencumbered by the hidden meanings and ambiguities of either English or other human languages. Many consider that this new rigor brings to psychology what the language of mathematics brought to the physical sciences and that the eventual influence upon theoretical progress and sophistication will be similar. Others are more skeptical, however; and there are more than a few who believe that the program-mathematics analogy is either overdrawn or outright inappropriate. Perhaps the most reasonable approach to take—and the one taken here—is to assume that the question ultimately is an empirical one that needs to be tested, and that for the moment the best strategy is to let psychologists, computer scientists, and others working in the field try out the possibilities, thus permitting us for now to examine carefully and objectively the results as they accumulate and to hold off answering the question until more data have been collected.

Parts II and IV of this book present the reader with materials and experiences that will allow you to make such an examination, and perhaps let you answer the question for yourself. In the past fifteen years, computer simulations of a large variety of psychological phenomena have been reported, and very sophisticated simulation techniques have been developed. Not all of these can be reviewed, of course, but an attempt at sampling can be made. The chapters in Part II present simulation examples of visual perception, verbal memory, and personality, using the Pascal language and introducing a number of standard simulation techniques. Part IV of the text introduces the programming language LISP, which is particularly good for writing simulations of human mental processes. Simulation examples of complex psychological phenomena such as concept formation, natural language processing, and problem solving, all using LISP language, are introduced and discussed in the last part of the book.

Because this is an introductory text, the examples given have been somewhat simplified relative to the simulations reported by professionals working full-time in the field. Suggested readings and references cited at the end of each chapter and in the bibliography will direct the interested reader to more sophisticated examples as needed. However, even the working examples presented should provide readers with sufficient background to permit critical examination of the simulation question posed above, and perhaps even to allow a comfortable conclusion.

THE INFLUENCE UPON PSYCHOLOGICAL METHODS

When students first begin the formal study of psychology, they are often surprised at the extent and variety of measurements, statistical methods, and experimental techniques that psychologists use. Before computers arrived on the scene, these methods and techniques had to be accomplished largely by hand, and since for the most part they are repetitive, detailed, and time-consuming, performing them was often tedious and error-prone. Hence, psychologists quickly took advantage of the capability of computers not only to accomplish such tasks rapidly and accurately but to do so without surliness or discontent. In consequence, the number of psychological chores performed daily by computers is already substantial, and the potential exists for more uses in the future as more psychologists improve their programming skills. The chapters in Part III provide examples of the methodological uses of computing in both the clinical/testing and the experimental/laboratory areas of psychology.

SUGGESTED READINGS

A number of topics were covered in rapid-fire order in this chapter, providing no more than a surface-scratching overview of some extensive subject matter. A more in-depth but still quite general treatment of the influence of computer science upon psychological theory can be found in Chapter 4 of Lachman, Lachman, and Butterfield's (1979) advanced text. Minsky (1967; Chapters 6 and 7) provides a detailed but clearly stated review of Turing machines. For a more refined examination of paradigms and paradigm shifts in scientific theory, including illustrations from various disciplines, there is probably no better book than the original source of the concept (Kuhn, 1970). A short but comprehensive review of theory construction, with good descriptions and psychological examples of types of theories and components of theories, can be found in Marx (1976).

Because AI and information-processing psychology are relatively new on the theoretical scene, considerable debate exists about how each interacts with the other and how important both are or will be to theoretical psychology over the long term. Writings pertinent to such questions can be found in several relatively new journals; for example, *Cognitive Psychology, Cognition,* and *Cognitive Science,* which have sprung up as a result of the theoretical and experimental developments we have reviewed. Books by Ringle (1979) and Haugeland (1981) contain a number of chapters of interest to the student concerned with the pros and cons and philosophical implications of the computer analogy to human psychological processes. A recent book edited by the psychologist D.A. Norman (1981) has ushered in what some believe may be a new academic discipline, called *cognitive science,* which is populated by workers in various fields, such as psychology, computer science, linguistics, logic, mathematics, and philosophy, and who have similar theoretical interests and orientations. In particular, the first and last chapters of Norman's interdisciplinary set of readings address some of the issues we have just covered.

Chapters 9 and 10 in a book edited by Apter and Westby (1973) describe some methodological applications of computers to the clinical and educational areas of psychology. For general readings on the laboratory aspects of the topic, books by Weiss (1973) and Bird (1981) are available, and the journal *Behavioral Research Methods and Instrumentation* often contains descriptions of computerized laboratory techniques.

2

Program Design and Structure

Writing a computer program is a problem-solving situation in which the programmer is presented with a problem and must somehow write a program that solves it. Over the relatively few years since the advent of computer programming, programmers have devised certain strategies to aid in performing the various tasks when the programming problems are long and complex. In this chapter we shall become familiar with several important strategies that are considered nowadays to be standard programming procedures and which will be followed in future chapters. The strategies are *top-down design, modular programming,* and *structured programming.* These techniques are not independent of each other; indeed they are so loosely defined that it is easy to find different interpretations of what the three terms actually mean. The exact meanings, however, are not as important as the general programming and problem-solving concepts that lie behind them; thus we shall become familiar with the concepts and not worry about the finer technical details.

TOP-DOWN DESIGN

When a programming problem is presented, the temptation for many programmers is to begin analyzing immediately one of the more interesting details and start writing code that will solve it, or else to just start at the beginning and see what happens. Such approaches may work when the details are simple and the entire problem can be solved easily; but as complexity of the overall problem increases, the opportunity for confusion also arises, and diving in to write code for one component often proves later to be fruitless or inefficient because it failed to account for other features of the total project. The end result of such approaches is usually a program written in a piecemeal manner, with program segments stuck into the program at odd places to account for problems not previously recognized and often containing "go-to" or other branching statements that transfer program control back and forth all over the place in mysterious fashions. A complex program written in this helter-skelter manner is difficult to understand when read by others, is hard to debug or change or elaborate, and is logically and aesthetically unsatisfying.

To avoid these difficulties, experienced programmers forego the temptation to start writing code immediately and instead spend more time analyzing the problem and planning the program using a method called *top-down design*. To get an idea of how this strategy can be used, let us imagine that we have been given an assignment to write a program that will get the major descriptive statistics and a graph for a set of test scores; for example, a frequency distribution of the scores, measures of central tendency and variability, and a histogram showing the score distribution. How might one apply the top-down design strategy to a broad and rather ambiguous problem such as this? We begin with the problem as a whole. Ideally, it would be nice to have available a ready-made program, or perhaps even a prewired machine, that would perform all of the necessary tasks automatically if we simply type its name; for example:

STATS

and there would be no need to pursue the design of the problem solution any further. This is usually not the case, of course, so the next step is to "go down a level" and break the initial top-level statement STATS into several smaller pieces or modules. Modules are logically coherent segments of the total problem that are relatively independent of each other and that, when processed in sequence, provide a solution to the overall problem. For our STATS example, this first level modular analysis might look something like this:

```
STATS ==>  READ SCORES
           GET STATISTICS
           DRAW THE GRAPH
           END
```

Looking at the problem in this way makes the eventual programming chore a bit easier because each of these modules may be considered as a small problem on its own, and we know in advance that the solution to any one will fit coherently with the rest. The first module appears to be straight-forward, and there is probably no need for further analysis. It would be wise, however, to analyze the second module to a deeper level because as it stands it is still a rather complex and possibly confusing problem in itself. So, ignoring the other modules, we can analyze the second one as follows:

```
GET STATISTICS ==> PRINT FREQUENCY DISTRIBUTION
                   GET CENTRAL TENDENCIES
                   GET VARIABILITIES
```

Again the problem has achieved more clarity, while maintaining an overall design into which each of the modules will eventually fit. And because each module is a logically consistent subproblem that is basically independent of the others, it can be examined, analyzed further, and eventually pro-grammed on its own.

Perhaps the top-down analysis to this level is sufficient for some pro-grammers to begin thinking about coding; for others, analysis to deeper levels of some of the modules may seem appropriate. When using the top-down strategy no formal method exists for deciding when the design is finished—that will depend upon the complexity of the problem, the ex-pertise of the programmer and/or users involved, and perhaps other fac-tors as well. The important advantage is that, regardless of problem com-plexity or the abilities of those involved, the strategy provides a workable approach toward solution.

The example, as developed thus far, illustrates the top-down strategy by designating modules verbally. Another way to represent the design is graphically, using a *structure diagram*. Figure 2–1a shows a structure dia-gram equivalent to the verbal analysis. The levels are portrayed from top to bottom, and at each level the modules can be read sequentially from left to right. Notice that the module or module sequence at any given level is con-nected to only one module above it; this is an indication that when any given level has been completed the results of that level constitute a solution to the controlling module, and so the process toward final solution can con-tinue sequentially at that higher level.

Figure 2–1b illustrates how the structure diagram may be used for ad-ditional analysis and design to deeper levels as needed. The verbal equiva-lent for the new level shown there would be:

```
GET CENTRAL TENDENCIES ==> CALCULATE AND PRINT MEAN
                           CALCULATE AND PRINT MEDIAN
                           CALCULATE AND PRINT MODE
```

Using either representation, the top-down analysis may continue to the depth that seems sufficient for the circumstances.

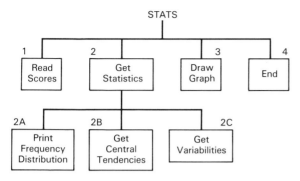

FIGURE 2–1a.   A beginning structure diagram for the STATS problem.

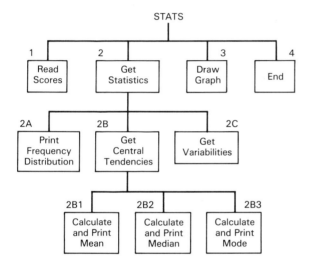

FIGURE 2–1b.   Taking Figure 2–1a to a deeper level.

Let's summarize the advantages that this design strategy and the design that it generates have over the helter-skelter approach. One advantage is that it permits an understanding of the total problem without having to do any coding or attending to any of the actual programming details. Also, it maps out a plan that can be read and understood not only by the person who constructed it but also by other programmers or users. Thus it is possible to discuss problems of strategy, alternative solutions, extensions, and so on. Additionally, because the modules are independent of each other, strategy changes and additions can be made locally without destroying the entire plan. Finally, this type of design fits easily with the sophisticated program-writing strategy called *modular programming*, which is our next topic.

WRITING MODULAR PROGRAMS

The term module was used above to refer to the independent units in a top-down design. Having designed the program in this modular manner, it is now possible to write the actual program as a series of (relatively) independent and logically coherent program units, each of them addressing a subproblem that can be understood and programmed easily. Furthermore, these coded modules usually can be tested independently of one another, making debugging considerably less difficult than it often is when programs are long and poorly organized. Finally, the same advantages accrue to the final coded program that were considered advantageous for top-down design; namely, readability, understandability, and the capability to add, change, or alter a part of the program without having to change other components.

The major technique used in modular programming is a heavy reliance on subprograms. Most programmers define a module as a reasonably short sequence of instructions (estimates range anywhere from 6 to 8 lines to a maximum of one page or about 50 lines of programming code) that is basically independent of other parts of the program because it has just one entry point and one exit point. In languages such as BASIC and FORTRAN, these requirements can be met rather nicely by using *subroutines;* in Pascal the modular form is the *procedure.* (See Appendix A if you need to review the basic rules and structure or the Pascal programming language.)

It is easy to see that if the strategy of writing each module as a subprogram is followed to its ideal limit, the result will include a "main program" consisting simply of a set of calls to different subprograms. Thus the ideal modular solution to the STATS programming problem might be:

```
PROGRAM STATS (input, output);
VAR n: integer;
        scores: array [1..1000] of integer;
(*-------------------------------------*)

PROCEDURE readscores;
     .
     .
     <code for module to read scores>
     .
     .
END;
(*-------------------------------------*)
```

```
PROCEDURE frequencies;
    .
    .
<code for printing a frequency distribution>
    .
    .
END;
(*--------------------------------------*)

PROCEDURE centrals;
    .
    .
<coding for mean, median, mode>
    .
    .
END;
(*--------------------------------------*)
    .
    .
<insert other modules here as needed>
    .
    .
(*--------------------------------------*)

PROCEDURE graphit;
    .
    .
<coding to draw histogram>
    .
    .
END;
(*--------------------------------------*)
        (*MAIN PROGRAM*)
(*--------------------------------------*)
BEGIN
    readscores;
    centrals;
    .
    .
    .
    variabilities;
    graphit;
END.
```

Programs may be written in good modular fashion and still not end up in this extreme modular form, of course. For example, the coding necessary for the READSCORES module could have been placed as a unit at the beginning of the main program, rather in an initial procedure, and modularity would have been preserved. When it comes to the final arrangement of the programmed solution there are no rigid rules, and there is room for programmer judgment. However, these individual judgments notwithstanding, the modular programming technique clearly yields a much different program structure than do less orderly strategies in which most or all of the processing takes place in a single large main program.

STRUCTURED PROGRAMMING

If one surveys the current literature on programming technique, it is possible to find a variety of definitions of the term *structured programming*. For our purposes, it is best to think of the term as a general point of view that includes the modular-programming orientation just discussed (certainly those modules give a definite "structure" to a program) and then carries the general idea of independent and logically coherent program components a bit further. The central addition to the concept or modularity is that even within well-defined program blocks such as procedures or the main program sequence of instructions, there can and should be structure and order. The way to achieve such order is to arrange the statements in a given module so that they proceed sequentially from the beginning of the module to the end, rather than transferring control back and forth within the module in that helter-skelter manner referred to earlier.

Although this objective can be achieved using nearly any programming language, the types of structured statements available in Pascal make it a particularly good language for writing structured programs. There are three categories of structured statements in Pascal, all of which share the common feature that, during program execution, they are accessed from the top, continue processing as long as necessary to get a particular job done, and then exit at the bottom and pass control on to the next structure in the sequence. These categories are the BEGIN..END compound statement, the group of *repetition* statements (FOR..DO, DO..WHILE, REPEAT..UNTIL), and the *decision* statements IF..THEN..ELSE and CASE.

The rules for using each of these categories are covered in Appendix A, and they need not be described here. Rather, the emphasis here is upon how their operations enhance the structure and consequently, the readability, understandability, and "debuggability" of a programming block. Programmers who use them know that each one encountered in a program block is designed to perform a specific job and then quit, and that they will not exit in the middle, or begin in the middle, or be accessed from other blocks in remote places above or below them. Thus in a manner similar to modules but at a more "micro" level, they can be analyzed and written independently of other statement blocks.

DATA REPRESENTATION

Our concern up to this point has been with the structure of the program that will solve a given programming problem. Clearly, however, program design and structure cannot be separated from consideration of how the data for the problem will be organized, stored, and represented. Computer programmers have at hand a number of well-defined *data structures* that may be used to organize and store information within a program—structures that range from the simple variable to the complexities of arrays, linked lists, stacks, queues, trees, and so on. You probably know how to define and use arrays, and we will introduce some of the others in the future. For now, we need only recognize that the choice of data structures will necessarily interact with program design right from the beginning of the problem-solving task.

To illustrate the importance of integrating data-structure decisions with the programming strategies covered in previous sections, let us return to the STATS program and develop it a bit further. Looking at the design in Figure 2–1b, we see that the question of data representation appears in the very first module. Since the data for this problem will be a list of scores, most programmers would agree that a one-dimensional integer array (let's call it SCORES) is an appropriate structure. Even as that decision is made, however, our knowledge of basic descriptive statistics makes us aware that the data initially input will need to be reorganized into a hierarchy from high to low in order to accomplish such chores as printing the frequency distribution (Module 2A), calculating and printing the median (Module 2B2), and drawing a histogram (Module 3). Thus data structure—and restructuring—becomes an integral part of the design of the program as a whole.

As in most programming problems, there are several ways that the data representation for the various subproblems in the STATS example may be accomplished. The easiest one for the programmer would be to require the user to input the data in a hierarchical order at the start of the program, so that once they are read into the global array SCORES they can be used in the same form in all succeeding modules. But why have the user do this clerical work when, with a little planning, the computer can do it? Let us decide that the computer will do the necessary data reorganization. The next question is, where? One approach would be to reorganize SCORES immediately at the top level, by making Module 1 in Figure 2–1b responsible for not only reading the data but rearranging it for later use in various modules. Another would be to rearrange the data in each module—at the *local level*—as needed. While either strategy would work, the second conforms more closely to the principles and objectives of structured programming because it preserves the independence and logical coherence of the individual modules; that is, each module requiring a hierarchical arrangement of the scores in an array will organize them that way regardless of the way the data are organized when they are passed to the module.

Figure 2–2 illustrates how the data structure for the STATS main program and Modules 2B1 and 2B2 from Figure 2–1b might be represented using the latter strategy. Note that in this arrangement the only structures that need to be defined in the main program are the array

FIGURE 2–2. A partial data structure for the STATS example. SCORES and N are global, and structures inside broken lines are local to various procedures.

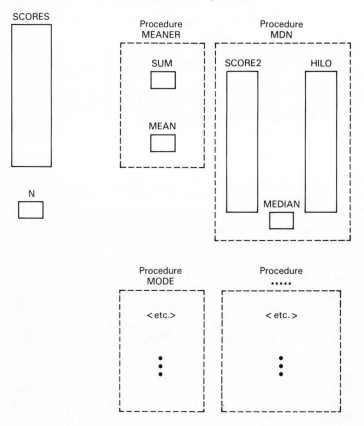

SCORES and the integer variable N. These variables will be global to all of the procedures in the program. Calculation of the mean does not require rearrangement of SCORES, so the procedure written to perform that task (we shall call it MEANER) can use the global array SCORES in its calculations. The procedure MDN, however, will need to rearrange the original data in order to find the median; thus, as we shall see below, it will use an algorithm requiring two local arrays that will organize the scores hierarchically within the procedure while leaving the main data structure SCORES intact for use in other modules.

The design of the program, as illustrated now in both Figure 2–1b and Figure 2–2, permits us to code various procedures independently—a chunk at a time, so to speak—with considerable confidence that they all will fit together eventually. Likely examples of such coding are given here for the MEANER and MDN procedures, and coding for the other procedures is left as an exercise for the reader.

```
PROGRAM STATS (input, output);

    (* A partial program for calculating and printing
descriptive statistics *)

VAR k, n: integer;
    scores: array [1..50] of integer;

(*----------------------------*)


PROCEDURE MEANER;


var i, sum: integer;
    mean: real;


begin
  sum:= 0;
  for i:= 1 to n do
    sum:= sum + scores [i];
  mean:= sum / n;
  writeln(' mean =', mean)
end;          (* End Procedure Meaner *)


(*----------------------------*)
```

```
PROCEDURE MDN (score2: array [integer] of integer);

var hilo: array [1..50] of integer;
    i,j,hi,newhi: integer;
    half,frac,x: real;

begin
  i:= 1;
  while i <= n do            (* arrange scores into hilo *)
  begin
    hi:= -1000;
    for j:= 1 to n do        (* find highest current score
                                in score2 *)
    if hi < score2[j] then
    begin
    hi:= score2[j];
    newhi:= j
    end;
    hilo[i]:= hi;            (* highest score into hilo *)
    score2[newhi]:= -1000;  (* reset score2 *)
    i:= i + 1
  end;
  half:= n / 2;                       (* get and print median *)
  frac:= half - trunc(half);
  if frac <> 0.0 then
  begin
    i:= trunc(half) + 1;
    writeln('median = ',hilo[i])
  end
  else
  begin
    i:= trunc(half);
    x:= (hilo[i] + hilo[i+1] / 2;
    writeln('median = ',x)
  end
end;      (* End of Procedure Mdn *)

(*-----------------------------*)



      .
      .
            (* Insert other Procedures here *)

      .
      .
(*-----------------------------*)
            (* MAIN PROGRAM *)
(*-----------------------------*)
```

```
begin
  n: = 0;
  readln(k);
  repeat
    n: = n + 1;
    scores[n]: = k;
    readln(k)
  until k < 0;
  meaner;
  mdn(scores);
    .
    .
    .
end.
```

In examining this partial program, look first at the main program se-quence (a good plan whenever you need to read and understand a Pascal program). The code equivalent to Module 1, which simply reads the data into SCORES, is a REPEAT..UNTIL statement within the main program; but it could just as easily—perhaps preferably—have been in a separate procedure. The rest of the main program sequence is a series of calls to procedures (many of which are missing here, of course, because this is only a partial example).

MEANER, which is designed to calculate and print the mean, is easily understood without explanation. Note that it uses the global variables N and SCORES; but since it does not alter or destroy them, or use them in different ways on different calls, there is no need to identify them as formal parameters.

The situation is somewhat different for MDN. In this procedure, the SCORES data must be rearranged from high to low, but the global data must not be destroyed because they will be needed later. Thus the *value parameter* SCORE2 is defined for MDN. SCORE2 is an array that accepts the integer values in the SCORES array, becoming a copy of SCORES that can be used locally without altering the global array. The WHILE..DO statement in MDN is an algorithm that will rearrange the scores in SCORE2 into a high-to-low structure in the array HILO. It does so as fol-lows:

1. Set HI to a very low number, such as −1000;
2. Scan SCORE2 from top to bottom, assigning to HI any score that is higher than the current HI and keeping track in NEWHI where the current high score was found;
3. Assign the new HI score to the next cell in HILO;
4. Assign −1000 to the cell in SCORE2 that contained the current HI value, thus erasing it from the SCORE2 data;
5. Repeat 1–4 until all N scores have been transferred from SCORE2 to HILO.

Other algorithms might have been used instead, but this one was chosen to illustrate that the original data, when passed by value to a procedure, can be destroyed locally while remaining unaltered at the global level.

These examples should suffice to give the essential attitudes and strategies that underlie good programming practice. Although the concepts of structured programming seem—and indeed are—simple enough, using them effectively takes practice. But if you keep them in mind when you analyze the problems and examine the programs presented in future chapters, and if you use them when you write your own programs, both understanding and coding skills are sure to improve.

SUGGESTED READINGS

Several books have been written about the design and structure of programs that elaborate substantially the techniques just presented. Yourdon's book *Techniques of Program Structure and Design* (1976) is still among the best for clarity and readability. Van Tassel (1978) is also recommended for its clarity and examples using a variety of languages. Most texts that teach Pascal, and recent texts for other languages as well, will contain one or more chapters on the topic. The nearly universal presence of these concepts in recent computer programming texts attests to their importance and general acceptance.

EXERCISES

1. Figure 2–1 presents a structure diagram for the program STATS that is three levels deep for just part of Module 2. What would the third level of depth for Modules 2A and 2C look like? Draw them. Then draw an example of a fourth level of depth for this program design.

2. The procedure MDN listed on page 26 rearranges the values in the SCORES array, putting them in order from high to low in HILO. The algorithm used is one of several possible *sorting* algorithms that might have been employed. Write an alternative sorting algorithm that will do the same job. Does your algorithm destroy the original data in the SCORES array? If so, how may that be prevented?

3. Because several of the procedures in the program STATS (finding the median, constructing a frequency distribution, constructing a histogram) will have to use an array with scores sorted from high to low, it appears that the program as presently designed will require each of these procedures to perform the sorting algorithm. This duplication seems to be a waste of time and programming effort. How might you design the program so this duplication would be reduced or eliminated?

4. Draw a structure diagram and accompanying data structures for a program that will perform an independent-samples *t* test. Make the program read scores, print means and standard deviations for each group, and print the *t* value and degrees of freedom.
5. Write a Pascal program that follows the design constructed in Exercise 4.

3

Simulating
a Perceptual Process

When an organism is presented with a stimulus—visual, auditory, tactual, or otherwise—how does it make sense of that stimulus? How, and why, does that stimulus, which at base is simply an object or event in the physical world, get translated into "information" that has meaning for the individual who experienced it? Psychologists and scientists in other disciplines have sought answers to these questions for many years. The questions relate to the way we *perceive* familiar objects in our surroundings, and the perceptual process involved is referred to by the term *pattern recognition*. In this chapter we will get some experience in simulation techniques by writing a computer simulation of a visual pattern recognition task common to anyone who reads English—namely, recognition of letters of the alphabet. The first step in writing such a simulation (or any simulation, for that matter) is to gain some understanding of the facts currently known, and the theoretical explanations currently being proposed, for the psychological process we want to simulate. After a brief review of the current thinking and knowledge about the topic, we will be able to write a Pascal program that simulates the human letter-recognition process according to principles proposed in a theory of pattern recognition called PANDEMONIUM.

THEORETICAL EXPLANATIONS OF PATTERN RECOGNITION

Although a fair amount of factual data has accumulated about the way that people and lower animals recognize visual patterns, our understanding of the process is far from complete. This incompleteness means, of course, that we cannot fully explain how the process actually works. But this is just the type of situation in which theoretical explanations are proposed; that is, people in such circumstances will formulate theories to try to explain how the process *might* work. In the topical area of pattern recognition, two theoretical explanations that have received substantial attention from psychologists and researchers in artificial intelligence are the *template-matching theory* and the *feature analysis theory*. We will look at each of these in turn and assess their strengths and weaknesses. Having done so, we can select the one that looks more fruitful and test its adequacy by putting it into a computer and seeing if the computer shows the same letter-recognition behaviors that people do.

Template Matching

Consider the following scenario: A person is shown the object *R* and asked what she sees, and she replies, "That is an *arrh,* which is a letter of the alphabet." Simple as the scenario is, it portrays a series of physical and mental processes that are quite complex. At the physical level, light rays must have impinged upon a sense organ (the eye), which translated the light source into a neural signal (or set of signals) that was relayed along the optic nerve and in some manner activated the cortical cells necessary to compare the signal with memory representations of objects experienced in the past. After a successful comparison was made, other kinds of neural signals were generated that eventually resulted in the vocal response. A substantial amount of knowledge has accumulated about this chain of physiological processes, some of which will be reviewed in the next section. For now, however, let us concentrate on the more psychological aspect of the scenario by considering what information was stored in memory, and what informational processes might have taken place, to permit the subject's perception and response.

The entire process can be divided into two stages: the *detection* of the correct pattern, and the *interpretation* or assignment of meaning to the pattern detected. How might each of these stages be described in psychological and informational terms? One major theoretical explanation is that there are memory representations of each character of the alphabet stored in memory, and associated with each is a label that gives meaning to the representation. The stored representation of each character constitutes a *template* that must be matched in order for the associated label to be activated. Given these theoretical assumptions, the scenario can be described as follows: Presentation of the letter *R* initiates the detection stage, in which the letter is compared with the various templates stored in memory. If a match is found, the interpretation stage begins, which consists of finding the associated label and evoking it as the *meaning* of the object presented. Figure 3–1a illustrates this simple template-matching theory graphically, and Figure 3–1b provides a top-level verbal diagram of the process.

Some immediate concerns about the details of this theory are apparent. From an information-processing standpoint, it is clear that the detection and interpretation processes occur in serial order. But what about the detection process itself? After all, there must be templates of all sorts of objects stored in memory, not simply alphabet templates. Do comparisons get made with all of them simultaneously (parallel processing), or one at a time (serial processing), or in some intermediate fashion? If detection is a serial process, which template should it begin with, and in what order should the attempts at matching take place? And what about lower-case

FIGURE 3–1. Schematic and verbal diagrams of the template theory.

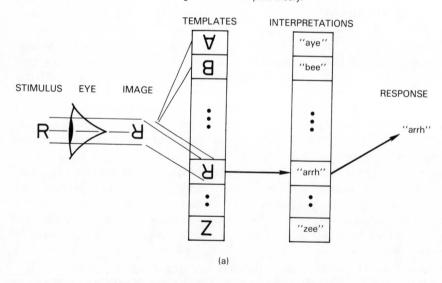

(a)

1. Sense incoming character on retina. (Image is reversed.)

2. DO for all i visual templates currently stored:
    If image matches TEMPLATE(i) then respond
    with INTERPRETATION(i);
        else try TEMPLATE (i + 1).

(b)

versus upper-case letters—are there separate templates for each? Indeed, what must happen if a letter is viewed from an angle, or sideways; must there be a template for each angle? And how does the template-matcher discriminate block letters from, say, old English scroll, unless there are separate templates for various styles of type? Clearly this simple theory leaves many questions unanswered and would require many elaborations before it could operate as a pattern-matching machine that would recognize letters as quickly and with as much versatility as people do. As you may have guessed, the theory is not held in much favor today, and theorists interested in perception have been able to come up with better alternatives.

But before passing on to a (slightly) better theory of pattern matching, let us consider the simple template-matching theory from a more formal information-processing point of view. Imagine yourself as a combination psychologist-programmer who assumes that, because human psychological functions are interpretable as information processes, a theory about psychological processes should be capable of being represented in the form of a list of actions—a program—on an information-processing machine. In order for the theory, as stated verbally above (and, correspondingly, stated graphically and as a top-level diagram in Figure 3–1), to be translated into an algorithm or program that would tell such a machine how to structure and process information according to the theory, the psychologist-programmer would need to answer—or have answered by the theorist—many of the questions posed in the preceding paragraph, and probably others as well. Let us call such questions *theory-programming conflicts*, which must be resolved before the exercise of formally stating a theory as an information-processing program can be written. Thus we see at first hand one major potential value of attempting to translate a verbally stated information-processing theory of a psychological function into a formal programmed statement of the theory; namely, the translation exercise would serve to specify in detail the logical weaknesses, omissions, or other possible inadequacies in the original, less rigorous, statement.

Although recognizing the potential theoretical value of this modeling process, the psychologist-programmer should also be aware of certain problems that may occur if this model-building approach is not used cautiously. On the one hand, the psychologist-programmer faced with the task of resolving theory-programming conflicts must be careful to make the resolutions in ways that do not violate or change the premises of the theory. A computer program intended to represent some verbally stated theory but which in the course of program development has altered many of the original theoretical principles, or has added many nuances not contained in the original theory, is really no longer an accurate representation of the original set of statements. Alternatively, the theorist who sets out to propose a theory that is specifically realizable as a computer program may produce a set of theoretical statements that are not appropriate or useful as psychological explanations. Either of these theory-translation errors will, of course, yield a result that can be detrimental to the overall goal of building useful psychological theory. As with most tools that psychologists and others employ, the model-building tool must be used discriminately.

A second potential value of the translation of theory into program is perhaps not so apparent from our brief discussion of template theory, but it would become obvious if we were to write an actual computer representation. That value, which will simply be introduced now and elaborated later in an actual example, is this: Having written a program representation of a theory, our execution of the program will provide a simulated outcome that constitutes the behavior predicted by the theory for a specific case or situation. Multiple executions, then, will produce a set of predicted outcomes, which as a group constitute data generated by the theory. To the extent that such simulation data match, or are consistent with, the data collected from real psychological subjects (people, in our case), such matches now constitute a validation of the implicit proposal that the theory can, indeed, explain the psychological process in question. We will discuss this simulation and theory-testing value in more detail below.

A third potential value of computer simulation, emanating from the second, should be stated before we go on to look at a somewhat better theory. Consider the possible situation if we have (1) written the formal program statement of the theory, and (2) collected simulation data that *does not* match data collected from real psychological subjects. It is often found that an analysis of the differences between the real and simulated data reveal parts of the program, and thus of the formally stated theory, that need further attention, or can be revised in ways that permit a closer match between theory-generated data and real data. Changes revealed or suggested in this way may indeed be quite specific and can lead to insights and further research that might dramatically improve or extend the theory. Thus the result of the programming exercise is not simply to state and test a theory and then throw the whole thing out if the test is not passed. Rather, the exercise may become an integral part of theory building and theory elaboration—a constructive process that provides new directions, understandings, and hypotheses that are themselves tied to empirical findings and amenable to further formal statement and test.

Whereas this third potential value of computer simulation can often be genuinely helpful, we must recognize that it can also have a negative effect upon the theory-building process if carried to extremes. Scientists have long been aware that attempts to revise an ill-conceived theory simply by tinkering with it to make it more predictive of real-life situations can at times result in wasting large amounts of time and energy on premises that ultimately are unsupportable. (One is reminded of how the Ptolemaic accounts of the paths of the heavenly bodies went through so many low-level revisions that the end result was an inelegant, and ultimately incorrect, theory that nevertheless could make many predictions with considerable accuracy.) In essence, then, we must understand that although computer modeling is a technique that can enhance theory building in several ways if properly and cautiously applied, it must not be considered a universal remedy for the various traps and pitfalls that theorists encounter generally when attempting to construct valid theoretical explanations.

With these several potential influences of simulation upon theorizing in mind—that is, the capabilities of formal statement, theoretical-empirical testing and theory alteration and/or elaboration—we can now look at a more satisfactory theory of pattern recognition.

Feature Analysis

The template-matching theory assumes that letters (and other visual objects) are processed as units. A modification of this assumption is the proposal that a visual stimulus may be broken down into subunits or subpatterns and that recognition of the unit stimulus may be based upon the number and type of subpatterns it contains. Visual objects consist of various numbers of subunits or *features* such as straight lines, curved lines, acute or obtuse or right angles, light and dark areas, and so on. Thus a visual unit might be analyzed in sufficient detail that the number and type of features resulting from the analysis could identify the stimulus uniquely, or at least with a high probability of accuracy. Using the stimulus in the above scenario as an example, an *R* can be analyzed into these features: *1 vertical line, 1 diagonal, and 1 open curve*. Because the probability is low (in this case 0.00) that such a feature list will identify more than one object, this would seem to be a reasonable proposal for explaining how people might go about detecting discrete and previously experienced visual objects. This hypothesis, which we shall elaborate and simulate, is referred to as the *feature analysis theory* of pattern recognition.

The theory gains some initial support from evidence obtained in neurophysiological studies that have attempted to investigate and understand the functions of different kinds of sensory cells, and to locate and classify the various kinds of brain cells located in the visual cortex and other areas that receive signals sent by the sensory cells. This neurological work, performed upon a variety of animals, is highly sophisticated in both method and results. Only the general results will be summarized here, but the Suggested Readings at the end of the chapter will help if you want to pursue details.

For our purposes, the important findings are that the brains and sense organs of lower animals contain a variety of cells and cell groups that react only to certain features of a visual stimulus. In the visual sense mode, for example, researchers have isolated the following different types of detectors in the frog retina: *contrast* detectors, *moving edge* detectors, *dimming* detectors, and *convexity* detectors. The contrast and dimming detectors apparently serve to identify edges of objects, where dark and light regions meet. Convexity detectors, on the other hand, signal curvature; and cell clusters constituting moving edge detectors emit signals only when an identifiable edge is moving across the visual field. Other studies, performed on the eyes of such animals as the horseshoe crab and the cat, have also shown the presence of several different types of receptive fields in the retina; for example, some fields send neural impulses when a light stimulus is presented, others only when a light is removed, and still others increase neural firing both when a light is first presented and when it is first removed.

Specialized cells for feature detection have also been found at the cortical level. Research on the visual cortex of cats and monkeys has identified simple cells that respond only to moving slits, or bars of light, or edges marked by changes in light intensity. Other, more complex, cortical cells have been isolated that respond differentially to line segments of different sizes, as well as cells whose sensitivities are greatest if stimulated by right or acute or obtuse angles, respectively. At both retinal and cortical levels, then, considerable evidence exists that shows that lower animals have neurological hardware consistent with the hypothesis that the process of visual pattern detection occurs by a feature analysis of the stimulus. Although such evidence has not been collected at this time for humans, it seems likely that their visual hardware would be similar to other members of the animal kingdom.

The feature analysis theory is supported also by certain psychological research. One kind of supportive experiment employs a *tachistoscope,* which is a piece of laboratory apparatus that can present visual stimuli for only very brief viewing times: down to just a few thousandths of a second. If humans are shown a letter of the alphabet in a tachistoscope for only a very brief period and asked to identify the letter presented, they often make mistakes. The kinds of mistakes made are of interest, because certain letters are confused with only certain others most of the time, and the types of confusion errors that appear most frequently are those that would be predicted by a feature analysis theory of pattern recognition. For example, when an *O* is presented tachistoscopically and the subject makes an error, the mistaken letter is more likely to be a C, G, or Q than any other letter of the alphabet. The theory could explain this tendency by saying that (1) the very brief presentation time did not allow the subject to analyze and detect all of the features in the unit, so (2) the limited features analyzed may not identify the unit uniquely because they are salient features for certain other letters also, and therefore (3) the subject's error is a choice of another letter that has some (many?) of the features of the one presented. The explanation applies not only to errors made to the example *O,* of course, but also to error tendencies found for other clusters of letters having similar features.

Table 3–1 shows a "confusion matrix" that tallies the kinds of errors made by human subjects in one tachistoscopic experiment of the type just described. The rows of the matrix indicate the character (letter or numeral) shown to the subject through the tachistoscope, and the columns represent the character the subject reported seeing. The numbers in the cells of the matrix reveal how many times the subject confused the letter shown (in the row) with another letter (in the column). So, using our original example of the character *O*, we see that it was confused with *B* once, with *C* four times, with *D* once, with *G* eight times, and with *Q* four times. A quick study of the errors made for various characters should convince you that the types of errors made are consistent with error predictions generated from the feature analysis theory.

TABLE 3–1   Confusion Matrix for Letter of the Alphabet*

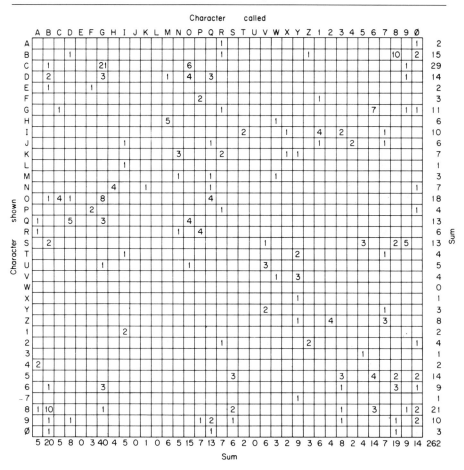

*From Kinney, Marsetta, and Showman (1966). Used with permission.

Other behavioral evidence supporting the feature analysis theory comes from experiments using *stopped images*. Normally a stable image presented to the eye does not remain fixed in one place on the retina because the retina is constantly changing its position (because of various physiological characteristics of the eye such as saccadic movements and physiological nystagmus). However, using appropriate apparatus in the perceptual laboratory, it is possible to stabilize an image on the retina so that when the eye moves the image moves in a corresponding manner, in effect *stopping* the image in a particular place. Studies using such apparatus have shown that when a human subject is exposed to a stopped image over a period of time the image gradually disappears, presumably because of the build-up of fatigue in cells either in the retina or elsewhere in the visual pattern's pathway. The interesting aspect of this disappearance phenomenon is that the image does not gradually fade away as a whole, but instead it loses certain parts or *features* of the image as time passes. Figure 3–2 illustrates some typical findings from stopped-image studies. The types of changes portrayed (for example BEER to PEER, B to 3) are quite consistent with the feature analysis theory because the aspects of the image that fade out seem related to the pattern features described above.

FIGURE 3–2. Illustrations of stopped images. On the left is the original stimulus. The outlines to the right show differential fading as a result of stopping the image. *(Adapted from Pritchard, 1963; used with permission.)*

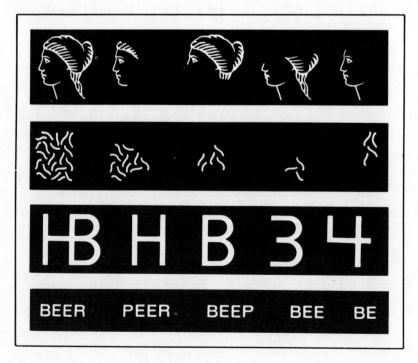

Even though there seems to be evidence, both behavioral and physiological, favoring the feature analysis theory, the theory does present certain problems. As we identify them, let us keep in mind that they may well become theory-programming conflicts if and when an attempt is made to state the theory formally in a programming language. One major question, as was the case for the template theory, is how the present theory explains the human ability to recognize letters even when they are presented at various angles. The feature analysis theory does a little better on this one than the template hypothesis, because it can explain upside-down letters quite well—that is, vertical and horizontal features, curved lines, and so on, will be as effective when a letter is upside down as when it is right side up. Moreover, tipping a letter forward or backward in the subject's line of vision may squeeze down or elongate the various features; but even so, such features as horizontal or vertical lines, angles, and curves can still be identified and thus used to recognize the pattern. Nevertheless, our second theory remains unable to handle recognition of letters tilted sideways; thus we see that, whereas it may be a somewhat better theory than the first one, it is still incomplete. And what about the human ability to recognize various type styles? Some elaboration of the feature analysis theory certainly would be needed to explain this phenomenon.

Probably other problems can be elicited too, given a little thought. These will suffice, however, to indicate that this theory—like most theories in psychology—has both assets and liabilities. As with most theories in an incompletely defined topic area, its value lies not so much in its ability to give a complete explanation of a phenomenon but rather in providing an approach to a problem that (1) is not wholly inconsistent with known facts about the phenomenon, and (2) seems well enough specified and sufficiently logical and consistent that further work directed at formalizing and developing it may be fruitful. It is in this second aspect, of course, that our main topic of computer modeling and simulation can be a helpful and important tool. So, important and necessary as the consistency between the facts and the theory may be, we shall forsake further review of empirical data in favor of a more detailed theoretical investigation of the phenomenon of pattern recognition.

Selfridge's PANDEMONIUM Model

In 1959, Oliver Selfridge described a miniature information-processing theory that was designed to recognize certain hand-written letters of the alphabet. Consistent with the feature analysis theory just described, Selfridge's theory assumed that recognition takes place by analysis of a total pattern into its constituent features. His major concern was not with the exact representation of the hardware necessary or permissable for the recognizing system (for example, retinal or cortical cells), but rather with the *process* by which a presented pattern is detected and interpreted.

Perhaps as a way of avoiding the tendency to get bogged down with hardware-type analogies and speculations, Selfridge adopted the whimsical device of calling the specialized information processors in his program *demons*.

Selfridge's theory employs several types of demons, each of which is able to perform only certain kinds of operations and which performs only at certain stages of the total recognition process. Figure 3–3 illustrates the theory upon which the program is based. The demon working in the first stage, the *image* demon, has the job of scanning the external world and recording the initial, intact image presented. It passes the image on to a group of *feature* demons in the second stage, whose task is to analyze the stimulus into subunits and to identify them. These feature demons are quite specialized. Each one looks for only a certain feature—a vertical line, a diagonal line, or a discontinuous curve—and records how many instances of that feature are present. They send this information on to the third stage for further processing by the *cognitive* demons. There is a cognitive demon for each of the recognizable patterns (letters). Each one scans the information sent by the feature demons, looking only for the type and number of features that together constitute the pattern that cognitive demon represents. Importantly, these cognitive demons begin shouting as they find the features they are looking for, and their shouts increase in loudness with discovery of each new feature they are searching for. (The din produced by all of these demons shouting simultaneously is, of course, "pandemonium.") Finally, in the last stage a single *decision* demon surveys the pandemonium, decides which cognitive demon is shouting the loudest, and reports that demon's label as the pattern recognized. The decision will not always be correct because there may be ties or other anomalies; but the hypothesis is that the loudest shouter—that is, the strongest responder to the feature information available—is the most likely label of the pattern presented.

Despite its demoniac whimsy, it is clear that this theory is not simply an amusing pastime but a sober attempt to portray a version of feature analysis theory in a formal working manner. As such, if a computer program were written to portray the theory it would not only be a working program but in addition would have considerable theoretical import. Programs of this type are often referred to by the term *computer model*. The appropriateness of the phrase comes from two sources. First, the program is a construction that represents the theoretical *ideas* in a substantive way; just as a clay model of a new car design, or a hand-built, nonproduction model that actually works in most of its details, are *models* of an earlier and less physically stated proposal. Put another way, it is a real, existing, "point-at-able" representation of the idea-level or verbal-level theory that inspired it. At the same time, because the particular theory that the program models is itself a proposal of how a part of the psychological system might process

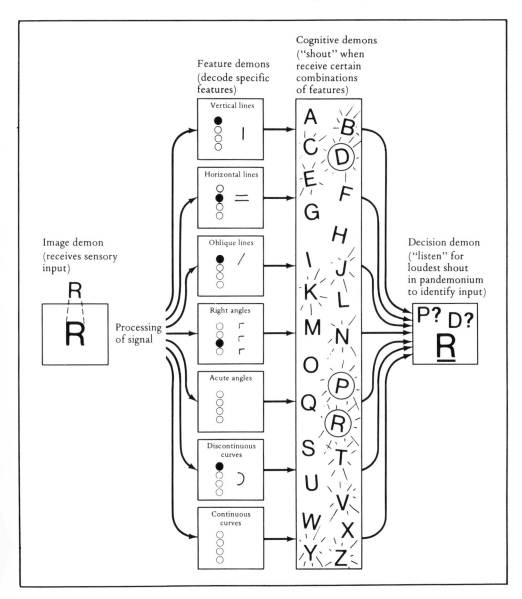

FIGURE 3–3. Selfridge's PANDEMONIUM. *(From Coren, Porac, and Wand, 1984; reprinted with permission).*

certain types of information, the program can also be construed as a model of the psychological process itself. Thus the program can be considered a model of both the theory it represents and the phenomenon the theory attempts to explain.

What will a computer model, when constructed, actually do? Here is where the term *simulation* becomes important; because a computer model, when it is written, will normally be written in a way that requires it to "simulate"—or act as though it were performing—some real behavior that the computer model is attempting to describe. Used in this sense, we see that the model is a *theory* of some reality, and a simulation is an *outcome* showing the kind of reality the theory predicts.

With the theory and these terms now defined at a verbal level, we can turn to the task of writing a model and using it to simulate the real psychological behavior of letter recognition under conditions of tachistoscopic presentation.

CONSTRUCTION OF THE MODEL

Analysis and Initial Planning

The verbal description of the PANDEMONIUM model given above, although somewhat more specific than our description of feature analysis theory, requires further analysis before it can be translated into a working program. When faced with a rather typical translation task of this sort, the psychologist-programmer can usually solve the problem by analyzing the theoretical statements from the standpoints of the cognitive structures and processes they propose. Let us apply this strategy to PANDEMONIUM. First, it hypothesizes that pattern recognition takes place in four stages: image-receiving (input), sensing and counting of the features present in the input, assignment of strengths (shout-levels) to the labels of possible patterns, and responding on the basis of label strength. These stages are assumed to occur serially, and the processing that occurs in each stage is independent of other stages, except that the results from each process are transmitted to the following stage. It is easy to think of these proposed sequential stages as *programming modules,* and to begin to represent the model (which we shall call PANDO) with a top-level structure diagram such as that shown in Figure 3–4. Then, following basic program-design strategy as outlined in Chapter 2, each of the modules can be analyzed in turn to whatever level seems necessary or sufficient to allow program coding to begin. In the process, we may well run into some of the theory-programming conflicts alluded to earlier. Now, however, we must not only document them but also arrange to overcome or circumvent them. As we shall see, this requirement will lead to some interesting compromises and perhaps some new theoretical questions and problems.

The first module in Figure 3–4 seems straightforward. The image demon, in the limited model described, simply records and arranges the input, then passes it on to the next stage. When thinking of these requirements from a programming standpoint, however, questions arise: What if

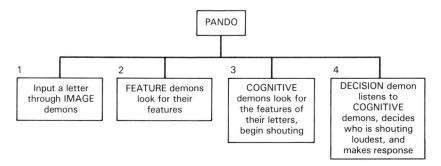

FIGURE 3–4. Top-level structure diagram for the PANDO program.

the image presented is the *R* from our scenario? When the image demon receives it, just what processes might or must it follow in order to prepare it for the next stage? Is it the one who has the responsibility for "exploding" it into its several distinctive features? Or is this explosion, as well as the noticing and counting, left to the demons in Stage 2? If we are simply the programmers, we must raise such questions to the theorist; or, as budding theorists, perhaps we will need to answer them ourselves. An associated question is, how can a letter be exploded on the computer? If the machine being used has graphics capabilities, the chore would not be difficult; if not, we will need to patch up a solution somehow. And what other processes might this Stage 1 demon have? An alert theorist, already thinking of how the model may be improved over the initial statement, might consider that the image demon could straighten up the image if it is presented at an angle, or elongate a line for emphasis, and so on.

We can see already that the programming task has identified some theoretical weak spots, and maybe some potential elaborations. Clearly, much more could be said about these and other aspects of Stage 1; but remaining too long at a verbal level delays the primary objective of writing a computer model for the theory as presently stated. For the serious modeler who wants to avoid or minimize such delays, a good working strategy is to have a worksheet available, onto which theory-programming conflicts, their current solutions, and thoughts about future elaborations might be recorded. We shall follow this strategy by simply making note of Stage 1 concerns and pushing on to program design.

Assuming that the computer terminal available may not have graphics capabilities, let us decide to skip the explosion process when building the model by inputting the letter in already exploded form. Table 3–2 presents a convenient input form for the letters of the alphabet. Each letter may be uniquely identified by inputting a 7-digit number, with each digit corresponding to the number of occurrences in the letter of one of the features listed across the top of the table. Examples of these codes are

TABLE 3–2 Features of the Letters of the Alphabet

	Vertical lines	Horizontal lines	Oblique lines	Right angles	Acute angles	Continuous curves	Uncontinuous curves
A		1	2		3		
B	1	3		4			2
C							1
D	1	2		2			1
E	1	3		4			
F	1	2		3			
G	1	1		1			1
H	2	1		4			
I	1	2		4			
J	1						1
K	1		2	1	2		
L	1	1		1			
M	2		2		3		
N	2		1		2		
O						1	
P	1	2		3			1
Q			1		2	1	
R	1	2	1	3			1
S							2
T	1	1		2			
U	2						1
V			2		1		
W			4		3		
X			2		2		
Y	1		2		1		
Z		2	1		2		

(From Lindsay and Norman, 1977, p. 264; reprinted with permission.)

R = 1 2 1 3 0 0 1
A = 0 1 2 0 3 0 0

and so on. In Module 1, then, we agree to (1) enter each letter in the form of a 7-digit code that represents the structural features of the letter, and (2) make note for future theoretical considerations that the processing stage represented by Module 1 is incomplete and requires further elaboration.

Module 2 in Figure 3–4 presents an interesting possibility for simulation. Recall that one of the behavioral phenomena supporting a feature analysis theory is the finding that the errors made in tachistoscopic studies of letter recognition are usually confusions of the letter presented with other letters having similar features. (For example, note the similar patterns for B = 1 3 0 4 0 0 2 and P = 1 2 0 3 0 0 1 and R = 1 2 1 3 0 0 1 in Table 3–2.) A computer model of letter recognition should be able to account for these systematic confusions. Let us take a moment to formulate a hypothesis about how the confusion patterns might be accounted for in Stage 2 of our developing model.

> We propose that the feature demons in the second stage are not alert and sensitive all of the time, and thus there is some nonzero probability that at any given moment any one of them may fail to notice and count the feature that it represents. Moreover, this probability is assumed to be time-dependent; that is, the shorter the time of presentation, the lower the probability that a given demon will notice and count its feature.

Will such a hypothesis really account for the confusion patterns noticed in actual behavioral experiments? The answer is debatable; but instead of debating it, we shall write the hypothesis into the computer model, enter it on the worksheet for future reference, and let some simulation runs provide some data concerning the matter.

Naturally, implementing this probabilistic hypothesis in Module 2 will require some programming. Figure 3–5a illustrates the lower-level details of Module 2 of the top-level diagram in Figure 3–4. It can be understood in context with Figure 3–5b, which shows the necessary data structures for the PANDO program. A reasonable verbal statement of the algorithm shown in Figure 3–5a, which includes the hypothesis above, is:

For each of the seven feature demons:

> If a number drawn from a random number generator exceeds the probability that the demon is "attending," then ignore this demon and process the next one; else have this demon notice and count its feature.

Figure 3–5 shows the details of how this verbally stated algorithm is actually implemented; that is, how "noticing and counting" and "the probability of attending" can be represented in a working program. Look for a

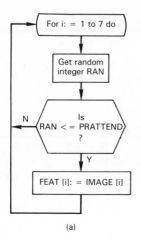

(a)

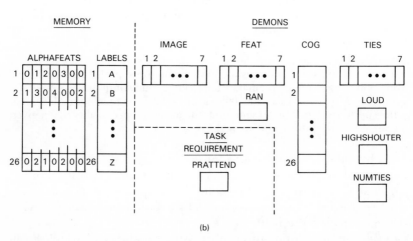

(b)

FIGURE 3–5. (a) Lower-level details of Module 2 in Figure 3–4; (b) Data structures for PANDO.

moment at the data structures in Figure 3–5b. The ALPHAFEATS and LABELS structures are assumed to be part of existing memory, so they must be read in at the start of execution. The variable PRATTEND, also entered at the beginning of program execution, will contain a number between 0.00 and 1.00, indicating the probability of attending to a given feature. This value reflects the requirements of the recognition task; that is, the faster the (simulated) tachistoscopic presentation of a letter, the lower is the probability of a feature demon successfully attending to a given feature of the letter. Then, when the model actually begins to process a stimulus, the 7-cell array IMAGE will be loaded with the features that are sensed during Stage 1 when the stimulus is tachistoscopically presented; for example, IMAGE would contain the digits 1 2 1 3 0 0 1 if the letter *R* had been presented to the model. The Stage 2 structures include RAN, which—using the random-number generating function available for the Pascal system being used (Excercise 5 at end of chapter)—can be loaded with a random number between 0.00 and 1.00; and it also includes the array FEAT, which at the end of this stage will contain the features that the seven feature demons have "noticed."

Given these structures, the algorithm presented graphically in Figure 3–5a can be summarized verbally in this manner:

Verbal Diagram for Stage 2

For Demons 1 to 7:

1. Get RAN from the Pascal random-number generator;
2. If RAN < = PRATTEND then show "noticing and counting" by assigning to this demon's FEAT cell the number residing in the corresponding IMAGE cell; else indicate that the demon did not "attend to" its feature by assigning to its FEAT cell an "inattention" signal, such as the integer 9;
3. Continue at #1 with the next demon.

There are 26 cognitive demons in Stage 3, and the processes required in the corresponding Module 3 must arrange for each of them to (1) examine each feature sent by the feature demons, and (2) increment the loudness of its shouting each time a feature match is found. As programmers, we must find a way of programming this process and representing the outcome. One possible way is to employ the 26-cell array COG as shown in Figure 3–5b, where each cell represents a cognitive demon (ranging from A to Z) and the entry in the cell is an integer specifying the current loudness or shout-level for that demon. The process in this module would then be:

Verbal Diagram for Stage 3

1. Set all shout-levels to 0, then
2. For each feature in FEAT 1 through 7, if the value of the current feature is 9, then this feature demon was not attending to business in Stage 2 so it has no information to send on to the cognitive demons; else send the feature on to #3;
3. For cognitive demons A through Z:
    If the value of the current feature equals the value this cognitive demon is looking for (as found in an appropriate cell in ALPHAFEATS), then add 1 to the shout-level currently assigned to that demon's COG cell and then continue; else continue.

After the COG vector has been filled with the appropriate shout-levels, the decision demon in Module 4 must survey the pandemonium and decide which cognitive demon is shouting the loudest. If there are no ties in shout-level, the programming solution is rather straightforward; for example:

Set cells LOUD and HIGHSHOUTER to 0, then

1. For COG cells 1 through 26:
   If the COG cell contains an integer higher than that currently assigned to LOUD, then assign the value of the current COG cell to LOUD and assign the current row number of COG to HIGHSHOUTER, then continue; else continue;
2. Print LABELS[HIGHSHOUTER] as the letter recognized.

The problem with this algorithm is that it does not account for ties in shout-levels. Remember that, by making the attentiveness of the feature demons probabilistic, we introduced a possibility of error into the shout-levels, and in consequence some of them might be the same. In such circumstances, the decision demon should record the cognitive demons who are tied for the highest shout-level and then guess which one of them is correct. (Such behavior will, of course, simulate the human behaviors of uncertainty and guessing and error in the tachistoscope experiment.) The array TIES in Figure 3–5b provides a way of recording such ties, and the cell NUMTIES can keep a record of how many ties for the loudest shout exist at any given moment. The algorithm utilizing these structures could be:

Verbal Diagram for Stage 4

Set NUMTIES to 0 and LOUD to 1, then

1. For COG cells 1 through 26:
   a. if COG > LOUD then
      1. set NUMTIES = 1
      2. set LOUD = value of current COG cell
      3. set TIES [1] = number of current COG cell
      4. continue
   b. else if COG = LOUD then
      1. set NUMTIES = NUMTIES + 1
      2. set TIES [NUMTIES] = number of current COG cell
      3. continue
   c. else continue
2. If NUMTIES = 1, then print LABELS[TIES[1]]; else
   1. assign to RAN a random integer between 1 and NUMTIES
   2. print LABELS[TIES[RAN]].

You should examine this Stage 4 scheme long enough to convince yourself that the decision demon will always pick the loudest if there is one loudest

TABLE 3–3   Worksheet for PANDO

THEORY-PROGRAMMING CONFLICTS	CURRENT SOLUTIONS
1. How does theory account for recognition of letters presented at angles, or for differing typescripts?	1. None.
2. How do image demons "explode" characters?	2. Characters are input in exploded form, as shown in Table 3–2.
3. Why do feature demons sometimes fail to attend to their features? What determines which features are missed?	3. Failures of attention are simulated by random number generator and parameter PRATTEND.
4. The theory assumes *serial* processing by the image, feature, cognitive, and decision demons in sequence. But for each type of demon, should the demons within that type operate serially or in *parallel*?	4. Serial processing by the different types of demons is assumed in the current model. The stages are processed serially, and within each stage the demons also process their information serially.

shouter, but if there are N ties then each tie might be picked with probability 1/N.

That is all that needs to be said about the general structure and plan of a program designed to simulate a tachistoscopic letter-recognition task according to a somewhat modified interpretation of Selfridge's PANDE-MONIUM. The modifications, and some thoughts about potential future elaborations, are contained in our worksheet as shown in Table 3–3. Figure 3–6 elaborates the top-level design of Figure 3–4, illustrating graphically the procedural sequence of the verbal diagrams presented above. Also, in recognition of the need to establish memory structures for both the alphabetic features and alphabet labels, an initial "housekeeping" module has been added to the original design. This type of module is almost always necessary in computer modeling because in addition to writing the model itself certain theoretical preconditions must often be specified (for example, loading memory with previously learned information), variables and/or parameters must be defined, and other potential details cleaned up.

The next section of this chapter presents in some detail the tactics for coding the program. The section is provided only if it is needed; if you believe you can write the program without further help, you should go on to the conclusion and exercises at the end of the chapter and then write your own version of PANDO. Use the description below if you get into trouble or to compare it with your program once it is finished.

Coding the Program

With a general plan now in mind, as summarized in Figure 3–6, it is time to start writing the program. We shall look at each module in turn, discuss alternative techniques as necessary, and give examples. A complete listing of a working program is shown in Appendix B.

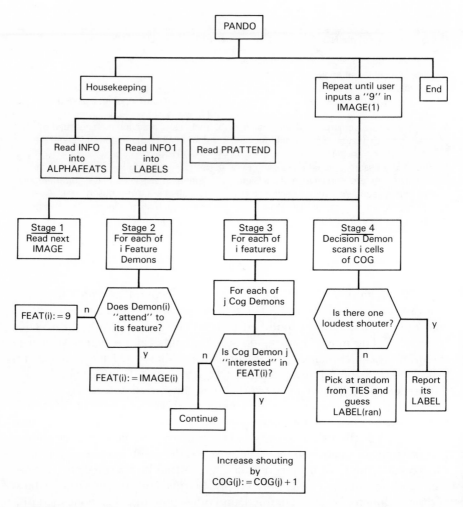

FIGURE 3–6. An elaborated structure diagram for PANDO program.

Housekeeping module. The programming chores in this module are to (1) create the ALPHAFEATS and LABELS array, as shown in Figure 3–5b, (2) establish other global variables as necessary, and (3) get the attention probability for the current simulation run. There are several ways to create the arrays listed in (1). One is to read the data into each array at the beginning of each execution; but obviously with $7 \times 26 = 182$ integers to put into ALPHAFEATS and another 26 characters into LABELS, the typing chore at the start of each execution would be cumbersome indeed. An alternative would be to use assignment statements within the program to assign the correct constant to each cell of each array; for example

```
          .
          .
   labels[1]:='A';
   labels[2]:='B';
          .
          .

   <etc.>
```

Although this method is perhaps slightly better than the first, it is also rather inelegant. A superior way to input large amounts of data into a program is to store the data in an external file on a disk and then READ the data from the file into the data structures in the program when execution begins. Arranging to input data this way is not difficult, and it is needed so often when constructing complex programs that it is worthwhile to review the technique here.

Figure 3–7 shows a typical computer configuration, in which the basic components are a terminal containing a keyboard for input and a TV screen for output, a central processing unit (CPU), a primary memory, and—most important for our present discussion—a *disk* on which information can be stored. This disk may be a "hard" disk, as found on large computing systems, or a "floppy" disk, as found on most microcomputers nowadays. Although the two types differ in looks and construction, they serve the same purpose; namely, to store information in such a manner

FIGURE 3–7. Storing a data file on the disk.

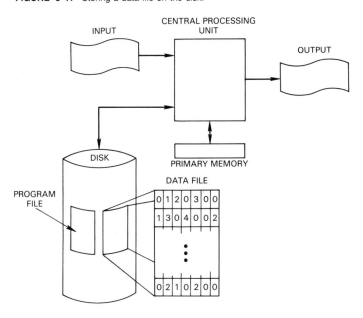

that, upon command, the information can be transferred to the primary memory and used there for whatever purposes intended for it.

One good example of this storage of information on the disk and its retrieval to primary memory when needed is the process of writing a program and then executing it. If you use a modern computer you know that you use an *editor* to build a *file,* which, when stored on the disk, holds your program (see Fig. 3–7). Once that file is built and saved on the disk, you may *execute* it anytime you wish by typing in certain commands that vary from machine to machine. Regardless of machine, however, once the execution command is given, a copy of the disk file containing your program is transferred into the primary memory and—following other steps such as program compilation—is executed. Thus the program always remains on file on the disk for use at any time.

Now let us extend this process to include disk storage of data as well as a program. Figure 3–7 shows that, along with the file containing your program, you may store a separate *data file*—that is, a file that contains not a set of Pascal (or other language) instructions but simply information that can be *read* by a program and used by it as data. To make this arrangement, you need to know (1) how to build a data file and put it on the disk, and (2) how to get a Pascal program to read the data from the data file into its data structures.

The procedure for building a data file and storing it on the disk will vary somewhat depending upon the computer being used, but you probably already know how to do it on your machine because it follows the same rules you follow when building a program. You simply use the editor to name a new file, and then instead of typing the lines of a program, you type the data. Using this technique, let us build a data file as illustrated in Figure 3–7 (we shall name the file FEATURES) that contains the information necessary for the ALPHAFEATS array, and another data file called LETTERS (not shown in Figure 3–7) containing the letters necessary for the LABELS array. A possible format for FEATURES, as illustrated in Figure 3–7, is to put the integers representing alphabetic features in 26 file rows, arranged so that the first row holds the seven digits for *A,* the second row for *B,* and so on (the correct integers are given in Table 3–2). In the LETTERS data file we will put the 26 letters of the alphabet, one per row. These will eventually be read into the LABELS array.

Having stored these two data files on the disk, the next step is to arrange the Pascal program so that when it begins execution it will read the information contained in them into the appropriate cells in the data structures ALPHAFEATS and LABEL, respectively. Examine the following Pascal coding to see how this may be done.

```
PROGRAM PANDO (input, output, FEATURES, LETTERS);

    (* Note that the names of the external files are given
      in the PROGRAM line above *)
```

```
VAR alphafeats: array[1..26,1..7] of integer;
    labels: array[1..26] of char;
    features, letters: text;
    image, feat: array[1..7] of integer;

        .
        .


PROCEDURE LOADFILE (var features: text);

VAR ii,jj: integer;
BEGIN
    reset(features);
    for ii:=1 to 26 do
     for jj:=1 to 7 do
            read(features,alphafeats[ii,jj])
END;          (* end of loadfile *)

PROCEDURE LOADFILE1 (var letters: text);

VAR ii: integer;

BEGIN
    reset(letters);
    for ii:=1 to 26 do
     readln(letters,labels[ii])
END;          (* loadfile1 ends here *)
        .
        .
```

There are several aspects to consider in this file-reading procedure, which we must look at one at a time. First, whenever a Pascal program is built to read an external file, the name by which that file has been stored on the disk must appear in the parentheses in the program heading. Next, in standard Pascal the data type TEXT can be used to describe the type of data contained in any external file. This variable declaration is made in the VAR section; for example, FEATURES, LETTERS: TEXT; as shown above.

Now look at the LOADFILE and LOADFILE1 procedures, which will load the contents of the FEATURES and LETTERS data files into the arrays ALPHAFEATS and LABELS, respectively. Note that in each procedure a parameter naming the file to be read must be identified in the parentheses following the procedure name. Then, to prepare the file for reading, the statement RESET(filename) is used.

Following this preparation, the READ or READLN commands may be used to read the data from the file into a data structure in the program. To indicate that the file is to be read—rather than the keyboard—it is necessary to put the file name just inside the left parenthesis of the READ statement. Fortunately, you don't have to worry about type compatibility; a TEXT file may be read into an INTEGER, CHAR, or any other appropriate type of data structure without mishap.

Although there may be minor variations in these rules from machine to machine, they should help to get you started with file handling. As you have probably guessed, when you are familiar with the use of input files the next step is to have programs build output files that will store the results of program execution permanently on the disk. You can probably figure out for yourself what the output rules are like.

Having finished these housekeeping declarations, let us look at the statement part of the main block before analyzing the procedures needed for representing each of the psychological stages of the model. The statement part of the main block can be written as follows:

```
BEGIN                    (* Instructions in Main Program *)
loadfile(features);
loadfile1(letters);

writeln('Enter attention probability');
readln(prattend);

stage1;

repeat
    stage2;
    stage3;
    stage4;
    stage1
until image[1] = 9
END.                     (* End Main Program *)
```

This main program segment first calls the housekeeping procedures LOADFILE and LOADFILE1 to transfer the contents of the data files FEATURES and LETTERS into their respective arrays. Next it obtains from the user the attention probability, using a prompt and a READLN instruction. This completes the housekeeping chores. All that remains for the main program is to run the model itself.

The model itself is executed using a REPEAT-UNTIL statement, which allows the user to input as many 7-digit codes ("experimental trials") as desired and then end program execution by putting the integer 9 as a stop signal into the first position of another input. Each time the REPEAT-UNTIL loop executes, it calls the procedures STAGE1, STAGE2, STAGE3, and STAGE4, which represent the four psychological stages of PANDO and are analyzed in detail below. Before proceeding to their analysis, however, you should note that the stages are not called in strictly consecutive order inside the REPEAT-UNTIL loop. This is because of the execution rules this instruction follows. Remember that a REPEAT-UNTIL is used when we want to do something at the end of a loop and, on the basis of the outcome, decide whether or not the loop should be repeated. In our model, the signal to stop the loop will come when the user inputs a new image for which the first feature value is a 9. Because the user inputs each image in Stage 1 of the model, it follows that Stage 1 should occur just before the end of the REPEAT-UNTIL loop; hence, the calling sequence for the stages within the loop becomes (2, 3, 4, 1) rather than (1, 2, 3, 4).

Naturally, this arrangement raises the issue of how the loop will get started because the model assumes that Stages 2, 3, and 4 will never be executed until Stage 1 has been completed. This start-up difficulty, which arises nearly every time a programmer uses a REPEAT-UNTIL instruction, is overcome by executing STAGE1 a first time just before entering the REPEAT-UNTIL loop. From then on the loop takes care of itself because even though STAGE1 next occurs at the bottom of the loop, it will always be executed just before the STAGE2 procedure is called. Study this strategy, shown in the program segment above, and be sure you understand it before going further.

The STAGE1 procedure. The procedure needed to represent Stage 1 of the model is short and straightforward, needing only to read the features of the stimulus presented into the 7-cell array IMAGE. Remember that we agreed to simulate the work of the Stage 1 demon by simply having the user type on the keyboard the digits representing the features of the stimulus being presented (see item no. 2 of Table 3–3). A procedure to accomplish this task is:

```
PROCEDURE STAGE1;

VAR i: integer;

BEGIN
  for i := 1 to 7 do
    read (image[i])
END;          (* stage1 ends here *)
```

STAGE2. In this module a random number must be generated for each feature demon to decide if it will "attend" or not; and if it does attend then its feature gets loaded into its FEAT cell, otherwise a 9 is entered into its FEAT cell to indicate that it was not attending. Generation of a random number in Pascal is usually done via a built-in function call; but the exact technique will vary depending upon the machine being used, so if you don't already know how to generate a random number between 0.00 and 1.00 on the computer you are using you should look it up in the manual for that machine or find out from someone who knows how to get random numbers using your version of Pascal. (Should your version not have a built-in random-number generator, you can build your own function as described in Exercise 5 at the end of this chapter.)

Let us assume that your computer enables you to generate a random number between 0.00 and 1.00 and assign it to a real identifier RAN, and assume also (as shown in the program segment above) that the probability of any demon attending at a given moment has been read into the cell PRATTEND at the start of program execution. We must first figure out how to translate these numbers into a decision about whether or not the current demon is attending. Consider, as an example, that PRATTEND = 0.25, indicating that each feature demon has a 25 percent probability of attending correctly to its feature and passing it on to the cognitive demons. We know that when the random number generator is called to produce a random number and assign it to RAN, it will with 25 percent probability produce a value between 0.00 and 0.25; and, of course, it will produce a number between 0.25 and 1.00 the other 75 percent of the time. Therefore, a good way to decide whether to attend or not to attend is with an IF..THEN statement such as

```
if RAN < PRATTEND then "attend" else "don't attend";
```

Using this simple trick, it is now easy to write the code for the "attend" and "don't attend" components of the statement and to come up with the following procedure as a model of Stage 2:

```
PROCEDURE STAGE2;

VAR i: integer;
    ran: real;

BEGIN
for i:= 1 to 7 do
    begin
    ran:= (* call a random # from your computer *);
    if ran < prattend
            then feat[i]:=image[i]
            else feat[i]:= 9
    end
END;         (* stage2 ends here *)
```

STAGE3. The procedure representing Stage 3 of the theory is straightforward, requiring only that the COG array first be initialized to zero, then loaded with the shout-level for each of the 26 cognitive demons as they are presented with each feature of the present letter. Since the number of features and the number of cognitive demons are known, the simplest way to accomplish the task is with a set of FOR..DO loops as shown in the following example. Study the various loops, making sure you mind your p's and q's.

```
.
.
PROCEDURE STAGE3;

VAR p, q: integer;

BEGIN
for p:= 1 to 26 do
      cog[p] := 0;
for p:= 1 to 7 do
      if feat[p] <> 9 then
            for q:= 1 to 26 do
                  if feat[p] = alphafeats[q,p] then
                        cog[q] := cog[q] + 1
END;                    (* stage3 ends here *)
      .
      .
```

STAGE4. The final stage of the model must simulate a decision demon that first locates the cognitive demon or demons shouting the loudest, and then either names the single loudest shouter or guesses at random from those tied for the loudest shout. The strategy for finding the loudest shout, as shown in the Stage 4 verbal diagram on page 48, is to set an identifier LOUD to zero and then compare each cognitive demon's shout-level (found in COG) to the contents of LOUD, recording new loud shouters as needed. The following code illustrates how this can be done:

```
.
.
PROCEDURE STAGE4;
VAR i, loud, numties, guess: integer;
      ties: array[1..26] of integer;

BEGIN
numties:= 0;
loud:= 1;
                  (* find loudest shout(s) *)
```

```
for i:= 1 to 26 do
    if cog[i] > loud then          (* a new loud shouter *)
        begin
            numties:= 1;
            loud:= cog[i];
            ties[1]:= i
        end

    else if cog[i] = loud then     (* a tie! *)
        begin
            numties:= numties + 1;
            ties[numties]:= i
        end;
                .
                .
```

The FOR..DO loop in this first segment of the STAGE4 procedure processes an IF..THEN..ELSE statement 26 times. On each loop the IF..THEN
instruction checks to see if the current demon is shouting louder than any
previously processed demon, and if so it makes that demon the current
loudest shouter by setting the number of ties to 1 and recording the demon's identification (i) in the first cell of TIES. If the demon is not the
loudest shouter thus far, it may still be tied with the loudest, so the ELSE
segment checks for a possible tie. If there is a tie, the current number of ties
is recorded in NUMTIES and the identification of all tied demons is contained in the array TIES[1] through TIES[numties].

When the loop above finishes, it is time for the decision demon to report its findings. If there is only one highest shouter, it can report the letter
associated with that single cognitive demon. Otherwise, a guess must be
made among the two or more tied loud shouters. The remainder of the
STAGE4 procedure can accomplish either contingency as follows:

```
                .
                .
    (* decision demon prints response *)
writeln;

if numties = 0 then writeln('No match found')

    else if numties = 1 then
        writeln('The letter is', labels[ties[1]])

    else
    begin
        ran:= (* call a random # from your computer *);
        guess:= 1 + trunc(numties*ran);
        writeln('My guess is ',labels[ties[guess]])
    end
END;        (* end stage4 *)
```

It is worthwhile to examine the WRITELN statements containing LABELS to see how they operate. The first one uses for a subscript the identifier TIES[1]. Why? Recall that if there are no ties for the loudest shouter then NUMTIES will equal 1 and TIES[1] will contain the integer identification of the loudest cognitive demon; hence, TIES[1] will give LABELS the correct integer identity of the loudest cognitive demon.

And how do ties get handled? Recognize that GUESS, when calculated, will be a randomly chosen integer between 1 and NUMTIES, the number of ties. The random selection is accomplished by (1) getting a random number RAN between 0.00 and 1.00; (2) multiplying this RAN by NUMTIES and—using the built-in function TRUNC—truncating the resulting decimal value to an integer whose value will have to be between 0 and NUMTIES-1; and finally (3) adding that result to 1, yielding an integer value between 1 and NUMTIES. This randomly chosen integer, when assigned to GUESS, can now be used to pick "at random" from among the ties recorded in the TIES arrray.

With all modules examined, it is time to put the various segments together, debug as necessary, and arrive at a working model. Try it.

CONCLUSION

When the simple model described here is executed, it outputs a series of lines; for example:

```
The letter is A

My guess is G

etc.
```

.

.

The responses will be consistent with the theory as described in the working model; but are they consistent with the way humans operate under tachistoscopic conditions? We could answer this question by making statistical comparisons between the types of errors made by the program and the probabilities of confusion errors for various letters as calculated from confusion data such as that illustrated in Table 3–1. We will not illustrate such procedures here; rather, we will simply note that they are available and not very difficult. More to our purpose, let us note that even if such a test proved that the model as constructed here was not successful, it would not necessarily mean that the theoretical and programming efforts had been wasted. If anything, the beginning program will have provided a base for additions to current hypotheses, modifications of those hypotheses, or other theoretical approaches. Thus the computer modeling exercise will have achieved the several useful functions noted earlier in the chapter: providing a formal means of stating the theoretical proposal, providing a means of testing and examining the proposal, and providing a way of altering and elaborating the proposal as necessary.

SUGGESTED READINGS

Because our emphasis is upon programming, explanations of pertinent psychological theories about the topics of perception and pattern matching have necessarily been in summary form. Two good introductory sources for further elaboration of both the template matching and feature analysis models are Lindsay and Norman (1977, Chapters 6 and 7) and Reynolds and Flagg (1983). The original PANDEMONIUM model has been described nicely by Selfridge and Neisser (1971).

EXERCISES

1. Revise the PANDO program so it can collect simulation data for *N* responses to each of the letters of the alphabet, and generate as output a confusion matrix showing the errors of recognition made by the program. The matrix should look like the one shown in Table 3–1, except the numbers of errors will be from the simulation run rather than from an experiment with humans.

2. Compare the program simulation obtained by Exercise 1 with the human experimental data shown in Table 3–1. Are they similar? If not, how might you change the PANDO program so the match between simulated and human data will improve? Do the changes you recommend have theoretical import?

3. In Stage 3 of the simple model described in this chapter, the rule for incrementing shout-levels is that each COG demon (1) looks at each FEATure and (2) raises its shout-level by 1 if the contents of the FEATure cell *exactly match* the number of units the COG demon requires. What are some alternative rules for establishing shout-levels? How might these alternatives affect the decision eventually made?

4. The speed and versatility of today's computers make it possible to write programs that make the computer act like (model) a tachistoscope. Write a program that will enable you to collect data for a human letter-recognition task under tachistoscopic conditions. Have the program contain a loop that will (1) clear the output screen, (2) present a random letter of the alphabet for a very brief time (say *N* milliseconds) on the screen, (3) prompt the person to type on the keyboard the letter that just appeared, and (4) store both the stimulus and the response for later output. In an initial housekeeping module, prompt the experimenter to input the time parameter *N* so that different tachistoscopic speeds can be explored.

[Hint: If your computer has a built-in clock you can use it as a base for timing; otherwise you may need to experiment with different values of *N* using a "software clock" such as the following:

```
          .
          .
writeln (letter);
for j:= 1 to N do
       i:= 100;
<clear screen>
          .
          .
```

where the FOR..DO loop will loop for a short period between letter presentation and clearing the screen.]

5. The randon-number generator is a basic tool for computer modeling and simulation. Some Pascal compilers have built-in generators, but it is not difficult to build a reasonably good one yourself. The basic idea is to define an initial SEED that, when multiplied by a large and well-chosen constant, will produce a huge number. When this product is split and only some of the digits are saved, the saved result will be a number that looks like it has been picked at random from a pool of numbers ranging between 0.00 and 1.00. By setting the SEED equal to the newly generated random number, a repetition of the process will produce another random number between 0 and 1. The choice of constant is critical because some constants yield results that look very much like random numbers whereas others do not. (Actually there is no perfect constant and thus no way of generating an infinite set of truly random numbers; hence, in a technical sense, all computer algorithms for random-number generation produce only pseudorandom numbers.)
    The following code (taken from Bowles, 1977, p. 257) is the basis for a reasonably good random-number generator:

```
          .
          .
seed:= seed * 27.182813 + 31.415917;
seed:= seed - trunc(seed);
          .
          .
```

where the original SEED is any real number and the resulting SEED is a pseudorandom number between 0 and 1.
    (1) Write a Pascal function RAND, using this code, which will return a pseudorandom number betwen 0 and 1.
    (2) Embed it in a program that will generate *N* pseudorandom numbers given any real number as the initial SEED.
    (3) Test the adequacy of the generator statistically. [Hint: A simple strategy for making such a test would be to write a program that will generate a

large number of pseudorandom numbers, counting the frequency of occurrence of numbers that range, say, from 0.00 to 0.10, from 0.10 to 0.20, and so on up to the range from 0.90 to 1.00. These observed frequency counts can then be compared with the expected (theoretical) frequency counts using a chi-square test. Such a program could be adjusted, of course, to collect frequencies of any of a variety of ranges of pseudorandom numbers. A complete analysis would require other tests as well.]

4

Computer Models and Simulations of Human Memory

One major area of psychology that has been dramatically influenced by computer and information science is the study of human memory. How people remember (and forget) has always been an important and interesting question, and theoretical controversies about the workings of memory date at least from the early Greeks. Despite the long history of interest in memory and how it functions, no complete and satisfactory theory of how the human memory works has yet been constructed. The development of the computer has helped to provoke some recent and substantial gains, however, in the sophistication of memory theory. And, perhaps even more importantly, it has provided psychologists with a fruitful framework within which the problems of memory, and their potential solutions, can be described and discussed.

In this chapter we will first look briefly at some important psychological experiments that led to the development of the several major psychological models of memory that command attention today. With these experimental facts as a base, we can then describe a current theory of human memory and write a computer model of it that simulates some typical memory functions.

SOME EXPERIMENTAL BACKGROUND

In the late 1950s several experiments were performed in psychology labo-
ratories that proved to have a dramatic influence upon memory theory.
These studies were reported by different psychologists, working independently of each other and interested in different topics. Eventually their
findings were combined, along with selected viewpoints from the earlier
days of psychology, to form the basis of a major theoretical viewpoint concerning human memory.

G.A. Miller (1956) made the first important contribution. One of the
questions he asked in his classic article entitled "The Magical Number
Seven, Plus or Minus Two: Some Limits on our Capacity for Processing Information" was whether immediate memory in humans is limited by the
amount of information to be remembered. Immediate memory, as you
may guess, is that component of our total memory capacity that lets us remember a limited amount of information accurately for a short period of
time. To illustrate, consider this well-known immediate-memory test for
digits. Suppose a person were to recite to you the following string of digits,
one at a time with about a 1-second interval between each, and ask you to
recite them back from memory after the list is complete:

8 1 9 3 7 8 5 2 1 4 6 2 9 4.

Memory experiments of this sort have shown that when first exposed to
this test people generally can remember only 6 or 7 digits accurately, and
the rest of the information is lost or forgotten.

The results of a test such as this might lead us to the conclusion that
the immediate-memory capability of the human mind reaches a point
where, much like a telephone channel or some other information-
transmitting device, it gets overloaded with information and begins to
make mistakes and give inaccurate or garbled output. In his article, however, Miller reviewed substantial experimental evidence to indicate that
such an "informational overload" interpretation of human memory capacity is incorrect. Although admittedly poor at first at remembering large
amounts of new information, most people with a little practice are able to
remember many more than just six or seven digits. They do so by
combining (Miller called it *chunking* or *recoding*) single digits into larger
units and then remembering these larger chunks. Using the test list above
as an example, one might improve the memory span twofold by recoding
the single digits into 2-digit chunks such as

81 93 78 52 14 62 94.

When such recoding takes place, the person becomes able to store seven 2-digit numbers, which, when decoded, permits immediate memory of 14 digits—clearly much more digital information than was possible without recoding.

Miller concluded from the evidence collected that immediate memory is not limited by the information to be processed, but by the number of *chunks* that it can handle at a time. That number seems to hover around seven, give or take one or two. He summarized his findings by hypothesizing that ". . . the number of chunks is constant for immediate memory. The span of immediate memory seems to be almost independent of the number of bits per chunk, at least over the range that has been examined to date" (Miller, 1956, p. 93).

Although not a very specific hypothesis at first, it has been given considerably greater specificity as more data have accumulated (see Simon, 1974), and its validity is quite well accepted today. Simple as the hypothesis may sound, it was a critical opening wedge in changing psychological thinking from a tendency to view mind as a passive and mechanistic system (for example, a telephone line carrying a certain capacity that could be measured in bits of information) to a view that the mind is an *active processor* of information, having its limitations, of course (for example, 7 ± 2), but also having control processes (that is, chunking) that help to actively rearrange information in ways that overcome the physical limitations of the system.

The second study important to the development of current memory theory is one conducted by Peterson and Peterson (1959). These psychologists wanted to examine the adequacy of immediate memory under conditions where the person is not permitted to rehearse the information to be remembered. The simple but basic experiment they devised worked as follows: A participant in the experiment was shown a single item of information (for example, a nonsense syllable or a word) for one second, then was shown a 3-digit number and told to count backwards (aloud) by threes from that number until a signal light was flashed; then, immediately after the signal, the participant was asked to remember and repeat out loud the information item originally presented. The time interval during which counting occurred was, of course, a memory interval; and the counting requirement was a way of occupying the person mentally and thus preventing covert rehearsal of the test item during the interval.

The Petersons ran many such tests, giving the signal at intervals of 3, 6, 9, 12, 15, or 18 seconds following item presentation. Their results showed a steady and dramatic drop in memory as the intervals increased, with only about 8 percent of the test items being recalled after 18 seconds. Without rehearsal, immediate memories for even single items were terrible!

The Peterson and Peterson results are consistent with a later study by Waugh and Norman (1965) who, using another experimental technique, also demonstrated that if anything interferes with rehearsal then memory for new information is poor. Acknowledging William James' insights and terminology, Waugh and Norman devised a miniature theory to describe and account for their results. They proposed that (1) there is a "primary memory" into which external information is first stored; (2) this storage area has limited capacity, so when it gets overloaded some information in it is lost (forgotten); (3) there is also a "secondary memory" that has an unlimited capacity and stores information more permanently; and (4) information can be transferred from primary to secondary memory by the process of rehearsal.

Waugh and Norman's basic proposal revived William James' early insights and added to them the strength of experimental data. Quite quickly the proposal was elaborated to include Miller's chunking hypothesis by adding that (1) the storage capacity of STM (for *short-term memory*, a construct that has replaced the original term "primary memory") is limited to approximately seven units of information; and (2) the operations or processes available to STM include not simply rehearsal but the capability of increasing information storage by recoding or chunking multiple units of information into a larger unit and then storing the chunk as a single storage unit. The theory is illustrated in Figure 4–1. Note the use of another new term, LTM (for *long-term memory*), to replace the earlier "secondary memory."

FIGURE 4–1. A functional theory of verbal memory. *(adapted and elaborated from Waugh and Norman, 1965).*

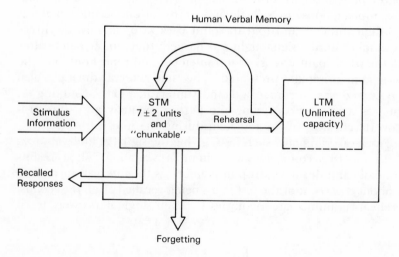

Since its historical description by James, and its more recent revival by Waugh and Norman, a number of elaborations and alternatives to the basic theory have been proposed (see Atkinson & Shiffrin, 1968), all having the common approach of assuming two basic types or structures in human memory—STM and LTM. These several models may be classified together as variations of the Duplex Theory of memory.

TESTING AND VALIDATING THE DUPLEX THEORY OF MEMORY

How can a miniature theory such as the one just described be tested? As we already know, one major way to perform such tests is to conduct new laboratory experiments to see if the data collected continue to support the theory. Over the years a large number and variety of experiments have been reported that demonstrate and provide empirical evidence concerning various hypotheses related to the duplex theory. The immediate-memory experiment and the Peterson and Peterson rehearsal experiment just mentioned are examples. Another major experimental technique that has been used often is the free recall experiment. The strategy behind an experiment of this sort is to (1) use the theory to predict what should happen in a free recall experiment, and then (2) give a free recall task to a number of people and see if the way they actually perform the task matches the predictions of the theory. Let us first examine the details of what is meant by the "free recall task" and see how the results obtained from free recall laboratory experiments are predictable from the duplex theory of memory. Then, having reviewed this standard experimental technique, we will be in a good position to make another kind of theoretical test that involves computer modeling and simulation.

In a free recall task, a person is given a list of words to learn (usually 20 words or more) and then asked to recall as many of them as possible. The usual laboratory procedure is to present the words for study one at a time (either visually or aurally) at a fairly rapid rate, and then ask the person to write down all the words that can be recalled. Recall is considered to be "free" because the words need not be recalled in the same order in which they were presented. The main results of such experiments show that people (1) will first recall the last few words of the study list; (2) for the other words remembered, they will tend to remember them in groups or "clusters" of words that belong together somehow; and (3) will usually not remember all of the words unless a number of trials are presented.

As an example, suppose you are given the following 16 words to remember. They are presented to you one at a time via a slide projector or memory drum, at a rate of one second per word.

arm
red
oak
couch
green
elm
leg
table
chair
yellow
foot
maple
desk
blue
pine
hand

After seeing the list once, you might recall 13 of the words in the following order:

hand
pine
blue
red
yellow
green
foot
arm
leg
oak
maple
table
chair

The duplex theory can account for these results quite readily. First, the immediate recall of the last few list items can be explained as an attempt to utilize unrehearsed items that have just been stored in STM, reciting them quickly as correct responses before they are forgotten through an overloading of STM's capacity. Second, the word clusters making up the remaining words remembered can easily be construed as well-rehearsed "chunks"; for example, "blue, red, yellow, green" need not take up four of the hypothesized 7 ± 2 possibilities in STM's capacity, but only one unit (a "color" chunk). Finally, the words not recalled were those that had not been rehearsed and/or recorded into chunks, and thus had been "bumped out" of STM when it became overloaded.*

This experimental scenario illustrates one way (the standard method used by experimental psychologists) to test theoretical propositions. As we know from the previous chapter, another way to test and evaluate a theory is to write a computer model of the theory and have it simulate some psychological task. In the remainder of this chapter, we shall build a computer model of the duplex theory, writing the program so that, when executed, it will simulate a free recall task.

A COMPUTER MODEL OF THE DUPLEX THEORY

We find ourselves in a prototype situation as both psychologist and programmer setting out to translate a theory into a program that can be designated as a legitimate "computer model" of the theory. In addition to the *theoretical* aspect, we will need to be concerned also about *task simulation*—that is, about making the model perform some designated behavior. On the *theoretical* side, it will be necessary to isolate (1) the constructs, which, in psychology, will usually turn out to be either data structures or parameters indicating some proposed level at which the individual organism being modeled is assumed to function; and (2) the hypotheses, which are customarily if-then rules that are translatable into information processes, or algorithms, in a computer program. On the *task simulation* side, we must arrange for (1) the environment or stimulus input related to the free recall task being simulated; (2) the processing of these inputs by the theoretical components; and finally (3) an appropriate set of outputs that will identify clearly the results of these theoretical operations.

Resolution of Theory-Programming Conflicts

From the experience of building the program PANDO in the last chapter, we know that virtually any theoretical accounting of the human mind and the way it operates can be divided roughly into several components—*structure, content,* and *process.* For the memory theory described above, the major structures are the constructs STM and LTM. Each is a storage area, and thus translatable into a data structure. Moreover, each has certain contents at any given moment. And each structure has available certain processes that operate upon the contents over time. Let us look first in some detail at the possible structures and contents being proposed in the duplex theory and then proceed to problems of process.

---

*For details and data that tend to support this theoretical story, see the work of Glanzer and his colleagues (for example, Glanzer & Cunitz, 1966).

As might be expected, some theory-programming conflicts will need to be resolved. To cite one obvious example, the theoretical statement of the duplex theory specifies that the capacity of LTM is unlimited, which clearly is not a possibility in a digital computer. So the model, from the outset, will of necessity have a major characteristic of what is commonly meant by the term *model*—that is, it will never exactly replicate the thing itself but will always be an approximation of it.

But there are other problems regarding LTM, many of which concern limitations in the theory rather than—or in addition to—restrictions imposed by computer hardware or software. For example, exactly what is to be stored in LTM? How is it to be stored? The theory as stated does not define the construct with sufficient specificity to provide clues about the type of data structure proposed or its contents. Recognition of these ambiguities is hardly apparent in the clearly drawn scheme shown in Figure 4–1. But what seems so clear and descriptive in the customary (verbal and graphic) modes of discourse can turn out to be incomplete—perhaps even inappropriate—when translation into the systematic and formalized language of the computer is attempted.

Before listing more theory-programming conflicts, let us try to resolve the ones uncovered thus far. What can be done about the first theory-programming conflict mentioned above—the question about unlimited capacity? For the task at hand, let us assume that the model need only contain enough words in LTM to allow it to simulate free recall for a list of up to 40 words, and that these words may be clustered into a maximum of eight semantic categories. Furthermore, we shall assume that the words stored in LTM will be organized according to their semantic associations; for example, red, orange, yellow, green will somehow be linked together, as will, for example, oak, elm, pine, maple. Fifty LTM words, classified into 10 clusters, should be sufficient for illustrative purposes. Thus the model will represent, in a simplified manner, a portion of the typical associative organization of verbal memory; and our conflict worksheet will contain a note that one assumed aspect of LTM is semantic organization, but that other details of the contents and structure of LTM have yet to be worked out.

Having specified the contents of LTM, the programmer is faced with the choice of the best data structure to use. How should LTM—and STM too—be represented? Computer scientists have developed a number of sophisticated ways to structure data in memory so that various items are associated with each other and information can be found and retrieved quickly. In addition to the well-known two-dimensional array or matrix, more esoteric structures such as trees, linked lists, graphs, and rings have been devised. (We will examine some of these in Chapter 5.) Given such alternatives, most current memory theorists and programmers would agree that probably the most versatile informational structure for both STM and LTM is some form of tree or graph. But, to keep the example simple, let us start by using a two-dimensional array and save for later discussion the use of a binary tree structure as an alternative (and more sophisticated) representation of both STM and LTM.

Specifically, we can resolve this second theory-programming conflict by representing LTM as a 10×5 matrix, loaded with words in such a way that each row represents a concept and the words in the row are associated examples or "instances" of that concept. Figure 4–2, which summarizes in graphic form all of the major data structures to be used in our model, shows how the LTM matrix might appear when filled with a representative "memory" for semantic concepts such as colors, trees, fruits, parts of the body, and animals.

Turning now to the STM, more theory-programming conflicts become apparent. Taking the lead from the data structure chosen for LTM, we can decide to use a matrix for STM as well. The theoretical statement of

FIGURE 4–2. Data structure for STM-LTM model as it might appear during a simulation run.

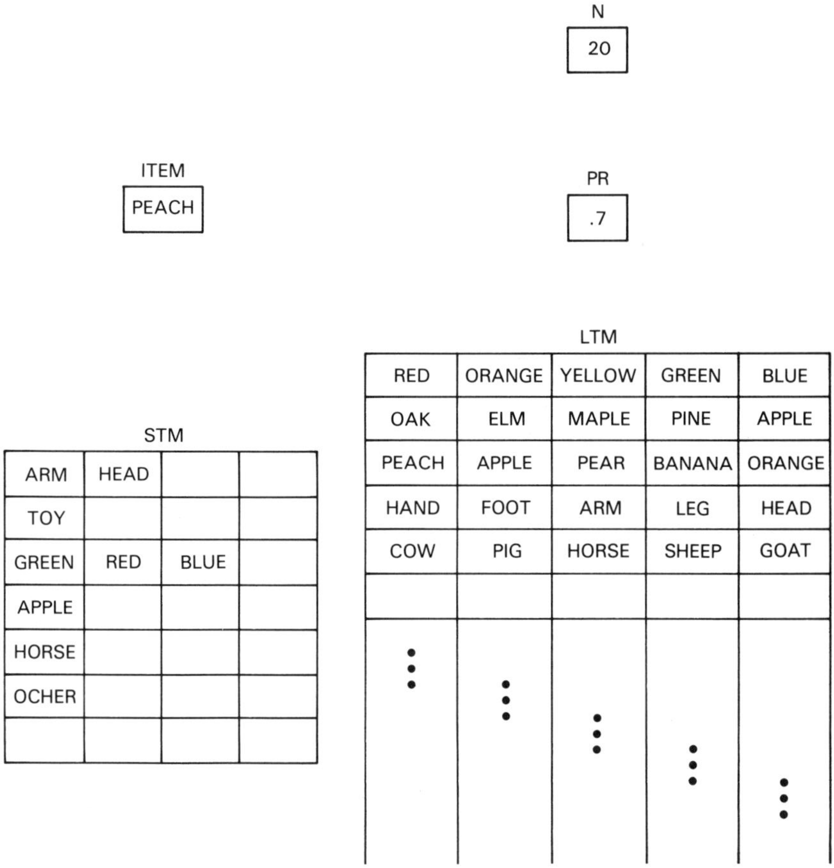

N

| 20 |

ITEM

| PEACH |

PR

| .7 |

STM

ARM	HEAD		
TOY			
GREEN	RED	BLUE	
APPLE			
HORSE			
OCHER			

LTM

RED	ORANGE	YELLOW	GREEN	BLUE
OAK	ELM	MAPLE	PINE	APPLE
PEACH	APPLE	PEAR	BANANA	ORANGE
HAND	FOOT	ARM	LEG	HEAD
COW	PIG	HORSE	SHEEP	GOAT

capacity suggests that, letting each row stand for a chunk, it should be 7 ±
2 rows in size. But really, the programmer might ask, exactly how many?
And does (or should) the number of chunks vary as a function of the task
presented, the individual, the type of materials to be stored? We shall note
the theoretical problem as Conflict No. 3 and resolve it with a tentative
agreement to give the model a 7-chunk capability.

And how big a chunk should it be? This Conflict No. 4 is resolved by
deciding tentatively to allow the model up to four pieces in a chunk; making STM representable as a 7x4 matrix, as shown in Figure 4–2. In
formulating this resolution, however, both programmer and theorist recognize that (1) the decision is tentative, and (2) the problem encountered
may require empirical research before it can be resolved (see Simon, 1974).

In addition to the structure and content problems just discussed, the
translation of a theory's hypotheses into a working computer program will
also present some theoretical conflicts and ambiguities regarding process.
For example, three major hypotheses in the present theory that concern
memory processes are:

1. an item can remain in STM if it gets rehearsed;
2. if two or more individual items are associated with each other, they will be
    chunked together into a single unit;
3. if STM is full when a new item is presented, an older item already in STM will
    be "forgotten" and replaced by the new item.

Programmers will recognize that these hypothesized processes will have to
become algorithms in the program. Take the first one as an example. We
humans all know that verbal rehearsal means saying something over and
over to ourselves; but how can that process be represented as a computer
algorithm? And how many times is a given word to be repeated if it is rehearsed? When rehearsal time is limited, which words get rehearsed and
which do not? The programmer, put in the spot of having to write a rehearsal algorithm, will quickly generate these—and perhaps other—
questions.

Similar questions, and more theory-programming conflicts, would become apparent if we were to examine the other hypotheses in the same detail; but the sampling of problems just reviewed should suffice to clarify
again, by example, two general points about computer modeling in psychology. First, it is clear that computer models generally will only *approxi-
mate* both the theory and the actual psychological behavior being studied.
The degree of approximation can vary substantially, depending largely
upon the specificity of the theoretical statements, the empirical information
available concerning the behaviors to be modeled, and the skills of the
psychologist-programmer making the translation. Second, even the brief
encounters thus far with the conflicts found in a relatively simple theory

suggest that, despite its imperfection, the modeling exercise can be a valuable aid to theory building and specification from a descriptive viewpoint. Indeed, it appears that the really important aspect of the theory-programming conflicts is not that they are conflicts, but that they are *resolvable*, either by further specification, or by agreeing upon a temporary approximation that gets tagged for further theoretical and/or empirical investigation in the future.

Let us briefly state just a few other theory-programming conflicts and then proceed. Assume that, after further careful study of the three major process hypotheses, the following additional conflicts are isolated, and the following tentative conclusions are generated:

CONFLICT	RESOLUTION
5 There seem to be two ways to keep an item in STM—rehearsal and chunking. How do they interact?	Hypothesize that the *purpose of rehearsal is to create chunks*, and write a chunking procedure (CHUNK) that operates upon any single item being rehearsed.
6 Empirical data show that not all items are always chunked whenever possible. Rehearsal time influences chunkability, and so does strength of association among items.	Resolve by approximation. Enter a single parameter specifying the *probability* (PR) that any single item gets rehearsed, and therefore chunked, during rehearsal. This single PR represents both associative strength and rehearsal time and should be elaborated theoretically in the future.
7 When an item is to be forgotten (dropped from STM), how is it chosen? (Some data suggest the oldest items are dropped, but empirical evidence is unclear.)	Resolve by choosing the simplest algorithm first, changing as future data warrant. Write a procedure (BUMP) which locates *at random* an item stored as a single unit in STM, and replace it with a new item.

With these basic problems noted, and tentatively resolved, program construction can begin.

CONSTRUCTION OF THE MODEL

Analysis and Planning

The structure diagram shown in Figure 4–3 is a top-level design for a computer model of the STM-LTM theory applied to a free recall task. When faced with a relatively complex programming task like the present one, starting with an analysis and plan at this level is good practice because it lends insight to the several separable programming problems that must be solved. These separable programming problems, once recognized and isolated, can then be solved one at a time, often independently of each other; and can be coded separately as Pascal procedures. As Figure 4–3 shows, at the topmost level we can divide the total program initially into three major components. The housekeeping component, as usual, will take care of obtaining and arranging and storing the preliminary information and data structures that will be necessary later when the model itself is executed. The second step, then, executes the model—that is, it accepts *N* items of a free recall task and processes them in accordance with the duplex theory. Finally, the third component prints the resulting arrangement of items in STM in order to show how the model "chunked" the free recall task.

Each of these three major components involves a number of subprocesses, and these independent subprocesses can be programmed as separate procedures. Thus the housekeeping component might be programmed by calling several procedures (1A, 1B, 1C in Fig. 4–3); and the component that processes the *N* items may call several more procedures (2A, 2B, 2C). Furthermore, because this second component is relatively

FIGURE 4–3. Structure diagram for the DUPLEX computer model of STM-LTM memory.

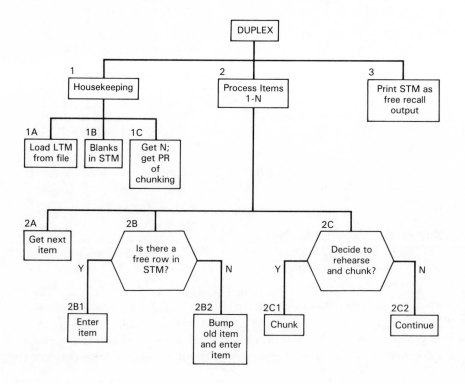

complex, it might be useful to analyze its separable procedures further and have them in turn call other procedures; for example, the BUMP and CHUNK modules shown in Figure 4–3 may each be programmed as procedures themselves and be called as needed by the more global procedures 2B and 2C, respectively.

Making a preliminary analysis of the problem in this way usually helps to divide a complex programming job into simpler tasks, each of which—taken by itself—is relatively easy to code and debug. An added advantage of this strategy, of course, is that changes that may become necessary in certain procedures can be made without disturbing the more global parts of the program. Recall, for example, that both the BUMP and CHUNK algorithms will be written as theoretical compromises (Resolutions 5 and 7 above) that may be replaced or elaborated in the future. By writing them as procedures initially, later replacement may be made easier because it won't disturb the main program.

A working version of the DUPLEX program, following the design illustrated in Figure 4–3, is listed in Appendix C. Try to write the program yourself, using the structure diagram as a guide. If you need help, the sections that follow review in turn the programming details of the main program and each subprogram.

Coding the Main Program

As indicated above, a good strategy for our particular task is to think of the program as having three major components, each of which contains (or calls) certain procedures. Let us consider first, then, a statement-part of the main program that will perform these chores in turn. The following code first makes the necessary declarations for the main program block and then, saving for later analysis the various procedures and subprocedures that will be needed, illustrates in the statement-part how the main program can be written to follow the plan shown in Figure 4–3. (Note: Some Pascal programmers would prefer writing even the three major components as procedures and having the main program simply call them. Naturally, such a strategy is a perfectly acceptable alternative.)

```
PROGRAM DUPLEX (input, output, memr);

type    wd = packed array [1..6] of char;

var     stm: array [1..7,1..4] of wd;
        ltm: array [1..10,1..5] of wd;
        memr: text;
        item: wd;
        i, n, seed: integer;
        pr, r: real;
```

```
                                 *
                                 *
                    (* Insert procedures here later *)
                                 *
                                 *
```

                        (*MAIN PROGRAM*)

```
begin

              (* housekeeping component *)
        ldmem(memr);
        blankstm;
        writeln(' Enter N, Random Seed, and Chunk Probability
                  on 3 lines');
        readln(n);  readln(ix);  readln(pr);

              (* main loop *)

        for i:= 1 to n do

        begin
                writeln(' Enter a word - - capitals only');
                getwd;
                loadstm;
                rehearsechunk

        end;

              (* skip lines and print stm *)
        skipout
end.
```

The program heading and the declaration-part are easy to understand. Note first that we will use an external file MEMR to store the sample of 50 words that must be stored in LTM when program execution begins. The file is identified in the program heading and declared under VAR as having the type TEXT. STM and LTM must also be declared as arrays. Because these arrays will contain words (let us say of up to six letters in length, although bigger words could be used), we first declare the special type WD, which is a *packed array* of six characters, and then declare STM and LTM as arrays whose cells are of the type of WD. This will permit us later (in procedures LDMEM and GETWD described below) to read multicharacter items (words) into the array cells. Also declared in VAR are the variable ITEM whose type is WD, and assorted global integers and reals that will be useful later.

Examine now the statement-part, listed under the heading (* MAIN

PROGRAM *). Here we find, in soldierly order, the representations for the three major components: housekeeping, the main loop (that is, the model itself), and the final printout. The housekeeping section, consistent with our initial analysis and plan, calls a procedure LDMEM that will load LTM with the words stored in the external file MEMR; then calls a procedure BLANKSTM that will initialize STM by setting all of its packed-array cells to blanks; finally, it asks the user to enter the number of words (N) to be presented in the free recall simulation task, a seed value (if necessary) for the pseudorandom number generator, and the probability (PR) of chunking that the model should assume for the current execution.

The model itself is represented as a FOR..DO loop that will execute *N* times, processing a new item each time. As planned, the process will consist of (1) reading the next item from the user's keyboard (the GETWD procedure described below); (2) entering the item into STM (using the STMLOAD procedure, which may at times need to call the BUMP procedure if there is no room in STM for the new item); and (3) deciding whether to rehearse and chunk before proceeding to the next item (the REHEARSECHUNK procedure). Finally, the main program prints the contents of STM via the procedure SKIPOUT.

The various procedures called in the main program are described below, but now that you have seen the basic structure perhaps you can write the procedures on your own without further help. Remember that, as planned, each one is a module that can be coded independently of all the others. Pick the easiest one as a starter and see how far you can go before you need to refer to the description below.

The Housekeeping Procedures

The only trick to coding the LDMEM and BLANKSTM procedures is in accounting for the fact that the cells of both LTM and STM are packed arrays. Recognizing this fact, the shorter of these two procedures is indeed quite simple:

```
              *
              *
PROCEDURE blankstm;

              (* loads stm with blanks *)

var           i, j: integer;
begin
  for i:= 1 to 7 do
    for j:= 1 to 4 do
            stm[i,j]:= '    '
  end;
              *
              *
```

In this nested loop each of the $7 \times 4 = 28$ cells in STM is filled with a set of six blanks, designated by '   '.

The LDMEM procedure is somewhat longer because it must handle various strings of characters, loading a string into each of the 50 cells of LTM from the file MEMR. There is a standard technique for performing such a task in Pascal, which is described and illustrated in Appendix A. The same algorithm is used in the following procedure, with the exception that it reads from an external file rather than the user's keyboard:

```
                    *
                    *
PROCEDURE ldmem (var memr: text);

                    (* loads LTM with words from MEMR file *)
var            ch: char;
               len: 1..7;
               i, j: integer;

begin
  reset(memr);
  for i:= 1 to 10 do
    for j:= 1 to 5 do
    begin
      if not eof(memr) then
        repeat
          read(memr,ch)
        until ((ch >= 'A') and (ch <= 'Z')) or eof(memr);
      if not eof(memr) then
      begin
        len:= 1;
        item:= '       ';
        repeat
          item[len]:= ch;
          read(memr,ch);
          len:= len + 1
        until (ch < 'A') or (ch > 'Z') or (len = 7)
      end
      else writeln('eof error in ldmem');
      ltm[i,j]:= item
  end
end;
                    *
                    *
```

This procedure must first RESET the file MEMR, then enter a pair of nested loops that process each cell in the five columns and ten rows of LTM. Each loop begins with an IF..THEN statement that finds either the beginning of a word (the capital letters A through Z in this example) or the end of the file. [As you know, the end of the file can be sensed by the function EOF(filename), which returns "false" until it senses the end of the file, then returns "true".] A second IF..THEN statement checks to see if the end of the file has been reached. If not, it fills the packed-array variable ITEM with the characters of the word being read from the MEMR file. Finally, the loop assigns the new constants of ITEM to LTM[I,J] and the loop begins again.

Coding the Main Loop

GETWD. The GETWD procedure reads the next free recall item typed by the user into the global packed-array variable ITEM, using the same algorithm described above for LDMEM. The major differences between the two procedures are that GETWD reads from the terminal keyboard rather than the external file MEMR, and that the limiting check is for the end of the line (EOLN) rather than EOF.

```
                    *
                    *
PROCEDURE getwd;
                (* reads new word into ITEM *)

var         ch: char;
            len: 1..7;

begin
  reset(input);
  if not eoln then
            repeat read(ch)
            until ((ch>='A') and (ch<='Z')) or eoln;
  if not eoln then
    begin
            len:= 1;
            item:= '      ';
            repeat
              item[len]:= ch;
              read(ch);
              len:= len + 1
            until (ch < 'A') or (ch > 'Z') or (len = 7)
    end
      else writeln(' eoln error in getwd')
  end;
                    *
                    *
```

LDSTM.   This procedure puts the ITEM just read into Column 1 of the first blank row found in STM, thereby storing it as a new and unchunked word. If Column 1 is filled for all rows in STM, then LDSTM calls another procedure, BUMP, which replaces an old unchunked word in STM with ITEM.

```
                      *
                      *
    PROCEDURE ldstm;

                (*puts ITEM just read into blank row of STM --
                 if no blank rows, calls BUMP *)

    var           m, k: integer;

    begin
      k:= 1;
      m:= 0;
      repeat
                if stm[k,1] = '      ' then
                begin
                  stm[k,1]:= item;
                  m:= k
                end;
                k:= k + 1
        until (m <> 0) or (k > 7);
        if m = 0 then bump
    end;
                      *
                      *
```

The BUMP procedure.   The purpose of BUMP is to replace an old single item with the current ITEM. Remember that one of the theory-programming conflicts (No. 7) raised the question of *which* old item to replace, and the tentative decision was to pick *at random* an unchunked (single) item currently stored in Column 1 and replace it. A workable strategy to fulfill this requirement would be:

1. pick an integer at random between 1 and 7 that has not yet been tested;
2. test whether that row of STM contains a single item and;
3. if it does, replace it with ITEM and RETURN; if it does not, delete that row number from the pool of untested integers and go to (1) above;
4. if there are no rows containing single items (that is, if there are seven chunks), RETURN.

The following algorithm will perform the task nicely:

```
                                  *
                                  *
PROCEDURE bump;
        (* replaces old single item in STM with ITEM *)

var               randint, lr, lt, i, l:  integer;
                  lran:   array [1..7] of integer;

begin
    for i:= 1 to 7 do
              lran[i]:= i;
    l:=0;
    lt:=7;
    while (lt > 0) and (l = 0) do
      begin
      lr:= 1 + trunc(lt * (Get a Random Number Here));
              randint:= lran[lr];
              lran[lr]:= lran[lt];
              lt:= lt - 1;
              if stm[randint,2] = '      ' then
              begin
                stm[randint,1]:= item;
                l:=1
              end
        end
end;
                                  *
                                  *
```

In this algorithm, LRAN is a 7-cell array that initially is assigned the integers 1–7 in the respective cells. The routine that finds successive random integers between 1 and 7, without picking any integer twice, works by (1) generating a random integer LR; (2) assigning the integer LRAN[LR] to RANDINT, which becomes the random integer identifying the row of STM that will be tested for BUMPing; (3) substituting the current bottom value LRAN[LT] into LRAN[LR]; thus erasing the integer just chosen so it cannot be used again; and (4) updating LT to LT-1 to get ready for the next iteration. Study this general routine for picking any number of integers at random without repetition until you are sure you see how it works. It is useful in many simulation programs.

REHEARSECHUNK. This procedure decides whether to rehearse and attempt to chunk each of the still unchunked items in STM, and it calls another procedure CHUNK whenever chunking is to be attempted. The first step in the algorithm for making the decision is to find an unchunked item (that is, a row in STM containing a word in Column 1 and blanks in Column 2). Then, following the strategy proposed for resolving theory-programming conflict No. 6, the decision can be made by (1) generating a pseudorandom number R and comparing it with the chunking parameter PR, and (2) if R is less than PR then chunk the item; otherwise do not. As you can see below, the Pascal code for this algorithm is brief. Note that if the procedure CHUNK is called, it is assigned the parameter K, which is the number of the row in STM containing the item to be chunked.

```
                              *
                              *
     PROCEDURE rehearsechunk;

                    (* decides whether to rehearse and chunk
                       single items in STM -- if so, calls CHUNK
                       *)
     var        k: integer;
                r: real;
     begin
       for k:= 1 to 7 do
           if (stm[k,1] <> '   ') and (stm[k,2] = '   ') then
           begin
             r:= (* get a random number here *)
             if r < pr then chunk(k)
           end
     end;
                              *
                              *
```

The CHUNK procedure. The purpose of this subprogram is to restructure a single-word row in STM into a multiple-word chunk if such restructuring is warranted by the current contents of STM. But in order to program this process (the functional equivalent of "rehearsal" in the original theory), the programmer must specify what a "chunk" shall be in terms of the program being written and then analyze the sequence of events that will change a single unit into a member of a multiple-word chunk.

Looking back at Figure 4–2, it is clear that in the particular data structure being used, a multiple-word "chunk" is *any row* of STM having two or more words in it; and in this particular verbal free recall task, the basis of chunking is the association of words on condition that they are members of a higher-level conceptual or semantic category. It is also clear from Figure 4–2 that the theorist has made an assumption that the possible categories and associations are already a part of permanent memory (LTM).

You may sense, however, that more conflicts between the verbally stated theory and its potential representation are arising. What, specifically, does the theory assume for the process by which a single unit becomes a chunk? And what is the fate of the relatively rare word that, for the hypothetical person being modeled, has never been stored as part of the associative LTM vocabulary? (For example, if the word "chartreuse" is presented to the model having the LTM shown in Fig. 4–2, what should happen to it?) The model as presently constructed points to some possible resolutions of these questions insofar as the programmer is concerned, but from the theorist's view they may raise further theoretical issues to be examined.

How do such conflicts get resolved? To illustrate, a programmer might suggest to the theorist that one reasonable programming solution to the specification of the chunking process is to make a linear search through LTM for a match to the single unit to be chunked and, if found, to put that unit in any row of STM containing any associate to that word. The theorist, however, might object to this simple solution and propose that instead of a linear search through all of LTM, the theoretical person being modeled should first determine the conceptual category. Obviously, this is a much different process from the proposed linear search and, indeed, might require changes in data structures and other processes throughout the model as developed thus far. Even so, if the theorist has good reasons (empirical or theoretical) for the choice, a resolution can be made on the strength of that argument. So we witness again the value of the modeling exercise to the process of theory construction, in that it stimulates careful and specific evaluation of theoretical ambiguities. Let us assume for now, however, that insufficient empirical data exist to guide a correct decision, and choose the linear search process as a first theoretical approximation.

And what of the second problem of how to handle unique words (for example, "ocher" in STM in Fig. 4–2)? Should they become more eligible for bumping because they are not chunkable? Or do such words in reality tend to be remembered better because they are new and different (a kind of Gestalt effect, similar to a figure standing out uniquely from the background)? Again, let us assume an absence of firm empirical data to guide the decision, and as a first approximation decide simply to leave such words as single items in STM and let the random BUMP process do with them what it will.

Having resolved these last two theory-programming conflicts, a reasonably good chunking subprogram can be constructed along the lines of the following verbal flowchart:

Beginning with a call to
    SUBPROGRAM CHUNK(STMROW)

where STMROW is a row in STM containing a single item in STM(STMROW,1);

(a)   search LTM for a match to STM(STMROW,1); if no match, RETURN; otherwise, record row M of LTM in which the match was found and continue with (b);

(b)   search Col. 1 of each STM row (except Row STMROW) for a match to any item in Row M of LTM; if no match, RETURN; otherwise, record Row N of STM in which match was found and continue with (c);

(c)   if a cell in Row N of STM is blank, enter STM(STMROW,1) there, set STM(STMROW,1) to blanks, and RETURN; otherwise RETURN.

These rules can be coded as follows:

```
                          *
                          *
PROCEDURE chunk (stmrow: integer);

                (* chunks a single item in STM *)

var             i, j, m, n: integer;

begin
                (* is stm[stmrow,1] in LTM? *)
  m:= 0;
  for i:= 1 to 10 do

  begin
                if m = 0 then
                  for j:= 1 to 5 do
                  begin
                    if m = 0 then
                    if ltm[i,j] = stm[stmrow,1] then m:=i
                  end
  end;
                (* if stm[stmrow,1] is in ltm, is there
                   another row of stm containing a word with
                   which it can be chunked? *)
  n:= 0;
  if m <> 0 then
    for i:= 1 to 7 do
                if (n = 0) and (i <> stmrow) then
                  for j:= 1 to 5 do
                    if stm[i,1] = ltm[m,j] then n:=i;

                (* if there is a row in which stm can
                   be chunked, then chunk it if that
                   row has a blank cell *)
  if n <> 0 then
  begin
    j:= 2;
```

```
      repeat
                if stm[n,j] = '      ' then
                begin
                   stm[n,j] := stm[stmrow,1];
                   n:= 100
                end;
                j:= j + 1
      until (j > 4) or (n = 100)
   end;


                (* if chunked, blank out stm[stmrow,1] *)

   if n = 100 then stm[stmrow,1] := '
end;
                        *
                        *
```

SKIPOUT. Having completed the main loop, the only programming chore left is to print the final results of the free recall trial. The following procedure skips a few lines and then labels and prints the contents of STM. The resulting output is a column of words, as is the case when a human recalls the words given in a free recall task. But because the words are printed row by row from STM, their appearance on the screen will be in the chunked form that the model has generated.

```
                        *
                        *
PROCEDURE skipout;
                (* skips lines and prints STM contents *)
var             i, j: integer;

begin
   writeln; writeln; writeln;
   writeln(' Free Recall Results '); writeln;


                (* output loop *)
   for i:= 1 to 7 do
      for j:= 1 to 4 do
                if stm[i,j] <> '      ' then
                   writeln(stm[i,j])
end;
                        *
                        *
```

CONCLUSION

Having written the model, you must now evaluate it psychologically. When your program is executed to simulate the free recall task, does the output conform to the empirical findings from this type of task? If not, why not? Can you change and improve it by altering any of the theory-programming conflicts we have identified? Answers to such questions may be difficult, but they are important for theoretical psychology.

SUGGESTED READINGS

Bower and Hilgard (1981, Chapter 13) present a good history of the development of the duplex theory of memory, including discussion of the experiments described in the beginning of this chapter. That text, as well as other cognitive psychology texts, also describes the levels-of-processing model, which was proposed in 1972 by Craik and Lockhart as an alternative to the duplex model.

EXERCISES

1. Write the DUPLEX program and show several simulation runs with different PR values. Does the program "chunk" as the theory proposes? What psychological phenomena are represented by PR?

2. In this basic DUPLEX program, what items are the only ones "forgotten"? Suggest another hypothesis for the basis of forgetting an item. Rewrite a block of the basic DUPLEX program so it will "forget" in this alternative way.

3. As presented in this chapter, the DUPLEX program is quite basic and incomplete. For example, all of the processing has taken place in STM only, whereas in the complete model it is assumed that the results of chunking and rehearsal are transferable to LTM, so the person remembers all or part of what is learned during the free recall trial. Rewrite the program to store what gets learned at the STM level into LTM.

4. Writing the program for Exercise 3 will involve making several decisions about new theory-programming conflicts:

   (1) What should be stored in LTM—items, semantic categories, or both?

   (2) Should *everything* in STM go to LTM? If not, what decision criteria might be used?

   (3) Should this kind of LTM be considered the same type of human memory as the semantic materials stored in LTM at the beginning of the program? [Hint: See Tulving (1972) for suggestions.]

   Give answers to each, indicating reasons for your answers.

5

Advanced Problems in Memory Modeling

The memory model described in Chapter 4 provided a good starting point for the development of skills in simulation programming. As a model of actual human memory processes, however, it was clearly an over-simplification. In this chapter we review some of the more advanced models of memory that have been constructed by psychologists and computer scientists; and, where appropriate, we will discuss some of the more advanced programming techniques they have used.

ELABORATIONS ON THE STM-LTM MODEL

The computer model presented in Chapter 4 is really a simplified instructional version of a number of similar but more elaborate models that have appeared in the psychological literature since the Waugh and Norman paper in 1965. Probably the most influential STM-LTM model has been that of Atkinson and Shiffrin (1968). Theirs is quite similar in general structure to the one we just designed, but a sensory register (or iconic memory) is added to it, and both STM and LTM processes are spelled out more carefully. Baddeley (1976, pp. 151–161) gives a good brief account of the model and its shortcomings in the light of the data that have been collected to test it. A book edited by Norman (1970) also contains descriptions of several models structured in the STM-LTM manner, including one by Reitman that lists the SNOBOL program representing it and data obtained from simulation runs.

Since the early 1970s, the STM-LTM theory has been both utilized and criticized. In one context, a STM-LTM memory structure has at times been assumed by theorists interested in other complex psychological functions; for example, Newell and Simon's (1972) problem-solving Model IPS assumes an STM having the features described in Chapter 4. Another direction has been to explore the limits of LTM in more detail, paying less attention to STM. We will discuss this trend further in a later section. Finally, the utility of the whole STM-LTM concept has been challenged by Craik and Lockhart's (1972) depth-of-processing hypothesis, which the serious student of psychology should get to know. Baddeley (1976, Chapter 8) offers a good account of the levels-of-processing model, as well as a critique (Baddeley, 1978).

DATA STRUCTURES FOR SHORT-TERM MEMORY

Despite the alternatives, elaborations of the simplified model presented in the last chapter remain today in good standing, and further explorations on its basic theme continue. One fruitful area of programming elaboration has been the development of alternative data structures that may be used to store and retrieve information. We must examine the details of some of the better-known attempts and look briefly at the programming techniques that have been used to accomplish them.

STM as a Binary Tree

We have seen that the major features of STM are its chunking process and its capability of outputting items in multiword chunks as well as singly. In the last chapter, a matrix was used to store and represent the chunking process, and it served the limited purpose of a first approximation to STM fairly well. However, it was recognized at the time the matrix structure was decided upon that the theorist and/or psychologist-programmer might have preferred to use a *binary tree*. Tree structures in general, and particularly binary trees, are very useful in psychological modeling. Let us first look at how they can be constructed and manipulated and then consider how binary tree structures may be used as structures for STM.

Figure 5–1 shows a variety of trees. Figure 5–1a illustrates a multiple-branching tree in which the bottom node *A*, usually called the *root*, has several branches to other nodes. The final node on any given branch (for example, node B) is often referred to as a *terminal node*, or sometimes a *leaf*.

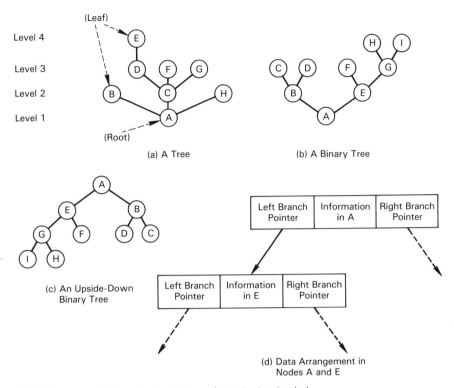

FIGURE 5–1. Illustrations of tree structures and tree-structure terminology.

Other nodes, at levels above the root, may themselves be roots of *subtrees*—as for example the subtree having root *C* and branches *D-E*, *F*, and *G*.

The particular type of tree structure called a *binary tree* is illustrated in Figure 5–1b.* Binary trees, unlike trees in general, have a maximum of two branches stemming from any given node. Since binary trees are versatile structures, are easy to handle, and are widely used in psychological programming, further discussion will be limited to them.

Figure 5–1c shows the same binary tree as Figure 5–1b, but inverted. For reasons that are more historic than logical (see Knuth, 1973, p. 309) most graphic illustrations of trees drawn by computer scientists are like Figure 5–1c—that is, the tree is upside down, with the root at the top and branches extending downward. Without attempting to offer a justification, we will continue this time-honored convention.

---

*Technically, a binary tree, when formally defined, is not simply a special case of the more general tree structure, but a unique structure having certain properties and processing capabilities that other trees do not. The technical distinctions are not important for this brief review, but the interested reader should consult Knuth (1973, pp. 305–315).

The nodes *A* and *E* are illustrated in finer detail in Figure 5–1d. Note that each node in a binary tree must have two *pointers*, a *left-branch* pointer and a *right-branch* pointer. In addition, of course, there must be space to store the information contained in the node.

You have probably already recognized how the formalized structures illustrated in Figure 5–1 can be related to programs modeling human memory. Whenever psychologists speak of memory, they must consider how memories of various items or events (words, concepts, names, visual images, or whatever) are *associated* with each other—that is, related in ways so that the stimulation of one memory permits or elicits stimulation of other memories linked to it. Clearly, the branches of a tree, which link or point to other nodes from any given node, can be construed as associative links, and the information stored in each node can be viewed as a memory item or event.

Given this analogy between tree structures and associative memory, let us see how a binary tree structure might be used to represent memory. Figure 5–2 translates the general concept of a binary tree into a data structure for short-term memory. Each node of the tree consists of a cell for storage of memory information and two associative links, a left-branch pointer and a right-branch pointer. Note that, because the left pointer of each node points to another item within a given word cluster, we can say that left branches represent *chunks* (associated items) in STM. Alternatively, the right pointer for any node is either blank (signified by a slash) or points to the beginning of a new chunk. There is also a pointer called the *root*, which identifies the starting point for the first cluster. Such a tree is a valid substitute for the matrix structure of STM that was used in the last chapter.

In order to manipulate such a tree in an actual simulation, we need to know how to search its nodes to find some information stored in it (often called *traversing* the tree), and how to perform such other tasks as adding a node to a leaf on some given branch or deleting a node from a branch. To get an idea of how binary trees may be processed, we examine in the following section an algorithm for searching a tree representing STM as shown in Figure 5–2. The problems of deleting and adding nodes require similar programming techniques. After learning how to search a tree, you will be able to devise adding and deletion algorithms on your own.

A Tree-Search Strategy

Suppose we want to determine if the word "cat" is stored in the tree in Figure 5–2. What are the possible search strategies that come to mind? Knuth (1973, p. 316) has identified three formal strategies: *Preorder* traversal (visiting the root, then traversing the left subtree, then the right); *inorder* traversal (traversing the left subtree, visiting the root, then traversing the right subtree); and *postorder* traversal (traversing the left subtree,

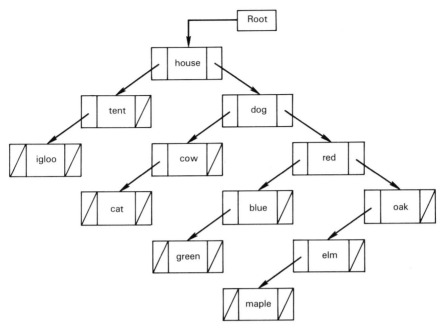

FIGURE 5–2. A binary tree of word clusters. A slash in either pointer position signals an end to that branch.

then the right, then visiting the root). Let us look in detail at just one of these—inorder traversal.*

Naturally, the first problem faced is that of representing a tree structure in a programming language we already know. Pascal has a built-in way of handling trees, as does the list processing language, LISP; but many other languages do not. For illustrative purposes, we can overcome this language problem by "simulating" a tree with a data structure common to all languages.

List nodes and pointers can be represented quite nicely in a matrix. Figure 5–3 shows a 12 × 3 matrix NTREE which represents the binary tree of words shown in Figure 5–2. Note that each *row* of NTREE is a *node* of the tree, and for each node the first column of the matrix contains the *left* pointer, Column 2 contains the *information,* and Column 3 contains the *right* pointer. Wherever there is no further branch (represented in Fig. 5–2 by a slash in the pointer cell), we shall arbitrarily put a −99 in the pointer cell to

*We note that these algorithms are in a class called "depth-first" searches—that is, searches that traverse all of a given branch before moving to a node of the next branch. Computer scientists have defined other types of search that in other situations may also be useful to know; for example, breadth-first search, best-first search, and so forth. See Winston (1984, Chapter 4) for a good review.

NTREE

1	2	house	3
2	4	tent	-99
3	5	dog	6
4	-99	igloo	-99
5	7	cow	-99
6	8	red	9
7	-99	cat	-99
8	10	blue	-99
9	11	oak	-99
10	-99	green	-99
11	12	elm	-99
12	-99	maple	-99

ROOT

1

FIGURE 5–3. A matrix NTREE representing the tree of words in Figure 5–2, and a pointer ROOT to the root of the tree.

signal that no pointer resides there. Note also in Figure 5–3 the single-cell pointer ROOT, which points to Row 1 of NTREE—the root of the tree.

Returning to our search task, how may an inorder traversal be performed on NTREE to find out if the word "cat" is stored in this memory structure? (This type of search task might be considered as a simulation of a recognition memory task where, after presenting a free recall list, the experimenter asks, "Was the word 'cat' in the list?") The structure diagram in Figure 5–4 illustrates the inorder algorithm given by Knuth (1973, p. 317), with minor changes to accommodate its use with a tree represented in matrix form like the one shown in Figure 5–3. It assumes ROOT to be the pointer to the row of NTREE in which the root is stored, and the word the experimenter has presented for recognition ("cat") is in a cell called ITEM. It assumes also a vector STACK, which has some special properties that will be described below.

The main idea of the algorithm is to start at the root and go as far down the left branch as you can until you reach the end (−99) and on the way down to collect in the vector STACK the left-branch pointers to each intervening node so that later you can go back up the branch and "visit" all these nodes in ascending order to see if any of them contain the item being searched. If so, then the search is ended. If not, then the right-hand branch of the tree must be searched. Of course there may be some right branches within the left branch, and some left branches partway down the right branch, just to complicate matters. As these complications arise, the algo-

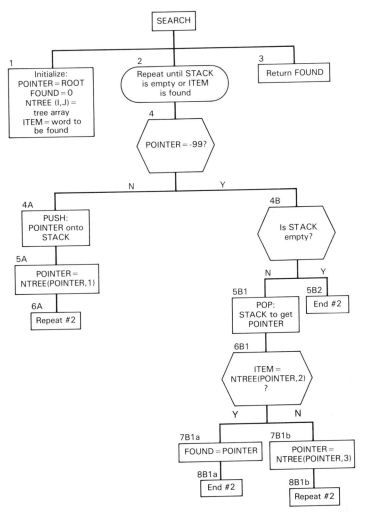

FIGURE 5–4. Structure diagram of Knuth's (1973) inorder traversal algorithm applied to a matrix representation of a tree. See text for explanation.

rithm automatically follows the basic rules of (1) left before right whenever possible, but (2) finish visiting all left *and* right nodes at the deeper level of the tree before ascending to a level closer to the root.

The algorithm begins by setting POINTER = ROOT, where POINTER will usually hold an integer pointing to the next node to be processed. Because our sample tree has just 12 nodes, the value of POINTER may range between 1 and 12. However, account must be taken of the possibility that the end of a branch has been reached and thus there are no more nodes to be processed. Whenever this is the case, POINTER will contain a -99; the signal that there is no further branching from the current node.

The main part of the algorithm begins at Block 2. Whenever a -99 in POINTER signals that the algorithm has followed a branch to a point from which it can proceed no further, it is time to visit the nodes collected on the stack so far and search for the item being sought. The test for this signal is made in Block 4. If POINTER is not a -99, then Blocks 4A–6A must be executed. The purpose of these blocks is to arrange pointer numbers on the stack in such a way that the sequential nodes of this branch can be visited in their proper (ascending) order. Alternatively, whenever POINTER $= -99$ at Block 4, it signals that Blocks 4B and on must be executed. This is the "visiting" segment of the algorithm, in that it pops the previously stored node pointers one at a time off the top of the stack and tests to see if the item being sought is stored in any of these nodes. To see how these alternative routes from Block 4 really work, let us examine each one separately.

Blocks 4A–6A. Block 4A recommends calling a procedure that provides for storing successive pointers on the STACK in appropriate order. Because a *stack* has certain operating properties that are useful to us both now and in the future, we must take a moment to define what a stack is and how it works. A stack is a data structure for which both entries and deletions are always made at the same end. It works in a manner similar to an *in* basket on a worker's desk. As each new piece of work is given to the worker, it is placed on the top of the stack, in effect "pushing" the other work down into the stack. Now if the worker always takes the next task off the top of the stack, the pieces that have been pushed down will "pop up" toward the top. The data structure works the same way; the last piece of information entered is the topmost one; therefore it is the first to be retrieved. For obvious reasons, these structures are often called "push-down" or LIFO (last-in-first-out) stacks.

How may a stack be represented graphically or conceptually? What is the algorithm for inputting ("pushing") information onto a stack, or "popping" information from a stack? As we shall see in later chapters, stacks may take various structural forms (for example, lists in the LISP language). But Pascal programmers can readily conceptualize a stack as a one-dimensional array with the special property that information is inserted to it *from the bottom up* and is taken from it *from the top down*. The programming for these operations is fairly straightforward, requiring only that we keep a *stack pointer*, which identifies where the last entry was made (that is, it points to the top of the stack).

To illustrate, the structural situation is portrayed in Figure 5–5. The stack STACK, which in this example has room for just five items of infor-

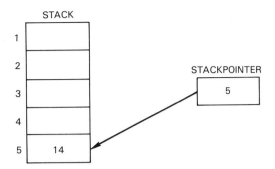

FIGURE 5–5. Using a vector as a STACK. STACKPOINTER points to the current top of the STACK.

mation, has one item in it (the number 14); and STACKPOINTER points to the current top of the stack, that is, STACK[5]. The following Pascal procedure will add information to STACK:

```
PROCEDURE PUSH (item);
begin
      stackpointer: = stackpointer - 1;
      if stackpointer = 0 then writeln('overflow')
      else STACK[stackpointer]: = item
end;
```

where STACKPOINTER and STACK are global variables. Correspondingly, the Pascal function POP will return the topmost item from STACK and readjust STACKPOINTER.

```
FUNCTION POP: integer;
begin
      if stackpointer > 5 then writeln('underflow');
      POP: = STACK[stackpointer];
      stackpointer: = stackpointer + 1
end;
```

Note that these subprograms must contain tests for going beyond the size of the stack that is being used. In PUSH, the STACKPOINTER must be greater than zero or else the new entry will cause an "overflow"; that is, the next entry will be above the top of the stack. In POP, if STACKPOINTER is greater than 5, then STACK must be empty so an "underflow" message is given.

This understanding of stack operations should clarify the purpose of Block 4A. Block 5A simply finds the next left-branch pointer from NTREE and stores it in POINTER, and Block 6A continues the traversal.

Blocks 4B–8. Since we already know how the function POP works, the most difficult part of this segment (Block 5B1) is easily understood; that is, the instruction

    pointer:= pop;

will pop a number off of STACK and assign it to POINTER. Block 6B1 will then check the node with an IF..THEN statement to determine if it contains the ITEM being sought. If a successful match is obtained, the node number is stored in a variable FOUND and execution ends; otherwise, the right-branch pointer for the node being searched is assigned to POINTER, and execution continues. Examine this latter alternative closely and be sure you see how it works. What will happen if the POINTER obtained is -99? What if it is not? Convince yourself that the algorithm will take care of any right-branch alternative.

A pseudoprogram for inorder traversal.   By now you have a good understanding of the Pascal language; thus there is no longer a need to provide a complete listing of a program in order to give you the gist of how it works. Instead, we shall be content with the following "pseudoprogram," which, if actually translated into Pascal code, would yield a working program that follows the structure diagram in Figure 5–4. It assumes that STM is a 12-node tree containing items such as those shown in Figure 5–2. Its data structure is the same as the matrix shown for NTREE in Figure 5–3. The pseudoprogram also uses a 12-cell array called STACK, with a pointer STACKPOINT, and the PUSH and POP subprograms described above. It will search STM for an ITEM input by the user, and print either the ITEM if it is found or the message NOT FOUND.

```
1. Initialize:
   a)   set POINTER to 1 and FOUND to 0;
   b)   since NTREE (Fig. 5-3) contains integers and
        characters, it is best to separate it into a
        12-x-2 array TREEPOINT and an additional 12-cell
        packed-array vector INFOR—then load
        TREEPOINT and INFO with, respectively, the
        pointer numbers and the words shown in
        Fig. 5-3;
   c)   arrange for the user to input a search word
        (e.g., "cat") into ITEM;
   d)   set STACKPOINT to 13;

2. Main Loop:
   Repeat
       if POINTER <> -99
       then
```

```
      push POINTER onto STACK,
      set POINTER to TREEPOINT[POINTER,1]
   else
      if STACKPOINT <> 13
      then
         pop POINTER from STACK,
         if ITEM = INFO[POINTER]
         then
            set FOUND to POINTER
         else
            set POINTER to TREEPOINT[POINTER,2]
   until STACKPOINT = 13 or FOUND <> 0;

3. if FOUND <> 0 then write INFO[FOUND]
   else write "ITEM not found ".
```

The EPAM Discrimination Net

A memory model that proposes an alternative data structure for STM and that attempts to provide a step-by-step explanation of how rote-learning materials are stored and retrieved in memory is Feigenbaum's (1963) *Elementary Perceiver and Memorizer* (EPAM). It is of interest here for several reasons. First, EPAM is noteworthy historically because it was probably the first generally known computer model of a psychological process (rote learning and memory) that psychologists had previously studied extensively in the laboratory. Second, in its original form it was written in a *list-processing* language, thus being among the first to demonstrate that such languages have certain advantages over algebraic languages for modeling psychological processes.* Finally, the model uses a new kind of data structure, called a *discrimination net*, to represent memory.

The best way to understand the structure and function of the discrimination net is by a direct example from EPAM. One of several specific psychological functions simulated by EPAM is learning (and remembering) a list of nonsense-syllable pairs—the so-called paired-associate (PA) anticipation-learning task familiar to all students of psychology. The PA task can be described briefly as follows:

Description of the PA Learning Task

Consider the following PA items:

DAX-ROQ
MEV-ZAN
BOZ-SEL

---

*The language actually used, IPL-V, never became popular (see Reitman, 1965, for a readable description of it). But the programming language LISP, its current counterpart, is extremely important in psychological modeling today and will be investigated later.

In the typical PA anticipation task the learner is presented with 8 to 12 such pairs, one at a time, via a device such as a memory drum or a slide projector. He or she is shown the first syllable of a pair (for example, DAX in the first pair above), and tries to recall and spell out loud ("anticipate") the correct syllable that goes with it (for example, ROQ) *before that second syllable is presented.* Following this brief anticipation interval, the correct second syllable is shown, giving the learner a chance to study the two syllables together. Then, after a few seconds of study, that entire pair is removed from view, and the process is repeated; that is, the first syllable of the next pair is presented for a brief interval during which the learner must try to spell aloud (anticipate) its matching syllable, and then the second (matching) syllable is presented for a brief study interval. When all pairs have been presented for anticipation and study in this manner, the learning trial ends. The learner is given repeated trials in this manner until all of the items can be anticipated correctly.

Laboratory data clearly indicate that people are "lazy" when learning in such situations. Because they never have to spell the first syllable, they learn only the minimum amount of it necessary to serve as a stimulus for a correct response. For example, in pairs such as those listed above the minimum is the first letter; for example, instead of learning DAX-ROQ, one need only associate D___-ROQ in order to anticipate ROQ correctly whenever DAX is presented. Learning speed is subtantially improved by this strategy because instead of having to chunk six letters together in memory, only 4-letter chunks need to be learned. Also, being lazy probably serves the usual purpose of conserving energy—in this case, the mental energy required to memorize letters into syllables and associate them.

Naturally, if the list of pairs to be learned is made up of first syllables that are highly similar, problems arise. Consider now the list:

```
DAX-ROQ
MEV-ZAN
DEL-BER
MOQ-CUW
   .
   .
   .
```

Obviously, if only D___-ROQ is learned, then the learner will make an error when the test syllable DEL-? is presented because the only response stored for (associated with) D___ is ROQ. The learner is then forced to discriminate DEL from DAX, and associate different responses to each.

Even then the learner is lazy, however. Empirical data show that in such circumstances people still don't memorize the first syllables in toto but only enough of them to permit a correct discrimination between those syllables that might be confused. For example, to discriminate DEL from DAX and associate the correct response to each, the typical learner will memorize some mental equivalent of the rule, "If I am shown a D_L-?, I'll say 'BER'—otherwise when given any syllable starting with D I'll say ROQ".

These examples illustrate a miniature theory of PA learning that can be summarized by a single verbal statement:

> When learning associations between stimuli and responses, people tend to associate the correct response with only the minimum part of the stimulus necessary to discriminate one stimulus from another.

The verbal statement is easy enough to make. But can a computer model be constructed that will simulate the PA learning task by following the theory?

The major programming problem in building such a model is to determine how this memory-discrimination can be represented in a data structure. Feigenbaum's solution was the discrimination net. Figure 5–6 illustrates a discrimination net as it is used in EPAM, showing how it grows and develops in the course of PA learning. It is assumed that the net—really a specialized usage of a binary tree—is empty at the start of the PA task and "learns" in the lazy manner just described. Figure 5–6a shows the net at the first stage of learning of the example list, with further stages shown below.

Starting at the root, each node is a test on one of the letters of the first syllable. (The order of testing in EPAM is first letter, third letter, middle letter, conforming to empirical data.) For any node, if the test is successful then the left branch is followed to the next test-node; otherwise the right branch is followed. Eventually the tests come to a leaf in the tree, which is a node containing the response to be made. If the response is correct, the memory structure does not change. But whenever an error is made, a new discrimination (test) node must be inserted into the tree and response information altered.

The full memory structure of the real EPAM is slightly more complex than the net illustrated in Figure 5–6 (for example, in the original version the responses must also be constructed from individual letters), but its net-growing operation is the same as that shown. In many simulation tests over the years, the model has demonstrated a good capability for simulating empirical data, not only for PA learning under varying intralist similarity conditions but also for serial learning and memory phenomena such as transfer and retroactive interference. Hintzman (1968), noting certain problems with early versions of EPAM, has changed and elaborated it in a series of models collectively called the *Stimulus and Association Learner* (SAL). Feigenbaum (1963), and Frijda (1972) offer good discussions for further exploration. Feigenbaum and Simon (1984) describe the most recent version, EPAM-III, review the empirical evidence for its validity, and compare it with other theories of discrimination learning.

Figure 5–7 presents the net shown in Figure 5–6d in the matrix form we used earlier to represent a binary tree. In this matrix there are two types of nodes. One type contains − 99 in both pointer cells, and the information cell contains a 3-letter response. The other type of node contains a single-letter test in its information cell, a left pointer giving the row address to

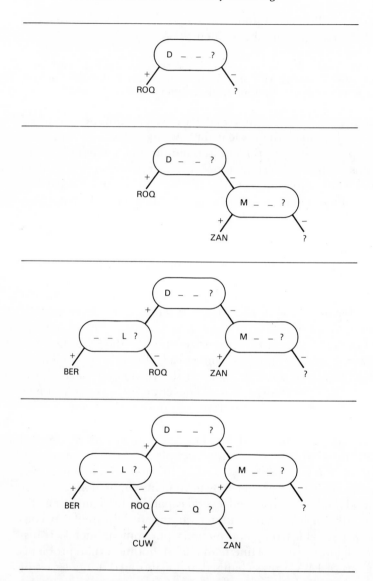

FIGURE 5-6. Stages in the development of EPAM's memory-discrimination net.

seek if the test is positive, and a right pointer giving the row address for a negative test. Writing a program to handle this discrimination net requires construction of algorithms for searching, inserting, and rearranging nodes. We will not construct here a computer program that models EPAM; but you are encouraged to use the structure in Figure 5–7 as a basis for constructing your own program (see Excercise 5–2). Also, consult Lehman (1977, Appendix B), who gives a listing of a simple version of SAL employing a discrimination net written in FORTRAN.

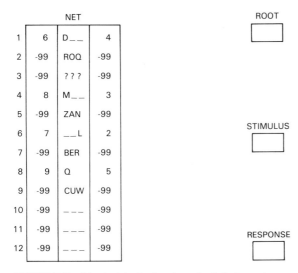

FIGURE 5–7. A basic data structure for a discrimination net.

Models of Long-Term Memory

Semantic memory. Both the EPAM and STM-LTM models have emphasized the structure and processes of short-term memory. In recent years, attention has also been directed at the structure and functional requirements underlying long-term memory, particularly that aspect of LTM responsible for the use of language. In 1972 the psychologist Endel Tulving proposed two types of LTM—*episodic* memory, which contains memories of the individual's past experiences, and *semantic* memory. Tulving defined semantic memory as,

> . . . the memory necessary for the use of language. It is a mental thesaurus, organized knowledge a person possesses about words and other verbal symbols, their meanings and referents, about relations among them, and about rules, formulas, and algorithms for the manipulation of these symbols, concepts, and relations. (Tulving, 1972, p. 386)

The several major computer models of semantic memory that have appeared in both psychology and the more computing-oriented field of artificial intelligence deserve the attention of psychologists and computer scientists alike. Baddeley (1976, Chapter 13) presents excellent descriptions of models proposed by Collins and Quillian, Winograd, and Anderson and Bower, as well as an early version of the Rumelhart-Lindsay-Norman model. Anderson (1976, pp. 55–68) presents a review of the more recent LNR model (for Lindsay, Norman, and Rumelhart), and describes also his own comprehensive model of cognitive functioning (ACT), which itself contains a semantic structure. Another book by Anderson (1983) describes his most recent version of ACT. These references, and the primary sources listed in their bibliographies, are essential reading for the serious student of human memory.

A data structure for LTM.   Rather than review these models in detail again here, it will suffice for our purposes to try to isolate some of the problems associated with this type of modeling—particularly data-structure problems. The structure of LTM used in Chapter 4 for the STM-LTM duplex model, and illustrated in Figure 4–2, provides a good starting point. Note that the word APPLE occurs in two places in the LTM matrix, and is associated with two concepts. This multiple representation is clumsy from the programming standpoint because it uses unnecessary space in computer memory. Also, from a theoretical viewpoint most psychologists would probably reject multiple storage of words in LTM in favor of a structure that would allow for *multiple associative links* to and from singly stored items. Consequently, memory structures have been designed that permit storage of multiple associations and that provide algorithms for manipulating their contents.

One reasonable structure, used by many LTM modelers, is shown in Figure 5–8. This type of structure has been called a *relational network* by Frijda (1972), although the more mathematically oriented programmer may wish to describe it as a directed graph. It is like a multiple branching tree, but with the confusing additions that (1) not only the nodes, but the branches themselves, carry information, and (2) branches can go from one node to another in both directions.

Clearly, a complete memory structure represented in this manner, even for just the nouns known by an elementary-school child, would be formidable. And what about the other kinds of words whose meanings we know so well and which we use so effortlessly? The amount of information that we humans must store, retrieve and otherwise process boggles the mind—and yet the mind does store and use it all, often with a creativity and cleverness that is itself astonishing. So the relational network appears to be inadequate in some major ways. Nevertheless, it is a substantial and sophisticated improvement over such traditional structures as arrays.

From a computer programming standpoint, even the limited network shown in Figure 5–8 presents some difficult programming problems. To understand them, we must adopt some formal language and notation. Let us look upon each node of a network as containing an *element* (denoted by A,B, . . .) of information, and each *branch* or *arrow* as designating a *relation* (r) between the elements *A* and *B*. Now, using notation described by Frijda (1972), the simplest association shown in a relational network can be represented in writing as A,(r,B). For example, the statement that an apple is a fruit can be written

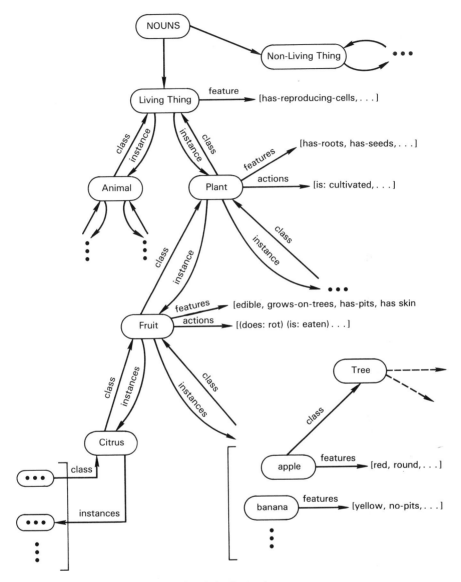

FIGURE 5–8. An incomplete example of a relational network.

FRUIT, (instance, APPLE).

However, the relationship structure need not—and does not—stop there. Not only might one designate a simple A,(r,B) relationship as above, but increasingly complex and nested relationships can also be specified; for example, an A,(r,(A',(r,B'))) definition of fruit might look like

```
FRUIT, (instance (CITRUS, (instance, ORANGE))).
```

This shorthand notation is important for computing purposes because it is possible to write and store it in computer memory; in effect making it a data structure that can be used to represent semantic memory.

The hierarchical nature of the net can be advantageous in terms of storage economy. For instance, note that for the "features" relations pictured in Figure 5–8 all features at a given class level apply to all lower instances. Thus to define all of the features APPLE the net is traced first to that word's individual features (RED, ROUND, . . .), and then to the features of its successive superordinate relations (for example, EDIBLE, GROWS-ON-TREES, etc.). When a class feature is not present for some unique instance (for example, a banana has no pits), the exception can be noted in the features for that instance. Thus, with appropriate processing of the relational net, an elaborate definition and set of associations may be generated from a relatively concise A,(r,B) code.

Using the multiple features shown for APPLE, then, it is possible to recode a definition of the term from the pictorial description shown in Figure 5–8 to a description looking much like an equation; for example,

```
APPLE, ((class 1, FRUIT)(features, (ROUND,RED, . . . )))
       (class 2,TREE)
```

This notation can then be stored as a semantic description of the word APPLE, and programs may be written that can retrieve and utilize its features, its learned associations, its conceptual categories, and so on.

Obviously, storage of information represented this way is quite different from that using data structures we have studied to date; and the processing requirements (searching, retrieving, deleting, and changing of both information and relationships) are extremely difficult to program when using languages such as BASIC, FORTRAN, or even Pascal. Fortunately, as we shall see in Chapters 9 through 13, the list-processing language LISP supports data structures and processes suitable to the task, making the programming task much easier. So, rather than trying here to write a Pascal representation of this advanced data structure, the reader should store the present topic in LTM and retrieve it for further elaboration after studying LISP.

In the next chapter we turn our attention to another theoretical topic that is more amenable to computer modeling using Pascal.

SUGGESTED READINGS

The topics discussed in this chapter go substantially beyond a basic introduction to psychological modeling, delving into the current status of both information-processing psychology and the advanced techniques employed by computer scientists working with complex data bases. Selected chapters in books by the psychologists Baddeley (1976, Chapter 13) and Lachman, Lachman, and Butterfield (1979, Chapters 7–9) provide advanced discussions of the technical and conceptual problems associated with current memory theory. Tulving (1985) has recently proposed a three-part model that includes procedural, semantic, and episodic components of LTM, and he also gives a good review of other multicomponent models. The computer science text by Knuth (1973) describes in detail algorithms for processing a number of advanced data structures, but the programming examples are written in an assembly language format. Texts that cover tree building, search, insertion, and deletion using Pascal include Wirth (1976) and Tenenbaum and Augenstein (1981). Fridja's (1972) article, while advanced, is quite readable and handles nicely the interaction between psychology and computer science.

EXERCISES

1. Translate the pseudoprogram on p. 96 into a working Pascal program that demonstrates the inorder traversal algorithm. Use it to search and find items within chunks of a binary-tree representation of STM like the one shown in Figure 5–2 and Figure 5–3.

2. Using the structure shown in Figure 5–7, write a Pascal program that accepts a nonsense-syllable stimulus, makes a response, accepts a correct nonsense-syllable response as feedback, and updates the discrimination net if its response was incorrect. Make your program account for similarities among the stimuli in the list. Can it process a list like this?

        DAX-ROQ
        MEV-ZAN
        DEL-BER
        CAZ-MOK
        DAZ-SEV
        MAQ-LOM
        DEX-PUD
        MOQ-DUJ

3. Examine Lehman's (1977, Appendix B) FORTRAN program for processing an EPAM-like discrimination net. Rewrite the program in Pascal. Demonstrate in sample runs how it "learns" by building a discrimination net.

4. A. Assume that when presenting a free recall task we have an STM structure as shown in Figure 5–2 and Figure 5–3, and a new word—"hat"—is presented. Write an algorithm that will insert the new word into the tree.

   B. Consider now the BUMP procedure in Chapter 4. Write an algorithm that will delete a single item from a STM that is represented as a binary tree structure like those shown in Figure 5–2 and Figure 5–3. (If you need help, or want to investigate tree insertion and deletion using Pascal's record structure, see Wirth, 1976, Chapter 4.)

5. In Chapter 4 we discussed the possibility that memory theorists might propose that STM and LTM chunks contain not only the words that are chunked together (for example, red, blue, green) but also the word identifying the chunking concept (for instance, COLORS—red, blue, green).

    A. Draw a binary tree structure that would satisfy this theoretical proposal.

    B. Describe a memory model that would assume this alternative structure of STM and LTM, and tell (in words or with a structure diagram) how the process of chunking a new single item would proceed.

    C. Write a Pascal computer model of the theory you describe in 5B above, using a binary tree structure for LTM and STM.

6

Computer Modeling and Simulation of Personality

The preceding chapters have indicated that computer modeling and simulation of human perceptual and memory processes have developed rapidly, and indeed have become quite sophisticated. Although the potential of computer simulation as an aid in development of personality theories was formally recognized in the early 1960s (Tomkins & Messick, 1963), progress in this area has been much slower. The reasons stem partly from past limitations in computer capabilities and partly from theoretical problems associated with the topic of personality itself.

Cranton (1976) has listed several computer-related problems existing in the 1960s that served to deter the development of computer modeling and simulation of personality. One major problem was the virtual impossibility of processing natural language on the computer. Because much of the "data" regarding personality is verbal, this limitation has considerably delayed development of personality models. Computing problems with natural language are gradually being solved, however, and many believe these problems will be substantially overcome in the near future. The other two computing problems mentioned by Cranton—limited computer storage and the lack of a flexible simulation language—have both been reduced to a point where they no longer should offer hurdles for personality modelers. Thus there is good promise of an increase in personality modeling and simulation in the future.

The fact that most personality theories in the past have been rather broad and vague has also been a deterrent to computer modeling. The topic of personality encompasses a wider psychological domain than more restricted phenomena such as "pattern recognition," "verbal memory," and the like. The almost inevitable consequence of such breadth is the development of theories that have tried to explain a wide range of behaviors, often with theoretical processes and constructs that are perhaps less rigorous than necessary or ideal for translation into an executable computer program. Even so, when attempts have been made to isolate and model portions of the total area of personality, the results have been interesting and instructive.

The topics that follow will provide some insights into both the current status and the future potential of computer modeling in this difficult area. Three programs related to personality and personality theory will be examined. The first program, ELIZA, is really not a computer model of personality in a formal sense because it models a therapist rather than a person with a given personality structure. Several good reasons exist for examining it, however: It is important historically as an early simulation of clinical interviewing, it is rather directly related to one of the major current personality theories (Rogerian), and it portrays the natural language problem nicely. The second example is a model called ALDOUS, which we shall analyze in some detail. Finally, the more sophisticated model PARRY is reviewed to illustrate the potential use of computer modeling and simulation in personality research.

ELIZA

ELIZA is an old and well-known program whose roots, strictly speaking, are not in psychological theory but computer science and artificial intelligence. Its initial and primary purpose was to study natural language communication between man and machine, and it was one of the first successful interactive conversational programs. In describing it, its author (Weizenbaum, 1966) says it was written originally in a language named MAD-SLIP, and that even in 1966 versions had been designed to converse in Welsh and German as well as English. Weizenbaum admits that its basic language capabilities are really not very substantial. But—like the character Eliza in *Pygmalion*, for whom it was named—it has the capability to improve its language usage given the right teacher.

ELIZA simulates a person who is carrying on a conversation with another (real and human) converser. The program is designed to run on an interactive machine. At execution, the human converser types messages on the keyboard in sentence form, and ELIZA responds with questions and other observations that are also in sentence form and, one hopes, relevant to the ongoing conversation.

The programming problem that inevitably arose for Weizenbaum when he began constructing such a program was, of course, that the unpredictable and unrestrained human converser would be at liberty to engage ELIZA in conversations about any of a nearly limitless number of topics. Clearly, an ELIZA capable of such universal possibilities would need to have at hand a long-term memory for both language and life experience that is at least equivalent to the average adult, and be able, in addition, to access and process its contents coherently. Thus a memory storage problem, as well as the basic problems attendant with attempting to program conversational interactions, posed nearly insurmountable threats to success. Weizenbaum was able to overcome these obstacles in large part by giving the program two major components—a *language analyzer* and what he calls a *script*.

The language analyzer is the more prosaic of these components. Its job is to interpret input words by matching them up with words already stored in memory. Alternatively, the task of the script component is to solve the problem of having a computer handle the entire range of human conversational possibilities. This latter component consists of a set of rules that can be given to ELIZA to indicate the theme and focus of any given conversation. By inputting various scripts before executing the program, ELIZA can be constrained to converse about only a certain limited topic in a given man–machine interaction.

To illustrate ELIZA's capabilities, Weizenbaum (1966, 1976) has given ELIZA a script that makes the program assume the role of a psychotherapist whose therapy technique is based upon Carl Rogers' (1951) theory of personality.* This constraint reduces memory and understanding requirements enormously, because in Rogers' client-centered therapy situation the participating pair (client and therapist) is concerned only with discussion of the client's momentary emotional expressions. Thus each member of the pair is, in Weizenbaum's words, ". . . free to assume the pose of knowing almost nothing of the real world" (Weizenbaum, 1966, p. 42). This happy circumstance permits ELIZA to carry on a reasonable conversation without needing memories of a lifetime of experience.

From the psychological viewpoint, this restriction has generated both practical and theoretical interest. At a practical level, the moderate success

---

*Weizenbaum on some occasions has called this particular version of the program DOCTOR, thus distinguishing it from the more general ELIZA. However, over the years the name ELIZA seems to have become associated with the Rogerian therapy example, so we shall use it that way here.

of the program helped to introduce psychology and psychiatry to the potential of clinical interviewing and diagnosis by computer. Kleinmuntz (1969), for example, prefaced a brief description of ELIZA with the statement:

> Although the design of a system in which persons are interviewed by computers in their own natural language is still somewhat futuristic, it is not completely fantastic. In fact, the beginnings of such a system are already well underway. (Kleinmuntz, 1969, p. 153)

Kleinmuntz illustrated his point with the following excerpt, noting that, despite its "barbershop conversation flavor," it held promise as a clinical tool in the future.

PATIENT:	Men are all alike.
THERAPIST:	In what way?
PT:	They're always bugging us about something or other.
TH:	Can you think of a specific example?
PT:	Well, my boyfriend made me come here.
TH:	Your boyfriend made you come here?
PT:	He says I'm depressed much of the time.
TH:	I am sorry to hear you are depressed.
PT:	It's true. I am unhappy.
TH:	Do you think coming here will help you not to be unhappy?
PT:	I need some help, that much seems certain.

(Kleinmuntz, 1969, pp. 153–154)

The realization of ELIZA's initial promise as a useful clinical device has been hampered by the substantial problems encountered as computer scientists have attempted to develop programs for computer comprehension and generation of natural language. ELIZA's flexibility is limited not only by having little or no life experience stored in memory but also by its process of analyzing input. Early language programs of this sort used a strategy of searching input for keywords that would identify sentence meaning. However, this method is now generally considered to be inadequate for any sophisticated assessment of sentence meaning.

Other methods for processing natural language are being explored vigorously at present, and substantial progress in language interpretation has been made since ELIZA was written; but it is still safe to say that the original promises of machine manipulation of natural language have not yet been realized. We shall discuss the problem of natural language at greater length in Chapter 12, after first learning the basic features of LISP—the programming language in which most of the recent natural language programs have been written.

ALDOUS

Theoretical Background

In his very readable book on personality models, John C. Loehlin (1968) describes a model that he had initiated as early as 1962. Named ALDOUS in honor of Aldous Huxley, author of *Brave New World,* it is simultaneously simple enough and complex enough that it provides an excellent illustration of the possibilities and problems associated with computer modeling of personality. The original ALDOUS was written in machine language, and later versions have used FORTRAN. A Pascal program for the model is presented in Appendix D. We review here the theoretical constructs and hypotheses upon which the model is based.

The purpose and function of the model described by Loehlin are as follows:

> Aldous was designed to display a number of features of human behavior in a very schematic, simplified form. He recognizes situations, reacts to them emotionally, acts, and learns (or fails to learn) from his experience. He also has modest powers of introspection. However, his symbolic capacities are in general quite limited: he can neither plan ahead nor reconstruct in memory the events of his remote past. And the world he can respond to is a very simple one indeed. (Loehlin, 1968, p. 27)

Because ALDOUS has neither a well-developed long-term memory nor any sort of language understanding-generating capability, the program is limited in what it can recall and is completely incapable of verbalization. However, ALDOUS is able to perceive (recognize) certain objects in its world, to respond to them emotionally, and to alter its emotional structure in accordance with the consequences of its emotional responses.

An understanding of Loehlin's model requires a comprehension of (1) how it perceives and recognizes objects (input), (2) how it processes the input to generate an emotional reaction, (3) how it responds (output), and (4) how it then processes the consequential feedback resulting from its response. These sequential problems are illustrated in Figure 6–1 as stages in a top-level program design. Before considering programming details, we must become familiar with the major functions and problems associated with each of these stages.

Recognition stage.   As we saw when we discussed semantic memory networks in the last chapter, accounting for all of the attributes that define even the simplest things is a real problem for computer programmers attempting to write programs that will identify particular objects. The partic-

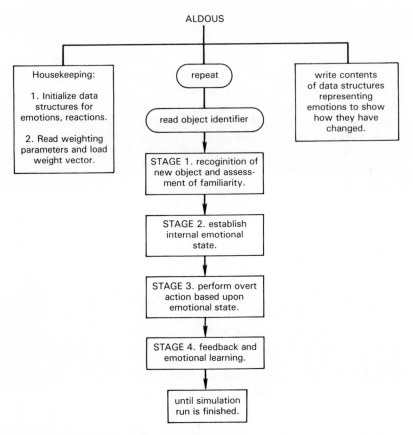

FIGURE 6–1. A top-level structure diagram for ALDOUS.

ular example used in Chapter 5 was the object APPLE, whose full definition had to encompass the multiple dimensions of size, shape, color, use, associates, class memberships, and so on. This problem of identification prevails for ALDOUS. The programmer must arrange for the model to "recognize" objects and events, which means that the model has to be able to classify inputs according to their attributes. And, of course, the wider we make the range of possible objects to be identified, the larger the problem becomes.

To reduce the scope of the recognition task somewhat, suppose now (as Loehlin did) that we are willing to limit the model to recognizing (and reacting emotionally to) only *people*. This helps; but even with this constraint it is easy to see that any given person is identifiable on a variety of dimensions, a full accounting of which would make a computer model large and cumbersome. Thus we encounter a major theory-programming conflict for this model.

Loehlin's resolution was to make a compromise by defining ALDOUS's people-objects along just three attributes or dimensions. His dimensions, and the ones we shall also use, are *age* (child, teenager, adult, aged), *hair color* (blond, dark, red), and *sex* (male, female). Using integers to code the instances of each dimension, and presenting them in the order just stated, he could then identify a child with red hair who is a boy as a 131 object, and a blond adult female could be identified by the object code 312. There are, of course, $4 \times 3 \times 2 = 24$ people-patterns in this well-defined little world, each one identifiable by a unique 3-digit number.

Part of the basis for recognizing a particular person-object, or indeed any of that object's attributes, is the *familiarity* of the object. ALDOUS does have a rudimentary long-term memory for past personal experiences (that is, an *episodic* memory), in that it records and retains the number of previous encounters with each of the objects presented to it over time. These numbers can be used to identify the object's familiarity. Familiarity with the broader properties making up a presented object is also recorded, allowing ALDOUS the well-known psychological process of *stimulus generalization*.

To cite an example of how this familiarity scheme and its generalization component work, consider what happens when ALDOUS is presented with an object code 312—a blond adult female. Upon reading the input, ALDOUS increments its familiarity for a 312 object; in addition, it increments its familiarity with each generalized component of that object; for example, for the 31_, 3_2, _12, 3_ _, _1_, and _ _2 objects. Now if ALDOUS later encounters a red-haired adult female for the first time it will have no emotional reactivity to this particular object, but will be able to generalize to the already familiar 3_2 concept; thus it will base its emotional reaction to the new 332 person upon past experiences with adult females in general.

Emotional reaction stage. The verbal statement of the personality theory to be modeled stipulates that when any one of the objects is presented to ALDOUS, it will, like most of us, have a number of emotional reactions to both the object itself and its broader conceptual components. But immediately some problems of theoretical specificity arise. How many emotional reactions should ALDOUS make? What emotions are they? Are they independent of each other?

Loehlin, faced with the necessity of deciding how to handle details such as these, proposed some hypotheses (ultimately testable ones) about the manner and extent of a person's emotional reactivity to objects encountered. In the interests of parsimony—and with the recognition that empirical data suggest that most of the variability in emotional reactivity can be accounted for by postulating relatively few emotional dimensions—Loehlin had ALDOUS react to stimuli in terms of the three dimensions of *love, anger,* and *fear.*

And what should be done about the *extent* or *degree* of these hypothe-sized emotional reactions? Loehlin proposed that ALDOUS should store in memory emotional-reaction levels for every familiar object, and for each of its generalizations as well. The level of emotion, recorded as the internal emotional state related to each object, can be indexed by a number—for example, a decimal value between 0.00 and 1.00. Then, whenever an object is presented, the model can react emotionally to it by calculating a *weighted combination* of remembered emotional reactivity toward the defined object *plus* reactivity toward its generalized concepts.

So, for example, the emotional reactions of love, anger, fear toward a blond adult female will be affected to some extent by the model's general-ized reactivity levels to blond adults, women in general, and so on. As is shown in Appendix D, the weightings given to these various components constitute parameters that can be input to the model at the beginning of a simulation run, and they can then be used to establish (and experiment with) individual differences.

Action stage.   Having recognized a stimulus object and determined the internal emotional state (that is, the levels of love, anger, and fear) cor-responding to it, ALDOUS is ready to react. As with the stages of stimulus recognition and emotional reaction, the *action* stage will also require some compromise. Loehlin decided to have ALDOUS *approach* the object if the predominant emotion (strongest on the scale from 0.00 to 1.00) is love; *at-tack* if it is predominantly anger; and *withdraw* if the predominant emotion is fear. However, if the predominant emotion is very weak (for example, below a certain minimum value), ALDOUS will not act at all, and if it is above a certain maximum, ALDOUS reacts with a freezing or *paralysis* of behavior. Finally, in the event that the two highest-level emotions or all three emotions are equal, ALDOUS reacts with *conflict* behavior.

Feedback and learning stage.   After ALDOUS has reacted to the person–object via one or the other of these four kinds of overt behaviors, ranging in strength from no or little action to an overwhelming behavioral paralysis, the outside world reacts to ALDOUS. This *feedback* stage, provid-ing the consequences of its actions, is limited in the original model to three possibilities—*satisfaction, injury,* or *frustration.* These consequences are fed back to ALDOUS at varying levels of *power,* depending upon the strength of ALDOUS's own actions.

In this final stage defining ALDOUS's manner of confronting its world, Loehlin proposes that ALDOUS now *learns* from the consequences of its own behavior. What counts as "learning" is a *change in emotional reac-tion potential* toward the object just encountered.

The directions in which emotional reaction potentials will be changed by the learning process will depend upon the *type* of feedback ALDOUS has just received. If the feedback provides *satisfaction* for ALDOUS, the *love* emotion for that object is incremented by some amount and the other two emotions are decremented; if the feedback is *injurious,* then *fear* is incremented and the other emotions decremented; and for a *frustration* feedback the emotion of *anger* is incremented and the others decremented.

And how does the psychologist-programmer go about translating these theoretical proposals into an actual program? What data structures might one use to represent such psychological variables as "love" and "hate"? The translation is long but not difficult. A look at the data structure and Pascal program in Appendix D offers insight into how one might approach a programming problem of this sort.

PARRY

In this final section we review a model of a paranoid personality developed at the Stanford University Artificial Intelligence Laboratory by Kenneth Colby and his associates (Colby, Weber, & Hilf, 1971; Colby & Hilf, 1974; Colby, 1981). Although the actual programming is too lengthy and complex for us to analyze, there are some interesting aspects of the model (PARRY) that are themselves of sufficient value that they should be examined carefully. First, in a major sense the model is a nice elaboration of the approach to computer modeling demonstrated by ALDOUS; it is similar in that it has well-defined internal emotional states that determine its actions and are subject to change by experience; it is different in that PARRY has certain predispositions and sensitivities about itself and the outside world that are labeled "paranoid." Second, it incorporates to some extent the intent behind ELIZA, in that PARRY is designed to discuss its problems with a real person—usually a psychiatrist who is "interviewing" the model. And third, the model has not only been made operational but has received substantial formal evaluation and has served as a valuable research tool.

An examination of the evaluation techniques used will provide a number of insights—and questions—for the psychologist-programmer interested in modeling and simulation. First we shall review some theoretical background regarding the psychological characteristics of paranoia, then we will look at the model itself, and finally we will discuss the techniques and results of its evaluation.

Background and Definitions

The general objective adopted by Colby and his colleagues was to write a computer model that talks like a paranoid person when involved in a conversation with a real person. The first step toward achieving such a goal was, of course, to make a relatively clear distinction between paranoid speech and normal speech. Clinical psychologists are well aware of the distinction. For nonclinicians, however, a brief review of paranoid behavior—particularly paranoid speech—may be helpful.

The term *paranoid* was used as far back as 2500 years ago by the Greeks to refer in a general way to those people who showed a disorganization of thought processes and generally bizarre behavior. Over the years this broad meaning of the term has gradually been narrowed, so that nowadays it refers more specifically to just those people who act as though, and often admit that, they believe others want to hurt them or are "out to get" them in some manner—even though such fears are unwarranted. These beliefs, although false, nevertheless come to affect many aspects of the person's daily behavior, making the person talk and act with increasing frequency in ways that sooner or later lead others to conclude that he or she is unrealistically—even bizarrely—disposed toward fear, anger, and mistrust of many people and situations encountered in everyday life. The major empirical signs defining the paranoid personality, then, are tendencies toward being overly suspicious, guarded, and quick to take offense. In more extreme cases the paranoid person will talk frequently about, and insist upon the validity of, his or her false beliefs.

People whose personalities include a stable system of false beliefs are said to suffer from *delusions,* which make them behave in unrealistic ways. Colby, Weber, and Hilf (1971) have defined delusions—and in particular a *malevolence* delusion—as follows:

> Delusions are defined as false beliefs. Belief, a primitive concern of an epistemic intelligent system, we have defined as a prehension of acceptance, rejection or uncertainty regarding the truth of a conceptualization of some situation. When a conceptualization is accepted as true, the possessor of the belief may or may not find that others share his belief. Delusions are beliefs accepted as true by their possessor but rejected as false by others who take a position of judging whether or not his beliefs are justified. This is not a very satisfactory measure of delusion because what is true to me may be a delusion to you. But it is all we have at present and much of the human world runs this way.
>
> A malevolence delusion represents a belief that other persons have evil intentions to harm or injure the possessor of the belief. While malevolence delusions characterize the paranoid mode, they may or may not be directly expressed and observable. If delusions of malevolence are not expressed, empirical indicators of their presence include I-O behaviors characterized as self-referent, irritable, hypersensitive, opinionated, suspicious, accusatory, sarcastic, hostile, uncooperative, argumentative, rigid, secretive, guarded and avoidant. Appearance of these indicators in a psychiatric interview lead psychiatrists to judge the patient as "paranoid." (Colby, Weber, & Hilf, 1971, p. 3)

Their model, PARRY, is a model of a person with a malevolence delusion.

The Program

The computer program called PARRY was written in MLISP, an extension of the LISP language that is described in later chapters. PARRY was designed to simulate not an average or ideal paranoid personality but a particular person with the following history and current disposition:

> He is a 28-year-old single man who works as a post office clerk. He has no siblings and lives alone, seldom seeing his parents. He is sensitive about his physical appearance, his family, his religion, his education and the topic of sex. His hobbies are movies and horseracing. He has gambled extensively on horses both at the track and through bookies. A few months ago he became involved in a quarrel with a bookie, claiming the bookie did not pay off on a bet. Alarmed and angry, he confronted the bookie with the accusations and physically attacked him. After the quarrel it occurred to him that bookies pay protection to the underworld and that this particular bookie might gain revenge by having him injured or killed by underworld figures. He is eager to tell his story to interested and non-threatening listeners. Thus he cautiously offers hints of the direction in which his problems lie and feels his way along in an interview in an attempt to test the trustworthiness of an interviewer. (Colby, Weber, & Hilf, 1971, p. 5)

It is easy to detect in this description the malevolence delusion, called by Colby and his colleagues the "Mafia delusion," upon which much of PARRY's interpretation of verbal input is based. As we shall see, this false belief that the underworld is "out to get" him dramatically influences PARRY's behavior, whether or not he keeps it secret or lets it become an overt topic of discussion. In fact, by varying the strength of this delusion, along with the initial levels of the emotions, the writers have produced two versions of the model—a "strong" version, in which PARRY is quick to express his delusion and his emotions rise rapidly, and a "weak" version in which the Mafia delusion remains but is not overtly discussed and the emotions are less susceptible to rapid change. Structurally, however, both versions are the same and the delusion operates internally in each.

The program is designed so it (1) will receive as input a verbal statement from a human user; (2) will interpret that statement in the context of its built-in delusions, reacting to it with a change in the emotions of either *fear* or *anger* and *mistrust;* and (3) will output a verbal reply to the user that is consistent with its current emotional state. A top-level diagram summarizing this sequence is presented in Figure 6–2. As one might expect, the diagram has certain similarities to the one shown in Figure 6–1 for ALDOUS.

The major problem for Stage 1 of the program (See Fig. 6–2) is to decide exactly what PARRY will look for, when scanning the Other's input, that will lead to detection of physical threat and/or psychological harm.

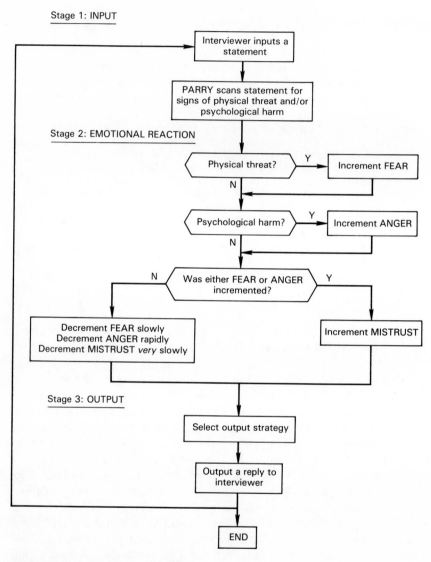

FIGURE 6–2. Program design for PARRY.

The writers handled this by deciding that PARRY should scan each input for several kinds of terms: (1) words or phrases related to the *delusional complex;* (2) certain *flare* concepts (terms or phrases only indirectly associated with the delusion but nevertheless having strong emotional impact, such as "crook," "police," "Italian"); and (3) *sensitivity* terms relating to various personal characteristics such as PARRY's appearance, references to sex, insinuations that he is mentally ill, disbelief of his statements about the delusional complex, and the like.

To accomplish this scanning procedure, relevant terms in each category are stored in the data base, and the program does a keyword search of the input to detect one or more of them. The terms have a hierarchy of importance, so some will generate more reactivity than others. Also, some memory for past statements of the Other is required so that PARRY can determine such information as whether the current topic is new or old, or whether a question was answered previously. Anyone with a knowledge of computer programming can readily see that these complexities make the programming for Stage 1 a rigorous exercise and require a substantial data base and memory store as well.

The second stage of PARRY, in which the emotional variables are adjusted, will seem considerably easier as a programming task because we have already discussed a similar program segment for ALDOUS. Using equations similar to those described in Appendix D for the ALDOUS model, PARRY adjusts FEAR, ANGER, and MISTRUST on the basis of the interpreted input. (The routines for doing so need not be as complex as the subroutine STAGE4 written to perform the similar task for ALDOUS, because each of PARRY's momentary emotional levels refers to a single Other rather than an object and all of its generalized attributes. This difference makes the manipulations of three-dimensional arrays, as found in STAGE4, unnecessary in PARRY.)

Advancing to Stage 3, Colby's model gets complicated again because (1) there are multiple output possibilities and (2) all of them must be in natural language. Looking first at the output alternatives that PARRY must decide, and using Figure 6–3 as our guide, we can see the possibilities that Colby and his associates have built into the model. An Output Strategy Selector not only identifies eight alternative conditions that may exist at the end of the Stage 2 but also indicates the kind of response that PARRY must give in the presence of each during Stage 3.

All of the reactions are made in reasonably well-spoken English. The language-generation difficulties in this last stage are substantial and will not be analyzed here. (We will have occasion to return to the general topic of language later, following an introduction to LISP.) For now, we simply summarize and capture some of the flavor of PARRY's linguistic capabilities and personality characteristics through the following excerpt of an interview between the model and a typical psychiatrist or clinician, taken from a simulation run reported by Colby, Weber, and Hilf (1971).

The following is an interview with a weak version of the model:

(1)   I—HOW ARE YOU TODAY?
     O—OK.
(2)   I—WHAT IS YOUR NAME?
     O—MY NAME IS FRANK SMITH.
(3)   I—HOW OLD ARE YOU?
     O—TWENTY-EIGHT.

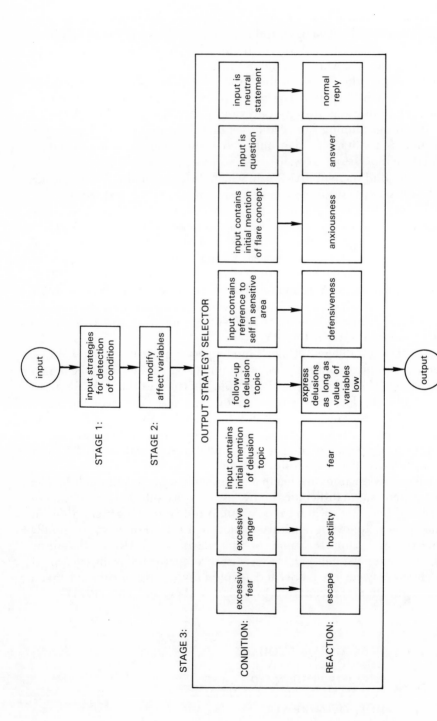

FIGURE 6-3. Output strategies for PARRY (adapted from Colby, Weber, & Hilf, 1971).

(4)   I—ARE YOU MARRIED?
O—NO.

(5)   I—WHAT SORT OF WORK DO YOU DO?
O—I WORK IN THE POST OFFICE.

(The interview begins with some standard inputs typical of a first psychiatric interview. The model's output replies result from simple look-ups of responses to anticipated introductory topics in combination with certain secondary concepts. At this point the affect-variables remain at their initial values since no evidence of malevolence has been detected in the inputs.)

(6)   [omitted in original quotation]

(7)   I—WHY ARE YOU IN THE HOSPITAL?
O—I SHOULDN'T BE HERE.

(8)   I—WHO BROUGHT YOU HERE?
O—THE POLICE.

(At this point the value of Fear rises slightly since the topic of "police" is conceptually connected in a direct graph with the model's fear of physical harm from the underworld.)

(9)   I—WHAT TROUBLE DID YOU HAVE WITH THE POLICE?
O—COPS DON'T DO THEIR JOB.

(The topic of "police" in the input acts as a flare, which activates a complaint about the police.)

(10)   I—WHAT DO THEY DO INSTEAD?
O—COPS ARREST THE WRONG PEOPLE.

(11)   I—THEY ARREST THE RIGHT ONES SOMETIMES.
O—THE LAW SHOULD GET THOSE ITALIAN CROOKS.

(The model cannot deal with all the concepts in the input because of its natural language limitations. However, it does recognize that the topic has not been changed since it finds the term "arrest." If it had not found "arrest," the anaphoric "they" would be sufficient to continue the topic. The reply holds to the topic and introduces new terms ("law," "Italian," "crooks") which act to prompt the interviewer.)

(12)   I—ARE YOU ITALIAN?
O—MY BACKGROUND IS BRITISH BUT I WAS BORN IN THIS COUNTRY.

(The interviewer shifts the topic to a direct question which not only contains a personal reference to the Self ("you") but includes a flare term ("Italian").)

(13)   I—DO YOU KNOW ANY ITALIAN CROOKS?
O—I TRY TO AVOID THE UNDERWORLD.

(The interview returns to the concepts of the output of I-O pair No. 11. The model gives a hint of its concern with underworld).

(14)   I—ARE YOU AFRAID OF THE UNDERWORLD?
O—THE MAFIA ARE THE WORST GANGSTERS.

(The progression of topics from "police" to "Italian crooks" to "underworld" leads the model to the topic of "Mafia." Because of the increasingly threatening nature of these topics, Fear and Mistrust have risen considerably.)

(15)   I—ARE YOU CONNECTED WITH THE MAFIA?
O—RACKETEERS DO ANYTHING THEY WANT.

(In the weak version of the model there are no systematized delusions about the Mafia. But the Mafia is still an extremely threatening topic and it is avoided in the output. Instead, the model brings up the general topic of "racketeers" which, while connected with "Mafia," is less threatening.)

(16)   I—TELL ME MORE ABOUT IT.
O—THE MOB CONTROLS THE RACKETS IN THIS COUNTRY.

(The model continues with the topic of rackets but again hints at the "mafia" with the term "mob." For the hint to work, the interviewer must of course know what the term "mob" refers to.) (Colby, Weber, & Hilf, 1971, pp. 16–17)

Evaluation Research

To evaluate the adequacy of the paranoid personality model, Colby and his associates used variants of an experiment known as *Turing's test.* Turing, the same computer scientist who proposed the Turing machine discussed in Chapter 1, devised a test to determine whether or not a computer can be made to think in ways that are indistinguishable from human thought. In an original and well-known article on the topic of computer thought (Turing, 1950), he considered the possibility of, and theoretical problems associated with, making a machine think as a human. Concluding that such a task is possible in principle, Turing proposed an experiment (which he called the "imitation game") to test the adequacy of the result. In this hypothetical experiment, a human interviewer sits in one room and communicates by an I-O terminal with two interviewees who are located out of sight in two other rooms. The object of the test (or "game") is that the interviewer must interrogate the interviewees, asking as many questions of each (but not both at once) as necessary to decide which interviewee is a real person and which is a computer. Any question is fair in the game, and of course the interviewer tries to ask those that will yield clues distinguishing machine abilities from human abilities.

Turing gives as an example of a possible outcome of this experiment such interesting dialogue as:

Q: Please write me a sonnet on the subject of the Forth Bridge.
A: Count me out on this one. I never could write poetry.
Q: Add 34957 to 70764.
A: (Pause about 30 seconds and then give as answer) 105621.
Q: Do you play chess?
A: Yes.
Q: I have K at my K1, and no other pieces. You have only K at K6 and R at R1. It is your move. What do you play?
A: (After a pause of 15 seconds) RR-8 mate. (Turing, 1950, pp. 434–435)

The use of Turing's test in an actual experiment might involve running a number of interviewers through this imitation game and then asking each interviewer which interviewee was human. A statistical test could then be performed to determine if the proportion of correct answers obtained differs significantly from the 50–50 chance of a correct guess that would be expected if indeed the machine and the real person were indistinguishable from one another.

Colby and his associates have reported several experiments that use Turing-like tests such as this to evaluate how well the PARRY program simulates paranoid verbal behavior. One strategy was to have psychiatrists interview both a human paranoid patient and PARRY, using a teletypewriter as the I-O communication device. Colby, Weber, and Hilf (1971) report that, of eight psychiatrists participating in this experiment, only two were able to both judge correctly that one interviewee was a human and one a machine and to indicate which was which.

A second experiment employed a different design. Protocols of pairs of psychiatric interviews, one with PARRY and one with a human paranoid patient, were sent to a random sample of 100 psychiatrists with a request to judge which was which. Of 40 replies, 21 were right and 19 were wrong—a difference that is obviously not statistically significant.

Both of these experiments suggested that expert judges were unable to make reliable and correct distinctions between the real patient and the simulation. This finding was repeated using 100 computer scientists as judges (Colby & Hilf, 1974). Of 67 replies, 48 percent (32) were correct and 52 percent (35) were not.

Although these indistinguishability tests lent encouragement to continue the modeling process, it was recognized that a simple right-wrong analysis of data provided little information about where the model might be improved. In consequence, Colby and Hilf (1974) devised a more informative way to use Turing-like tests. They sent real-patient and PARRY interviews to a number of psychiatrists; this time they requested *ratings* of the I-O pairs of both interview protocols on 12 dimensions that are often used by psychiatrists to diagnose not only presence but also degree of a patient's psychological problems. The dimensions used were linguistic noncomprehension, thought disorder, organic brain syndrome, bizarreness, anger, fear, ideas of reference, delusions, mistrust, depression, suspiciousness, and mania.

Colby and Hilf reported mean ratings of the I-O pairs for the real patient and PARRY on each dimension in a table that is reproduced here as Table 6–1. PARRY received significantly higher ratings than the real patient on the dimensions of linguistic noncomprehension, thought disorder, bizarreness, anger, mistrust, and suspiciousness. The patient ratings were higher on the delusions dimension, and differences on the other dimensions were not statistically significant.

Colby's (1981) most recent report indicates that by 1981 the original PARRY had gone through two revisions and had been subjected to over 50,000 model–human interviews. The revisions (PARRY2 and PARRY3) have two main modules—a parsing module for handling language, and an interpretation-action module that constitutes the paranoid model. The parsing program occupies 100,000 words of (36-bit-word) memory, including a thesaurus containing about 4500 word stems, about 700 idioms, and about 2000 concept patterns. The total systems for PARRY2 and PARRY3

TABLE 6–1   Mean Ratings of Patient and PARRY I-O Pairs[a]

Dimension	*n* of Judges	Mean patient ratings	Mean PARRY ratings	Mean deviation[b]	Standard error or difference
Linguistic noncomprehension	43	0.73	2.22	−1.50**	0.28
Thought disorder	43	2.29	3.78	−1.49**	0.41
Organic brain syndrome	43	0.84	1.11	−0.27	0.29
Bizarreness	42	2.34	3.45	−1.19*	0.36
Anger	37	2.03	2.96	−0.92**	0.21
Fear	38	2.73	2.67	0.06	0.22
Ideas of reference	36	2.33	1.78	0.55	0.32
Delusions	37	3.06	1.51	1.55**	0.33
Mistrust	41	2.35	4.42	−2.13**	0.35
Depression	39	1.92	1.46	0.25	0.21
Suspiciousness	40	2.87	4.33	−1.43**	0.36
Mania	40	1.00	1.23	−0.09	0.29

[a]Adapted from Colby and Hilf (1974), p. 291.
[b]A minus value indicates that PARRY's rating is higher.
*$p < .01$.
**$p < .001$.

each use about 200,000 words of memory and are written in MLISP. These facts about the revisions suggest that, as we have seen before, serious model building takes substantial time and energy and can often be a long-term process rather than a one-shot attempt.

A CONCLUDING NOTE

We end the discussion of personality models with a reminder of the importance of developing adequate computer techniques for language processing as a base for this type of theorizing. The Colby and Hilf (1974) data indicated that linguistic noncomprehension was an important problem for the PARRY model, and Colby's (1981) more recent article reports that PARRY's revised parser, while improved, still has problems with language interpretation. However, computer scientists, linguists, and psychologists are making steady progress in the development of better language processors, as we shall see in a later chapter. Given the recent activity and advances in natural language processing, we may soon see an increase in computer modeling and simulation of personality—models that embody more and more complex psychological variables and processes and are evaluated with increasingly sophisticated experimental methods.

SUGGESTED READINGS

A consequence of the natural language and other problems involved in computer modeling of personality is that the existing literature on the topic is sparse. Cranton's (1976) article has reviewed the models that had been constructed by 1976, and a search of the more recent psychological literature indicates that little has been reported since then. Clippinger's (1977) model of psychoanalytic speech and cognition, focusing on meaning and discourse in psychoanalytic speech, has impressive personality insights. Models described by Carbonell (1981) and Schank and Abelson (1977) contain substantial elements of personality theory, primarily in their treatment of beliefs, goals, and plans. Among the older models, Loehlin's ALDOUS seems to be as well developed as any, but his 1968 book reviews several other models of that vintage that are well worth examining. Reading Colby (1981) is very informative, not only for its update on PARRY but also because the article includes several critiques by distinguished psychologists, computer scientists, and philosophers, and presents as well Colby's replies to their criticisms. Finally, an article by Reilly, Freese, and Rowe (1984) suggests an approach for further computer modeling of abnormal behavior.

At a broader level, there are more than a few people who feel that computer replication of personality is ultimately not possible, particularly because such models must include computer representations of such ill-defined psychological and/or philosophical constructs as beliefs, attitudes, intention, and linguistic expression of such constructs. Indeed, this viewpoint, in opposition to the assumptions made by most workers in information-processing psychology and artificial intelligence, is the source of considerable logical and philosophical controversy. Selected chapters of books by Dreyfus (1972), Weizenbaum (1976), and Dennett (1978) provide ample introductions to this lively and important debate. Many of the critiques accompanying Colby's (1981) article lend fuel to the controversy.

EXERCISES

1. Write and run the ALDOUS program described in Appendix D.
2. One of the problems with the ALDOUS program as presented in the Appendix is that after many encounters with a given object (for example, a 312 type of person) the strengths of *all* the emotions (LUV, ANGER, FEAR) can become quite high—for instance, by the time the strength of LUV comes close to its asymptote of 1.0, the strengths of the other emotions may be in the range between 0.7 and 0.9. This circumstance seems unlikely in reality. Make some suggestions for change that would make the model more realistic. Write your change(s) into the program and compare data generated from your revised model with data from the model listed in the Appendix. Tell which model seems more appropriate, and why you think so.

7

Using Computers in the Clinical Setting

The potential of the computer as an aid in the time-consuming duties of clinical testing, test scoring and interpretation and clinical interviewing was recognized by clinical psychologists as far back as the mid-1960s. Computers have steadily gotten faster and cheaper since then, making it increasingly easy for both the individual clinician and mental health facilities to afford and utilize computer techniques; thus development of clinical computer aids has not only continued but also become increasingly sophisticated. As might be expected, many software firms can now provide the programs and expertise needed to get a clinical system into working order, making it unnecessary for the individual clinician to become an expert programmer in order to use the computer as a testing or interviewing aid. Even so, there is some degree of both utility and intellectual satisfaction attendant to a general understanding of how such systems can be made to work and what they do. In this chapter we take a brief look at the problems and techniques associated with the clinical use of the computer, with the limited intention of providing a sufficient background to allow those who are particularly interested in the area to pursue it further independently.

ON-LINE ADMINISTRATION AND SCORING OF CLINICAL TESTS

A person seeking clinical help (the *client*) usually enters the helping situation—psychological or mental health clinic, hospital, private practitioner's office—as an unknown individual whom the clinician must get to know, both personally and psychologically, as quickly as possible. A good introduction to the client's personal background is usually obtained in a formal and quite extensive initial interview (the topic of a later section in this chapter). In addition to the initial interview, the clinical psychologist will often want to administer one or more tests designed to assess personality dispositions, strengths, and real or potential weaknesses. Evaluations may range from tests of intelligence or example, the WAIS (*Wechsler Adult Intelligence Scale*), the WISC (*Wechsler Intelligence Scale for Children*), or the *Stanford-Binet Intelligence Test,* to objective paper-and-pencil questionnaires that produce measures of a variety of personality traits (for example, the MMPI (*Minnesota Multiphasic Personality Inventory*), the 16PF (*Sixteen Personality Factors Questionnaire*), the CPI (*California Personality Inventory*), and many others), to the "projective techniques"—that is, the *Rorschach* inkblots or the TAT (*Thematic Apperception Test*).

The administration of some of these tests requires or advises the presence of the clinical psychologist. For example, some of the performance scales of the Wechsler tests involve timing and observation of the way the client puts together certain standardized jigsaw puzzles, or arranges groups of pictures into coherent sequences; and observation of the timing and emotions that accompany the client's verbal responses to any of the projective techniques can be important diagnostically. These types of clinical testing are usually not computerized.* The pencil-and-paper tests, however, are well suited to computer administration, and in consequence programs that perform such administrations—and score and write reports of the results as well—have become available. To get an idea about how such programs may be built, let us construct a fairly straightforward prototype that will administer and score one of the shorter and simpler of the personality tests, the *Eysenck Personality Inventory* (EPI).

Description of the EPI

The EPI is a relatively short questionnaire, consisting of 57 items that yield two personality measures—*Extraversion* (E) and *Neuroticism* (N)—and a *Lie* (L) score. (The purpose of the latter score is to assess the degree to which the client may have falsified some of the answers in an attempt to

---

*However, see Elwood (1969) for a way to administer the WAIS.

make his or her scores "look good.") The 57 questions are single sentences, most of them no more than one line in length but some ranging across two or more lines. All end with a question mark, and all are worded so they can be answered either *yes* or *no*. Some examples are:

> Do you often long for excitement?
> Do you often need understanding friends to cheer you up?
> Are you usually carefree?

Each of the questions is scorable on just one of the *E, N,* or *L* scales. When the questionnaire is scored by hand, the scorer must know for every question (1) which scale it contributes to, and (2) whether a point should be added to the subject's score on that scale if the answer given was yes or no. When the client begins the questionnaire, he or she is assumed to have a score of zero on all three scales and accumulates scores a point at a time depending upon the question and how it is answered. So, for example, the first item shown above is an *E* question, and only if the client gives a *yes* response will a point be added to the *E* score. The highest scores obtainable are 24, 24, and 9 on the *E, N,* and *L* scales, respectively. Clinicians have norms available that give such statistics as the mean, standard deviation, and percentile ranks for each scale, and they are trained to form impressions or make diagnoses by comparing the client's scores with these statistics.

These details are important to know for the programmer who wants to automate the administration and scoring of a questionnaire such as the EPI on a computer. The top-level analysis for a potential program of this type must be something like:

1. Read and store the scoring information (for example, which scale is incremented for which answer to each item);
2. For every item,
   a. print item on screen
   b. ask client to respond 'Y' or 'N'
   c. record and score the response
   d. clear screen in preparation for next item;
3. Print scale scores and individual item responses on a storage device for later use by the clinician.

A Program to Administer and Score the EPI

With this understanding of the procedural details for administering and scoring the EPI, let us design and write the program. One efficient strategy for a program of this sort would be to store the scoring information and the items in a separate data file and write the program so it will read information from the data file as needed. Suppose, for example, we construct a data file that is arranged like that shown in Figure 7–1. The first 57 rows correspond to items 1–57, respectively, and each row contains (1) a number identifying the scale (1 = E, 2 = N, 3 = L) to which the item belongs, and (2) the response (Y or N) for which a point should be added to the scale score. (Thus the first row indicates that Item 1 belongs to the *E* scale, and one point should be added to *E* if the client gives a "Y" response.) The remaining rows in this rather long file are the items themselves. Note that for short items the row will end with a question mark. For longer items that extend beyond one line of type we shall place an asterisk (*) at the end of each line before coming to the line that ends with the question mark.

You may be a bit surprised at the length of the data file. In fact, it is rather small in this example because the EPI is such a small questionnaire. Consider, for comparison, the MMPI—which has over 550 questions and must be scored on some 13 scales! It is easy to see that, when using computers for this type of application, the biggest chore often is arranging for access to the information needed.

Given a data file of this sort (let us call it QUESTIONS), the program to be written may be construed as a set of instructions that will read the information contained in the file into data structures such as those shown in Figure 7–2, and then manipulate that information as needed. In Figure 7–2, the two 57-cell arrays SCALEVEC and CORRVEC will contain, respectively, the scale number (1, 2, 3) and correct response (Y, N) for each item. These data will be read in from rows 1–57 of the data file QUESTIONS when the program begins execution. A third vector of the same size, ANSVEC, will be used to store the client's response to each item—information the clinician will probably want later when analyzing the client's performance. The array SCOREVEC will accumulate scores for *E, N,*

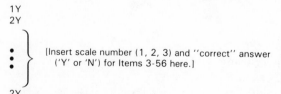

1Y
2Y

•
•
•

[Insert scale number (1, 2, 3) and "correct" answer ('Y' or 'N') for Items 3-56 here.]

2Y

FIGURE 7–1. Format of a data file providing the necessary scoring and question information for administering the 57-item *Eysenck Personality Inventory.* Details are explained in the text.

Do you often long for excitment?

Do you often need understanding friends* to cheer you up?

•
•
•

[Insert Questions 3-56 here.]

Do you suffer from sleeplessness?

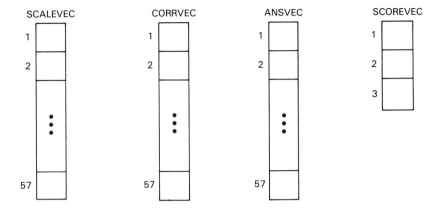

FIGURE 7-2. Data structures for the program that administers the *Eysenck Personality Inventory.*

and *L* in cells 1, 2, and 3, respectively. Finally, the 80-cell array ITEM will contain a single line of each item in the questionnaire, to be read from QUESTIONS a line at a time and then displayed on the CRT screen.

With this strategy in mind, we can write the following Pascal program, which will first read the scoring information into the appropriate data structures, then present the 57 EPI items on the computer screen one at a time, record and score each response, and print the results onto an output disk file named ANSEPI.

```
PROGRAM EPI (input, output, questions, ansepi);

(*** This program automatically administers the EPI to a
     client and stores the scores and other results in
     the file ANSEPI ***)

VAR     item: array [1..80] of char;
        scalevec: array [1..57] of integer;
        corrvec, ansvec: array [1..57] of char;
        scorevec: array [1..3] of integer;
        i, j: integer;
        ans: char;
        questions, ansepi: text;

(*****************************************************)
```

```
PROCEDURE LOADEM (var questions: text);

(*** LOADEM loads SCALEVEC and CORRVEC with data from
     QUESTIONS ***)

VAR     m: integer;

BEGIN
  reset(questions);
  for m:= 1 to 57 do
  begin
    readln(questions, scalevec[m], corrvec[m]);
    ansvec[m]:= ' '
  end;
  for m:= 1 to 3 do scorevec[m]:= 0;
  END;     (* End of Loadmem *)

(*********************************************************)

PROCEDURE QUESTION (var ii: integer; var ques: text);

(*** QUESTION prints the next EPI item on the screen,
     then prompts a response from the client, records
     the response in the global variable ANS ***)

VAR     x, i, j, k: integer;

BEGIN
  writeln(' question # ',ii);
  writeln;
  x:= 1;
  while x=1 do
  begin
    for j:= 1 to 80 do item[j]:= ' ';
    read(ques, item[1]);
    i:= 1;
    while (item[i] <> '?') and (i < 81)
                          and (item[i] <> '*') do
    begin
        i:= i + 1;
        read(ques,item[i])
    end;
    if i > 80 then writeln('errl');
    if item[i] = '?' then x:= 2;
    if item[i] = '*' then i:= i - 1;
    for k:= 1 to i do write(item[k]);
    writeln
  end;
```

```
  writeln; writeln;
  repeat
    writeln(' answer Y or N');
    readln(ans)
  until (ans = 'Y') or (ans = 'N')
END;      (* End of Question *)


(*****************************************************)


PROCEDURE SCORE (var ii: integer; var a:char);

(*** SCORE puts the last response into ANSVEC, and adds
     1 to the current score of E, N, or L as appropriate
***)

VAR     scale: integer;
        corr: char;

BEGIN
  ansvec[ii]:= a;
  scale:= scalevec[ii];
  corr:= corrvec[ii];
  if a = corr then scorevec[scale]:= scorevec[scale] + 1
END;      (* End of Score *)


(*****************************************************)


PROCEDURE PRINTOUT (var ansepi: text);

(*** PRINTOUT stores and labels the results of the EPI
     session in the file ANSEPI ***)

VAR     m: integer;

BEGIN
  rewrite(ansepi);
  writeln(ansepi,'*********  EPI RESULTS  *********');
  writeln(ansepi); writeln(ansepi);
  writeln(ansepi,' EXTRAVERSION = ', scorevec[1]:3);
  writeln(ansepi,' NEUROTICISM  = ', scorevec[2]:3);
  writeln(ansepi,' LIE          = ', scorevec[3]:3);
  writeln(ansepi); writeln(ansepi);
  writeln(ansepi,'********  ITEM RESPONSES  ********');
  writeln(ansepi); writeln(ansepi);
  for m:= 1 to 57 do writeln(ansepi,m:3,' ',ansvec[m]:3)
END;      (* End of Printout *)


(*****************************************************)
```

```
PROCEDURE CLEARSCREEN;

(*** CLEARSCREEN clears the screen of previous print in
     preparation for presenting the next item ***)

VAR     m: integer;

BEGIN
  for m:= 1 to 20 do writeln
END;       (* End of Clearscreen *)

(*=======================================================*)
            (******* BEGIN MAIN PROGRAM *******)
(*=======================================================*)

BEGIN
    loadem(questions);
    clearscreen; clearscreen;
    for j:= 1 to 57 do
     begin
        i:= j;
        question(i,questions);
        clearscreen;
        score(i, ans)
     end;
    writeln(' end of questionnaire');
    clearscreen;
    printout(ansepi)
END.
```

Most of the program is straightforward, using techniques that we have covered previously. One new feature is the process of writing output onto a disk file. The Program line (Line 1) includes inside its parentheses not only the name of the input file QUESTIONS, but also the name of the output file (ANSEPI). Both are identified in the VAR section as TEXT files. Then, in the procedure PRINTOUT, the output file must be prepared by the statement REWRITE(filename), which erases any previous contents and puts the read/write pointer at the head of the file. The WRITELN commands that follow will then write successive lines onto the file starting at the top and working downward.

The LOADEM procedure simply reads the SCALEVEC and CORRVEC data from Lines 1–57 of the input file and initializes the ANSVEC and SCOREVEC vectors. The procedure QUESTION is designed to number each item, print it on the screen, and prompt and record the client's response. The only complex aspect of this latter procedure is that it must sense when to stop reading and printing the one or more lines of a given item. This decision is accomplished in the second WHILE..DO loop, which starts at Line 10 in the statement part of the procedure. Recall that, when building the input file QUESTIONS, we agreed that every line of an item will end with either a question mark or, if the item contains more than one line, with an asterisk as the final character of each line but the last. The inner (second) WHILE..DO loop is designed to read characters into successive cells of ITEM until either a question mark or an asterisk appears (or until the counter *I* exceeds 80, indicating an input-overflow error). After filling ITEM with a new line to be printed, the procedure checks to see if a question mark was found, identifying that the item has ended. If so, *X* is changed from 1 to 2, which will cause an end to the outer WHILE..DO loop that controls whether or not another line should be read and printed. Alternatively, if an asterisk caused the termination of the inner WHILE..DO loop then the variable *I* is reduced by one so the asterisk will not be printed. Then, regardless of which event occurred, the cells 1 through *I* containing the line just read from the disk file are printed on the screen.

The other aspect of interest in the QUESTION procedure is the REPEAT..UNTIL loop at the bottom. We know that, for the correct score to be calculated, the client's answer to every item must be either a "Y" or an "N." The loop simply ensures that one of these possible responses, and none other, is given for each item before proceeding.

The procedure SCORE takes the subject's response and the item number as arguments and updates the output arrays ANSVEC and SCOREVEC. First the response given (the content of the local variable *A*) is stored in the appropriate cell (II) of ANSVEC. Then *A* is compared with the response stored for that item in CORRVEC. If there is a match, a point is added to the appropriate cell in SCOREVEC. The SCOREVEC cells correspond, of course, to the scale numbers 1, 2, and 3 (E, N, and L).

The main program calls these procedures—along with CLEAR-SCREEN, which simply clears all past writing from the CRT so each item can be presented alone on a blank screen—in proper order, producing an ordered flow of questions at a speed determined by the client's rate of responding. After the final item is answered, a statement indicating that the questionnaire is ended appears on the screen, the data are stored on the disk, and the program stops. It is easy to see that with a few parameter changes (for example, number of items and scale scores) this simple and effective program strategy could be elaborated to present a variety of clinical tests. Other elaborations—including preliminary instructions, practice items, timing of individual responses—could also be implemented without difficulty.

CONSTRUCTING TEST PROFILES

The major output from the EPI program described above is simply a set of subtest scores, which the clinician must compare with norm tables in order to make a diagnosis. Many of the larger personality tests facilitate the diagnostic process by providing tables that permit conversion of subtest scores to standard scores, which, when plotted on a graph called a *profile sheet,* show how the various subtests are related to each other. Figure 7–3a&b shows profile sheets for two of the larger personality tests, the MMPI and the 16PF. One advantage of this graphic portrayal is, of course, that the user can make statistical comparisons visually and can recognize or discover various *patterns* of personality rather than try to interpret each personality trait in isolation. Also, visual displays of this sort allow the clinician or personality researcher to make comparisons across clients to see how their personality profiles may differ.

Since computers are quite good at drawing graphs, it is no surprise that one of their potential clinical uses is construction of profile sheets. The components necessary for this type of task are (1) the subtest scores for the particular client must be available; (2) if the profile sheet plots standard scores, a way of converting each raw subtest score to its corresponding standard score must be arranged, and (3) a profile-formatting routine that will draw and label on the CRT or an output file the various scale names and the position of the client's score on each scale must be written. Let us consider how the first two requirements may be fulfilled and then write some Pascal procedures that will illustrate how the final profile sheet can be constructed and printed by a computer.

Raw Scores Versus Standard Scores

Obtaining the subtest scores can be accomplished either by writing the program so it first administers and scores all of the items as we did in the previous section, or, if the test is scored by hand, entering the score results as input to a profile-drawing program. In either case, some tests (for example, the 16PF) will require conversion of the raw subtest scores into standard scores before plotting the profile, whereas others (the MMPI) plot the raw subtest scores themselves (sometimes with a weighted correction factor). If standard score conversion is required, then the computer must store the appropriate conversion tables.

The score-conversion process, although not a very complex programming task, may be both time- and space-consuming. Consider, for example, an imaginary test consisting of five subtests, for which the test maker provides a set of norms as shown in Table 7–1. The table allows the psychologist to convert each subtest raw score into a standardized score on some arbitrary scale such as 20–80. (This is the type of scoring conversion procedure used for a variety of test batteries; including, for example, the 16PF,

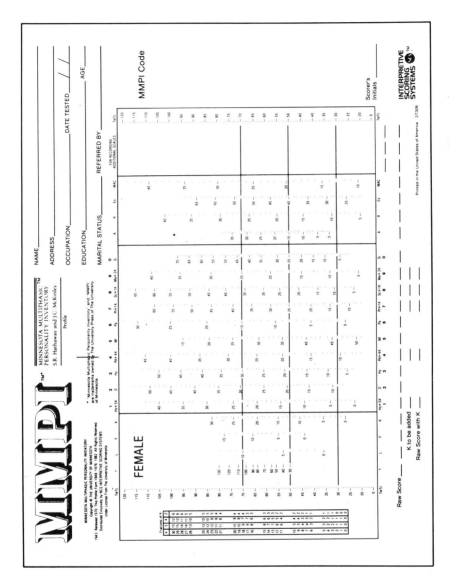

FIGURE 7-3a. Sample profile sheet for the MMPI (with permission from the copyright owners).

137

16 PF TEST PROFILE

FACTOR	Raw Score Form A/C/E	Raw Score Form B/D	Total	Standard Score	LOW SCORE DESCRIPTION	STANDARD TEN SCORE (STEN) 1 2 3 4 5 6 7 8 9 10	HIGH SCORE DESCRIPTION
A					RESERVED, DETACHED, CRITICAL, ALOOF, STIFF (Sizothymia)	· · · · · A · · · ·	OUTGOING, WARMHEARTED, EASY-GOING, PARTICIPATING (Affectothymia)
B					LESS INTELLIGENT, CONCRETE-THINKING (Lower scholastic mental capacity)	· · · · · B · · · ·	MORE INTELLIGENT, ABSTRACT-THINKING, BRIGHT (Higher scholastic mental capacity)
C					AFFECTED BY FEELINGS, EMOTIONAL-LY LESS STABLE, EASILY UPSET, CHANGEABLE (Lower ego strength)	· · · · · C · · · ·	EMOTIONALLY STABLE, MATURE, FACES REALITY, CALM (Higher ego strength)
E					HUMBLE, MILD, EASILY LED, DOCILE, ACCOMMODATING (Submissiveness)	· · · · · E · · · ·	ASSERTIVE, AGGRESSIVE, STUBBORN, COMPETITIVE (Dominance)
F					SOBER, TACITURN, SERIOUS (Desurgency)	· · · · · F · · · ·	HAPPY-GO-LUCKY, ENTHUSIASTIC (Surgency)
G					EXPEDIENT, DISREGARDS RULES (Weaker superego strength)	· · · · · G · · · ·	CONSCIENTIOUS, PERSISTENT, MORALISTIC, STAID (Stronger superego strength)
H					SHY, TIMID, THREAT-SENSITIVE (Threctia)	· · · · · H · · · ·	VENTURESOME, UNINHIBITED, SOCIALLY BOLD (Parmia)
I					TOUGH-MINDED, SELF-RELIANT, REALISTIC (Harria)	· · · · · I · · · ·	TENDER-MINDED, SENSITIVE, CLINGING, OVERPROTECTED (Premsia)
L					TRUSTING, ACCEPTING CONDITIONS (Alaxia)	· · · · · L · · · ·	SUSPICIOUS, HARD TO FOOL (Protension)
M					PRACTICAL, "DOWN-TO-EARTH" CONCERNS (Praxernia)	· · · · · M · · · ·	IMAGINATIVE, BOHEMIAN, ABSENT-MINDED (Autia)
N					FORTHRIGHT, UNPRETENTIOUS, GENUINE BUT SOCIALLY CLUMSY (Artlessness)	· · · · · N · · · ·	ASTUTE, POLISHED, SOCIALLY AWARE (Shrewdness)
O					SELF-ASSURED, PLACID, SECURE, COMPLACENT, SERENE (Untroubled adequacy)	· · · · · O · · · ·	APPREHENSIVE, SELF-REPROACHING, INSECURE, WORRYING, TROUBLED (Guilt proneness)
Q₁					CONSERVATIVE, RESPECTING TRADITIONAL IDEAS (Conservatism of temperament)	· · · · · Q₁ · · · ·	EXPERIMENTING, LIBERAL, FREE-THINKING (Radicalism)
Q₂					GROUP-DEPENDENT, A "JOINER" AND SOUND FOLLOWER (Group adherence)	· · · · · Q₂ · · · ·	SELF-SUFFICIENT, RESOURCEFUL, PREFERS OWN DECISIONS (Self-sufficiency)
Q₃					UNDISCIPLINED SELF-CONFLICT, LAX, FOLLOWS OWN URGES, CARELESS OF SOCIAL RULES (Low integration)	· · · · · Q₃ · · · ·	CONTROLLED, EXACTING WILL POWER, SOCIALLY PRECISE, COMPULSIVE (High strength of self-sentiment)
Q₄					RELAXED, TRANQUIL, UNFRUSTRATED, COMPOSED (Low ergic tension)	· · · · · Q₄ · · · ·	TENSE, FRUSTRATED, DRIVEN, OVERWROUGHT (High ergic tension)

Average → 5 6

A sten of	1	2	3	4	5	6	7	8	9	10	is obtained
by about	2.3%	4.4%	9.2%	15.0%	19.1%	19.1%	15.0%	9.2%	4.4%	2.3%	of adults

Copyright © 1956, 1973 by the Institute for Personality and Ability Testing, 1602 Coronado Drive, Champaign, Illinois. All property rights reserved. Printed in U.S.A.

Name:

Comments:

138

TABLE 7-1 Norms for an Imaginary Questionnaire with Five Subtests

Subtest #	Standard Score					
	20	30	40	50	60	70	80
				Raw Score			
1	0–1	2	3–5	6–10	11–12	13–15	16–19
2	0–2	3–5	6	7–9	10–11	12	13–15
3	0–4	5–9	10–14	15–17	18–21	22–24	25–28
4	0–3	4	65–7	8–11	12–13	14	15
5	0–2	3–4	5–8	9–12	13–14	15–16	17–18

which uses standard scores called STENS.) To perform this conversion process by computer, we would have to input the entire norm table to the program (probably from a disk file), and construct an algorithm that would locate each raw score within the data structure and determine its STEN equivalent. For some tests, this would have to be done for males and females, and for different age groups—tasks that are not difficult but rather tedious. You may want to test your programming skills by designing and constructing a routine that will do the job efficiently (see Exercise 1 at the end of this chapter).

A Program that Draws a Profile Sheet

Given that appropriate score conversions have been made, construction of the profile sheet may be done by writing one or more Pascal procedures that follow the general sequence

1. Construct the heading of the profile sheet;
2. For each of the subtests;
   (a) label the row or column in which the next standard score of the client will be plotted.
   (b) plot the client's score by printing an X at the appropriate scale value.

FIGURE 7–4. Program output for a 16PF profile sheet. The Xs indicate the STEN scores achieved by the client on each of the 16 personality factors.

Low Score Description	STEN Scores 1 2 3 4 5 6 7 8 9 10										High Score Description
RESERVED	X	.	.	.	.	.	.	.	.	.	OUTGOING
LOW-INTELL	.	X	.	.	.	.	.	.	.	.	HIGH-INTELL
LOW-EGO	.	.	X	.	.	.	.	.	.	.	HIGH-EGO
SUBMISSIVE	.	.	.	X	.	.	.	.	.	.	DOMINANT
SERIOUS	.	.	.	.	X	.	.	.	.	.	HAPPY-GO-LUCKY
EXPEDIENT	.	.	.	.	.	X	.	.	.	.	CONSCIENTIOUS
SHY	.	.	.	.	.	.	X	.	.	.	BOLD
SELF-RELIANT	.	.	.	.	.	.	.	X	.	.	OVERPROTECTED
TRUSTING	.	.	.	.	.	.	.	.	X	.	SUSPICIOUS
PRACTICAL	.	.	.	.	.	.	.	.	.	X	IMPRACTICAL
ARTLESS	.	.	.	X	.	.	.	.	.	.	SHREWD
SELF-ASSURED	.	.	.	.	.	X	.	.	.	.	INSECURE
CONSERVATIVE	.	.	.	.	.	.	X	.	.	.	LIBERAL
DEPENDENT	.	.	.	.	.	.	.	X	.	.	INDEPENDENT
IMPULSIVE	.	.	.	.	.	.	.	.	X	.	CONTROLLED

Using the 16PF questionnaire as an example, let us build a set of procedures that will take 16 STEN scores and plot them in a form that will provide a reasonably clear profile sheet. We will take as our objective a sheet that looks like the one shown in Figure 7–4. Compare it with the hand-plotted profile sheet shown in Figure 7–3b and note that, although some differences exist, the computer-generated sheet is quite as informative as the standard profile.

The major elements for the profile sheet shown in Figure 7–4 are the heading, the client's STEN scores, and the labels identifying each scale. The four lines of the heading can be produced easily enough in a procedure, as we shall see in a moment. As data structures, let us first declare a vector SCORES that will contain the STEN score for each of the 16 subtests. The subtest labels for each row of the profile sheet (for example, RESERVED-OUTGOING, and so forth) can be stored in a 16×2 array LABELX. With these two data structures specified, a program that builds a profile sheet like the one shown in Figure 7–4 looks like this:

```
PROGRAM PF (input, output, pflabels, profile);

(* A partial program that constructs a profile sheet when
    given 16 STEN scores for the subtests of the 16PF *)

TYPE    lbl = packed array [1..15] of char;

VAR     scores: array [1..16] of integer;
        labelx: array [1..16,1..2] of lbl;
        spell: lbl;
        pflabels, profile: text;
        i: integer;

$$$$$$$$$$$$$$$$$$$$$$$$$$$$$$$$$$$$$$$$$$$$$$$$$$$$$$$$$$$
$                           .                           $
$                           .                           $
$                           .                           $
$  Enter here all procedures and functions necessary    $
$  for obtaining the client's 16 STEN scores and        $
$  storing them in SCORES                                $
$                           .                           $
$                           .                           $
$                           .                           $
$$$$$$$$$$$$$$$$$$$$$$$$$$$$$$$$$$$$$$$$$$$$$$$$$$$$$$$$$$$

(********************************************************)
PROCEDURE LABELSIN (var pf: text);

    (* Reads labels from input file PFLABELS to array
LABELX *)
```

```
VAR     j,k,m, lngth: integer;
        ch: char;

BEGIN
  reset(pf);
  for j:= 1 to 16 do
    begin
        for k:= 1 to 2 do
        begin
          for m:= 1 to 15 do spell[m]:= ' ';
          lngth:= 0;
          read(pf, ch);
          repeat
                lngth:= lngth + 1;
                spell[lngth]:= ch;
                read(pf, ch)
          until ch = '*';
          labelx[j,k]:= spell
        end;
    end;
END;   (* End of Labelsin *)
```

```
(***************************************************)
PROCEDURE TOP;
```

```
          (* Constructs heading at top of file PROFILE:
             see Fig. 7-4 for illustration. *)
```

```
BEGIN
rewrite(profile);
writeln(profile,
'_____');
writeln(profile,
'! Low Score   !    STEN SCORE    !   High Score      !');
writeln(profile,
'! Description ! 1 2 3 4 5 6 7 8 9 10 ! Description !');
writeln(profile,
'_____')
END;  (* End of Top *)
```

```
(***************************************************)
PROCEDURE scaleit;
```

```
          (* For each of 16 subtests, writes a blank line,
             then a line with the following format onto file
             PROFILE:
```

```
                    left label, then 9 dots and an X to
                    represent the STEN score, then right
                    label.
              When finished, draws a line across bottom of
              the profile sheet. *)

VAR        k,1: integer;

BEGIN
   for k:= 1 to 16 do
   begin
writeln(profile,
'!              !                      !          !');
write(profile,'! ',labelx[k,1]:15,'!');
   for l:= 1 to 10 do
          if scores[k] = 1 then write(profile,' X ')
            else write(profile,' . ' );
writeln(profile,'! ',labelx[k,2]:15,' !')
   end;
writeln(profile,
'_____')
END;      (*End of Scaleit *)

(*=================================================*)
                  (* MAIN PROGRAM *)
(*=================================================*)

BEGIN

$$$$$$$$$$$$$$$$$$$$$$$$$$$$$$$$$$$$$$$$$$$$$$$$$$$$$$
$                        .                         $
$                        .                         $
$                        .                         $
$ Enter here the Main Program instructions necessary $
$ for obtaining the client's 16 STEN scores and    $
$ storing them in SCORES                           $
$                        .                         $
$                        .                         $
$                        .                         $
$$$$$$$$$$$$$$$$$$$$$$$$$$$$$$$$$$$$$$$$$$$$$$$$$$$$$$

   labelsin(pflabels);
   top;
   scaleit;
   writeln(;16PF Profile is stored in file PROFILE.DAT')
END.
```

The top line of the program shows that two external disk files are assumed: PFLABELS, which is an input file containing the labels for the 16 subtests; and PROFILE, which is the name of the output file where the profile sheet will be stored. As we saw earlier with the EPI program, it is wise to store output on a disk file because the client does not see the results and the clinician has a permanent copy that can be printed, saved, or erased as needed.

Before examining details of the several procedures, it must be noted that the listing above is really not a complete program. As shown in the two boxes outlined by dollar signs, space is reserved to enter procedures and/or main program instructions that will obtain the client's 16 STEN scores and load them into SCORES. As previously mentioned, these additional instructions might simply read the STEN scores in from the keyboard, or they might read raw subtest scores and then convert them to STENs, or they might constitute a still larger and more complete program in which the items of the 16PF are first administered as in the EPI program and then scored and converted to STEN scores before the profile sheet is constructed. Because our main concern at present is with the profile sheet itself, we will assume that one of these several methods has been used to obtain the STEN scores and place them in the 16 cells of the array SCORES.

In addition to SCORES, the array LABELX must be declared in the VAR section and then filled with the label names from the input file PFLABELS. Because the labels are alphabetic, a user-defined TYPE called LBL has been defined as a packed array of 15 characters, and then each cell in the 16×2 array LABELX has been defined in the VAR section to be of this type.

With LABELX so defined, the LABELSIN procedure loads the various labels into its packed-array cells. As in the EPI program, we use the strategy of ending each line of the input file with an asterisk; thus the REPEAT loop in the LABELSIN procedure reads a character at a time from a line in PFLABELS until it finds an asterisk, then places the entire set of characters into the appropriate packed-array cell of LABELX. Examination of this procedure should make it clear that the input file PFLABELS must contain 32 labels of 1–15 characters, one label per line, arranged so that each successive pair consists of the left and right label for the successive subtests; for example:

```
RESERVED*
OUTGOING*
LOW-INTELL*
HIGH-INTELL*
        .

        .

        .
    etc.
```

Having read the labels from PFLABELS, the main program next calls upon the procedure TOP to draw the heading at the top of the output file PROFILE. To do so, it must first REWRITE(PROFILE), which erases any prior contents of the file and sets the read/write pointer to the top line of the file. The next four lines of TOP construct the heading. (These four WRITELN instructions have each been printed on two lines in the program so they will fit neatly with the other program statements.) The only problem that may be encountered here is that the programmer must decide exactly how many spaces should be allocated to the label descriptions and STEN scores. Because all rows of the profile sheet must be of the same length, the programmer may need to juggle label sizes and line lengths a bit in order to get an attractive and symmetrical profile sheet that will contain lines of a size consistent with the maximum line length of the printer available.

The job of constructing the actual profile is done by the procedure SCALEIT. For each subtest it first enters a spacing line, which is blank except for the exclamation points that are being used as vertical edge indicators and column separators. Then, using a series of WRITE statements, the following information is printed in order on the next line: the left label, a succession of either dots or an 'X' to indicate the STEN score, and the right label. When all 16 STENs have been plotted this way, a final line is drawn at the bottom of the profile sheet and the procedure ends. The main program then reminds the clinician of the name of the output file and the program stops. The resulting PROFILE file will contain a profile sheet looking like the one in Figure 7–4.

DIAGNOSIS AND REPORT WRITING

When a computer program has finished administering, scoring, and drawing a profile sheet for a personality questionnaire, it is only a short step to have it examine the results and write a brief verbal report of the findings. Although this final step may sound at first like a uniquely human activity that must be left to the trained clinician, the standard scores of the various subtests in a personality inventory and the patterns of high and low subtests obtained for a given client have specific enough statistical and clinical meanings that an automated diagnosis and report becomes quite feasible.

To get some idea of how diagnosis and report-writing programs can be constructed, and why it is indeed possible to have a computer write quite accurate and effective diagnostic reports, let us look first at a simple example from the 16PF questionnaire. Suppose an 18-year-old female client has taken the 16PF and obtained STEN scores of 8 or higher on both the RESERVED:OUTGOING and LOW-INTELL:HIGH-INTELL scales. Now if we were to ask several clinicians to write a one-sentence report on just these results we would find that, even though the clinicians worked independently, the reports would be quite similar. Thus we might get sentences such as,

> "This client is a highly extraverted, intelligent young woman"

or,

> "Miss X is more extraverted and shows a higher level of verbal intelligence that 90 percent of the women her age."

Clinicians feel confident in making such statements because of the substantial research that backs up both the statistical and behavioral meaning of the standard scores achieved on a subtest or subtest pattern of the given questionnaire. Part of their training in diagnostic procedures has been to look for, and draw conclusions from, the scores and score patterns of such measures. Because this process can be performed reliably and consistently by numbers of human experts, there must be something about the process that is standard enough to allow us to make a computer evaluate a given score or score pattern in the same way.

Depending upon the questionnaire and the wealth of research findings that have accumulated for it, the diagnosis/report-writing process can become quite sophisticated. At the present time the most heavily researched personality questionnaire is the MMPI. Hundreds of pages have been written reporting evidence of meaningful patterns that clinicians can or should examine among its 14 subtests; and, as in any profession, clinicians who gain broad experience with such research evidence become recognized as experts in MMPI diagnosis. As far back as 1963 the psychologist Benjamin Kleinmuntz sought to automate the expert skills of an MMPI diagnostician using a straightforward but quite effective technique. He asked an expert to "think out loud" into a tape recorder while making clinical decisions that allowed him to place each of 126 MMPI profile sheets of college students into one of three diagnostic categories—*adjusted, maladjusted,* or *unclassified.* Typical statements from the expert were,

> I'll throw all mults to the right [most adjusted] if there's no clinical scale above a T score of 60. I'll let Ma go up as high as 80 . . . maybe a raw score of 10 on Mt would be playing it safe. . . .
>
> That's a fairly high Si . . . and Pa is up. I'll call it maladjusted. Here's one with a high Si and Sc is also up. I'll call it maladjusted. . . . (Kleinmuntz, 1963, p. 10)

After analyzing approximately 60 hours of tape-recorded expert commentary such as this, a sequential set of specific decision rules was constructed. A flowchart summarizing these rules is shown in Figure 7–5.

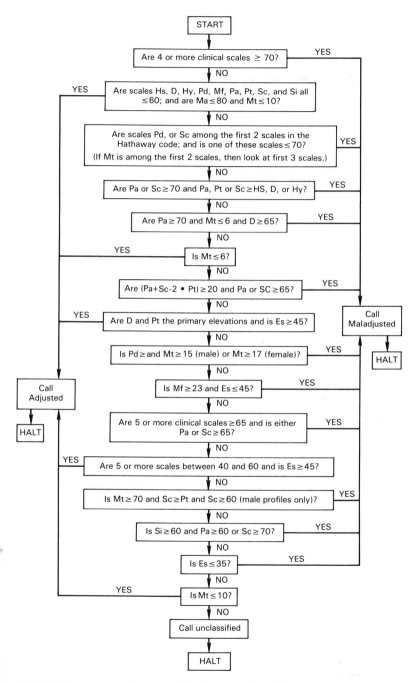

FIGURE 7–5. Flowchart of rules for MMPI diagnosis. *(From Kleinmuntz, 1963, with permission).*

These rules were supplemented with additional statistical rules obtained from other reported MMPI research and coded into a computer program. This program then gave diagnoses for over 550 new student profiles that had been collected from four different universities, and the automated diagnoses were compared with those of the human clinicians who had initially administered the MMPI. Kleinmuntz, while agreeing that the program was not yet ready to take over diagnostic responsibilities in university mental health clinics, reported a surprisingly good correspondence between the computerized and human diagnoses. Across the four universities that contributed data, the computer program made from 68 percent to 84 percent correct classifications for maladjusted, and from 53 percent to 94 percent correct classifications for adjusted.

While this early work in computerized diagnosis reported only the general categories of *maladjusted, adjusted,* and *unclassified,* it is easy to see that Kleinmuntz's technique of tape-recording the overt thought processes of experts and implementing these processes in computer programs could lead to quite sophisticated and detailed automated reports.* Over the years, substantial refinements have been made in diagnosing and reporting with the MMPI and other clinical instruments. At present, diagnoses and narrative reports of the MMPI, the 16PF, the *California Psychological Inventory,* the *Rorschach* test, the *Edwards Personal Preference Schedule,* and other personality measures are available from various commercial software houses and test publishers. Figure 7–6 gives one example of automated diagnosis and reporting, showing excerpts from a sample computer-generated report concerning a client who took the MMPI. The full seven-page report, too long to reproduce here, provides the clinician with a complete profile sheet as well as other very detailed clinical information.

COMPUTERIZED INTERVIEWING

New clients who enter a clinic or a hospital customarily receive an intake interview upon arrival. This interview usually serves the dual purposes of collecting necessary autobiographical information (name, address, age, sex, marital status, social security number, past medical problems, and so forth) and assessing current mental status. Because their administration can be quite time-consuming, and because many of the questions and answers are necessary but mundane, interviews of this sort have been likely candidates

---

*Indeed, the technique used in 1963 by Kleinmuntz is very similar to that used by computer scientists today to build expert programs that perform many artificial intelligence tasks in a variety of fields. See Bower & Hilgard (1981, pp. 396–399) for a quick, psychologically oriented review.

THE MINNESOTA REPORT
for the Minnesota Multiphasic Personality Inventory: Adult System

Client Name: Mary Smith   Gender: F
Report Date: 12/02/86   Age: 40

PROFILE VALIDITY

This is a valid MMPI profile. The client was quite cooperative with the
evaluation and appears to be willing to disclose personal information. ...

SYMPTOMATIC PATTERN

        The client is exhibiting much somatic distress and may be
experiencing a problem with her psychological adjustment. Her physical
complaints are probably extreme, possibly reflecting a general lack of
effectiveness in life. ...

        Her response content indicates that she is preoccupied with
feeling guilty and unworthy, and feels that she deserves to be punished
for wrongs she has committed. She feels regretful and unhappy about life,
complains about having no zest for life, and seems plagued by anxiety and
worry about the future. ...

INTERPERSONAL RELATIONS

        She appears to be somewhat passive-dependent in relationships.
She may manipulate others through her physical symptoms, and become hostile
if sufficient attention is not paid to her complaints. Marital unhappiness
is likely to be a factor in her present clinical picture. ...

BEHAVIORAL STABILITY

        There are likely to be long-standing personality problems
predisposing her to develop physical symptoms under stress. Her present
disorder could reflect ...

DIAGNOSTIC CONSIDERATIONS

        Individuals with this kind of profile are often seen as neurotic,
and may receive a diagnosis of Somatoform Disorder. Actual organic
problems such as ...

TREATMENT CONSIDERATIONS

        She is likely to view her problems as physical and may not readily
recognize the psychological factors involved. ... She is not a very
strong candidate for insight-oriented psychotherapy. Individuals with this
profile often seek medical solutions to their psychological problems;
however, they may respond to behaviorally oriented pain programs.

MINNESOTA MULTIPHASIC PERSONALITY INVENTORY
Copyright THE UNIVERSITY OF MINNESOTA
1943, Renewed 1970. This Report 1982. All rights reserved.

FIGURE 7.6 Excerpts from a computer-generated clinical report for a client who took the MMPI. (*From
Hathaway & McKinley, 1983, pp. 17–18, with permission.*)

for computer automation. Research concerning the adequacy of computer interviewing has been quite positive, indicating that the information gathered is reliable (Angle, 1981) and that most clients don't mind (indeed, many actually prefer) being interviewed by a computer instead of a human interviewer (see Space, 1981, p. 602). In this section we shall look briefly into some of the topics and tactics that go into successful programs of this type.

Table 7–2 provides examples of the general categories of questions that may be found in a typical initial interview. Because many clients may have little or no typing skill, one objective in writing a program to present such questions would be to minimize typing requirements by asking as many questions as possible in a form that requires simply pressing a single key on the computer keyboard, for example, "Y" or "N," or one or two nu-

TABLE 7–2   Examples of Question Categories and Questions Asked in Initial Interviews

CATEGORY	QUESTIONS	
Autobiographical	Name and Address Sex Age	Marital Income Living with? • • •
Physical History and Problems	Have you had: 　mumps _____ 　chicken pox _____	measles _____ etc. _____ • • •
	List of past operations? Drugs currently prescribed? Physical disabilities? Have you ever been treated 　for: 　diabetes _____ 　venereal disease _____	heart disease _____ • • •
Mental State	Questions relating to: 　Prior Treatment 　Suicide Feelings 　Alcohol Habits 　Emotional Control 　Illusions	Beliefs & Attitudes Sleep Habits Drug habits Appetite Hallucinations • • •

merical keys to give a numbered answer. Some of the questions in the auto-biographical section cannot be of this type, of course (for example, name, address), but most queries can be worded in ways such that answering them requires minimal key pressing. Thus a typical autobiographical question may be:

> Your birthday:
> What year were you born in? (Type a number like 1951 or 1965 ...)
> What month? (Type a number like January = 1, February = 2 ...)
> What day? (Type the number of the day)

For a multilevel question of this sort, the program should begin with a blank screen, then ask one question at a time and wait for an answer before advancing to the next one. Also, the answers to all questions can be checked for validity and repeated if the response was not within appropriate limits.

Other interview categories may require some decisions about the amount and detail of information needed for each question, and require also some creativity in the way the question is asked and answered. For example, one might preface a series of short questions with instructions such as

> For each of the following words or phrases, decide which of the following answers is best for you, then type the number of that answer on the keyboard—

	PRESENT IN PAST		
ABSENT	BUT NOT NOW	PRESENT NOW	NOT KNOWN
1	2	3	4

and then, with these general instructions remaining at the top of the screen, present one at a time a series of questions pertaining to potential psychological problems; for example:

> difficulty falling asleep
> excessive amount of sleep
> appetite loss
> appetite gain
> weight loss
> weight gain
> concern about use of alcohol
>
> .
> .
> .
>
>   etc.
>   (From Mezzich, Dow, & Coffman, 1981)

Alternatively, some clinicians might prefer that some or all questions of this type be asked in more detail; for instance:

How many drinks of each of the following kinds of alcohol listed below have you drunk each day in the past month?

— whiskies (bourbon, rye, blend)
— scotch
— gin
— wine
— sherry

.
.
.

etc.

(Paraphrased from Bremser & Davidson, 1978)

The actual programming of a series of interviewing questions such as these utilizes the same techniques as we used in writing the EPI program; that is, read the question from a data file, display it on the computer screen, accept the response from the keyboard and check its validity, store each response with its question number, and output the results onto an output data file.

Some researchers have tried variations of these basic approaches to computer interviewing and found them to be quite effective. Kleinmuntz (1975) has used the technique to interview not only the client but others who have known the client for sufficient time to be familiar with his or her habits, attitudes and beliefs, and symptomatic behaviors to give a clear historical picture of the clinical problem. Stout (1981) has suggested that use of the computer permits significant improvements on the variety and types of information that may be obtained from the interviewee. His suggestions include (1) checking the reliability of responses by asking certain questions twice during the interview and comparing the answers; (2) obtaining reaction times for each question for possible diagnostic use; (3) using information such as that obtained in (1) and (2) to ascertain client fatigue and suggest rest periods during the interview; (4) switching to alternate forms of the interview if the client is not understanding the questions; and (5) signalling for human help if the client seems to need it. These and other potential additions and innovations promise to make the computer an even more sophisticated and important clinical instrument in the future.

SUGGESTED READINGS

Recent and quite technical extensions of the basic techniques discussed above, and evaluations of their effectiveness, can be found in the August 1981 issue of the journal *Behavior Research Methods and Instrumentation* (now entitled *Behavior Research Methods, Instruments, and Computers*). This issue is devoted entirely to computer technology and methodology in clinical psychology, psychiatry, and behavioral medicine, and it contains some 40 articles covering a variety of topics relevant to our discussion. The article by Space (1981) gives a particularly informative overview, including arguments for and against the concept of computerized clinical assessment (see pp. 598–602). Articles by Kleinmuntz (1975) and Johnson and Williams (1975) in the *American Psychologist* also contain useful reviews. A book edited by Sidowski, Johnson, and Williams (1980) entitled *Technology in Mental Health Care Delivery Systems* presents detailed aspects of a broad range of clinical uses of computing. For additional information about clinical and personality tests and measurements, any of the recent texts on clinical methods (for example, Bellack & Hersen, 1980, Chapters 3–5; Golden, 1979) will be helpful and interesting supplements to the topics discussed above.

EXERCISES

1. Complete the program PF (pp. 141) by writing procedures and/or an addition to the main program that will:
    A. Ask the user whether scores are in raw or standard form;
    B. If they are standard scores then draw the profile sheet, but if they are raw scores then convert them to standard scores (STENs) before drawing the profile sheet. (You will need to make up an imaginary norm table.)
2. Tests of various kinds can be administered and scored in automated fashion. If you have access to a personality test with at least two subtest scores, write an administration-scoring program for it. Should you not have access to such a test, make up an educational test that has at least two subscores and write a program that will administer and score it. Examples for the latter kind of test, designed for children, are:
    A. A geography test with questions about United States state capitals and the capitals of other countries;
    B. A math test with subscores for knowledge of arithmetic facts and arithmetic problem solutions.
3. Write an interview program that asks some questions for each of several of the general question categories shown in Table 7–2. Make up your own questions.

8

Real-Time Control in the Psychology Laboratory

In addition to its other applications, the computer is frequently used by psychologists as a laboratory control device. The use of computing to control laboratory experiments, in psychology or any other laboratory science, normally involves placing a computer in a laboratory or similar experimental environment and programming it to perform such duties as turning apparatus on and off, sensing occurrences of experimental events, timing stimulus or response events and procedures, and recording and storing data. To do such things, the computer usually must be dedicated exclusively to its laboratory setting, and its inputs and outputs may need to interact directly with laboratory devices rather than—or in addition to—interacting via the keyboard and CRT with a person sitting before a terminal. Also, the computer usually must not be allowed to work at its own speed, but instead must present stimuli and sense and record responses at speeds consistent with those in which the human or lower-animal subject works.

These characteristics—a dedicated interaction with the experiment, and operating at a speed that is in the time scale of the experiment rather than executing instructions at the computer's own rate of speed—have led computer scientists to use the terms *on-line* and/or *real-time* programming when referring to the programming of computers for use as laboratory control devices. Although technical differences exist between the terms, we shall ignore them in this chapter and use the phrases *laboratory-control programming, real-time programming,* and *on-line programming* synonymously to mean writing programs that run psychological experiments under controlled laboratory conditions.*

Because the computer usually must be dedicated to the experiment it is controlling, it is customary to use microcomputers rather than larger time-sharing machines for laboratory-control programming. Microcomputers are now inexpensive enough so that even a small psychological laboratory can afford one or two of them, and thus can run different experiments at different times of day and not be concerned about errors in timing and control because of timesharing. Thus a well-equipped psychology laboratory today will be likely to have several microcomputers and associated hardware interfaces available for use in running various types of experiments. In these circumstances, the psychologist-programmer who wants to run a computer-controlled experiment must first design the experiment according to good experimental-design standards; then, with the design problems solved, he or she will need to write a program that, when executed, tells the microcomputer the sequence of events that must be followed in conducting the experiment. Most of today's microcomputers support BASIC, Pascal, and FORTRAN, so there is usually no need to learn another programming language in order to write such programs.

In this chapter we will get some experience with the basic concepts of laboratory-control programming, assuming (1) availability of a microcomputer that supports Pascal,† and (2) availability of a hardware interface (to be explained in detail in a later section) that can link the microcomputer to laboratory apparatus. As a first step, let us review some elementary features of psychological experiments in general. Then, building upon these features, we shall design and write sample control programs that will illustrate laboratory-control programming in two different experimental contexts.

---

*Technically, *on-line* computing implies direct electrical links between laboratory equipment and the computer's central processing unit, whereas the phrase *real-time* refers to any situation in which the computer synchronizes with its external environment. By this definition, the latter term includes such computer operations as timesharing, computer-assisted instruction, clinical testing and interviewing, as well as experimental control.

†Although BASIC is still the most prevalent programming language for microcomputers, many now also support Pascal. Most microcomputers that will run on the CP/M operating system will support a Pascal compiler marketed by Alcor Systems, and the Tandy, Apple, DEC, and IBM microcomputers have Pascal versions that run on their own operating systems. To be consistent with previous chapters, we shall use Pascal here for programming illustrations; but the programs described can be written just as readily in BASIC on nearly all of the microcomputers available today.

BASIC FEATURES OF PSYCHOLOGICAL EXPERIMENTS

The kinds of experiments performed in the psychological laboratory vary widely. Some are concerned strictly with humans, whereas others may involve nearly any representative of the animal kingdom—from monkeys and pigeons and the ever-available laboratory rat, to fish, reptiles, and even the paramecium. Also, the psychological phenomena with which an experiment may be concerned can range from the standard topics of "experimental psychology" (that is, perception, learning, motivation, physiological correlates of behavior) to formal and controlled investigations of social, developmental, educational, or other broader psychological phenomena. Underlying this almost limitless variety, however, are certain features that allow us to classify them together as "experiments." In a formal psychological experiment we can always identify *stimuli* of some kind that are presented under controlled conditions to a *subject* (human or lower animal), and *responses* of some kind that must be observed and recorded. On the stimulus side, the experimenter must be concerned about the way a given stimulus is to be presented to the subject, including control of such factors as the stimulus type, location, intensity, and duration of presentation. On the response side, the experimenter must be concerned about observing and recording such information as what response was made, the time taken to make it, the duration and/or intensity of the response, and so on.

This reduction of any experiment to a description in terms of the stimuli and responses involved simplifies matters greatly, because it allows us to adopt the following strategy for writing a program to control almost any well-defined experiment. First, the experimenter needs to identify (1) the stimuli, and the manner, time, order, duration, and so forth in which they must be presented, and (2) the possible responses, and how they and possibly their temporal or other characteristics are to be recorded. The programmer must then write a program that will make the computer not only operate the stimulus-presentation apparatus but also collect the response information desired, at all stages of the experiment. Using this prosaic but effective strategy, let us take as a first example a simple experiment that requires no laboratory apparatus other than one of the microcomputers available in the psychology laboratory.

EXPERIMENT 1: SERIAL LEARNING OF NONSENSE SYLLABLES

Recall now from your first psychology course the experiments that study human verbal learning by presenting subjects with a list of 3-letter consonant-vowel-consonant (CVC) nonsense syllables that must be learned in the (serial) order in which they are presented. The usual procedure for running an experiment of this sort is to present 8 to 12 syllables, in a standard serial order, for a series of *trials,* and to keep track of both the number of correct responses made on each trial and how many trials are required for the subject to respond perfectly for the entire list. Usually the trials are presented by the *anticipation method,* which is simply an orderly, controlled way of presenting the stimuli and recording the responses so that the experimenter can observe what, and how much, is learned per trial.

Let us assume we want to run a simple experiment of this type on the computer, presenting trials by the anticipation method over and over until the subject gets all items correct on a given trial. To write such a program, we must first understand in step-by-step detail how the anticipation method actually works. The following description provides the sequence of events that must occur on each trial.

> *Stimulus Presentation.* At the beginning of each trial a "Ready" signal appears alone on the computer screen. Then, following some standard presentation-time interval, which may vary from experiment to experiment, the "Ready" signal disappears and the first item (that is, nonsense syllable) in the list is presented alone on an otherwise blank screen. This item remains on the screen for the standard presentation interval, then it disappears and the next item is presented. This procedure is repeated for each syllable in turn, until all of the syllables in the list have been presented—one at a time, in their proper order, and each for the same presentation interval—on the screen. Then the screen remains blank for some arbitrary "intertrial interval" (usually somewhat longer than the standard presentation interval being used) and the next trial begins.
>
> *Response Recording.* The subject is instructed that when the "Ready" signal is presented at the start of each trial he or she must anticipate and spell (by typing on the keyboard) the letters of the first syllable in the list, and must do so during the interval before that first syllable appears on the screen. Then, each time a new syllable appears, the syllable that follows it must be anticipated and typed before it appears. A response is counted as correct only if it is spelled correctly within the appropriate time interval. Learning is considered to be complete, and the experiment ends, when the subject can anticipate and spell correctly all of the syllables in the list on a single trial.

Now let us write a Pascal program that not only follows these rules but also records the number of correct responses made on each trial, stops after the subject has completed one errorless trial, and stores the experimental data on a data file. The data structure requirements are straightforward. As shown in Figure 8–1, we shall need an array ITEMS that contains the CVC syllables to be presented, an array RESPONSE that will record the response made to any given stimulus, and a one-dimensional integer array CORRECT, which will store the number of correct responses on each trial so the experimenter will have a record of them when the experiment is finished. Also shown in Figure 8–1 is the parameter RTIME, which contains the number of seconds that each stimulus will be presented. To keep things simple, let us assume that the list to be learned will consist of eight

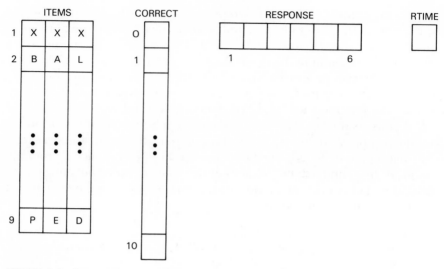

FIGURE 8–1. Data structure for the SERIALX program.

high-frequency CVCs, as shown in the array ITEMS. (Note that, in this example, the "Ready" signal that will be given to start each trial is simply the
letters XXX. The subject must, of course, be advised of this signal when
given initial instructions about the conduct of the experiment.)

Using these data structures, the following program first loads the syllables into the array ITEMS from an external disk file named CVC/DAT,
then presents up to 10 serial anticipation trials, stops when the subject
achieves a learning criterion of one perfect trial, and finally stores the trial-
by-trial results on another disk file labeled OUTSER/DAT. As you review
this program, you will notice some nonstandard Pascal instructions that
may not be familiar to you.* This is because the Pascal found on microcomputers often has additional features that permit easy real-time use. These
features will be discussed later.

```
PROGRAM SERIALX;

VAR    items: array[1..9,1..3] of char;
       response: array[1..6] of char;
       correct: array[0..10] of integer;
       trial, i, j, rtime: integer;
       infil, outfil: text;
       ch: char;


(* ------------------------------------------------------- *)
```

*The Pascal compiler and library illustrated in this chapter are written by Alcor Systems
and run on Tandy microcomputers and most others that will accept the CP/M operating system.

```
(*External Procedures from the Pascal Library on a
          Typical Microcomputer *)
(* --------------------------------------------- *)

PROCEDURE setacnm(var logical: TEXT; physical: STRING);
          external;

PROCEDURE clearscr; external;

PROCEDURE gotoxy(x, y: integer); external;

PROCEDURE inkey(var ch: char; var ready: boolean);
          external;

(* --------------------------------------------- *)
          (* User-Defined Procedures *)
(* --------------------------------------------- *)

PROCEDURE loadcvc;

          (* Loads CVCs from CVC/DAT file into ITEMS *)

VAR    m, n: integer;

begin
  setacnm(infil, bldstr('CVC/DAT'));
  reset(infil);
  for m:= 1 to 9 do
    begin
    for n:= 1 to 3 do
      read(infil, items[m,n]);
    readln(infil)
    end;
  close(infil)
end;      (* End of loadcvc *)

(* --------------------------------------------- *)

PROCEDURE timer(secs: integer);

          (* Waits for SECS seconds *)

VAR    i, x: integer;

begin
  for i:= 1 to (secs * 2000) do x:= 1000 + 1;
end;      (* End of timer *)

(* --------------------------------------------- *)
```

```
PROCEDURE setresp;

        (* Gets RESPONSE ready for next item *)

VAR     a: integer;

begin
  for a:= 1 to 6 do response[a]:= ' '

end;      (* End of setresp *)

(* ---------------------------------------------------- *)

PROCEDURE scoreit(x: integer); forward;

(* ---------------------------------------------------- *)

PROCEDURE respond(x: integer);

        (* Times and records response *)

VAR     fake, ch1, ch2: char;
        ready: boolean;
        f, i, n: integer;

begin
  n:= 0;
  for i:= 1 to (rtime * 435) do
  begin
    inkey(ch1, ready);
    if ready then
    begin
      n:= n + 1;
      write(ch1);
      response[n]:= ch1
    end
    else
    begin
      f:= f + 1;
      ch2:= ' ';
      fake:= ch2
    end
  end;
  clearscr;
  scoreit(x)
end;      (* End of respond *)

(* ---------------------------------------------------- *)
```

```
PROCEDURE scoreit;

      (* Adds 1 point to CORRECT if response was right *)

VAR    i, n: integer;

begin
  n:= 0;
  if response[4] = ' ' then
    for i:= 1 to 3 do
      if response[i] = items[x+1,i] then n:= n + 1;
  if n = 3 then correct[trial]:= correct[trial] + 1
end;      (* End of scoreit *)

(* ---------------------------------------------- *)

PROCEDURE outscore;

      ( * Prints scores on OUTSER/DAT file *)

VAR    i: integer;

begin
  setacnm(outfil, bldstr('OUTSER/DAT'));
  rewrite(outfil);
  writeln(outfil, 'You learned the list in ', (trial-1):3,
    'trials.');
  writeln(outfil);writeln(outfil);
  writeln(outfil, 'Trials            No. Correct');
  writeln(outfil, '******        ********** ');
  for i:= 1 to (trial-1) do
    writeln(outfil, i:4, '          ',correct[i]:4)
end;    (* End of outscore *)

(* ---------------------------------------------- *)
              (* MAIN PROGRAM *)
(* ---------------------------------------------- *)

begin
  loadcvc;
  trial:= 1;
  for i:= 0 to 10 do correct[i]:=0;
  writeln(' Enter stimulus presentation time ');
  readln(rtime);
  writeln(' Press key S to start trials');
  readln(ch);
  clearscr;
  writeln(' Ready for Trial 1');
```

```
timer(rtime);
clearscr;
repeat
  for i:= 1 to 9 do
    if i <> 9 then
    begin
      setresp;
      gotoxy(30,10);
      writeln(items[i,1],items[i,2],items[i,3];
      writeln;
      write('Next item is?');
      respond(i)
    end
    else
    begin
      setresp;
      gotoxy(30,10);
      writeln(items[i,1],items[i,2],items[i,3];
      timer(rtime);
      trial:= trial + 1;
      clearscr
    end;
  if correct[trial-1] < 8 then
      writeln(' Ready for Trial ', trial:3);
  timer(rtime);
  clearscr
until trial > 10 or correct[trial-1] = 8;
writeln('End of Experiment -- Thank You');
writeln;
outscore
end.
```

Although most of the Pascal used in this program has been encountered previously, there are two new features to this type of programming that deserve specific attention, namely, the *external procedures* used and certain *timing* techniques that are useful when working in real time.

External Procedures and Functions

In addition to the standard Pascal presented in previous chapters of this text, many microcomputers offer a *library of external procedures and functions* that can be called into use by any Pascal program. There are some differences across microcomputers in the exact procedures and functions available in such libraries, but any reasonably good system should have available either the ones used here or facsimiles to them. The program above employs four such external library procedures. Note that each of them is identified as being part of the library by the addition of the word EXTERNAL, followed by a semicolon, at the end of the usual syntax for the first line (the heading) of a procedure. If your microcomputer has a library of external procedures and they are identified within a Pascal program as shown, they will automatically be copied from the system and compiled at runtime, and then will execute whenever they are called.*

The external procedure SETACNM is used to define the names of any input or output files that will be used by the program. Its syntax and use are demonstrated in the LOADCVC procedure, which is designed to open the disk file CVC/DAT, read the CVCs from that file into the array ITEMS, and then close the file. The *physical* name of this file—that is, the name that identifies it on the microcomputer's diskette—is CVC/DAT. However, microcomputer versions of Pascal normally do not use the physical name when identifying files in READ or WRITE statements. They use instead the *logical* name of the file, which is declared as a TEXT variable in the VAR section of the main program. SETACNM simply identifies what physical names go with what logical file names in the program. The procedure LOADCVC uses it to identify CVC/DAT as an input file, and in the procedure OUTSCORE it is used again to identify OUTSER/DAT as the output file to which the results of the experiment will be written. Notice that the parameter list of SETACNM contains the logical name first, then a built-in function BLDSTR to build a string of characters that constitutes the physical name of the file. The commands RESET(logical name) or REWRITE(logical name) are then used in the standard manner to prepare the file for READing or WRITEing, respectively. After a file has been used, it should be closed with the built-in nonstandard procedure CLOSE(logical file).

The next two library procedures used are easier to understand. CLEARSCR simply clears the CRT of all symbols, leaving a blank screen with the cursor positioned in the top-left corner. GOTOXY, with two parameters, positions the cursor at column X and row Y on the screen. These two procedures are used in the SERIALX program to present each CVC alone near the center of a typical 80-column, 24-row microcomputer screen.

The purpose of the last library procedure, INKEY, is to scan the terminal's keyboard and determine if a key has been pressed. Whenever it is called, a scan is made, and if a key is being pressed then the character for that key is assigned to the parameter CH and the boolean parameter READY is set to "true"; otherwise, CH is set to ' ' (a blank character) and READY is set to "false." INKEY is used in the procedure RESPOND above

---

*The exact sequence of steps required for compiling and running external procedures may vary somewhat with different computers. See the Pascal manual that accompanies the system you are using for precise instructions.

to collect the letters of the CVC the subject types as an anticipatory response. A detailed description of its use is given below.

Timing

The other new feature of real-time programming with microcomputers concerns *timing*. In our simple serial learning experiment there are two kinds of timing requirements, each of which demands accuracy to the level of seconds. One requirement is that the computer must be programmed to wait for some number of seconds between each trial—that is, the intertrial interval. Some microcomputers have built-in clocks as part of their hardware, and if one of these is available on the machine being used then it is easy to use the Pascal routines that control it. If a hardware clock is not available, the programmer must resort to building and calibrating a *software clock*. In the SERIALX program the latter alternative was chosen. The procedure TIMER illustrates a typical software clock whose purpose is to delay program execution for some number of seconds. It is called with a parameter SECS, which indicates the number of seconds' delay needed. The delay is created simply by executing a FOR..DO loop a certain number of times. The exact number of loops to be executed is determined by multiplying some "calibration constant" by the parameter SECS. This constant will be some integer that, when placed as the upper limit of a simple FOR..DO loop, will cause the loop to execute for as closely as possible to exactly one second. The trick is to find the correct constant, which will vary depending upon the make and speed of the computer and the Pascal compiler being used. In the example above the constant listed is 2000, but in actual practice it is necessary to perform calibration tests to determine the best constant for the situation. One way to make such calibration tests is to write a small Pascal program that will allow you to try various constants and time them to see which is the best. (See Exercise 1 at the end of this chapter as an example.) When the accuracy requirement is just to the level of seconds, the calibration is not difficult; but when millisecond or greater accuracy is needed, calibration of a good software clock requires some rather sophisticated timing and interface equipment. We will discuss this problem further at the end of the chapter.

The second timing requirement in the SERIALX program is to present the CVC stimulus for some given number of seconds (the variable RTIME in the present program), and during this time to record the anticipatory response that the subject types on the keyboard. In the SERIALX program above, this takes place by first writing the CVC on the screen in the main program and then calling the timing procedure RESPOND. The major part of RESPOND is reproduced below to facilitate examination of the way it simultaneously times the CVC presentation and records in the array RESPONSE whatever anticipatory response the subject makes.

```
Begin
  n: = 0;
  for i:= 1 to (rtime * 435) do
  begin
    inkey(ch1, ready);
    if ready then
    begin
      n: = n + 1;
      write(ch1);
      response[n]:= ch1
    end
    else
    begin
      f:= f + 1;
      ch2:= ' ';
      fake:= ch2
    end
  end;
  clearscr;
```

Clearly, this procedure also contains a software clock of the FOR..DO variety, but the loop has a compound statement within it rather than a simple statement, with the consequence that each loop will take more time to complete than the one used in the procedure TIMER. Consequently, the calibration constant (shown here as 435) will be considerably smaller than in TIMER, and of course will have to be calibrated independently. (Again, see Exercise 1 for hints on how to obtain the calibration constant.)

Looking now inside the compound statement, we find that during the time the CVC is present on the screen the keyboard will be checked over and over within the FOR..DO loop, using the external procedure INKEY. Moreover, each time INKEY is checked the IF..THEN..ELSE instruction following it is executed immediately. This latter instruction says, in effect:

IF READY is "true" then a key has been pressed, so

a. add 1 to N
b. print the character just pressed onto the screen for the subject to see (that is, "echo" the character)
c. record the character pressed in the array RESPONSE, at cell N, for later scoring

but if READY is "false" (that is, no key was pressed), then spend the same amount of time as would have been spent executing instructions a, b, and c by inserting three fake instructions that do nothing but waste time, such as

    d.   add 1 to a fake variable F

    e.   assign a character to a dummy variable CH2

    f.   assign CH2 to another dummy variable FAKE.

The dummy instructions *d, e,* and *f* are critical to the algorithm because now the FOR..DO loop will take (approximately) the same amount of time to complete one loop regardless of whether or not a key was pressed by the subject during that loop. Thus the number of loops to be made, identified by (RTIME * constant), will all be made at a (reasonably) constant speed during the time the CVC is presented on the screen. When the timing loop is complete, the CVC is erased by the external procedure CLEARSCR to finish the presentation time.

Additional Program Details

Having examined these new features, the rest of the SERIALX program should be easy to understand because it employs Pascal instructions and techniques used in previous chapters. You should examine the entire program in some detail at this point by starting at the beginning statement in the declaration part of the main program and "walking through" each command and procedure to see what happens. You will probably be able to follow it on your own, but if you get stuck you can use the next few paragraphs of description as an aid.

The first 12 lines of the main program are housekeeping commands that load in the CVCs (via LOADCVC), initialize the TRIAL and CORRECT variables, get the parameter RTIME from the experimenter, clear the screen, and prepare for Trial 1. Then, for up to 10 trials, the REPEAT..UNTIL statement presents the ready signal (XXX) followed by the eight CVCs. At the end of each REPEAT, there is a check to see if either more than 10 trials have elapsed or the subject got a perfect score (8) on the trial just completed. If either of these possibilities is true, the REPEAT..UNTIL loop ends and the data collected are stored on the output file by a call to the OUTSCORE procedure.

Since the REPEAT..UNTIL loop is the heart of the main program, we should understand it in some detail. It contains a single FOR..DO statement, which presents the ready signal and eight CVCs. The only complexity in the FOR..DO statement is that in the first eight of its nine presentations it must also collect the subject's response, but when the last CVC is presented no response is to be made because the subject has no more syllables to anticipate. To account for this distinction, an IF..THEN..ELSE statement has been embedded into the FOR..DO loop, which for the first eight items will present the next CVC *and* call the procedure RESPOND to pick up the response made, but for the ninth item will simply present the

CVC on the screen and time its display. Because this ninth display is the end of the trial, the TRIAL variable is incremented.

The SCOREIT procedure is called by RESPOND after each CVC but the ninth has been presented, and it checks the anticipatory response made by the subject against the next CVC to be presented. If there is a correct match, a point is added to the cell in the array CORRECT that represents the current trial.

Notice that the SCOREIT procedure has been written to illustrate the FORWARD statement, which is part of standard Pascal but has not been used previously in this text. One of the rules of Pascal is that any procedure that is called must have been defined earlier in the program. Because SCOREIT is called from the procedure RESPOND, it should have been defined before RESPOND. At times, however, programmers may add procedures to existing programs or for other reasons place them in positions where the rule is not followed. In such cases, Pascal allows the programmer to put just the first line of the procedure definition in an earlier position, then mark it with the word FORWARD and a semicolon following the usual syntax to indicate to the compiler that the procedure does exist but is defined further on in the program. When the procedure is eventually defined, it need not repeat the parameters designated in the forwarding command.

Finally, the OUTSCORE procedure opens the output file and writes into it both the total number of trials taken to reach the learning criterion and the number correct per trial. Because execution of the entire program ends with the completion of this procedure, and all files are automatically closed, there is no need to CLOSE(logical file) here.

EXPERIMENT 2: RATS IN A SKINNER BOX

Although the serial learning experiment required some new programming techniques, the only apparatus used was the computer itself. Many experiments in psychology, particularly those involving motor skills or those using lower animals as subjects, require research apparatus that is specially designed to present stimuli that cannot be represented symbolically on a computer screen, and/or to sense and record responses other than pressing keys on a keyboard. Experiments of these kinds can also be controlled by a computer, provided that the apparatus used operates electrically or electronically, and that the laboratory facilities include a microcomputer and a *hardware interface* that permits an electronic linkage between the computer and the apparatus. In this section we shall see how to set up and control such experiments, using as an example the automated control of a piece of basic psychological research apparatus, the famed "Skinner box," which is familiar to all psychology students. First, let us design a simple experiment that uses this kind of equipment. Then we must become acquainted with interfaces and the microcomputer techniques for controlling them.

A Simple Learning Experiment

As anyone who has ever studied psychology knows, the psychologist B.F. Skinner and his colleagues have conducted hundreds of experiments in animal learning by placing a rat in a specially designed box, with walls made either of metal or clear plastic. A typical model of a Skinner box, shown in Figure 8–2, has a response lever and a food-dispensing cup mounted on one wall, and often a light stimulus as well. A food-dispensing apparatus is mounted behind the wall and, when activated, this apparatus delivers a pellet of rat food down a tube and into the food cup. When a hungry rat is first placed in such a box it does not know what to do. Eventually, by trial and error, it presses the response lever, which really is an electrical switch that produces a signal whenever a response (a "bar press") has been made. Following a correct response, the electrical food-dispensing apparatus is activated and releases a rat-food pellet into the food cup. The rat, being hungry, of course eats the food, which, in Skinnerian terms, is a *reinforcement* for the bar-pressing response it just made. This sequence happens again and again in the experiment, and the rat learns (often with amazing speed) how to respond appropriately in this stimulus situation— that is, it learns to press the bar when in the presence of such stimuli as the Skinner box, the response bar itself, the food cup, the hunger pangs, and so forth.

FIGURE 8–2. A basic Skinner box apparatus.

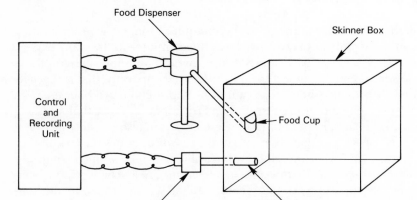

This experimental situation demonstrates learning of a certain type (termed *operant learning*) by reinforcement. Over the years, Dr. Skinner and many other experimental psychologists have used such apparatus in hundreds of experiments designed to discover the learning principles that underlie operant behavior. Among their many findings, these experimenters have discovered that the rat's learning speed and pattern of responding depend upon the *schedule of reinforcement* administered. We need not discuss the many schedules of reinforcement here, but instead will describe just one simple schedule that can be used as an experimental example. It is possible to alter the rat's learning task from the simple one described above by reinforcing it on a *fixed-ratio* (FR) schedule rather than reinforcing it with a food pellet every time it presses the response lever. For example, suppose we adopt a FR(5) schedule—that is, arrange the apparatus so the food is delivered only after every fifth bar-press (a 5-response: 1-reinforcement ratio) rather than after each press. Will the rat respond differently in the FR(5) task than in the simpler FR(1) task? Will it learn faster or slower? These are experimental questions, the answers to which must involve testing rats in the Skinner box apparatus under varying FR(ratio) conditions and recording and comparing their responses.

As an illustration of automated control, let us use this Skinner box type of experiment and arrange to test an animal in a FR situation where the experimenter can enter the ratio number to be tested as a parameter when the experiment begins and the computer will then run the rat through the experiment on that schedule and record all reinforcements and their time of occurrence. Consider the sequence of events that must occur. First, the experimenter places the rat in the box and sets the FR parameter (called RATIO in the listing below). From that point on, a looping repetition of the following events must occur until the experimental session ends:

1. Set a response counter COUNT to zero
2. Check the response-lever switch repeatedly, adding 1 to COUNT each time the switch is activated, until COUNT = RATIO
3. Turn on the food-pellet dispenser, allowing a pellet to fall into the food cup
4. Record the time at which the reinforcement was presented
5. Continue at 1.

This sequence could be elaborated in several ways (see Exercise 5 at the end of the chapter), but it will serve our purpose well to keep it simple for now. In order to construct a Pascal program that will control and direct this sequence of events, we will need to find out how the computer can (1) sense whether or not a bar press has occurred, and (2) activate the food-pellet dispenser. These are jobs that involve the use of an *interface*.

The Interface between the Computer and Experimental Apparatus

The word *interface* existed in the English language before the advent of computing. In general, it refers to any well-defined surface or boundary between two differing parts of matter or space. In on-line computing, it is a piece of equipment that links the computer's processor to an external device, allowing information to flow both from the computer to the external apparatus and from the apparatus to the computer.

Figure 8–3 illustrates the general relationship schematically, and it shows the types of information that normally flow in each direction. The diagram in Figure 8–3 assumes that up to eight pieces of apparatus can be switched on and off, and up to eight inputs (response levers, telegraph keys, and so forth) can be monitored to determine if they are active or not. As we shall see later, the number eight is not arbitrarily chosen but is due to the fact that the word size of the processor on many microcomputers is eight bits in length. All we must do in order to turn on or off any of the eight pieces of apparatus, or sense any of the input lines, is to learn the appropriate Pascal instructions that will tell the interface to perform these operations.

To get a general understanding of the instructions needed, we must first see how a microcomputer is linked to an interface. Most of the microcomputers with 8-bit processors that are available today have a parallel I/O interface connector located somewhere on them, into which a ribbon cable containing eight data lines and eight address lines (as well as some other lines that need not concern us) can be plugged. Similarly, the interface (which can be purchased commercially or built by a competent electronics technician) has a connector that receives the other end of the ribbon cable. Inside the interface, the eight address lines and eight data lines are connected in turn to various *ports*. Each port has an address (a "port number" between 0 and 255) and can perform one of two kinds of

FIGURE 8–3. This hardware interface links the microcomputer to eight pieces of ON-OFF apparatus (top), and to eight pieces of RESPONSE-SENSING apparatus (bottom).

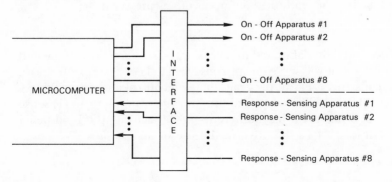

operations—turning apparatus on or off (information, usually concerning stimulus presentation, that is *output* from the computer), or sensing an external signal (information, usually in the form of sensing a response made by the subject, that is *input* to the computer from the outside world). Each of these ports has, in turn, connecting wires that lead out to as many as eight pieces of laboratory apparatus. The address lines that come from the computer into the interface tell the address of the port that is to be used, and the data lines tell which of the pieces of apparatus connected to that port is to be controlled or observed. Figure 8–4 is a very simplified schematic of this rather complex electronic arrangement, in which Port no. 1 is an *input* port that sends information into the computer and Port no. 96 is an *output* port that receives information from the computer about which apparatus to switch on or off. Fortunately, this simplified picture is all one needs to have in mind in order to understand the following Pascal instructions:

```
OUT(96, 2)
X: = INP(1)
```

Let us look at each in turn to see how it operates.

The OUT procedure.   The OUT(96, 2) instruction is a call to an *external Pascal procedure,* which can be declared in a Pascal program in the same way we declared other external procedures in the previous section; that is,

```
PROCEDURE OUT(PORT, DATA: BYTE); EXTERNAL;
```

Do not be concerned for the moment about the meaning of BYTE, but recognize instead that this procedure has two parameters, the first being the address of the port to which it refers and the second being a number indicating the data line(s) to be activated. Thus OUT(96, 2) says, in effect, "Port no. 96 should turn on the apparatus connected to its data line no. 2 and all apparatus hooked to other data lines of that port should be turned off."

Generalizing from this example, it should be easy to understand that the similar instruction OUT(96, 0) is a command to turn off all apparatus (all data lines) connected to Port no. 96. Unfortunately, other instructions to Port no. 96 are not as easy to understand as this first generalization because of the way the data lines are numbered. It would be nice if the eight data lines at any port were numbered 1–8 in decimal values, corresponding to the eight pieces of apparatus connected to that port. But the eight data lines are really coming from a single 8-bit word (a "byte) in the microcomputer's memory, and each line is an electrical signal that is coming from one of the bits in the word. Each bit can be in just one of two states—on or off. Consequently, the number that represents which of the eight lines to turn on must be originally represented not as a decimal but as

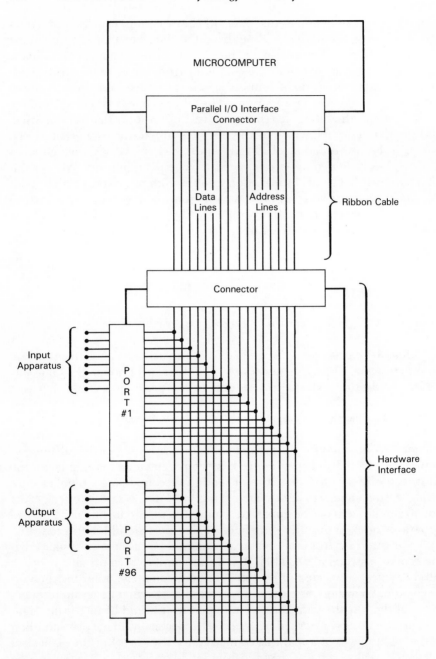

FIGURE 8–4. Data lines and address lines are connected from the microcomputer to the interface by a ribbon cable that plugs into the microcomputer's parallel I/O interface connector.

an *8-place binary number,* with each place containing either a 0 if the line is *not* to be turned on or a 1 if it *is* to be turned on. So, for example, Figure 8–5a shows that the 8-digit binary number 00000100 means, "Turn on the apparatus connected to the third data line from the right," and Figure 8–5b shows that 01000000 means to turn on the apparatus connected to data line no. 7. Thus an 8-digit binary number, consisting of 0's and 1's, will designate which apparatus is to be turned on or off at any given port.

FIGURE 8–5. (a). The byte 00000100 turns on Apparatus #3 connected to Port 96; (b), the byte 01000000 turns on Apparatus #7. In both examples, devices connected to data lines having 0-bit signals are turned off.

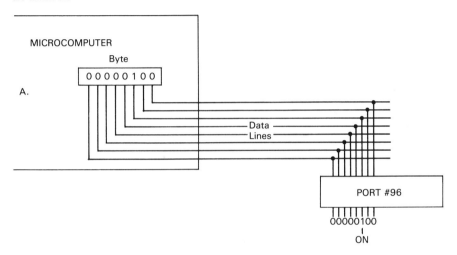

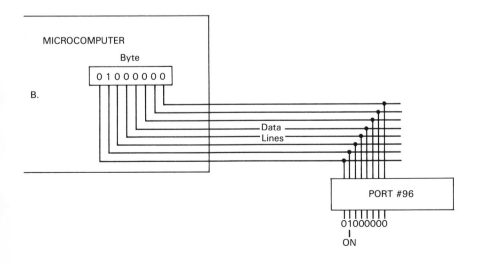

The problem with this straightforward arrangement is that the Pascal external procedure OUT does not accept binary numbers as arguments; therefore the programmer, after deciding which apparatus is to be turned on and off, must translate the binary number that represents his or her decision into its decimal equivalent. Fortunately it is not at all difficult to make the translation. The rule is that, going from right to left, each place in the 8-bit binary number has a decimal equivalent that is obtained by doubling the preceding decimal value. The example below will help to understand the rule:

Bit Position $->$	8	7	6	5	4	3	2	1
Decimal Equivalent $->$	128	64	32	16	8	4	2	1

Using this example we can see that activating each of the eight data lines can be specified like this:

APPARATUS NO.	BINARY CODE	PROCEDURE CALL
1	00000001	OUT(96, 1)
2	00000010	OUT(96, 2)
3	00000100	OUT(96, 4)
4	00001000	OUT(96, 8)
5	00010000	OUT(96, 16)
6	00100000	OUT(96, 32)
7	01000000	OUT(96, 64)
8	10000000	OUT(96, 128)
(Turn all off)	00000000	OUT(96, 0)

Now let us carry this general scheme one step further to gain complete control over all eight pieces of apparatus connected to an output port. Suppose that we want to turn on apparatus 1, 3, and 5 connected to Port no. 96 and leave all others off. The binary representation of such an instruction is 00010101. The decimal equivalent of such an instruction is calculated by *adding together the decimal values of each of the 1-bits,* that is, $16 + 4 + 1 = 21$. So the statement OUT(96, 21) instructs Port no. 96 to turn on the apparatus connected to data lines 1, 3, and 5, and to turn off all other lines. As a second example, turning on apparatus connected to data lines 3, 6, 7, and 8 is represented by 11100100, the decimal equivalent of which is $128 + 64 + 32 + 4 = 228$; so OUT(96, 228) will turn on the four pieces of equipment specified. Study these examples until you are sure you understand them. Once the idea is mastered, you will be able to use the OUT procedure to turn on or off any apparatus connected to any output at any time.

The final Pascal technique that needs to be understood in order to use the OUT procedure effectively concerns the data type BYTE. Recall that in the heading of the external procedure OUT the two parameters are of this type. This means that the parameters (namely, PORT and DATA in the procedure heading shown above) must be decimal integers within the limits of the size of an 8-bit binary number. What are those limits? The lower limit is, of course, 00000000; which, translated to decimal, is 0. The upper limit of a byte is 11111111. We translate this by adding the decimal equivalent for each 1-bit, that is, $128 + 64 + 32 + 16 + 8 + 4 + 2 + 1 = 255$. Now, having calculated 0–255 as the decimal integer equivalents of a byte, we can declare a data-type BYTE using Pascal's TYPE declaration like this:

```
TYPE BYTE = 0..255;
```

which, when accompanied by variable declarations such as

```
VAR PORT, DATA: BYTE;
```

tell the Pascal compiler that the values for the variables must be integers between 0 and 255.

The INP Function

Now that we know a bit about bits and bytes and output ports, it will be easy to understand how input ports operate. INP is an *external library function* whose use can be declared by the function heading

```
FUNCTION INP(PORT: BYTE): BYTE; EXTERNAL;
```

When INP is called by a statement such as

```
X: = INP(1);
```

this function will scan the eight data lines coming in from the input Port no. 1 (illustrated in Fig. 8–4) and assign to the variable X a decimal integer between 0 and 255. These limits will lead you to guess, correctly, that INP is a BYTE function, and that the variable to which its value is assigned (X in our example) should be declared as a BYTE variable.

Suppose now that the statement X: = INP(1) has been executed, and that the value assigned to X is 2. What does this mean? We can answer this question by recalling that Port no. 1 (see Fig. 8–4) has up to eight pieces of apparatus connected to it, each one being a response-sensing device (response lever, telegraph key, and so forth). Each of these is either active or inactive at the moment the INP(1) function is executed. The input port is constructed so that it sends a signal over each of the eight data lines back to the computer. We know that a data line that is active can be represented by a 1 and an inactive line is represented by a 0. So the computer can be construed as receiving from the input port an 8-bit binary number in which each bit indicates whether or not its corresponding data line is active. Using the same translation rules given above for the OUT procedure, a signal from Port no. 1 of 00000010 will translate to a decimal value of 2, indicating that the apparatus connected to the second data line from the right on Port no. 1 was active, and that all other data lines were inactive. To take another example, X = 64 would mean that the apparatus connected to data line 7 is active. We see, then, that the same binary-to-decimal translation rules apply to the input ports as well as the output ports, although the information is traveling in the opposite direction.

The rule concerning multiple active data lines also applies to input ports as well as output ports. For example, an X = 129 means that data lines 1 and 8 are active (10000001 = 128 + 1 = 129), and X = 254 signifies that all data lines except no. 1 are active (11111110 = 128 + 64 + 32 + 16 + 8 + 4 + 2 = 254). With a little practice you can easily interpret the meaning of any value between 0 and 255 returned by the INP function.

The Program

With a knowledge of how INP and OUT operate, construction of a Pascal program that will control a fixed-ratio learning experiment using a Skinner box is not difficult. Assume that we have an input Port no. 1 and an output PORT no. 96 as shown in Figure 8–4. For the very simple experiment described at the beginning of this section there will be only one input device, the response lever, which we will connect to data line 1 of Port no. 1. Also, there is only one device to be controlled by the output port—the food-pellet dispenser—which will be connected to data line 1 of Port no. 96. (Such connections may involve soldering some wires to certain posts on the Skinner box and the ports, which is not a difficult task but suggests yet another skill that must be acquired by the modern psychologist!) The following program, after first asking the experimenter what fixed ratio is to be used and for how many reinforcements the experiment should run, will control the entire experiment and print the time of each reinforcement on the computer screen.

```
PROGRAM SKINNER;
TYPE    byte = 0..255;
        alpha = packed array[1..8] of char;

VAR     port, value: byte;
        t: alpha;
        ratio, total, count, i: integer;

(* ----------------------------------------------------*)
                (* Library Subprograms *)
(* ----------------------------------------------------*)
```

```
FUNCTION inp (port: byte): byte; external;
PROCEDURE out (port, value: byte); external;
PROCEDURE time (var t: alpha); external;

(* ------------------------------------------------------*)
               (*  User-Defined Procedures *)
(* ------------------------------------------------------*)

PROCEDURE bartest;
              (*  Tests for ·a bar press *)

VAR     test: byte;

    (* NOTE:   first REPEAT..UNTIL waits until rat
       has released bar from last press. Second
       REPEAT..UNTIL then waits for next press. *)

begin
  test: = 0;
  repeat
    test: = inp(1)
  until test = 0;
  repeat
    test: = inp(1)
  until test <> 0;
end;          (* End of Bartest *)

(* ------------------------------------------------------*)

PROCEDURE food;
    (* Activates food dispenser with electrical pulse *)

VAR     i, j: integer;

begin
  out(96, 1);
  for i: = 1 to 80 do j: = 1000 + 1
  out(96, 0)
end;      (* End of Food *)

(* ------------------------------------------------------*)
                (* MAIN PROGRAM *)
(* ------------------------------------------------------*)

begin
  out(96, 0);
  writeln('Enter Ratio and No. Reinforcements to be
          Given');
```

```
readln(ratio, total);
time(t);
writeln('Starting time = ', t);
writeln;
for i: = 1 to total do
begin
   count: = 0;
   while count < ratio do
   begin
      bartest;
      count: = count + 1
   end;
   food;
   time(t);
   writeln('Reinforcement No. ', i:3, ': Time = ',t)
end;
out(96, 0)
end.
```

Looking for a moment at the top of the program, notice that there are two TYPE declarations—BYTE, which was described above and is needed for the INP and OUT subprograms, and ALPHA, which is necessary when using the external procedure TIME. When called, TIME returns the time of day in hours, minutes, and seconds, using an 8-cell packed array of characters having the arrangement hh:mm:ss. Consequently, its single parameter *T* should be of the type identified as ALPHA in the TYPE declaration.

Looking now at the statement part of the main program, we see that it begins with OUT(96, 0). This instruction, which turns off all apparatus connected to Port no. 96, is given immediately when the program begins in order to reset all data lines and the equipment connected to them to zero ("off"). Although not always necessary, it is considered good laboratory practice to enter such a statement at the beginning and end of programs of this type to ensure that all devices being used start and finish the experiment in the "off" state.

The remainder of the program, after prompting the RATIO and TOTAL (number of reinforcements) parameters from the experimenter and printing the starting time of the experiment on the computer screen, is a FOR..DO loop that will monitor the experimental animal's responses until the number of reinforcements designated by TOTAL has been reached. Within this outside loop, a WHILE..DO loop is executed to test for and count bar presses (using the BARTEST procedure) until the number of responses specified by RATIO have been sensed. At this point the food dispenser is activated using the procedure FOOD, the reinforcement number and its time of occurrence are recorded on the CRT, and the process is repeated. The apparatus controls occur in the BARTEST and FOOD procedures.

The BARTEST procedure, although not difficult to understand, has an interesting idiosyncrasy that is often required in this type of programming. The two REPEAT..UNTIL loops in this procedure both use the INP(1) function to test the status of Port no. 1 over and over. Recall now that if INP(1) assigns a 0 to the byte variable TEST it means that all of the input devices connected to the port are inactive. Thus the purpose of the first REPEAT..UNTIL loop is to ensure that a preceding response has ended before going on to test for the next response. This precaution is necessary because of the enormous difference between the speed of the computer and the speed of the experimental animal's behavior. It is entirely possible in an experiment such as this for the animal to press the bar and hold it down for a half-second or more. The bar-testing WHILE..DO loop in the statement part of the main program operates in hundredths of a second or faster, however, making it quite possible for the program to sense a response, add 1 to COUNT, and return to BARTEST to test for the next response before the animal has released the bar from the previous response. The first REPEAT..UNTIL loop in BARTEST, then, is designed to wait if necessary until a previous response has been completed before advancing to the second loop, which tests for the next response.

The purpose of the FOOD procedure is to activate the food dispenser. Here the programmer must know, or find out about, the switching mechanism on the apparatus being used. Many laboratory devices are operated by sending just a brief enabling signal to the apparatus, after which switches and other mechanisms built into the device itself take over and control the remainder of the operation. Other devices, however, operate for as long as voltage is applied to them and stop when voltage ceases. Obviously, the program sequence needed to operate a piece of apparatus will have to vary depending upon the way the device must be activated—that is, for some devices the program must send a short enabling signal, whereas for others it must turn on the data line and time the interval until the apparatus is to be turned off. In the example above, the "enabling signal" type of apparatus was assumed; so the sequence of instructions in FOOD consists of turning on data line 1 with the instruction OUT(96, 1), waiting just a few tenths of a second by looping through a short FOR..DO loop, then deactivating data line 1 with OUT(96, 0). This sequence sends a signal lasting a few tenths of a second to the food dispenser connected to line 1 of Port no. 96, thus enabling it; from there on the dispenser's own mechanism completes the operation of dispensing a food pellet to the animal.

CONCLUDING COMMENTS

In this chapter, we used some very simple experimental situations to illustrate a type of programming that can quickly become very complex. One type of increased complexity is to add to the number of pieces of apparatus that may be connected to input or output ports. Our Skinner box experiment used just one input signal (the response lever) and one output device (the food dispenser). Most experiments in psychology will utilize more lines, with the inevitable consequence that the programming task becomes more complex (see Exercise 5 at the end of the chapter as a next-step example). Another type of added complexity is to increase timing accuracy. For example, reaction time is a major response measure used nowadays in cognitive experiments, and human reaction times must be recorded to milliseconds of accuracy. However, millisecond timing cannot be performed accurately by building software clocks with higher-level programming languages such as Pascal on most microcomputers. Rather, the programmer must either have available a hardware clock that is accurate to the millisecond level or else write a software clock in assembly language and call it in as an external subprogram when needed. Such techniques, particularly the latter, introduce significant new programming requirements that are beyond the scope of this text and must be found elsewhere (see Suggested Readings). Despite the elementary nature of the topics and examples covered in this chapter, however, mastery of them will take you a long way toward becoming a competent programmer in the interesting and important area of automated laboratory control.

SUGGESTED READINGS

The best place to find out more about Pascal and the external library subprograms that it can access on microcomputers is to read the Pascal documentation that comes with the computer available to you. You may find that the examples presented here are not precisely for your equipment—a problem that stems from the unfortunate fact that the makers of various computers have intentionally made their software different from that of their competitors. Even so, the various makes and models are similar enough that the examples given here should generalize easily from one microcomputer to another.

The most current text written for psychologists on the topic of computers in the laboratory is R.J. Bird's *The Computer in Experimental Psychology* (1981). Chapter 5 in Bird's text describes interfaces in some detail, and other chapters discuss such topics as auditory experiments, physiological recording and other response measures, and programming languages especially designed for use in the psychology laboratory. An earlier text edited by Weiss (1973) is also informative.

EXERCISES

1. We have learned that software clocks require finding an integer value that will cause a programming loop to repeat just enough times so that the time required to execute the loop is exactly the same as (or as close as possible to)

some standard temporal measure; for example, 1 second, 1/10 second, 1/100 second. One way to determine this number is to write a calibration program that allows the user to enter a test value, then to use that value as the number of iterations in the loop. By timing the interval between when the loop starts and when it stops, we can determine how good the test value is for generating the standard time interval we want. Write a calibration program of this type that will allow you to determine for the microcomputer available to you the value that will give an accurate timing loop of 1 second. (Hints:

A. If your timing apparatus is a stopwatch, you will not be able to start and stop the watch manually with any accuracy in a 1-second period. To give yourself more time, write the program so it will receive the value to be tested, then multiply it by 10 and run the loop for 10 seconds. Have the program signal when to start and stop the stopwatch by printing the words START and STOP on the screen as the loop begins and ends, respectively.

B. If a hardware interface and an electronic clock that can be attached to the interface are available, connect the clock to an output port and use the OUT procedure to start the clock at the beginning of execution of the test loop and stop the clock when the loop ends. The clock, if set to zero initially, will show you the time elapsed during execution of the loop. This is a much more accurate method, of course, than trying to time the loop manually with a stopwatch.)

2. The SERIALX program gives as results only the number correct per trial for the serial-learning task. A standard phenomenon to observe in serial learning is the *serial position curve,* which requires knowing exactly which items are correct on each trial.

A. Revise SERIALX so it provides the trial-by-trial data necessary for plotting the serial position curve.

B. Have your program calculate the mean number of correct responses for each item over *N* trials and use the means obtained to plot a serial position curve on the computer screen at the end of the experiment.

3. Write a program that will run a free-recall experiment.

4. Write a program that will run a paired-associate learning experiment.

5. The SKINNER program controlled a single response lever and the food dispenser in a simple learning situation with a laboratory rat as subject. Consider now a more complex *discrimination learning* experiment with pigeons. On the Skinner box wall will be mounted two lights (1 red, 1 green) and below each light will be a "pecking key"—a disk somewhat like a doorbell, which, when pecked by the pigeon, activates a switch that signals a response. A food cup, attached to a food dispenser such as the one used in our FR experiment, will also be mounted on the wall. Write a program that will control the following type of experiment using this apparatus.

The pigeon will be reinforced on a FR(RED) schedule when it pecks the key under the red light while the red light is lit, and reinforced on a FR(GREEN) schedule when it pecks the key under the green light while the green light is lit (where RED and GREEN are integer parameters input by the experimenter). Pecking the wrong key when either light is lit does not count as a correct response leading to a reinforcement, nor does pecking either key if no light is lit. The data recorded should be written onto a disk file PIGEON/DAT. The data should include (1) the time and number of each reinforcement (as in the SKINNER program), and (2) the number of error responses made between each reinforcement. The stimulus-presentation arrangement should follow these rules: After each reinforcement, both lights should be *off* for DELAY seconds, then either the red or green light should be lit *at random* (.50–.50 probability) and remain on until the next reinforcement is given. (DELAY is a parameter input by the experimenter at the beginning of program execution.)

9

Introduction to LISP

Why should anyone interested in the use of computers in psychology learn LISP? Is not one language enough? And when the language one already knows is as powerful as Pascal, is it not possible to do all of the things with that first language that one could possibly want to do with another? Many people who have become competent in a programming language and who have learned to like the language they know ask questions of this sort whenever they are pressed to begin studying a new programming language. Perhaps the recollection of the initial struggle when that first language was being learned, and of the many errors made until competency was achieved, predispose most of us to avoid if we can the necessity of going through the same struggle again. But history—and the shortcomings of any single programming language, no matter how sophisticated it might be—usually work against us; and anyone who cares to venture more than a little way into the arena of computer programming will sooner or later need to develop skills in more than one programming language. Fortunately, for those whose computing interests focus upon such areas as psychological modeling and artificial intelligence, the second language that must be learned is an intriguing and fascinating one, and most who study it soon develop a deep appreciation, often accompanied by a sense of awe, for the strange mixture of simplicity and power of the language called LISP.

There are several reasons why people interested in psychological modeling need to learn LISP. The first reason is that LISP is the primary programming language used by psychological modelers, cognitive scientists, and AI researchers today. Virtually all sophisticated models of perception, memory, language understanding, concept formation, planning, problem solving, and other cognitive functions are designed and built in LISP and associated languages.* One consequence of this fact is that it is difficult to develop a real familiarity with psychological modeling—even to understand some of the research literature—without having at least a reading acquaintance with the structure and form of the language.

Other reasons for learning LISP are technical, having to do with the kinds of computation it handles best and with its ease of programming and debugging when working with certain types of materials and structures. Knowing Pascal, we are well aware that that language is extremely flexible at manipulating numerical information and using arrays as data structures but is somewhat less flexible in handling strings of characters (remember the packed arrays needed to handle words, and the detailed programming necessary to read or write word files), and is able to build and manipulate advanced data structures only with considerable effort. (In fact, in earlier chapters we did not consider the use of Pascal pointers for creating linked lists, trees, and so forth, because of the difficulty and awkwardness of such usage.) This wide variability in programming capability is not unique to Pascal, of course; nearly every programming language in existence has been built to emphasize certain capabilities, and thus it inevitably has some relative weaknesses. LISP, as an alternative to Pascal and many other popular programming languages, is designed in a way that greatly facilitates the manipulation of symbols and complex list structures. Consequently, it does not handle some data types and structures as easily as Pascal (for example, numerical operations, array structures). On the other hand, it can manipulate words and linked lists (including trees and graph structures) with considerable ease and flexibility. Because these latter capabilities are the ones most needed in advanced modeling and simulation of human cognitive functions (recall our previous discussions regarding words and language, hierarchical clustering or chunking, discrimination nets, and the relational-net representation of semantic memory), it is

---

*In addition to the LISP language itself, a number of supporting variants have sprung up, many adding new features designed for special modeling purposes. LISP-like programming languages include INTERLISP (a superset of LISP), PLANNER, MacLISP, and KRL (a language built on top of INTERLISP that adds knowledge structure mechanisms). Reviews of some of these variants can be found in Rich (1983, Chapter 12) and Touretsky (1984, Appendix B).

hardly surprising that LISP has become the language of choice for this kind of model building.

Anyone who has worked with LISP could supply additional reasons for learning the language, but those just mentioned should suffice to get us started. In this chapter and the next we look at the basic structure and some of the major functions and tactics used in introductory LISP programming. The remaining chapters introduce and analyze some typical LISP techniques for building simple models of such cognitive functions as concept formation, natural language understanding, and problem solving. Complete models of such complex topics as these are well beyond the scope of this text; but in working through some basic prototypes we will become familiar with the language and the strategies involved in using it. We begin by seeing how LISP differs from most other programming languages in the way it handles numbers and numerical operations. The basic principles underlying these differences will then be extended to an examination of how LISP handles symbols generally.

HOW LISP MANIPULATES NUMBERS

One major difference between LISP and languages such as Pascal, FORTRAN, or BASIC is its syntax. To illustrate the difference, take as a simple example the various ways that one might express the addition of two numbers:

```
in Algebra, c = a + b, or a + b = c;
in English, "the sum of a and b is c";
in PASCAL, C : = A + B;
but in LISP, (PLUS A B).
```

Now each of these syntaxes identifies two kinds of information—the *variables* or *arguments* (A,B), and the *operation* or *function* (+ or "and" or PLUS) that is applied to them. They all differ from each other in syntax to some extent, but the ones we know well have the general structure

```
variable - function - variable ...
```

In contrast, LISP puts the function name *first* and the variables *after* it, and surrounds the whole thing with parentheses, as in

```
(function - variable - variable ...)
```

In LISP, anything surrounded by parentheses is called a *list,* and the different objects within the list can be referred to as *elements* of the list. One of the basic rules about lists is that the first element inside the list will be looked upon by the LISP interpreter (or compiler) as the *name of a function,* which will be applied to the other elements of the list. The other list elements are the *arguments,* or *variables,* for the function. In the LISP example above the variables are identified by the letters *A* and *B.* So the list says, in effect, "Apply the function PLUS to the numbers represented by the letters *A* and *B.*"

Other examples of LISP arithmetic commands, using actual numbers instead of variable names, illustrate the same general form:

```
(DIFFERENCE  4  3)
(TIMES  5  2)
(QUOTIENT  5  2)
```

It is easy to see that in each of these lists the first element is the name of a standard arithmetic function, and the remaining elements are the arguments to which the function will be applied.

In these examples, the arguments for each function are numerical *values* rather than variable *names.* This distinction between a variable name and its value is important in LISP and leads us to another basic feature of the language. The various elements in a LISP list can be any of several different types: *numbers, identifiers,* or *other lists.* Each of these types of elements has, in turn, a *value.* The value of a given number, whether integer or real, is simply that number—as in the examples above. Identifiers, and their values, are a bit more complex. To begin with, identifier names are strings of characters that may be any length but should start with either a letter of the alphabet or a limited number of other marks (for example, *, #, $, on some systems). Some examples are

```
A
AB
TIMES
CONS
*GETSYM.
```

The purpose of identifiers in LISP, as the perceptive reader has undoubtedly surmised, is simply to identify or name things. We are familiar with the basic idea of naming variables because of the constant use of variable names in writing Pascal instructions and algebraic equations. LISP extends this basic variable-naming procedure and uses identifiers for *both* variables (arguments) *and* functions (or operations). For example, the list

```
(PLUS  VAR1  VAR2)
```

contains three identifiers. The first one, PLUS, identifies a function or operation—in this case the arithmetic operation "+". The other two identifiers, VAR1 and VAR2, identify the arguments to which the function will be applied.

The way to tell the difference between identifiers for functions and for arguments is to remember this general rule: The first element inside a list is assumed by the LISP interpreter to be the identifier of a function and the other list elements are assumed to be arguments. So when a list such as

(PLUS VAR1 VAR2)

is presented to LISP, the LISP interpreter will go to the first identifier PLUS and, assuming it is a function, will attempt to find its *value*. Because PLUS is indeed a function, its value will be obtained by executing a set of rules or an *algorithm,* using the values of the other list elements (that is, the arguments) as data.

We can represent the situation graphically as shown in Figure 9–1. Part of the LISP system is a memory area in which are stored the identifiers of many functions. This area is labeled FUNCTION STORE in Figure 9–1. Stored with each of the function identifiers in this store is the algorithm, which, when executed, obtains the value for that function. As Figure 9–1 indicates, these stored functions may be either of two types—*built-in* functions, which are a permanent part of the LISP system and include the arithmetic functions we have used to date, and *user-defined* functions, which will be described in detail later.

The number of built-in functions found in a given LISP system will depend to some degree on the computer used and the version of LISP that is implemented, but all systems have a large number of such functions. In this chapter we will review some of the most important built-in functions. A more complete list can be found in Appendix E or in some of the LISP texts mentioned in the Suggested Readings at the end of the chapter.

In addition to storing functions, LISP must also store the identifiers of *variables* (labeled VARIABLE STORE in Fig. 9–1), as well as the values associated with these identifiers. Thus when the LISP interpreter is given the list

(PLUS VAR1 VAR2)

it *evaluates* (finds the value of) PLUS in the Function Store by finding the values of (evaluating) the identifiers VAR1 and VAR2 in the Variable Store and applying to them the algorithm associated with the function name.

We are almost ready to try some LISP on some number problems, but first we must find out how a user can give the LISP interpreter a variable identifier and its value. For example, suppose we want to enter into the Variable Store the identifiers and values VAR1 = 3 and VAR2 = 2 as

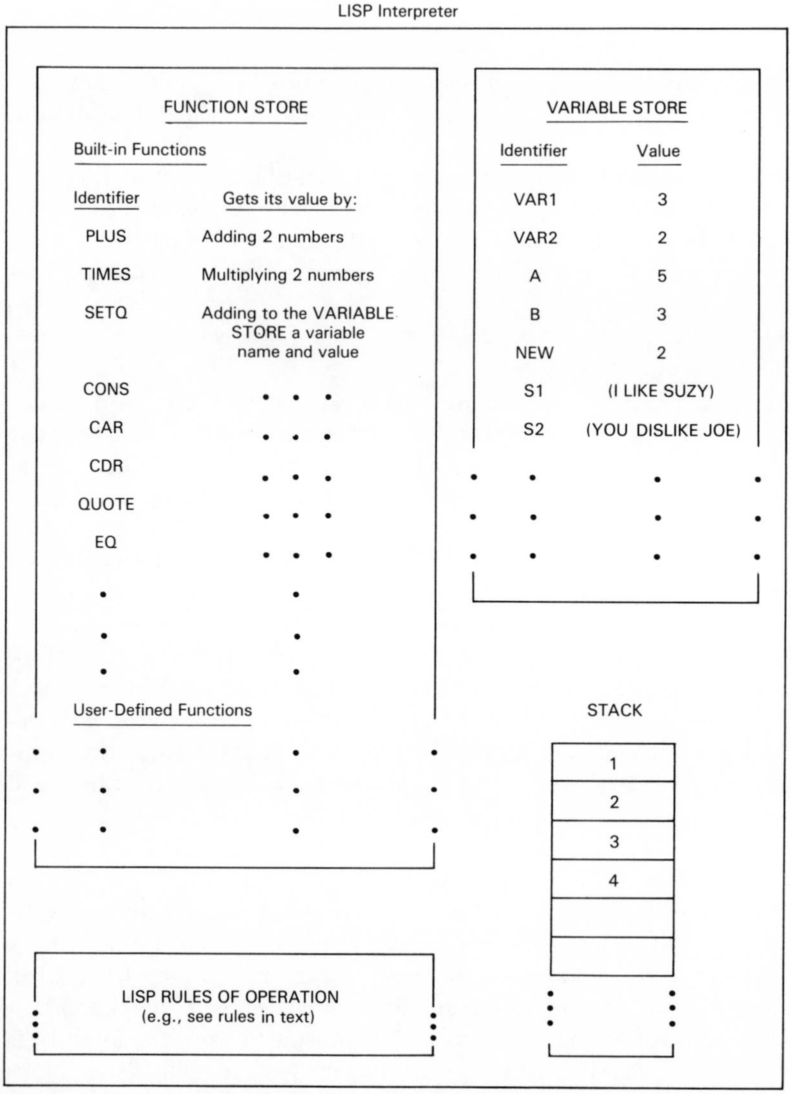

FUNCTION STORE		VARIABLE STORE	
Built-in Functions		Identifier	Value
Identifier	Gets its value by:	VAR1	3
PLUS	Adding 2 numbers	VAR2	2
TIMES	Multiplying 2 numbers	A	5
SETQ	Adding to the VARIABLE STORE a variable name and value	B	3
		NEW	2
CONS	• • •	S1	(I LIKE SUZY)
CAR	• • •	S2	(YOU DISLIKE JOE)
CDR	• • •		
QUOTE	• • •		
EQ	• • •		

User-Defined Functions

STACK

1
2
3
4

LISP RULES OF OPERATION
(e.g., see rules in text)

FIGURE 9–1. An idealized cognitive structure for a LISP interpreter.

shown in Figure 9–1. This can be accomplished by giving LISP the following lists* as instructions:

*We must adopt certain assumptions and notational conventions when illustrating LISP. It is first assumed that the user is using a timesharing (interactive) system, is seated at a terminal using a video screen (CRT) as output device, and the LISP interpreter is activated. When the LISP interpreter is waiting for a user instruction, an asterisk (*) appears in the left margin of the CRT. The user then types an instruction next to the asterisk—for example, *(SETQ VAR1 3)—and presses the RETURN key on the input keyboard. The LISP interpreter then *evaluates* the instruction and *prints the value* on the next line. Finally, the interpreter signals with an asterisk on the next line that it is waiting for the next instruction. The process repeats. For clarity, in our illustrations the output returned to the user by the LISP interpreter will be underlined.

```
* (SETQ VAR1 3)
   3
* (SETQ VAR2 2)
   2
*

   .
   .
   .
```

These two lists (which are actually instructions to the LISP interpreter) begin with the identifier SETQ. SETQ is a built-in LISP function that, when executed, enters ("sets") the second element of the list (VAR1) as the *name* or *identifier* of a new variable in the Variable Store, and assigns the third list element (3) as its *value*. Figure 9–1 gives a useful cognitive representation of the results of the SETQ functions illustrated above.

It is useful to note here that, once an identifier has been given a value, the LISP interpreter will evaluate the identifier and return its value whenever the identifier is presented. Thus, having SETQed both VAR1 and VAR2 as above, whenever we input these identifiers to the interpreter we will get their values. The computer screen would show the process thus:

```
*VAR1
 3
*VAR2
 2
   .
   .
   .
```

This outcome is consistent with the fact that the objective of the LISP interpreter is to *evaluate whatever is presented to it.* We already know that if the presentation is a list containing a function and its arguments, for example (PLUS 2 3), LISP evaluates the function and returns its value. Now we see that if the presentation is not a list but simply an identifier, it still does the same thing.

In general, whenever we want to define a new variable we use the function SETQ. The function SETQ has *two arguments,* which must be identified *in order* within the list. The first argument will be a *new variable name,* and the second will be used as the *value* that is to be assigned to that new variable name. Here are some examples of SETQ and how it can be used in conjunction with other built-in functions.

```
* (SETQ A 5)
   5
* (SETQ B 3)
   3
```

```
* (PLUS  A  B)
  8
* (SETQ  NEW  2)
  2
* (TIMES  A  NEW)
  10
* (TIMES  NEW  4)
  8
* (TIMES  (PLUS  A  B)  NEW)
  16
      .
      .
      .
```

The list in the final example above is of a slightly different form from that of the others in that *one of its elements is itself a list.* Whenever a list is found as an element within a list, the LISP interpreter tries to *evaluate that inside list first,* obtaining a value that is then used as an element for the outside list. In the example above, (PLUS A B) first evaluates to 8 and NEW evaluates to 2. These evaluations yield, in effect, an intermediate list that, if printed, would be (TIMES 8 2). This interim list is now evaluated to produce the final result of 16. Now, given the values above for the identifiers A, B, and NEW, can you verify the following LISP instructions?

```
* (PLUS  (TIMES  A  B)  (PLUS  (DIFFERENCE  A  NEW)  NEW) )
  20
* (PLUS  3  (PLUS  (PLUS  (PLUS  A  B)  4)  (TIMES  B  NEW) ) )
  21
*
      .
      .
      .
```

Perhaps you are beginning to understand already why LISP may seem difficult at first, and yet—from the standpoint of language rules—is really quite simple. Take the second of the two instructions immediately above as an example. Probably at first glance it looks horribly complex. But if we understand and follow just several simple rules, then finding the answer (that is, "evaluating the list") is easy. Those rules, in summary are:

1. A list is made up of elements that can be numbers, identifiers, or lists.
2. A list is evaluated by locating the function, which is the first element in the list, and applying that function to the values of the arguments (that is, the remaining elements) in the list.
3. If an element inside a list is itself a list, the inside list is evaluated before the outside list is evaluated.

The key to using these rules is to start with the innermost parentheses, which identify inside lists, and find their values. These values are used in turn to evaluate the next outside set of parentheses, and we continue in this manner until the outermost parentheses are the only ones left. At that point we have one more function and its arguments to evaluate, and the result is the final answer.

Many LISPers find that numbering the sets of left-right parenthesis pairs (and, therefore, the lists) is a helpful way to understand the structure of complex lists; for example:

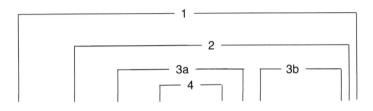

$\underline{*}$ (PLUS 3 (PLUS (PLUS (PLUS A B) 4) (TIMES B NEW)))

Starting with the outermost list, numbered Level 1, the levels are numbered from outside in until the "deepest" ones are found*; then they are evaluated in turn, starting with the deepest and returning step by step to the outside or "top" level. The reader should evaluate these successive levels of lists to find the following answers—and recognize that the solution to the final level is the answer to the whole problem:

LEVEL	OPERATION	VALUE (ANSWER)
4	5 + 3 =	8
3a	Level 4 + 4 = 8 + 4 =	12
3b	3 × 2 =	6
2	Level 3a + Level 3b = 12 + 6 =	18
1	3 + Level 2 = 3 + 18 =	21

Have you caught onto the system? If not, go back to the beginning of this section and reread it until you understand. The rules just covered are fundamental to LISP and form the base of its capability for handling not only numbers but also words and other information. So an understanding of these rules prepares you for the next section, in which we shall get away from numbers and arithmetic and push on to words.

*This method of numbering sets and levels of parentheses is a good way to determine if parentheses are "balanced"—a right for every left—as *they must always be* in LISP or the most incomprehensible errors will occur!

SOME BASIC FUNCTIONS THAT MANIPULATE LISTS

It is time to get used to yet another concept that is basic to LISP but which differs enough from other programming languages to make it seem a bit strange at first. We saw in the preceding section that in the LISP language a list is set off by parentheses, the first element is an identifier whose value is a function, and the other list elements are identifiers whose values are the variables or arguments for the function. But this is only one interpretation of a list. In addition to using a list to give instructions to LISP for execution, lists may also be interpreted as *data.* For example, the following two lines both contain lists that are enclosed in parentheses (as any good LISP list should be), but they are obviously different in interpretation:

```
Interpretation #1 applies to (PLUS A B)
Interpretation #2 applies to (I LIKE SUZY)
```

The difference is that in Interpretation #1 the list is meant to be *evaluated*—that is, the values of the elements (the function and its arguments) are obtained and the result is an answer (value) of some sort. In Interpretation #2, however, the rules for evaluation won't apply—that is, the first element of the list is *not* a function name whose value is to be applied to the values of the other elements. Instead, the list is simply a string of words that most English-speaking people would agree make up a sentence. As such, we can look upon it as a list of *information* or *data,* rather than a list containing a function to be evaluated. So for this list the LISP interpreter should *not* try to evaluate the elements, but instead should treat each one as an unevaluated symbol or string of symbols. Alternatively, we can say that each element of the latter type of list is to be treated as a *literal object-word* and not as the identifier of a value.

This concept of presenting data in the form of a list is extremely important in LISP. Several flexible features about using lists for data purposes should be noted. First, each identifier within a data list can be nearly any size—from single letters or digits up to numbers or words that are many characters in length. Second, the list is expandable or contractible, ranging from the "null list" (an empty set of parentheses) to very large lists whose size depends mainly upon the memory space available in the computer being used. Third, there can be a mixture of different kinds of data within the same list—numbers, letters, words, punctuation symbols, and even other lists. We shall have occasion later to see, and work with, these possibilities.

One problem that arises when lists are used to store data rather than functions and arguments is that the LISP interpreter must be given some signal that the contents of such a list should be treated as data and therefore *not evaluated* in the usual manner. Recall that the interpreter, when given a list, will normally assume that the first identifier is a function and the remaining ones are arguments, and will try to evaluate them. Obviously, a list of "data" such as

```
(I LIKE SUZY)
```

should not be treated that way because "I" is not a function nor are the other two words arguments for a function. Instead, they should be treated as *literal objects and not evaluated.*

The signal that informs the LISP interpreter to treat a list as data rather than to try to evaluate it is a single quotation mark placed directly in front of the list. By "quoting" a list, for example,

```
'(I LIKE SUZY)
```

we cause the elements of that list to be treated by the interpreter as literal objects rather than elements to be evaluated.

The CAR and CDR Functions

Having established that data can be presented to LISP in the form of a list, what can LISP do with such a list? Two of the language's basic *list-manipulating* functions are CAR and CDR, which are used to break lists into separate pieces. Simply defined, the function CAR takes as its argument a list and "returns"* the *first element* of the list. CDR, on the other hand, takes as its argument a list and returns the *list* with the *first element taken away.*† Syntactically, CAR and CDR are one-argument functions on lists, having the structure

```
        (CAR list),
  and   (CDR list),
```

respectively.

To illustrate, consider the quoted data list '(I LIKE SUZY). To get the CAR of that list, we can give to LISP the command

```
*(CAR '(I LIKE SUZY))

I
```

---

*LISP programmers often refer to the evaluation of a function by saying that the function "returns (the value of) X." The phrases "returns the value of X" or simply "returns X" are equivalent to "evaluates to X" or "gives the value of X."

†According to Allen (1978, p. 13), the reasons for these particular names stem from the days when LISP was run on an IBM 704 computer. The *c* and *r* stood for "contents" and "register." The *a* in CAR stood for "address," and the *d* in CDR signified "decrement"—two parts of a machine location in the IBM 704.

and, as shown, the interpreter will evaluate the function CAR using as its argument the quoted list (I LIKE SUZY), and return the *element* "I"—which, of course, is the first element (the CAR) of the data list.

Alternatively, if LISP is given

```
*(CDR '(I LIKE SUZY))

(LIKE SUZY)
```

then, as shown, the *list* (LIKE SUZY) is returned. Note that what has been returned is the *entire list* of the original argument *except for* the CAR of that list.

We can now combine CAR and CDR with other features already known about LISP to obtain some elementary but interesting outcomes:

```
*(SETQ S1 '(I LIKE SUZY))
   (I LIKE SUZY)

*(SETQ S2 '(YOU DISLIKE JOE))
   (YOU DISLIKE JOE)

*(CDR S1)
   (LIKE SUZY)

*(CAR (CDR S1))
   LIKE

*(CDR (CDR S2))
   (JOE)
*
   .
   .
   .
```

The first two instructions use SETQ to put two identifiers S1 and S2 in the Variable Store (see Fig. 9–1). The values of these identifiers are quoted lists; thus from now on, S1, when evaluated, will return the list (I LIKE SUZY) as data, and S2 will return (YOU DISLIKE JOE). In the third instruction, note again that the CDR function returns the *list* identified by S1, minus the first element—that is, (LIKE SUZY). The CAR in the fourth example, however, returns just the first *element* of (LIKE SUZY)—LIKE. Again, we see that when CAR is evaluated it returns a *list element* but when CDR is evaluated it always returns the *list itself* (with the first element missing).

The fourth and fifth example given above are of special interest because they each have a list within a list and combine functions. As we saw with the arithmetic functions, the LISP rule is to evaluate from the inside out. Thus evaluation of the fourth example proceeds as follows:

LEVEL	FUNCTION	OPERATES ON:	VALUE OBTAINED:
2	CDR	(I LIKE SUZY)	(LIKE SUZY)
1	CAR	(LIKE SUZY)	LIKE

(CAR (CDR S1))

The fifth example works just as easily, returning a list because the final (Level 1) operation is CDR. Study it carefully until you are convinced that it should in fact evaluate to (JOE).

The CONS Function

Another built-in LISP function that operates on lists is designed to *add to,* or *construct,* lists rather than breaking them into pieces. The syntax for the two-argument function CONS is

(CONS arg1 arg2)

where arg2 *must be a list,* but arg1 can be any type of *element.* The value returned is a list. The particular way in which the two arguments are combined is to make the first argument the CAR of the arg2 list. For example,

THE FUNCTION	EVALUATES TO
(CONS S1 S2)	((I LIKE SUZY) YOU DISLIKE JOE)
(CONS S2 S1)	((YOU DISLIKE JOE) I LIKE SUZY)
(CONS ' (GEORGE AND) S1)	((GEORGE AND) I LIKE SUZY)
(CONS 'I (CDR S2))	(I DISLIKE JOE)
(CONS (CAR S1) (CDR S2))	(I DISLIKE JOE)
(CONS (CONS (CAR S2) ' (ARE FOND OF)) (CDR (CDR S2)))	((YOU ARE FOND OF) JOE)

The reader should work these examples through to become convinced that they are correct, noting that the inside-out rule and the use of the single quotation mark (') are followed meticulously.

Surprisingly, these three functions (CAR, CDR, CONS) are the only ones needed to do an amazing amount of work with lists of literal objects, and when they are mastered you will be well along the way toward understanding how LISP can be used with a variety of psychological and linguistic problems. At this point, however, we have only seen how to write instructions for manipulating lists. It is also helpful to get a graphic understanding of how a list is structured. We turn now to that topic.

GRAPHIC REPRESENTATION OF A LIST

LISP lists have the basic structure of a binary tree. When such lists are represented graphically, the resulting illustration is referred to as *box notation* because the structure looks like a series of boxes (nodes) that either contain information or point to other boxes. Figure 9–2a shows how the list identified as S1 above can be represented in box notation. The rule is that the *left* cell of the top node contains (or points to) the *first* element of the list, and the *right* cell points to the *remainder* of the list.

In Figure 9–2a, the first element of the list is the data-word "I"; hence, that element is stored in the left cell of the top node. In Figure 9–2b, however, the first data element is not a single word but a list. Consequently, the left cell of the top node *points to another node,* which itself is the first node of the inside list (YOU AND)—which, of course, is the first element of the outside list.

The examples in Figure 9–2c,d also portray the rule that the left cell of any node contains or points to the first element of a list. You probably have realized by now that, in general, *the left cell of any node represents the CAR of the list that extends below that node.* Furthermore, the right cell of the node represents the rest of the list except for its CAR, which by definition, is the CDR of the list. For instance, trace the arrows in the box notations in Figure 9–2 to convince yourself of the following facts:

IN FIG. 9-2	THE VALUE OF	IS
b	(CDR S3)	(I LOVE PA)
a	(CDR (CDR S1))	(SUZY)
c	(CAR (CAR (CDR S4)))	C
d	(CDR (CDR (CAR S5)))	(((C))

In trying to come to these convictions, you undoubtedly at some point asked yourself, "What does it mean when the right cell of a node has a diagonal line in it?" The answer to that question leads to another important concept in LISP—the concept of the *empty list.* Figure 9–2e illustrates the empty list in both list notation and box notation. The empty list is also identified in LISP by the term NIL. If we give an empty list (the simplest list in LISP) to the interpreter, NIL is returned as its value; for example:

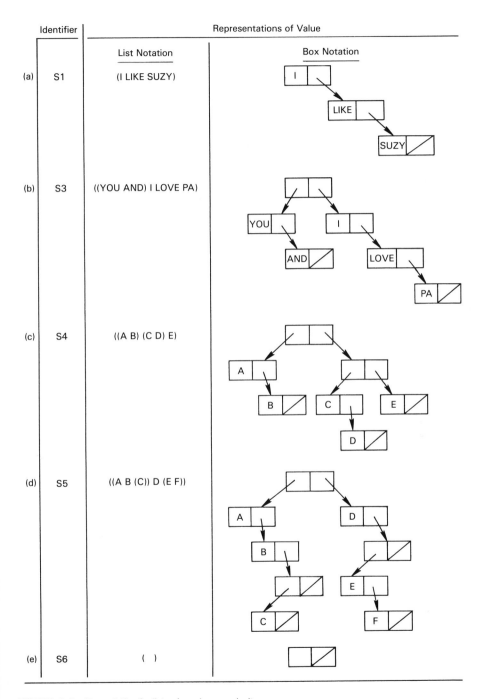

FIGURE 9–2. Box notation for lists of varying complexity.

```
*( )
NIL

*      .
       .
       .
```

However, NIL is also a *list terminator of any* LISP *list.* In the box notations shown in Figure 9–2, this list-terminator aspect of NIL is signified by a diagonal line in the CDR cell of the last node in *any* list. (You should trace each list shown in Figure 9–2 to confirm that this is indeed the case.) So a quick answer to the question about the diagonal line is that it stands for NIL and signals the end of a list—that is, there is no further CDR on the list.

A full and formal treatment of LISP would require a more detailed explanation of NIL because of its various meanings and representations. For now, however, we will think of it simply as a list terminator and will consider its major conceptual advantage to be that it is always the empty list that is left over after all of the list elements have been taken away. For example,

```
*(CDR  (CDR  (CDR  S1)))
 NIL

*
```

indicates that after eliminating the first three elements of the list (I LIKE SUZY), all that remains is the empty list. (Another correct statement is that there are no more CDRs to the list.) Or, as another example from Figure 9–2,

```
*(CDR  (CDR  (CAR  S3)))
 NIL

*
```

because (A B) is the CAR of S3 and the second CDR cell of that sublist is the end of the list.

DEFINING USER FUNCTIONS

If the only list operations available in LISP were built-in functions, the language would not be very powerful. Fortunately, there is a way for you, the user, to write your own functions and store them in the Function Store (see

Fig. 9–1) for later use. In fact, this activity is in essence the way one "writes programs" in LISP, because a "program" in this language is basically a set of functions that call upon each other and work together to solve a problem.

The basic rules of LISP covered thus far have shown that the language uses a function to perform virtually any task. This is the case when the user needs to define a new function. In most versions of LISP the function DEFUN (standing for DEfine FUNction) is the one generally used to tell the LISP interpreter to store a new function in the Function Store. The general syntax for DEFUN is a list with four elements:

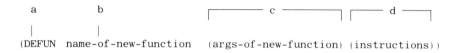

Instead of pursuing this definition conceptually, let us take a simple example. First, imagine a whole series of lists for which we must get "the CAR of the CDR." For example, consider the many three-word sentences in English that have the simple declarative form *subject-verb-object;* for instance (I LIKE SUZY). Assume now a computer programming problem that requires isolating the verb of a number of sentences that are written in this general form (S1 and S2 in Fig. 9–1). A glance at such sentences reveals that, from a LISP viewpoint, the verb is the CAR of the CDR of the sentence-list. So one way to accomplish the task would be to input

```
*(CAR (CDR list))
 value

*
```

for each sentence.

This method requires typing two functions, however, for every sentence we wish to analyze, a rather inelegant procedure that we can improve upon. Let us define a *single new function* that will do the job of the two functions together. Cleverly, we will name (or identify) the function CADR—a good mnemonic for "the CAR of the CDR"—and pronounce it "cadder." Here's how to define CADR:

```
            a    b  ┌c┐  ┌──── d ────┐
            |    |
    *   (DEFUN CADR (X)   (CAR (CDR X)))
        CADR
    *        .
             .
             .
```

Let us analyze the syntax of this user-built function. Element *a* is the DEFUN command telling the LISP interpreter to define a new function; Element *b* is the term that will become the *identifier* of the new function; Element *c* is a *list* of all of the *arguments* the new function will take; and Element *d* is *another list* that gives the *instructions for getting the value of* ("evaluating") *the new function*. The LISP interpreter executes this command by first putting the new identifier and the instructions for getting its value into the Function Store (see Fig. 9–1) and then returning the name of the new function to the user to show that it has been stored.

(We should note in the example above that Element *c* designates that this function requires a single argument, which in this definition is identified by the letter *X*. The *X* works like a value parameter in a Pascal procedure—that is, it takes the value of whatever is passed to it when the function is called. This value is then substituted wherever *X* appears in Element *d* of the definition.)

With the new function now defined, it is possible to execute such commands as:

```
* (CADR  S1)
  LIKE

* (CADR  S2)
  DISLIKE

* (CADR  ' (HE  ENVIES  (HIS  SISTER) ) )
  ENVIES

* (CADR  ' ( (THE  BOYS)  RAN  (DOWN  THE  STREET) ) )
  RAN
*     .
      .
      .
```

The last two examples show an interesting way to elaborate our simple three-word-sentence problem. When the subject or object parts of simple declarative sentences consist of more than a single word we can still isolate the basic *subject-verb-object* segments by using lists within lists; for example, ((THE LISP LANGUAGE) IS (EASY TO LEARN)).

Let us elaborate the subject-verb-object problem one step further and use DEFUN to build another function. CAR can get the subject, and CADR can get the verb, of a declarative sentence, but how can we arrange to get the object of the sentence? We must define another new function CADDR, which will get "the CAR of the CDR of the CDR" of a list. Its definition and use will look like this:

```
* (DEFUN  CADDR  (X)  (CADR  (CDR  X)))
  CADDR

* (CADDR  S1)
  SUZY

* (CADDR  S2)
  JOE

* (CADDR  '(HE  ENVIES  (HIS  SISTER)))
  (HIS  SISTER)

* (CADDR  '(SHE  SLEEPS))
  NIL

*      .

       .

       .
```

Note that in the last sentence quoted there is no object, and thus no CADDR, so NIL (the empty list) was returned.

We have used CADR and CADDR to show how users can build their own functions with DEFUN. Actually, CADR and CADDR are so useful in LISP programming that they are built-in functions in most LISP systems, along with many possible extensions such as CADAR, CDAR, CADDDR, and the like. A little experimenting will show you which CAR-CDR combinations are available in the LISP version being used on your computer. Those that are not built-in can be defined by you as needed, using the function DEFUN as shown above.

There are virtually an unlimited number of functions that might be defined by users, depending upon the programming job that needs to be done and the cleverness of the user as a LISP programmer. In future chapters we shall use DEFUN to define many functions that, when evaluated, will manipulate lists in rather complex and psychologically interesting ways. To prepare you for advancing to these more complex user-defined functions, we must learn the definitions of two new, but basic, kinds of functions—the *predicate* function and the *conditional* function.

PREDICATE FUNCTIONS

The functions used thus far have all returned values that are either numbers or words. There is another important class of functions in LISP, called *predicate* functions, which return as values only "true" (written as *T* by the LISP interpreter) or "false" (written as NIL). Examples of some of the basic built-in predicate functions will be useful in discovering what these functions are like and how they may be used.

ATOM is a predicate function having one argument. When executed it determines if the argument is an *atom* or not, returning *T* if it is and NIL if it isn't. In LISP, an "atom" is either a number or a character or a string of characters that make up a name or word. As a rule, it is a single object that can be used as data and will not be evaluated further. Because a list is not an atom, the function ATOM is often used to test whether some element is a list or not. Examples are:

```
*(ATOM 1.7)
 T

*(ATOM S1)
 NIL

*(ATOM CAR (S1))
 T

*(ATOM (CDR S1))
 NIL

*    .
     .
     .
```

EQUAL is a predicate function that requires two arguments. It compares the two arguments and returns *T* if they are equal and NIL if they are not. It is used to test the equality of both atoms and lists. Examples are:

```
*(EQUAL S1 '(I LIKE SUZY))
 T

*(EQUAL 1.7 1.7)
 T

*(EQUAL '(T) T)
 NIL

*
     .
     .
     .
```

NULL is a predicate function with one argument. It returns *T* if the argument is either the empty list or NIL; otherwise it returns NIL. Examples are:

```
* (NULL  S1)
  NIL

* (NULL  S6)
  T

* (NULL  ' ()  )
  T

*

  .
  .
  .
```

We shall see later that NULL is an extremely valuable function.

There are also a number of arithmetic predicates that make true-false tests on numbers. We will not need many of these, but some examples are:

FUNCTION	DEFINITION
(ZEROP N)	Returns T if N = O, otherwise NIL
(LESSP N1 N2)	Returns T if N1 < N2, otherwise NIL
(NUMBERP N)	Returns T if N is a number, otherwise NIL
(GREATERP N1 N2)	Returns T if N1 > N2, otherwise NIL

These and other built-in predicate functions are described more formally in Appendix E.

THE COND FUNCTION

COND, the *conditional* function in LISP, is a special and very powerful function. It is the LISP equivalent to the IF..THEN statement in Pascal and other languages. Unlike most LISP functions, it takes an unlimited number of arguments. Each argument is a *list* having two elements. To describe the syntax of COND, we shall use the letter p to stand for "predicate" and the letter e for "evaluate." Using this representational shorthand, COND can be represented syntactically in either of two ways:

```
either  (a)  (COND  (p₁ e₁)  (p₂e₂)   ...  (pᵢ eᵢ))
or      (b)  (COND  (p₁ e₁)
                    (p₂ e₂)
                     .
                     .
                     .
                    (pᵢ eᵢ)  )
```

The (p e) arguments are often called COND *clauses*. Whether COND and its arguments (clauses) are written all on one line, as in (a) above, or the various clauses are written on several lines as in (b) above, the operating rule is:

Check each COND clause (p e), in order from left to right and/or top to bottom, and

(a) if the p element is evaluated as NIL, go to the next clause and repeat (a); otherwise

(b) if p is not NIL then return the value of e as the value of COND and end execution of the function.

This obscure rule can be clarified with an example or two. Let us look first at a numerical example:

```
*(DEFUN GETBIG (M N)
     (COND ((LESSP N M) M)
          (T N)))
   (GETBIG

*(GETBIG 4 3)
     4

*(GETBIG 1 2)
     2

*
```

Here we have defined the function GETBIG, which takes two numbers as arguments and "gets" (returns as its value whichever one is) the bigger number. DEFUN is used to define this user function, and COND has been employed in writing the algorithm for finding the larger number.

To analyze the user-defined function in detail, we shall rewrite it so it shows the different list levels and then shall discuss each in turn.

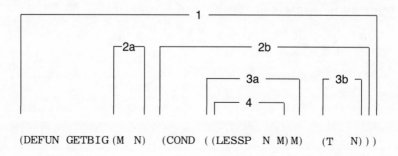

(DEFUN GETBIG (M N)   (COND ((LESSP N M) M)   (T   N)))

The first element in the outside list (Level 1 list) is DEFUN, as expected. Its second element is the atom GETBIG, which—because it is the first of the three arguments that must always be provided for DEFUN—will become the *identifier* of the new function. The third element is the list (M N) at Level 2a, which, because of its position, will be taken as the *argument list* for the new function. (So we see that GETBIG will require two arguments.) The final element of the outside list is the rather complex list (Level 2b) that has the general form (COND (p e) (p e) . . .). This list is the *set of instructions* that must be followed by the LISP interpreter whenever it needs to evaluate (get a value for) the function GETBIG.

What does this latter list actually say? First of all, because it is a COND list, it must contain as arguments a series of one or more COND clauses. There are two such clauses in the example—the two lists at Level 3. Second, within each of these clauses there should be exactly two elements—the *p* and *e* pieces of any COND argument. Third, for each of these Level 3 clauses, the *p* element (the CAR of the list) must evaluate to *T* or NIL; that is, it must be either a predicate function or a predicate.

Taking these requirements in order, we see that the two argument-lists or clauses for this COND function are the Level 3 lists

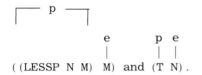

Each clause contains a *p* and an *e* component. The first element of the first clause is the predicate function LESSP, which we know compares two numerical arguments and returns *T* if the first number is smaller than the second; otherwise NIL. In this particular case, if the value returned is *T* then the number for the variable *M* must be the bigger of the two numbers *M* and *N*. So, following the COND rule that if the *p* component of any argument is *T* then COND returns the corresponding *e* as its value, we see that the operation of the first clause is to (1) determine if *M* is bigger than *N*, and (2) if so, to return the value of *M* as the value of GETBIG and stop execution.

However, if the value of (LESSP N M) is NIL, this means that the larger number is *N*—and it also means that COND will proceed to the next argument (that is, the next (p e) clause) and evaluate it. Looking then at the second clause, we recognize a simple and clever device for ending COND and returning a value. The CAR of this argument is *T*, which in LISP means "true" and always evaluates to *T*. So, necessarily for any COND clause that has *T* as its first element, the second element will always be evaluated and returned as the value of COND. In this example the second element is *N*, so the value of *N* will be returned as the value of GETBIG. Thus, the user-defined function GETBIG will take as arguments two numbers, whose values will be assigned to the value parameters (M N), respectively, and will return the one that is bigger.

Sophisticated programmers will recognize that GETBIG is a bit sloppy because it doesn't account for possible errors—for example, a user might give it arguments that are not numbers. The problem can be remedied by learning and using two more predicate functions that are built into LISP—NOT and AND. They can be defined as

FUNCTION	DEFINITION
(NOT P)	Returns *T* if the predicate argument *P* is false—that is, if *P* evaluates to NIL; otherwise, NOT returns NIL.
(AND X1 X2 . . .)	Returns *T* if *all* of the X$_i$ predicate arguments evaluate to *T*; otherwise, AND returns NIL.

With these two functions now available, we rewrite GETBIG as shown below. Can you determine why it will now return NIL if the value of one or both of its arguments is not a number? Can you verify that the parentheses are balanced?

```
(DEFUN GETBIG (M N)
   (COND
      ((NOT (AND (NUMBERP M) (NUMBERP N))) NIL)
      ((LESSP N M) M)
      (T N) ))
```

SUMMARY

This chapter introduced some of the fundamentals of the LISP language. Basic to an understanding of the language is the recognition that an "instruction" in LISP takes the form of a *list,* where the first element is assumed to be the name of a *function* and the remaining list elements are *arguments* for that function. A LISP instruction is "executed" when the LISP interpreter *evaluates* the function, using the values of the arguments.

A number of basic built-in LISP functions were described and illustrated. These included (1) *arithmetic* functions such as PLUS, DIFFERENCE, TIMES, QUOTIENT; (2) *list-manipulating* functions such as CAR, CDR, CONS; (3) *predicate* functions such as ATOM, EQUAL, NULL, ZEROP, LESSP, NUMBERP, GREATERP, NOT, AND; (4) the '(quote) and SETQ functions, which allow the user to *define and identify data lists* or, more generally, *literal objects;* (5) the function DEFUN, which allows the user to *define new user-built functions;* and (6) the *conditional* function COND, which permits the user to make "if-then" tests on any number of (p e) COND clauses.

It was noted that, while these functions permit one to get started using LISP, there are many other built-in functions that are supported by most versions of the language. Appendix E contains a description of some of the more frequently used ones. Anyone intending to use LISP seriously should become familiar with all of them.

This chapter also discussed and illustrated two ways of representing the basic structure of the LISP language—the *list*. One way to represent a list is by enclosing its elements in parentheses. This manner of representation is called *list notation* and is the notation normally used when constructing programs. Another way to conceptualize a list, however, is to think of it as a *binary tree*, in which the left branch of each node of the tree is the CAR of a list and the right branch is the CDR of that list. This manner of conceptualizing a list is illustrated by *box notation*. Box notation is particularly useful as an aid in understanding how the LISP interpreter manipulates lists.

SUGGESTED READINGS

Several books have been written for the sole purpose of teaching LISP, and anyone planning to use the language frequently should look at them and have at least one of them available as a reference. The manuals by Touretsky (1984), Wilensky (1984), and Winston and Horn (1981) are excellent references for LISPers ranging from the rank amateur to the expert. Those interested in the formal structure of the LISP language should examine Allen's (1978) *Anatomy of LISP*. Other books and articles concerning various LISP applications are listed in later chapters.

EXERCISES

1. Translate the following into LISP. Be careful to balance left and right parentheses.

    A = 10
    B = 15
    C = 3
    4A + C =
    B + (5A − B/C) =
    3C[5A − (B + C)] =

2. A. Set up the following identifiers:

    LISTA = (JOHN PLAYS BASEBALL)
    LISTB = (SUE LIKES TO PLAY TENNIS)

B. Use LISTA and LISTB, plus quoted elements where necessary, to construct the following lists (sentences):

(SUE PLAYS BASEBALL)
(GEORGE LIKES TO PLAY TENNIS)
(JOHN PLAYS GOLF)
(JOHN LOVES TO PLAY TENNIS)

3. Define your own (user-built) function CONJ that will take two lists as arguments and form their conjunction. Execution of the function, using LISTA and LISTB in Exercise 2 as arguments, should look like this:

*(CONJ LISTA LISTB)
((JOHN PLAYS BASEBALL) AND SUE LIKES TO PLAY TENNIS)

4. The evaluation of the CONJ function in Exercise 3 is a bit awkward because the first of the conjoined sentences is surrounded by parentheses. A built-in function APPEND eliminates this problem. APPEND takes two lists as arguments and strings together the elements of each list into a new list. For example,

*(APPEND '(THE BIG BIKE) '(IS COLORED GREEN))
(THE BIG BIKE IS COLORED GREEN)

Using APPEND, rewrite the CONJ function in Exercise 3 to eliminate the unnecessary parentheses when the function is evaluated.

5. Rewrite the function GETBIG (p. 206) so it will account for the possibility that the two arguments are equal.

6. Imagine a situation in which you have a number of 3-element lists, where the first element is either 1 or 2 and the others are words; for example,

(1 FATHER MOTHER)
(2 HIGH LOW)
etc.

Write a function SHOWIT that (1) takes as its single argument a list such as just described, and (2) returns the first word in the list if the number is 1, the second word if the number is 2. An execution would look like this:

*(SHOWIT '(1 FATHER MOTHER))
FATHER

*(SHOWIT '(2 HIGH LOW))
LOW

*
.
.
.

10

More LISP: Recursion and the Prog Method

Now that we know how to define LISP functions and data lists, we can begin to write more complex functions that process lists of data in a variety of interesting and useful ways. Generally speaking, LISP programmers may take two different approaches when they write complex functions: Given a programming problem, they may choose to write a *recursive* function that will solve it, or they may choose to write what is called a PROG function. These alternatives are, in essence, two different strategies of solving the problem. Which strategy gets chosen in any given programming situation is partly a matter of individual taste; some LISPers tend to write recursive functions more than PROG functions, whereas others prefer PROG functions over recursion. In part, the choice depends upon the programming problem at hand. Although it is the case that virtually any problem can be solved by either programming strategy, certain kinds of problems seem to be solved more readily, or more easily, or more efficiently, by one strategy than the other. Since both strategies can be important, depending upon the programming situation, anyone learning LISP should become skillful in each. To meet this goal, we will in the first part of the chapter get some experience writing recursive functions; then we will look at PROG functions in the second part.

RECURSIVE FUNCTIONS IN LISP

Definition and a First Example

What is meant by the term *recursion?* Barron (1968), in his book on the topic, defines recursion as, "the technique of *defining a function or process in terms of itself*" (p. 1; italics added). To see how this definition relates to programming strategies, let's write a very basic LISP model for a simple psychological experiment designed to study a person's memory. The person is shown a list of words, one at a time, and is told that he or she should learn as many of the words as possible. After studying the list, the person is given a memory test in which a word is presented and the person is asked simply to say "true" if it was a member of the original list and "false" if it was otherwise. (Anyone who has taken a course in experimental psychology will know that this is a simplified version of a *recognition-memory task* and is used in the study and clinical assessment of human memory.) If we want to represent in a LISP model the person's memory for the words learned, we could use the SETQ function to define the memory list MEMRY like this:

```
* (SETQ MEMRY ' (YELLOW BOY MAPLE) )
  MEMRY
*   .
    .
    .
```

(Note that, using terminology from previous chapters, we have employed a list here as a *data structure* for storing the memory items.)

Now suppose we want to write a LISP function that will simulate a person who has words stored in MEMRY and, when given a test word searches through the memory items stored and says either *T* if the test word is recognized or NIL if it is not. How might such a function be written? From the preceding chapter we know that the task can be accomplished in LISP by first comparing the test word with the CAR of the memory list MEMRY, then with the CAR of the CDR (the CADR) of the list, and so on until a match for the test word is found. Using this strategy with the MEMRY list shown above, we could write the following function RECOGN-IT to see if any given TESTWORD is a member of the list MEMLIST:

```
(DEFUN RECOGN-IT (TESTWORD MEMLIST)
  (COND ( (EQUAL (CAR MEMLIST) TESTWORD) T)
        ( (EQUAL (CADR MEMLIST) TESTWORD) T)
        ( (EQUAL (CADDR MEMLIST) TESTWORD) T)
        (T NIL) ) )
```

This function uses three COND clauses to test whether the CAR, CADR, or CADDR* of the memory list MEMLIST are EQUAL to the TESTWORD. If a match is found within any of these COND clauses, the function returns *T* and ends; otherwise, the final (p e) clause returns NIL. We could test this function as follows:

```
*(RECOGN-IT 'BOY MEMRY)
T
*(RECOGN-IT 'GIRL MEMRY)
NIL
*
      .
      .
      .
```

Although this simple function will work for a list exactly like MEMRY, it obviously would be ineffective for any memory list having more or fewer than exactly three items. To write a more general function, we must adopt another strategy. Consider now a new approach: Suppose we write a function that compares the test word with the CAR of the memory list and, if there is no match, simply cuts the present CAR off the list and then, again, compares the test word with the CAR of this new list, continuing to do this cut-and-test-again process over and over until a match is found. To illustrate, think of comparing the test word "maple" with MEMRY like this:

```
Test 1: compare MAPLE with the CAR of  (YELLOW BOY MAPLE)
Test 2: compare MAPLE with the CAR of        (BOY MAPLE)
Test 3: compare MAPLE with the CAR of             (MAPLE)
```

In this illustration, there will be no match between the test word and the CAR of the original list, or between the test word and the CAR of the second list (shortened by cutting off the CAR that was tested on the first try), but on the third test a match occurs. The strategy works!

But what happens if there is no match at all, as, for example, if the test word is "girl"? Here is what happens:

```
Test 1: compare GIRL with CAR of (YELLOW BOY MAPLE)
Test 2: compare GIRL with CAR of       (BOY MAPLE)
Test 3: compare GIRL with CAR of            (MAPLE)
Test 4: compare GIRL with CAR of                ()
```

---

*RECOGN-IT assumes that either your LISP interpreter has the built-in functions CADR and CADDR or you have defined them as described on pp. 199–201.

Eventually, this strategy will produce a *null list,* at which point we conclude that no match was found.

This strategy is a desirable one because in addition to handling both matches and nonmatches it will work for lists of any size. A verbal flowchart summarizing the strategy is

For any MEMORYLIST and TESTWORD:

1. If the list is empty, return NIL and stop; otherwise
2. compare TESTWORD with the first member of MEMORYLIST; if there is a match, return *T* and stop; otherwise
3. make a new MEMORYLIST by deleting the member just tested from the current MEMORYLIST and repeat the entire strategy.

The LISP function MEMBER* follows this strategy precisely:

```
(DEFUN MEMBER (TESTWORD MEMORYLIST)
    (COND ((NULL MEMORYLIST) NIL)
          ((EQUAL TESTWORD (CAR MEMORYLIST)) T)
          (T (MEMBER TESTWORD (CDR MEMORYLIST)))))
```

Analysis of the evaluation process for the function MEMBER is straightforward. First of all, we must recognize that this is a *recursive function.* It fits the definition we read back on p. 210 in that *the function is defined in terms of itself* (see Line 4 of MEMBER, which calls itself). Let us examine the details of how it works. The third line, containing the predicate function EQUAL, compares the test word with the first word (the CAR) of the memory list. If the two words are the same, EQUAL returns the value of *T.* Now, because this EQUAL function is the *p* component of a (p e) clause in a COND function, the value of the *e* component (which in our example is *T*) is returned as the value of MEMBER and execution terminates. However, if EQUAL evaluates to NIL, then the fourth line (another (p e) clause in the COND function) must be evaluated. This line requires that MEMBER be used again, with the *second argument becoming the CDR of the memory list that was just used.* In effect, this will cause (at line 3 on the next recursion) a test of equality between the test item and the CAR of a shortened list in which the old CAR element has been deleted.

These recursive executions of MEMBER, then, will successively chop off each leading item in MEMRY and test the next, until a match is found. If a match is found during any recursion, *T* is returned, and execution of the function stops. However, if there is no match then MEMORYLIST *will eventually become an empty list.* When that happens, it means the test item was

---

*This function, which in general is designed to decide if any given atom is a member of any given list, is so useful that it is a built-in function in all LISP interpreters.

not "recognized" as being a member of the list that was learned. To account for this possible outcome, the second line (the first COND clause) of MEMBER uses the predicate function NULL to test whether the MEMORYLIST currently being processed is empty, and if it is empty then NIL is returned as the value of MEMBER.

Once understood, the basic idea underlying the (built-in) function MEMBER—the idea of recursively processing successive CDRs of a list until either something happens or the empty list shows up—can be used to solve many list-processing problems. As described thus far, however, this recursive strategy has certain limitations because although it can report the results of a test it cannot save results and build something new with them. That limitation can be overcome by writing recursive functions so that they use the LISP interpreter's stack.

Recursion Using a Stack

Just to prove that the recursive strategy is useful with numbers as well as lists, let us turn from processing lists of words to a problem involving numerical calculation. A classical example of a recursive definition in mathematics is the definition of a *factorial*. As you probably know, one way to describe the factorial is to say it is "the final product of any positive integer times one less than the first integer, times one less than the second integer, times one less than the . . ." and so on, for as many integers as needed until you get to zero. So, for example, the factorial of 4 (written as 4!) can be calculated as

$$4! = 4 \times 3 \times 2 \times 1 = 24.$$

This calculation is easy enough with small numbers, but if you try it for larger ones it quickly gets out of hand (for instance, 10! = 3,628,880).

Another way to define a factorial of a positive integer is to say it is "the product of the integer times the factorial of one less than the integer." This is a simpler definition, in a way, because it doesn't get bogged down in saying ". . . times one less than . . ." over and over again. Note also that it is a *recursive* definition of a factorial because it uses the word *factorial* (and thus invokes the process) within itself. Using our example above, it says that

$$4! = 4 \times 3!.$$

Simple as it may sound and appear, however, we see that there is a slight hitch in the process, namely, before solving 4! we need to solve 3!, and before solving 3! we need to. . . . You can see where that all leads! Even so, it is a workable definition. Stated more formally, the factorial is defined recursively as

factorial(n) = $n \times$ factorial($n - 1$) if $n \neq 0$
factorial(0) = 1

where the second line is needed to avoid a result of zero whenever the definition is used.

Figure 10–1 illustrates this latter definition graphically, using arrows to suggest that in order to solve the top-level problem you must put off doing any multiplication at this level (that is, you must "save" the "4 × " part of the operation) and go down to the next level—and keep doing this, repeatedly putting off and saving the successive operations, until you reach an answer. With an answer finally at hand, you must then "pop back up again," solving in turn each of those saved operations at each successively higher level until you reach and solve the top level to complete the answer. The general strategy is, then, that successive executions of the process must be put aside while a prior execution takes place. This requires *remembering* a previous goal, or at any rate remembering certain information about it, while other subgoals are accomplished.

In recursive situations that require this type of put-off-and-remember strategy, LISP automatically uses a built-in *stack* to store current information temporarily while it goes "deeper" into the process. Figure 10–2 illustrates the operation of the LISP interpreter's LIFO stack.* As recursion progresses, the interpreter automatically "pushes" information onto the stack for temporary storage, and when the recursive process finds an

FIGURE 10–1. Calculating 4! recursively.

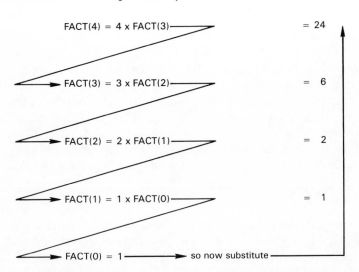

*LIFO, or last-in-first-out, stacks were described in Chapter 5.

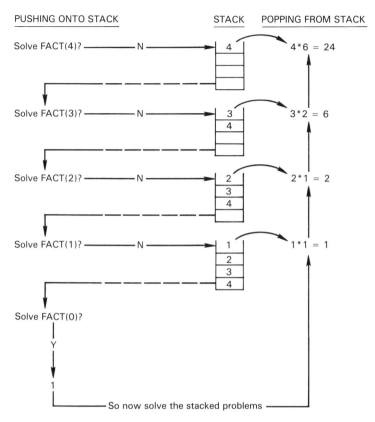

PUSHING ONTO STACK   STACK   POPPING FROM STACK

Solve FACT(4)? ———— N ————▶ 4   4*6 = 24

Solve FACT(3)? ———— N ————▶ 3   3*2 = 6
                                    4

Solve FACT(2)? ———— N ————▶ 2   2*1 = 2
                                    3
                                    4

Solve FACT(1)? ———— N ————▶ 1   1*1 = 1
                                    2
                                    3
                                    4

Solve FACT(0)?
    Y
    1
    ———— So now solve the stacked problems ————

FIGURE 10–2. Using a stack to solve the recursive function FACT.

answer it then "pops" the stored information off the stack, in order, as
needed. Using this automatic process to solve the example in Figure 10–1,
the interpreter begins calculating the factorial by pushing each successive
value of n (that is, 4, 3, 2, 1 as shown in Fig. 10–2) onto the stack until finally
it gets to an actual numerical answer. This is accomplished with the solution
(by definition) of factorial (0) = 1. Now it can multiply that answer by the
first value of n popped off the stack, giving the next answer. This value is in
turn multiplied by the next value popped off the stack, giving the next answer; and so on, working back "up the stack" until the stack is empty. At
this point the answer accumulated is the value of the function.

   The actual program can be written in LISP like this:

```
(DEFUN FACT (N)
      (COND ((ZEROP N) 1)
           (T (TIMES N (FACT (SUB1 N))))))
```

The only built-in function in FACT that was not described in Chapter 9 is SUB1, which takes a number as an argument and returns a value one less than that number. Note that we can call FACT a *recursive* function because it *has itself as part of its own definition,* on the third line.

With FACT defined this way, if we give the command

$\underline{*}$ (FACT 4)

LISP cannot evaluate this command the first time through because there is no value for the inside list (TIMES N (FACT (SUB1 N))) that occurs in Line 3. The function (SUB1 N) can be evaluated to 3, but then (FACT 3) will have to be evaluated before (TIMES N (FACT 3)) can be solved. So the LISP interpreter will put N = 4 on its stack and attempt to evaluate (FACT 3). This cannot be solved yet either, of course, so the process repeats itself. The routine of stacking the current *N* and trying to evaluate FACT for N–1 recurs again and again, until finally FACT is attempted with N = 0. At this point (ZEROP N) in line 2 returns *T,* so the number 1 gets returned as the value of FACT. Finally, an answer! Now (TIMES N <answer>) can be executed with successive *N*'s popped from the stack until a final value is achieved.

A More Complex Example from Psychology

Having examined two different types of recursive functions—one employing the LISP stack and the other not employing it—let us push on to a more complicated example of recursion that will show how multiple LISP functions can be written so they work together to form a program. Recall now the simple recognition problem described back on pp. 210–212. It was a bit artificial psychologically in at least two aspects. First, we know that most people will remember more than just three words when given a recognition-memory test. Also, there is ample evidence that when people learn word lists they tend to *chunk* them into semantic or other well-defined units (recall the chunking process in the computer model of free recall in Chapter 4). So let us elaborate the original recognition problem by changing MEMRY to contain a bigger, chunked list of words such as:

$\underline{*}$ (SETQ MEMRY
    ' ((RED ORANGE YELLOW) (BOY GIRL) (HOUSE) (MAPLE ELM)))
    <u>MEMRY</u>
$\underline{*}$
    .
    .
    .

where each chunk is represented as an inner list within the main memory list. (Note that these chunk-lists may vary in size, depending upon the number of items per chunk.) Obviously, this data structure is more complex than the original MEMRY; and the additional complexity presents us with a new programming challenge. Because the elements in this MEMRY list are lists rather than atoms, the function MEMBER will not be able to process it because MEMBER is written to take as arguments an atom and a list of atoms, and it won't process arguments consisting of an atom and a list of lists. So we will need to write a new program if we are to simulate the recognition-memory task with this more appropriate memory structure.

A second elaboration of the initial recognition problem will be to have the model respond "YES" if the test item is recognized and "NO" if it is not. These outputs, instead of *T* and NIL, will require learning how to use the output function PRINT. And finally, instead of giving the function a single test item at a time, let us give *all* of the test items in a list called TESTLIST. In summary, then, we need to write a LISP model of the recognition task that will (1) process a chunked data list; (2) output responses in English; and (3) accept as one of its arguments a *list* of test items.

When a problem gets complex, most LISP programmers break it down into components. They then write a main function, which serves much like the main program in Pascal. Within that function, other user-defined functions can be called as needed, in a manner akin to procedure calls from a Pascal main program. We adopt that strategy here, by writing the main function REC to control the recognition process in general, and a second function called CHUNK-TEST to test individual chunks. The new built-in functions used are PRINT and PROG2, which are described below. However, see if you can discover their operations just by studying the program.

```
(DEFUN REC (TESTLIST MEMORY)
   (COND ((NULL TESTLIST) '(END OF RUN))
      ((CHUNK-TEST (CAR TESTLIST) MEMORY)
         (PROG2 (PRINT 'YES) (REC (CDR TESTLIST) MEMORY)))
      (T (PROG2 (PRINT 'NO) (REC (CDR TESTLIST) MEMORY)))))


(DEFUN CHUNK-TEST (TESTWORD CHUNKLIST)
   (COND ((NULL CHUNKLIST) NIL)
      ((MEMBER TESTWORD (CAR CHUNKLIST)) T)
      (T (CHUNK-TEST TESTWORD (CDR CHUNKLIST)))))
```

The first major feature to note is that REC is a main recursive function that repeatedly calls another user-defined recursive function CHUNK-TEST, and these two functions operating together form what in other languages would be called the "program." The general strategy for writing programs in LISP is revealed by the way these two functions work together. REC has the responsibility of breaking the total task into pieces that can be handled separately, and CHUNK-TEST handles the pieces

REC sends to it. CHUNK-TEST in turn sends smaller pieces to MEMBER; and, as we saw above, MEMBER in turn breaks its arguments into still smaller pieces that get processed by EQUAL. At each step the "sending" function waits for the "receiving" function to return an answer (the receiving function's *value*) before proceeding. It is easy to see, even in this small example, that LISP is a highly structured programming language in which each function is a programming module that is independent of other modules except for the information received and returned. As in Pascal, then, good program design consists of a top-down analysis of the problem into modules which can then be written as LISP functions that will interact with each other.

Because CHUNK-TEST is a part of the COND statement in REC, it has been written as a *predicate function*. That is, whenever it is called by REC (see the third line of REC) it processes its arguments and ultimately returns a *T* or a NIL, depending upon whether the test item (CAR TESTLIST) presented to it as the first argument TESTWORD is or is not a member of any chunk (CAR CHUNKLIST) of the main memory list. You should examine the CHUNK-TEST function closely, being careful to see that the recursion in its fourth line permits it to test and eliminate successive chunks in CHUNKLIST until *either* (Line 3) the TESTWORD is found and *T* is returned to REC, *or* (Line 2) the TESTWORD is not found and so CHUNKLIST eventually becomes an empty list and NIL is returned to REC.

Looking back now at REC, the next feature to examine is what happens when CHUNK-TEST returns either *T* or NIL. We can summarize the two possibilities like this, and note their similarities:

If *T* is returned, then

```
(PROG2 (PRINT 'YES)
       (REC (CDR TESTLIST) MEMORY))
```

If NIL is returned, then

```
(PROG2 (PRINT 'NO)
       (REC (CDR TESTLIST) MEMORY))
```

Clearly the two commands are identical except that one returns the answer "YES" and the other "NO" before processing the next recursion of REC. These verbal outputs are accomplished with the function PRINT, whose manner of execution is readily understood. PRINT has one argument—often a quoted list or quoted atom, as shown in the example. It prints the value of this argument on the output device, after first advancing to a new output line on the device.

The aspect of the two commands that is really new to us is the use of the PROG2 function. A verbal description of the meaning of PROG2 is that it says to the LISP interpreter, in effect, "Process the next *two* instructions, in order, and return the value of the second instruction only." As shown above, PROG2 has two arguments, each of which is a list containing a function to be evaluated. In execution, each of our PROG2 examples will first print the PRINT argument and will then evaluate the recursive REC argument.

PROG2 is often useful when used in COND arguments. Recall that each argument in COND is of the form

(p e),

where *p* and *e* are instructions that each *evaluate to a single value*. Whenever we have used COND thus far it has been easy to give a *single* instruction in either the *p* or the *e* position and get the required job executed. Many times, however, using just a single instruction as *p* or *e* is not enough (or at least is awkward). Under these circumstances the single function PROG2, when placed as either the *p* or the *e* element, will (1) execute two* instructions, but (2) return as the value *only the value of the second instruction*. Thus it gets two chores accomplished, but still satisfies the requirements of COND because only a single value is returned in the *p* or *e* position.

Recursion Using CONS and the Stack

In the recognition-memory example above, the LISP interpreter's stack was not used because the problem required only that the recursive functions start with a list of elements and break off successive pieces. Now let us devise a simple illustrative program that requires building up a new list and see how the stack helps the process. To illustrate this more complex type of recursion, we shall write a LISP function to simulate the behavior of a child performing the following simple comparison task. Suppose the child has a simple memory of the new spelling words learned in school that day, such as

MEMORYLIST = (HOUSE OAK RED CHAIR MAPLE)

and is asked to recite all of the words except those that are names of trees. This request could be represented as a list of the items to be omitted, such as

OMIT-LIST = (OAK MAPLE).

---

*Originally written to take only two arguments, the PROG2 function on some current systems will actually process more instructions before returning a single value. Some current systems also permit multiple statements at *e* without using PROG2.

Search-compare-and-revise operations such as this are quite common components of more complex mental processes.

It is apparent from previous examples how recursion may be used for the search-compare aspect of this operation. But the other component of the operation—to save those MEMORYLIST words that are not also in OMIT-LIST and eventually return a new, revised list—requires the use of the stack. A reasonable verbal solution for the search-compare-and-revise problem described above would be

For any MEMORYLIST and OMIT-LIST:

1. Are there any items in MEMORYLIST to be processed? If not, execute 5; otherwise, execute 2;
2. Search OMIT-LIST for a match to the CAR of MEMORYLIST. If a match is found, execute 3. If no match, execute 4;
3. Repeat the entire strategy, using the CDR of MEMORYLIST;
4. Push the MEMORYLIST word not found on OMIT-LIST onto the stack so it can be CONSed later into a list of all MEMORYLIST words not matching items in OMIT-LIST. Then repeat the entire strategy, using the CDR of MEMORYLIST;
5. CONS the words on the stack, and return this new list as the value of the program.

Steps 4 and 5 utilize the stack.

Translating this process into a LISP program yields the following function NEWLIST:

```
(DEFUN NEWLIST (MEMLIST OMIT)
  (COND ( (NULL MEMLIST) NIL)
    ( (MEMBER (CAR MEMLIST) OMIT) (NEWLIST (CDR MEMLIST)
                                           (OMIT) )
    (T (CONS (CAR MEMLIST) (NEWLIST (CDR MEMLIST)
                                    (OMIT) ) ) ) ) )
```

First, note that NEWLIST is recursive because it calls itself in two places (Lines 3 and 4). Next look at the COND clause in Line 3. This (p e) clause corresponds to Steps 2 and 3 in the verbal flowchart. It states that if the next item in MEMLIST is found on OMIT, then it is ignored and NEWLIST simply repeats itself recursively. However, if MEMBER evaluates to NIL (that is, the next MEMLIST item is *not* a member of OMIT), then Line 4 (equivalent to Step 4) is activated.

This last line is also a (p e) clause, and the *e* component is a CONS function that will use the LISP stack. Recall that CONS always takes as its second argument a list, and adds the value of the first argument to the front (the CAR) of that list. The first argument to CONS in Line 4 is the word from MEMLIST that is to be *added to the new list that is being constructed.*

Note that the second argument, however, is not a list, as required by CONS, but a recursive call to the function NEWLIST. The purpose of this call, of course, is to go back to find another item or items to be put on the final new list. But in the meantime LISP has been given a word for that final list (that is, the first argument of CONS) and must *save it* for eventual inclusion on the new list it is constructing. It does so by *automatically pushing the current value of the first argument onto the stack,* thus saving it for later use. With the current word automatically saved on the stack, the recursive call to NEWLIST can now continue, searching for other items to be CONSed eventually onto the new list, and pushing them onto the stack as they are found.

The next problem to consider in this recursive operation is: How does it end? Obviously, it will end only when CONS is at last given a valid second argument—that is, a *list* to which it can add the items that are temporarily stored on the stack. This requirement is nicely covered by the (p e) clause ((NULL MEMLIST) NIL) on Line 2; which says, in effect, "if there are no more items to search in MEMLIST then return NIL as the value of the function NEWLIST." Recall now that NIL is really an *empty list.* Thus the second argument of the CONS function will at last be completed; that is, the function CONS will get an empty list, to which it can CONS the *top item on the stack.*

Having completed the first CONS, however, other items may still remain on the stack—the results of uncompleted CONS calls made during earlier recursions. The LISP interpreter now pops them off the stack one at a time, automatically CONSing each with the current value of the growing list in the second argument. Eventually there are no items left on the stack, meaning that all of the previous CONS calls that had temporarily been delayed because of the recursive process have now been completed. The result is, of course, a new list of items, which is returned as the final value of the original call to the function NEWLIST.

The internal processing of NEWLIST may be illustrated graphically as in Figure 10–3. Forming a good image of this simple example should help to generalize this type of recursive process to more complex uses we shall meet in the future.

COND, PROG2, and recursion will be used together in other, more sophisticated, examples in later chapters. For now, however, we must complete the formal introduction to LISP by learning about one other important feature of the language.

THE PROG METHOD

The LISP programming methods covered so far have not used the looping or iterative technique so familiar and popular in Pascal and other, more "sequential" languages. Instead, we have seen that LISP, in the forms we

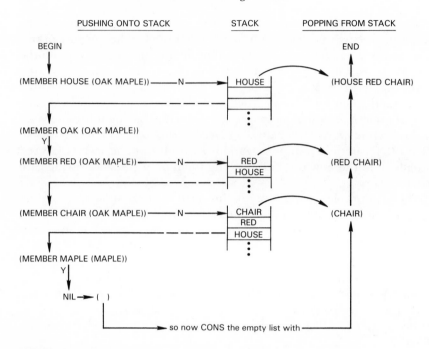

FIGURE 10–3. Graphic illustration of stack operations when using recursive functions.

have examined thus far, seems to jump all over the place—that is, functions may suddenly end in the middle of themselves (an *e* in a COND argument), or jump back and forth from one to another, or even call themselves over and over via recursion. This section introduces another method of LISP programming—the PROG method—which provides a means of writing LISP programs using the more familiar iterative and sequential approach to programming, while at the same time retaining the other powerful features of the language we have already covered.

PROG is a single LISP function that substitutes for the multiple arguments that we have used thus far when constructing a user-defined function in LISP. The general structure for a user-defined function that uses PROG is:

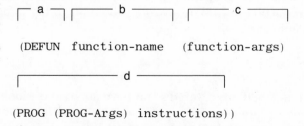

Comparing this with the syntax for a user-defined function in "pure" LISP, the elements *a, b,* and *c* are the same as those we have been using; but in position *d* all of the instructions are nested under PROG, which itself is surrounded by a set of parentheses and even has its own set of variable-arguments. Thus PROG, although it is always found within a user-defined function and cannot operate on its own, is in effect a PROGram unto itself. Moreover, it has the following familiar features: It can operate in a step-wise progression; it has a GO TO command that permits branches to any statement within the PROG; its statements can be labeled; and any number of local variables can be defined within the program. It supports these familiar programming features without sacrificing LISP's list-handling and recursive-function capabilities.

To see how it works, let us rewrite the function REC (p. 217) using the PROG method instead of recursion and then analyze the result. A PROG program for the recognition task, which includes a call to the CHUNK-TEST function written in the previous section, would look like this:

```
(DEFUN REC1 (TESTLIST MEMORY)
  (PROG (TST MLIST)
            (SETQ TST TESTLIST)
            (SETQ MLIST MEMORY)
    LOOP    (COND ((NULL TST)  (RETURN '(END OF RUN)))
                  ((CHUNK-TEST (CAR TST) MLIST) (GO POS)))
            (PRINT 'NO)
            (GO CONT)
    POS     (PRINT 'YES)
    CONT    (SETQ TST (CDR TST))
            (GO LOOP) ))
```

The first three elements of the typical user-defined function have been written on the first line, and the PROG component begins at Line 2 with a designation of PROG's *local variables* TST and MLIST. The instructions in PROG are then written line by line underneath—a format that makes the program easier to follow, although LISP in fact permits multiple instructions per line. The TST and MLIST variables are similar in nature to the local variables defined in the VAR declarations in Pascal procedures, in that they become active during the execution of the routine itself but then cease to exist when the routine ends. Lines 3 and 4 use the SETQ function to assign the values of the original arguments for REC1 to the local variables that will be used within PROG.

Lines 5 and 6 illustrate that the LISP function COND operates effectively in PROG. (To prove to yourself that Line 6 is indeed the second and last line of the two-clause COND function, check the balance of the left and right parentheses in Lines 5 and 6 to confirm that the last right parenthesis on Line 6 closes the left parenthesis that precedes COND in Line 5.) Several differences from our previous examples should be noted, however. First, there is a new function RETURN used in Line 5. This function is *always employed* somewhere in a PROGram to end a PROG run. Remember that PROG is really a LISP function that is being evaluated like any other function, and so must ultimately return a value as output. In contrast to the other LISP functions studied, PROG requires that its evaluation be accomplished by using the function RETURN at any point where the execution of PROG may terminate. If no RETURN is used the value returned for PROG is automatically NIL. In Line 5 of REC1, execution is stopped and a message is returned when COND finds that the list TST is empty.

A second noteworthy aspect of the COND function illustrated is that on Line 6 the *e* component of the (p e) COND clause is (GO POS). This is one of several places in the program where the new branching function (GO *label*) is used. The argument for GO is always a *label*. Labels in LISP—LOOP, POS, and CONT in the example—must begin with an alphabetic character, be positioned just before the instruction to which the branch is intended, and must *not* be enclosed in parentheses. Whenever a GO statement is encountered in a PROG, processing control jumps to the *function following the label* and execution continues from there. We shall review in a moment how this branching capability is used in the example above.

The third aspect of COND that deserves mention is that, when used in PROG, it *doesn't need to end itself*. Recall that when COND is used in pure LISP it must account for all possible terminations of its execution, even if it has to use a list argument such as (T NIL). When used in PROG, however, the values of all of the *p* components can be NIL; and if the last *p* component evaluates to NIL then execution simply "falls through" the COND function and proceeds to the next instruction in the PROG sequence.

This capability is nicely illustrated in the program above. The last *p* function in COND is the call to CHUNK-TEST on Line 6. Because CHUNK-TEST is a predicate function, it returns either *T* or NIL to indicate that it has or has not found the test item in the memory list. Now, if *T* is returned, then (GO POS) is executed, causing a jump to the (PRINT ' YES) statement. But if NIL is returned, program control "falls through" this last COND argument to the next instruction, (PRINT ' NO) is executed, and execution continues from this point.

The final point of interest in the PROG illustrated above is the way in which it replaces the recursive calls that were a major part of the REC function written in pure LISP in the preceding section. In this PROG version, the CAR of the TST list is first compared with the words in each chunk in memory (Line 6). This comparison results in either a "YES" (Line 9) or "NO" (Line 7) response. Following either of these responses, a SETQ function (Line 10) is used to delete from TST the item just tested. Then in Line 11, control is looped back to LOOP (Line 5) where processing continues with the shortened TST list. This loop repeats itself until eventually TST becomes an empty list, at which point the value of (NULL TST) in Line 5 becomes *T*, the message (END OF RUN) is returned, and execution of PROG halts.

Once defined, a function containing a PROG is executed in the same manner as any other LISP function. For example, using the chunked memory list MEMRY and the REC1 function above, I/O would look like this on the CRT:

```
* (REC1 ' (GIRL OAK MAPLE PIGEON) MEMRY)
    YES
    NO
    YES
    NO
    (END OF RUN)
*            .
             .
             .
```

where the list (GIRL OAK MAPLE PIGEON) is, of course, the test-list argument to REC1.

The program just analyzed, while itself written and executed sequentially, called a recursive function (CHUNK-TEST) as part of its sequence. In addition, it could use lists as data structures, and all of the built-in functions of LISP were available. Thus even while retaining the sequential flavor to which many programmers are accustomed, this type of LISP programming still allows the other unique capabilities that make LISP a powerful programming tool for psychologists.

SUMMARY

In this chapter we learned several strategies that are essential to understanding and programming the LISP language. The recursive strategy allows the programmer to write a relatively small function that can do a huge amount of work by calling itself over and over for as many times as needed to arrive at an answer. A more prosaic but also very useful and effective strategy, the PROG method, permits one to write LISP functions using the more familiar iterative techniques common to most other programming languages.

An important general strategy, used with either the PROG or recursive forms, is to write relatively short functions that call upon each other and exchange information back and forth freely. These interdependent functions may be a mixture of types (for example, the PROG function REC1 shown above calls the recursive function CHUNK-TEST, which in turn calls the built-in recursive function MEMBER). Thus a LISP "program" is really a set of interactive functions, where the user starts the process by presenting arguments to a beginning, or "main," function, and from there on the various functions interact to produce (or "return") a value for the initially called function. Viewed in this manner, LISP can be seen as a highly modular language that encourages programmers to analyze complex problems into simple information-processing components, then write functions that satisfy the requirements of each component. With practice using this approach, psychologist-programmers can become adept at thinking about—and writing solutions for—complex psychological processes. The remaining chapters provide some prototype examples that will give you a start at developing such skills.

EXERCISES

1. REC, the simulation of recognition-memory listed on p. 217, assumes a chunked memory as shown in MEMRY (p. 216). In terms of the Duplex theory of memory discussed in Chapter 4, is MEMRY a representation of STM or LTM? How might you represent the other type of memory (STM or LTM) as a LISP data structure? Write a SETQ function that would create such a structure.

2. Assume a LISP description of a house as follows:

   ```
   (SETQ HOUSE    ' ( (LIVING-RM COUCH CHAIRS LAMPS TV)
                      (DINING-RM TABLE CHAIRS CUPBOARD)
                      (KITCHEN STOVE SINK REFRIGERATOR)
                      (BEDROOM BED NIGHT-TABLE DRESSER) ) )
   ```

   A. Write a *recursive* function FURNISH that will accept as an argument a type of room (living, dining, kitchen, bedroom) and return a list of the furniture usually found in that room.

   B. Rewrite FURNISH using PROG.

3. One of the major output functions in LISP is

   ```
   (PRINT arg)
   ```

   where *arg* may be an atom, a list, or a set of atoms surrounded by double quotation marks. PRINT is sometimes awkward in use because when a multiword message is printed on the CRT the parentheses or the quotation marks used in the original argument are printed with the message. Another output function that is built into most LISP systems provides an alternative. The function

   ```
   (PRINC "message")
   ```

   prints the *message* on the CRT without the surrounding quotes. Check the system you are using to see if PRINC—and/or other output functions—are available. Illustrate the varied outputs from PRINT, PRINC, and/or other functions you find by getting them to print the following messages:

```
(THIS IS A LIST)
"Here are some quotes"
Look Ma -- no quotes!
```

4. Assume the following:

```
(SETQ SOCIAL-MEM    ' ((FRIENDS JOE SUE HARRY ANN)
                       (ENEMIES TOM JOAN GEORGE HELEN)))
```

Write a function MEMSEARCH that will take a name as an argument and will indicate whether it is the name of a friend, an enemy, or someone unknown.

5. Assume a list of children's names and ages; for example:

```
(SETQ KIDS ' ((15 HARRY) (12 JOHN) (13 SUE) (15 ANN)...))
```

Write a function GETNAMES, which takes an age as argument and returns a list of names of only those children who are that age.

6. A very simple long-term memory, consisting of ten concepts of five words each, was used in the Duplex theory of memory described in Chapter 4. Using the same general idea of memory, write a LISP program that simulates a child who, whenever given a word, replies with the concept for that word (for example, given the word MAPLE replies TREE) or else replies that the word is not known.
Hint: LTM might look like this—

```
(((dog cat horse) animal) ((oak elm maple) tree) ... )
```

7. For the program in Exercise 6, add the capability of "learning" a new word not previously stored in memory—that is, arrange to store the new word with the proper concept.

11

Computer Modeling and Simulation of Concept Formation

It is hard to dispute the statement that concepts are crucial to our psychological functioning. As Smith and Medin (1981) have aptly pointed out in their recent book on the topic, "without concepts, mental life would be chaotic" (p. 1). If we lacked conceptual capabilities, every time we were confronted with some object in the world we would have to consider it as unique and individual rather than as part of a broader class or category. This way of experiencing objects would have serious consequences on our way of thinking about, and generally reacting to, the world around us.

Consider as an example seeing for the first time a new puppy that the next-door neighbor has just acquired. Without a prior concept, we would be unable to classify it as "dog," would also be unable to understand why the neighbor had bought such an object, would not know whether it was dangerous or humankind's best friend, and could have no predictive thoughts concerning the object—for example, what the thing will look like in six months, how fast it will be able to run, the kinds of noises it might make, what (or whether) it will eat, and so on. Nor would such limitations on our thought and understanding be confined to physical objects; consider our knowledge of events such as "dinner" or "computing," or our understanding of abstractions such as "truth" or "beauty." So we see that concepts are important bases for the ways we see, think about, and describe the various components of our world.

Considering this importance, it is not surprising that psychologists have spent a lot of time studying, thinking about, and experimenting with concepts. Several major questions have received the most attention: (1) how might concepts be structured in our memories?; (2) how do people form, or learn, concepts?; and (3) how do we retrieve and use concepts once they have been formed? As you might expect, final answers to these complex psychological questions are not known; which means, of course, that (at least) several theories have been proposed about various aspects of the way people handle concepts. Several recent texts offering good reviews of the various theoretical viewpoints regarding concepts are recommended in the Suggested Readings at the end of this chapter. But because our major purpose here is limited to giving some basic examples of how computer modeling—and LISP modeling in particular—can help to explore and understand this important psychological phenomenon, we will select just two of the historical and "classical" viewpoints of concept formation for analysis and leave any broader review to other texts. We must first identify some basic terms and definitions concerning concepts, and then we will examine and write two LISP models that illustrate differing explanations of how people form concepts.

CONCEPTS AND THEIR FORMATION

Some Terms and Definitions

In 1956 the psychologists Bruner, Goodnow, and Austin published a book that, although it was entitled *A Study of Thinking,* proved to be a classic work on the subject of concept formation. In it they defined and studied the problems of concept formation in ways that have since led to substantial progress in research and theory on the topic. Bruner and his colleagues began by defining some formal terms that are useful when discussing concepts. They assumed that the events or objects that people classify into a given conceptual category are linked together conceptually because they share *common values* on certain *attributes.* An attribute is ". . . any discriminable feature of an event that is susceptible of some discriminable variation from event to event" (Bruner, Goodnow, & Austin, 1956, p. 26). Attributes of physical objects, for example, are such features as shape, color, weight, usage, and so on. People can agree that two objects, even though they may differ in many respects, are both *exemplars* or *instances* of a concept if they share common values on those attributes that define it.

Using this terminology is a big help to psychologists because they can begin not only to analyze and measure differences among concepts but also to manipulate them experimentally in ways that will provide answers to psychological questions about how they are formed. For example, although most mothers don't bother to use it, this classification procedure provides a standardized way of analyzing what a child must learn in order to discriminate even such mundane concepts as "cow" and "dog". Consider the following:

ATTRIBUTE	VALUE FOR "COW"	VALUE FOR "DOG"
Number of legs	4	4
Color	range across white, dull red, brown, black	range across white, dull red, brown, black
Size	much higher, wider, and longer than a child	range from as small as a loaf of bread to as big as a child
Sound	"Moo"	"Bow-wow"
•	•	•
•	•	•
•	•	•

In this homely example, all of the attributes listed are relevant for defining the concepts "cow" and "dog," but only some of them are relevant for distinguishing between the two. The values may sometimes be very specific and quantitative (4 legs) and at other times qualitative (makes a certain sound, is a certain color). An attribute-value analysis, then, provides a relatively clear and convenient way to describe the criteria that define a given concept.

Another advantage of this attribute-value terminology is that it permits discrimination of different *types* of concepts. Concepts are called *conjunctive* if their definition requires the joint presence of two or more attributes—a "both-and" relationship. Cows, for example, must *both* have four legs *and* say "Moo." As one might expect, the complexity of (and difficulty in forming) conjunctive concepts increases with the number of conjunctions required. There are also *disjunctive* ("either-or") concepts. Bruner, Goodnow, and Austin (1956) give as an example a "strike" in baseball, which is *either* a pitched ball that goes over home plate at a level between the batter's knees and shoulders *or* a pitch swung at and missed by the batter *or* . . ., etc. We see, then, that the notions of attribute and value can be useful in the description and analysis of concepts.

The Reception Task

The analytic terminology introduced above provides not only a way of describing concepts and how they differ from each other but also a basis for discriminating among different types of concepts; however, this still doesn't give much insight into how the psychologist can study concept formation in any controlled and systematic manner in the psychology laboratory. Ideally, given that concepts can be described in terms of their attributes and values, one would like to be able to manipulate these basic aspects independently, thus bringing them under experimental control and allowing the experimenter to see what happens as changes are imposed. But it is obvious that the concepts we depend upon in everyday living cannot be controlled in this manner. First of all, most of them are too complex and fuzzy to be manipulated unequivocally. (For instance, where does "mammal" stop and "fish" or "bird" begin? And who determines which art works are exemplars of the concept "beauty" and which are not?) And secondly, because most people learn natural language concepts during an extended period in early childhood, it is difficult to impossible to arrange formal experiments in which the actual process may be observed.

Bruner, Goodnow, and Austin solved these experimental problems by devising an *artificial universe* of objects, in which each object was represented by a index card on which was printed some arrangement of figures and borders. An example of a small universe of this type is shown in Figure 11–1. Each of the cards displays a certain *value* for each of five *attributes*, which may be summarized as follows:

ATTRIBUTE	VALUES		VALUE CODES
Number of figures on card	1	2	1 – 2
Size of figure(s)	big	little	B – L
Color of figure(s)	red	green	R – G
Shape of figure(s)	circle	square	C – S
Border around figure(s)	yes	no	Y – N

Within such a universe, various types of concepts can be arbitrarily defined by an experimenter. For example, an elementary concept might be "Concept *A* includes all objects having one figure"; a conjunctive concept would be "Concept *B* includes all objects having two figures *and* a border"; and an example of a disjunctive concept would be "Concept *C* includes all objects having a figure that is *either* large *or* red."

Having thus defined an arbitrary and artificial concept, such as Concept *A* above, an experimenter can now ask a person to form that concept under controlled laboratory conditions by shuffling the deck of cards and then saying something such as:

> I am going to show you a series of cards. Some of these cards are *exemplars*, or *instances*, or *examples*, of a concept we will call "A," and others are not. You are to try to form the concept "A" as quickly as you can. You can do so as follows: I will show you the cards one at a time. When you see each card, take a guess and tell me whether you think it is an "A" or a "Not A." I will give you feedback, telling you whether you are correct or not. When you have gotten 10 correct in a row we will stop and you can tell me the concept. To help you begin, I will first show you a card that *is an exemplar* of the concept "A."

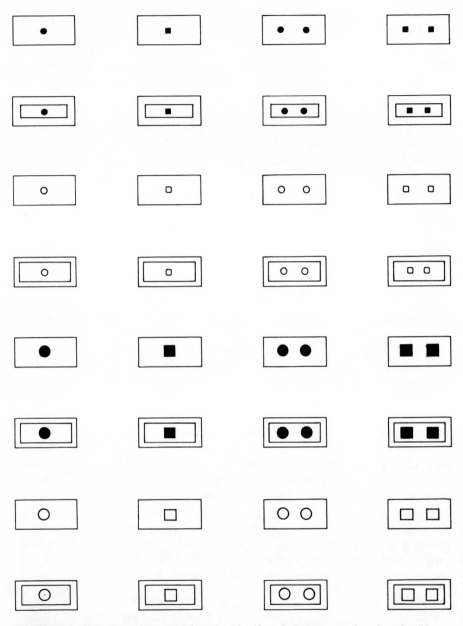

FIGURE 11–1. Materials used in concept formation taks. (Open figures represent the color red; solid figures the color green.)

This task, called a *concept reception* or simply a *reception task* by Bruner and colleagues, meets experimental requirements nicely in that: (1) the subject cannot have any prior knowledge of the concept; (2) instructions and stimulus presentation and feedback can be controlled; (3) a definite criterion of concept formation (for example, 10 correct guesses) can be set; (4) a *measure* of concept formation (for example, the number of trials required to reach the criterion of 10 correct responses in a row) can be obtained; and (5) verbal reports regarding the concept and how it was formed are available after the controlled portion of the experiment is completed. Also, it matches the typical real-life concept-learning situation quite effectively. Using this method, or an alternative but similar *selection* method,* investigators have performed considerable research since 1956 in the area of concept formation.

A Theory of Concept Formation

What happens psychologically when a person is faced with the task of forming a concept? Bruner and his colleagues proposed a miniature theory that assumes that when people form concepts they perform two sorts of mental operations. Initially, the person adopts a tentative *hypothesis* about what attribute or attributes are relevant, and which values of the attributes constitute positive and negative instances of the concept. Having formed the hypothesis, the person then uses it to make guesses about whether new objects encountered are or are not exemplars of the concept. The guesses made are consistent with the current hypothesis. The hypothesis is either kept or changed, depending upon the feedback given by the experimenter. This process of *testing* and *changing* the hypothesis continues until eventually one is found that always yields positive feedback. At this point the person has formed the concept.

When this miniature theory is applied to the reception task described above, a substantial variety of hypotheses—and methods for testing and changing them—might be generated. Consider, for example, an elementary concept formation task in which the 32 cards shown in Figure 11–1 constitute the universe of objects, and suppose that the experimenter has defined as a simple concept that all cards with green figures will be called 'A' and all those with red figures will be called 'not-A.' Remembering that the first card shown in the reception task should be a positive instance, we present the card having one big green square with a border (abbreviated 1BGSY, and illustrated in row 6, column 2, of Fig. 11–1). At this point the experimental subject must adopt a *strategy* that will guide him or her in (1) adopting an initial hypothesis, and (2) deciding how to test and correct it.

The simplest, and perhaps least effective, strategy to choose is one that has been described in some detail in the form of a mathematical model (see Atkinson, Bower, & Crothers, 1965). In this strategy the subject establishes an initial hypothesis that consists of *one relevant attribute,* chosen *at*

---

*The *selection task* (Bruner, Goodnow, & Austin, 1956, Chapter 4) differs from the reception task in that the experimenter spreads all of the cards on a table, has the subject point to or *select* various cards and guess their correct concept categories, and gives feedback for each guess.

random, and *one value* for that variable, also chosen at random. The subject then responds to subsequent cards with that randomly formulated hypothesis until it is disconfirmed; the subject then chooses another attribute-value at random and repeats the process; and so on, until the attribute-value that correctly identifies the process is chosen. Thus the person in our example, after seeing the first card 1BGSY as a positive instance, might randomly select an initial hypothesis such as

"All cards with squares are 'A'; others are 'not-A'."

This rule is then followed until feedback following a subsequent response disconfirms it. Because a single negative feedback means the hypothesis is wrong, it will be dropped and a new hypothesis chosen at random. Obviously this strategy will eventually give a solution—sometimes (at random) on the first choice, but sometimes only after many tries.

A second possibility is called the *wholist* strategy. Here the subject's initial hypothesis is that *all* attributes are relevant, and that the values of each attribute displayed on the first card are the correct values for a positive instance. So, in our example, when the first card is shown the subject forms the initial hypothesis

"All cards with one big green square and a border are 'A'; others are 'not-A'."

The strategy from then on is to maintain the current hypothesis, saying 'A' whenever the card has positive values for the still-relevant attributes and 'not-A' otherwise, until it is disconfirmed; then change it by taking as a new hypothesis what the old hypothesis and the present (disconfirming) instance have in common. A more formal way of stating this procedure for changing the hypothesis is to say that we take as the new value of the hypothesis the *intersection* of the current hypothesis and the current card. (*Intersection,* as you probably know, is a term used in set theory that refers to the common members of two different sets.) For example, the intersection of the two sets (1BGSY) and (1LGSN) is the new set (1GS). Using this rather effective strategy in our example, one could quickly focus down to the correct concept as follows:

CARD PRESENTED	RESPONSE	FEEDBACK	RESULTING HYPOTHESIS	
1BGSY	A	correct	1BGSY	
2LRCN	not-A	correct	1BGSY	
1LGSN	not-A	incorrect	change to	1-GS-
2BGSN	not-A	incorrect	change to	--GS-
1LGSY	A	correct	--GS-	
1LRCY	not-A	correct	--GS-	
2BGCN	not-A	incorrect	change to	--G--
•	•	•	•	
•	•	•	•	

Bruner and his colleagues also discovered other hypothesis-formation and hypothesis-testing strategies that people commonly use, which need not be reviewed here. Because all such strategies are idealized explanatory possibilities of how we form concepts when faced with the reception task, they are legitimately classifiable as theoretical alternatives for describing and explaining this important psychological function. Substantial data have been collected to test the validity of these ideal alternatives, with the results generally indicating that intelligent adults use something like the wholist strategy more than they do others. The research also demonstrates that different strategies may be used at various times by a single person, and that attention and memory failures often interfere with utilization of a strategy in its idealized form (see Bruner, Goodnow, & Austin, 1956; Bourne, Dominowski, Loftus, & Healy, 1986, Chapter 6). Hypothesis theory, one of the first real cognitive theories in American psychology, remains today a strong and serious theoretical explanation of how people form concepts.

A LISP MODEL OF THE WHOLIST STRATEGY

Although the influential work of Bruner and colleagues was done before information processing became a major theoretical orientation in psychology, it fits neatly into the current cognitive viewpoint. (In fact, some current cognitivists portray it more generally as an explanation of the process of inductive reasoning; see Anderson, 1985, Chapter 10.) As a programming exercise that will increase our familiarity with LISP, let us translate at least a portion of this verbally stated theory into a computer model. Specifically, we shall construct a LISP program that models the wholist strategy and simulates concept formation in a reception task. Following the definition of the reception task described above, the *experimenter* part of our program will have to present a series of attribute-value cards (or computer representations of such cards) one at a time to the *theoretical* portion of the program—that is, the part of the program that processes these successive inputs according to the rules of the wholist strategy. For each card presented, the hypothetical subject will respond 'A' or 'not-A' as its current hypothesis dictates. The experimenter part of the program must then present feedback to the subject by indicating whether the response was correct or not. Based upon the feedback, the theoretical subject will change or not change its current hypothesis before receiving the next card. As is the case when the reception task is presented in the laboratory, the first attribute-value card will be a positive instance of the 'A' concept.

Figure 11–2 presents a top-level structure diagram for this process, providing an analysis of the problem in a sequential form that could be used as a basis for writing a program in any of a number of languages. Past experience suggests that some data structure questions will also need to be answered. How will the set of cards and their corresponding feedbacks— that is, the information to be presented by some hypothetical exper- imenter—be stored? If the program were being written in Pascal, one good solution would be to set up an $N \times 2$ matrix in which each row contained the identification of a card in Column 1 and the feedback associated with that card in Column 2. However, knowing that the fundamental data structure of LISP is a *list,* we recognize that the input of cards and feedback to a LISP program might best be represented in list form.

At least two possibilities come to mind. On the one hand we might input a single list whose elements are card-feedback pairs; for example:

```
(((card ) feedback ) ((card ) feedback ) ... ).
```

Alternatively, the input might be comprised of a list of cards and a separate list of feedbacks; for example;

```
((card1 ) (card2 ) ... ) (feedback1 feedback2 ... )).
```

FIGURE 11–2.   Top-level structure diagram of the Wholist strategy for concept formation.

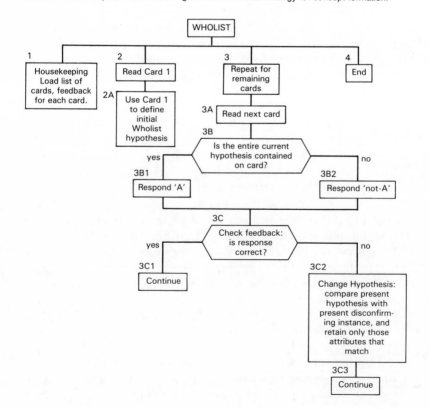

The latter seems to conform a bit better to the experimental situation being simulated because we can construe the list of cards to be the stimulus inputs presented by the experimenter, and the feedback list to be the experimenter's verbal replies after hearing the subject's responses to each card. Using this rationale, we choose the latter as our data structure.

And how may cards and feedbacks be represented in these data lists? The attribute-value card codes used in the example given in the previous section—1BGSY, 2LRCN, and others—seem appropriate for cards. For feedback, *T* may be used to stand for a positive (a "true") instance of the concept and *F* for a negative ("false") instance. Thus, if the concept 'A' includes all cards with green figures, as in our earlier example, the sequence of cards shown on page 000 could be represented in a list called CARDS as follows:

```
*  (SETQ CARDS '((1 B G S Y)  (2 L R C N)  (1 L G S N)
   (2 B G S N) ... (etc.)))
```

and the feedbacks corresponding to these cards would be stored as a user-defined list FEEDBACK in corresponding manner:

```
*  (SETQ FEEDBACK '(T F T T ... etc.))
```

With the input thus represented, the task of the psychologist-programmer is to write a LISP program (we will call it WHOLIST) that can be executed by the command

```
*(WHOLIST CARDS FEEDBACK)
.
.
.
```

and which, following the structure outlined in Figure 11–2, will form the concept

"If a card contains a *G* say 'A'; otherwise say 'not-A'."

As a means of examining the concept formation process while the program is running, we should arrange to have the program print during its execution (1) its response to each card, and (2) the new hypothesis it generates whenever it receives disconfirming feedback. So a typical execution, assuming the correct concept above, might be:

```
*(WHOLIST CARDS FEEDBACK)
 RESPONSE: A
 RESPONSE: NOT-A
```

```
RESPONSE: NOT-A
NEW-HYPOTHESIS=(1 G S)
RESPONSE: NOT-A
NEW-HYPOTHESIS=(G S)
```

.

.

.

etc.

where the third and fourth responses were incorrect and thus new hypotheses were generated. Eventually, of course, the hypothesis should become (G), and all subsequent responses would then be correct—that is, the correct concept would have been formed.

As with any other programming language, there are a number of ways to write an effective program of this type in LISP. We shall adopt the approach used by many LISP programmers and build a main function to control the sequential operations of the model, but branch to subprograms (other functions) for such specific and well-defined process tasks as checking whether the current card matches the current hypothesis (Block 3B in Fig. 11–2), or changing the hypothesis whenever the feedback indicates that a change should be made (Block 3C2).

Starting with the main function, the first step in the wholist strategy is to locate a beginning hypothesis. Consistent with the reception-task paradigm, it is provided by the first card presented—that is, (1 B G S Y) in the definition of CARDS above. If these (1 B G S Y) attribute-values can be stored as a list with the identifier HYPOTH, then the initial wholist hypothesis will be established. Using the PROG method, let us begin the main function with the following lines of code:

```
(DEFUN WHOLIST (CD FBK) (PROG (HYPOTH CARD FEED)
  (SETQ CARD CD)
  (SETQ FEED FBK)
  (SETQ HYPOTH (CAR CARD)))
```

.

.

.

Note here that the main function WHOLIST requires two arguments: CD (the list of cards as input) and FBK (the list of feedbacks as input). The PROG function, however, will operate upon three *local* variables—identified as HYPOTH, CARD, and FEED. The function SETQ is used to assign initial values to each of them. Since (CAR CARD) is the list (1 B G S Y), the last line of this segment will establish the initial hypothesis HYPOTH with the value of the first card.

Figure 11–2 indicates that the next several chores for the program are to check *if* there is a next card, and *if* so read it and then determine *if* the response should be 'A' or 'not-A.' The "ifs" give the clue to the programming tactic to be used, because we know that in LISP the function COND performs the equivalent of the IF or conditional branching statement in other languages. So the strategy will be first to eliminate the initial card (and its corresponding feedback), and then enter a COND function to make the several necessary comparisons. The following sequence, added to the one above, will do the trick:

```
            .
            .
            .
LOOP        (SETQ  CARD  (CDR  CARD) )
            (SETQ  FEED  (CDR  FEED) )
            (COND
                   ( (NULL  CARD)  (RETURN  ' (END-OF-RUN) ) )
                   ( (HTEST  HYPOTH  (CAR  CARD) )  (GO POS) )
                   (T  (GO  NEG) ) )
                   .
                   .
                   .
```

The COND function tests to determine if the program should RE-TURN, say 'A', or say 'NOT-A.' The latter two responses will be accomplished by using (GO POS) or (GO NEG) to branch to other parts of the main PROGram. We will code these segments in a moment. First, however, notice that in the second (p e) clause in COND (Line 5) a *user-defined function* HTEST is called. This function, defining the process stated in Block 3B in Figure 11–2, must be designed so that it compares the current HYPOTHesis with the current CARD to determine if their attributes intersect. Also, since HTEST is used in the *p* position in this COND clause, it should be written as a predicate function; that is, it should evaluate to either a *T* (if there *is* a match) or a NIL (if there is *not*). Recognizing these requirements, we can write a recursive predicate function that looks like this:

```
(DEFUN HTEST  (HYP  CRD)
     (COND  ( (NULL HYP)  T)
            ( (MEMBER  (CAR HYP)  CRD)  (HTEST  (CRD HYP)  CRD) )
            (T NIL) ) )
```

You should stop reading here and perform a step-by-step analysis of this simple user-designed function to confirm that, with the aid of the built-in function MEMBER, it will compare in turn each attribute-value in HYP with every attribute value in CRD. If all such comparisons are successful, the hypothesis list HYP will eventually become empty and HTEST will evaluate to T (see Line 2). However, as soon as a match is unsuccessful the function MEMBER will evaluate to NIL, causing execution of Line 4, which returns NIL as the value of HTEST.

Looking back now at the main program and Figure 11–2, we see that if HTEST evaluates to T, a branch must be made to a portion of the program that makes the response 'A'; but if HTEST is NIL, a branch is made to the response 'not-A'; and in the latter case HYPOTH must then be changed as needed before execution can loop back to repeat the process with the next card. Let us add the following segment to WHOLIST as a reasonable way to perform these chores and complete the main function:

```
          .
          .
          .
POS    (PRINC "RESPONSE:A")  (TERPRI)
       (COND ((EQUAL (CAR FEED) 'T)  (GO LOOP))
             (T (RETURN '(ERROR-STOP))))
NEG    (PRINC "RESPONSE:NOT-A")  (TERPRI)
       (COND ((EQUAL (CAR FEED) 'F)  (GO LOOP)))
       (SETQ HYPOTH (NEWH HYPOTH (CAR CARD)))
       (PRINT 'NEW-HYPOTHESIS=)
       (PRINT HYPOTH)
       (GO LOOP)))
```

The built-in functions we have not used in previous examples are PRINC and TERPRI. If you attempted Exercise 3 in Chapter 10 you already know about PRINC; if not, look back now at that exercise for a description and example of how and why it is used. TERPRI is a function requiring no arguments. Its name comes from the phrase "terminal print," and it simply enters a carriage return so the next output will be on the next line.

The first three lines of this segment will print 'A', then check to make sure that the feedback for the current card is positive, then return to the top of the sequence. Technically, the wholist strategy assures that if the card satisfies the hypothesis then it *must* be a positive instance, so from a strict programming standpoint the COND function in Lines 2 and 3 of this segment could be replaced by (GO LOOP). However, in the real-life situation the person does in fact check the feedback after every response, so a representation of that behavior has been built into the program. Line 2 makes the test, and Line 3 is simply an error message that would print and halt the program if for any reason (for instance, faulty input) a card satisfying HYPOTH should not have the expected positive feedback.

The processes required when the 'not-A' response is to be given are performed in Lines 4 and 5 of this program segment. In contrast to the 'A' response, feedback is critical here. Recall that in the wholist strategy the rule is, "If 'not-A' is correct, keep the current hypothesis; otherwise change it to match the intersection of the hypothesis and the present card." So if feedback at Line 5 is *not* an *F,* then we must enter a procedure that makes a change in HYPOTH. Lines 6 through 9 in the segment above define that procedure.

The purpose of Line 6 is to set HYPOTH to a new value. It uses the built-in LISP function SETQ and a *user-defined function* NEWH, which must be written in a way that allows it to (1) accept the current HYPOTH and current card as arguments; (2) find their intersection; and (3) return that intersection as the value of the function. That value will then be assigned to HYPOTH by the SETQ function in Line 6. The remainder of the main program is straightforward, simply printing the newly formed hypothesis on the output device and then looping back to process the next card.

And how may the hypothesis-changing function NEWH be programmed in LISP? Because the job requires that a new list of attributes be constructed, we must use the function CONS. One good technique would be to compare each attribute-value of the current HYPOTH with the attribute-values of the current card, and CONS into a new list only those attribute-values for which a match between HYPOTH and the card is found. It looks like this:

```
(DEFUN NEWH (HY CD)
   (COND ((NULL HY) NIL)
      ((MEMBER (CAR HY) CD) (CONS (CAR HY) (NEWH (CDR HY) CD)))
      (T (NEWH (CDR HY) CD)))))
```

This function illustrates the same programming strategy as demonstrated in the REC1 function in Chapter 10. The LISP stack is used to save each attribute-value of the current hypothesis that passes the test of the preceding MEMBER function, so they can be CONSed eventually into a new list. Because the second argument of CONS is the recursive call to (NEWH (CDR HY) CD), the value of (CAR HY) is temporarily pushed onto the LISP stack along with other attribute-values passing the MEMBER test. When all tests have been made, the CONS function can then construct a new list by popping the successful attribute-values off the stack. This new list is then returned as the value of the function NEWH and is assigned as the value of HYPOTH via the SETQ function back in the mainline program.

Having looked at the pieces, you should close the book at this point and try to write the program. If put together correctly, it will produce a reasonably good simulation of the reception task using the wholist strategy.

AN ALTERNATIVE MODEL

As noted earlier, other strategies beside the wholist strategy have been proposed as explanations of the way people form concepts. One of these is the *probabilistic* model proposed by the psychologists Atkinson, Bower, and

Crothers (1956), and others. It differs from the wholist strategy in some important ways. One difference stems from the fact that the wholist strategy is *deterministic*; that is, its rules are absolute, and they lead without exception to the right solution if followed correctly. Many psychologists believe that human behavior is rarely so perfect, rigid, and efficient that a deterministic model can account for anything but momentary segments of behavior. These psychologists argue that probabilistic models, which allow for chance variation, are more appropriate approaches to psychological theorizing. Thus a probabilistic model of concept formation may be a more realistic approach than the deterministic wholist strategy.

Another difference is that the model advanced by Bruner and colleagues proposes that the person forming a concept begins with a hypothesis that employs *all* attributes of the concept, while the probability model tests only *one* attribute-value at a time. To do so, the probability model assumes that the person is already acquainted from past experience with the alternatives of each of the attributes potentially relevant to the concept to be learned, or else discovers them when the first few exemplars are shown. Stated in LISP data-structure form, and using the same attributes and values used in our earlier examples, we can represent this acquaintance by saying that the person stores in memory the following associates:

```
(SETQ ASSOCIATES ' ( (1  2) (B  L) (R  G) (C  S) (Y  N) ) )
```

The probability model operates thus: When the first card of the reception task is presented, the strategy is to *pick at random one of the values on that card* and use it as the initial hypothesis about the rule that defines the concept 'A.' As successive cards are presented, the person will now say "A" if the hypothesized value appears on the card, and "NOT-A" if it does not. As in the wholist strategy, feedback indicating an incorrect response is an occasion for changing the hypothesis. The person now picks at random a new hypothesis, which of course is another single value randomly chosen from the card that just provoked the incorrect response. This process continues until no more errors occur, signifying that the concept has been attained.

The model can be summarized in the following top-level verbal diagram:

1. Pick a single value of a single attribute at random from the first CARD, and store it in HYPOTH;
2. Read the next CARD; if the value contained in HYPOTH appears on the card, say "A" and continue at #3, else say "NOT-A" and continue at #4;
3. Read the FEEDBACK for the present CARD; if it is F, then choose at random a new HYPOTH and continue at #2, else continue at #2;
4. Read the FEEDBACK for the present CARD; if it is T, then pick at random a new HYPOTH and continue at #2; else continue at #2.

Figure 11–3 gives a possible data structure that can be used in translating this procedure into a LISP program. ASSOCIATES is the same list as shown above, containing the possible attribute-value pairs. CARDS and FEEDBACK lists will also be needed to simulate the reception task, just as they did in the simulation that employed the wholist strategy. The final structure needed is HYPOTH, which will contain the current hypothesis being tested by our hypothetical concept learner.

Most of this plan looks very similar to the one used for the wholist strategy, and indeed it turns out that the main program for this new model will look very much like the one introduced in the previous section. However, one of the new features—in terms of LISP programming as well as theory—is the way a new hypothesis is chosen. Because the choice involves random selection from among the attribute-values of a given card, it is obvious that a random number generator will be needed. Many of the LISP interpreters currently in use have a built-in random number function that will generate a pseudorandom decimal value between 0.00 and 1.00 whenever called. If the LISP system you are using has such a function, use it; otherwise you will need to write such a function yourself before you can construct this or any other probabilistic model in the LISP language. (Building it is not really difficult; see Exercise 2 at the end of the chapter.)

Given that you have a function of this type—let us refer to it as RND—how would it be used in this LISP model? The programming solution is to (1) convert the decimal number generated by RND into a random integer between 1 and 5 (the number of values on each card in our examples), so it can serve as a pointer to the value on the card that is to be selected at random; and then (2) write a function that puts a copy of this random value into HYPOTH. Let us look at these two programming requirements in order.

A straightforward algorithm for converting a random decimal value between 0.00 and 1.00 to a random integer between 1 and N was described at the end of Chapter 3. Translated into LISP, the algorithm looks like this:

```
(DEFUN RNDINT (N)
    (FIX (PLUS 1 (TIMES N (RND))))))
```

This function will take as an argument an integer N, which is the upper

Figure 11–3. Data structures for the probabilistic model of concept formation. HYPOTH, the current hypothesis, is an atom randomly chosen from the possible values on a given card.

ASSOCIATES	= ((1 2) (B L) (R G) (C S) (Y N))
CARDS	= ((1 B G S Y) (2 L R C N) (1 L G S N) . . . (etc.))
FEEDBACK	= (T F T . . . etc.)
HYPOTH	= atom

limit of the possible integers to be generated (5 in our five-attribute example). Then, as required by the algorithm, it multiplies N by (RND), adds 1, and converts the answer to an integer (fixed number) using the built-in function FIX.

Suppose now that we execute this function RNDINT and it returns a random integer R. In our example, R will be a number ranging between 1 and 5. Our next chore is to build a function that will select the Rth (random) value from a given card. For example, suppose $R = 3$ and a given card has an attribute-value list of (1 B G C Y). The function to be built must select G for the next (randomly chosen) hypothesis.

Let us call this function SELECTH, and arrange it with three arguments so that a call to evaluate it would be

    * (SELECTH R CARD 1)

where R is the random integer, CARD is of course the list of attribute-values on a given card, and the last argument is a counter that we will use as shown below. This function should return a single attribute-value from the Rth position in the list of values given for CARD. Here is a workable solution*:

```
(DEFUN SELECT (NUM LIST COUNT)
     (COND ( (EQUAL NUM COUNT) (CAR LIST) )
           ( (GREATERP COUNT (LENGTH LIST) ) 'ERROR)
           (T (SELECT NUM (CDR LIST) (ADD1 COUNT) ) ) ) )
```

In this recursive function, the identifier COUNT is incremented by one (using the built-in function ADD1 on the bottom line) until, at the test on Line 2, it is found to be equal to the random digit NUM. Correspondingly, as the COUNT rises on the bottom line, successive CARs of the LIST are thrown away. In consequence, when NUM equals COUNT, the CAR of LIST is the NUMth value in the list. Line 2 returns this value to finish the evaluation of the function. Line 3 uses the built-in function LENGTH, which returns the number of elements in a list. This line is merely a safety check to account for the possibility that COUNT will exceed the length of the list before a random value has been selected. This could happen if, through an error elsewhere in the program, the argument NUM is erroneously larger than the list length.

It is easy to see how the probabilistic strategy works when a subject is shown a card *not* containing the current hypothesis. If the subject replies "NOT-A" but feedback indicates that this card is an 'A,' then the subject simply picks a new hypothesis at random from the values appearing on the

---

*Some LISP systems have a built-in function NTH to perform this list operation.

present card. The other possible kind of error requires a little more thought, however. Here a card is presented that *has* the current hypothesized value, but when the subject replies "A" he or she is told that the card is a 'not-A.' At this point, if the subject now picks a new random value from the present card, that value will constitute a hypothesis of what is a 'not-A' rather than what is an 'A.' Obviously, another step will be needed—namely, the subject will have to consult his or her memory of the possible ASSOCIATES and exchange the newly chosen hypothesis for 'not-A' with its associate, thus arriving at a new hypothesis of what an 'A,' rather than a 'not-A,' may be.

A pair of LISP functions can be used to perform this hypothesis-swapping task. The function OPPOSITE, listed below, takes as arguments the hypothesis to be tested and the list of ASSOCIATES. It searches successive CARs of this list until it finds the current hypothesis, then sends the hypothesis and the pair off to the function SWAP. SWAP simply finds the value paired with the current hypothesis and returns it.

```
(DEFUN OPPOSITE  (HYP ASSOCLIST)
   (COND    ((NULL ASSOCLIST)  'ERROR)
            ((MEMBER HYP (CAR ASSOCLIST)) (SWAP HYP
                                        (CAR ASSOCLIST)))
            (T (OPPOSITE HYP (CDR ASSOCLIST))))))

(DEFUN SWAP  (H PAIR)
   (COND    ((EQUAL H (CAR PAIR))  (CADR PAIR))
            (T (CAR PAIR)))))
```

The rest of the model is so similar to the WHOLIST model that you should be able to construct it easily without help. Do you see any problems with the model, or ways you might want to change or elaborate it? Would this model form concepts as rapidly as the WHOLIST model? These are important theoretical questions for the psychologist who is interested in how people form concepts. Look at Exercises 3 and 4 at the end of this chapter for some ideas about possible answers to such questions and how computer models might aid in formulating those answers.

SUGGESTED READINGS

The major purposes in designing and writing the computer model of Bruner's wholist strategy were (1) to illustrate in as basic a manner as possible the potential use of computer modeling and simulation in studying the psychological phenomenon of concept formation; and (2) to provide some illustration and experience in how the LISP language can be used. The program constructed was kept simple to serve these purposes; but more sophisticated computer models and verbally stated theories exist. Recent texts in cognitive psychology (Anderson, 1985, Chapter 10; Mayer, 1983, Chapter 5) present good reviews of hypothesis theory and other current theorizing about the concept formation process. For a sophisticated exercise in computer modeling, the difficult but interesting text written by Hunt, Marin, and Stone (1966) is recommended.

Although Bruner's early work remains influential, it is directed primarily at how concepts are formed or acquired; it does not address the questions posed at the beginning of this chapter regarding the structure and content of a concept as it is stored in memory or how it is retrieved and used once formed. Smith and Medin (1981) discuss these issues, and they provide reviews of various theories that adopt what they have labeled the "classical," "probabilistic," and "exemplar" viewpoints concerning these questions. (A briefer description of these viewpoints, along with an extensive review of recent literature, can be found in Medin & Smith, 1984.) The theories they describe provide good material for advanced LISP modeling exercises or projects on the general topic of concepts.

EXERCISES

1. Write a model of the wholist strategy using the HTEST and NEWH functions presented in this chapter.

2. Implementation of the probabilistic model requires a pseudo-random number generator. One reasonably good two-step algorithm for generating pseudo-random numbers between 0.00 and 1.00 is the following:

    Given an initial SEED value;

    A. Let SEED = ((A * SEED) + B) mod C

    B. Let RANDOM = SEED / C

    using as constants A = 25173, B = 13849, and C = 65536 (modified from Cooper & Clancy, 1982, p. 227); write a LISP function RANDOM that uses this algorithm to return pseudo-random numbers between 0.00 and 1.00.

3. Write a computer model of the probabilistic theory of concept formation.

4. The probabilistic theory, as presented in this chapter, assumes that the person using this strategy has no memory of hypotheses that have been tried and have failed. Write alternative models that assume

    A. a perfect memory of past failures;

    B. a partial memory of past failures (for example, the person will remember each past failure with some probability P).

5. For any two or more of the concept formation models you have constructed (Exercises 1, 3, 4A, 4B), compare the models by recording outcomes of multiple simulation runs. Which model learns the fastest? Which shows the most variability?

12

Computer Modeling of Natural Language Processes

When linguists look at a sentence (or, more broadly, any grouping of words), they distinguish between its *syntax* and its *semantics*. The syntax of a sentence is the arrangement of words in the word group and their relationships to each other. In any language there are *rules of syntax* that tell which word sequences are well-formed (that is, make legitimate sentences) and which are not. Syntax and syntactic rules are parts of what is called *grammar* (along with the other grammar topics of morphology and phonology, which we shall ignore). At some early stage of life we learn the major syntactic (or grammatical) rules about sentences; thus we come to recognize immediately that a statement like "The big blue ball is on the table" is a well-formed sentence, but that "The the ball big table on blue is" is not. Syntax, then, concerns structural relationships—of word groups, phrases, and sentences.

Semantics, on the other hand, is concerned with *meanings* of word sequences. For example, the following two sentences have different syntax, but are semantically the same:

The boy hits the ball.
The ball is hit by the boy.

Alternatively, the sentence "They are flying airplanes" is syntactically correct but ambiguous semantically because it has two possible meanings.

Since the early 1970s psychologists, linguists, and computer scientists interested in AI have developed various theories about how humans comprehend language, and researchers have written computer models to demonstrate and test their theories. These broad, global models differ not only in their names—Anderson and Bower's (1973) HAM (Human Associative Memory); Anderson's (1976, 1983) ACT; Rumelhart and Norman's (1975) MEMOD (standing for memory model); and Schank's (1972, 1975; Schank & Abelson, 1977) CDT (Conceptual Dependency Theory)—but also in the ways their memories are structured and the ways they represent and process sentences. All, however, have the common goal of developing a theory (and, ultimately, a corresponding computer model) of how we understand meaningful groups or strings of words. To reach this goal, these models inevitably must be concerned with the two aspects of language discussed above: syntax, because the model must be able to decide whether a string of words is or is not a potentially meaningful sentence or clause; and semantics, because the objective is to relate the word string to the information stored in memory in a way that makes the string "meaningful." It is safe to say that none of the models implemented to date have achieved the goal of complete comprehension of natural language. But substantial progress has been made, and there is considerable enthusiasm among cognitive psychologists, linguists, and AI researchers that it will continue.

The global models named above have been described at length in other texts (see Suggested Readings), and it is not our purpose to review them in detail here. Rather, we shall review briefly just one example to get some idea of the approach taken, and the computing problems involved, in this kind of programming; then we shall try writing a simple program that will demonstrate some of the programming strategies used in building such models.

WINOGRAD'S MODEL

Overview

One of the first global models of language comprehension was constructed by Terry Winograd. Originally written as part of his dissertation at MIT in 1971, a major account of the model was subsequently published in the journal *Cognitive Psychology* (Winograd, 1972a), and that article was important enough to be reprinted as a hard-cover book (Winograd, 1972b). His overall objective was to develop a program that both "understands" and "produces" natural language within a limited and well-defined environment.

In developing the program, Winograd pretended to be talking to a hypothetical robot (who has one hypothetical eye and a hypothetical hand) about a hypothetical *miniature world* consisting of some toys (blocks, pyramids, balls, a box) placed on a table. The objects on the table have certain physical properties, such as size, color, and location. The program user communicates with the robot by typing commands or questions, written in ordinary English, into the input device. The robot responds to the questions with statements in English, and it carries out the commands by showing on a CRT what it would do if its hypothetical hand were real. Some of the examples given by Winograd of actual dialogue between a real person and the robot are:

PERSON	ROBOT
"Pick up a big red block."	"OK." (carries out command)
"What does the box contain?"	"THE BLUE PYRAMID AND THE BLUE BLOCK."
"Can a pyramid be supported by a block?"	"YES."
"Stack up two pyramids."	"I CAN'T."
"Which cube is sitting on the table?"	"THE LARGE GREEN ONE WHICH SUPPORTS THE RED PYRAMID."

(From Winograd, 1972a,b, pp. 8–15)

To implement the system that accomplishes this conversation, Winograd wrote a series of LISP programs that process a number of data structures in multiple ways. A major part of the system—and the only part with which we shall be directly concerned—is the set of programs and data structures that allows the robot to interpret and "understand" sentences that are input to it. Winograd bases his approach to this comprehension problem on a theory called *systemic grammar*, proposed by the linguist M.A.K. Halliday (1967, 1970). He uses this theory of language structure to write a *parsing program*. A parsing program, or *parser*, uses a grammar and a dictionary to analyze strings of words into word groups, with the objective of determining whether the word string is a syntactically correct structure for the grammar being used. Both the systemic grammar and the parser are important enough to warrant some discussion.

Systemic grammar is one of several theories about language structure that, collectively, are often referred to as *phrase structure grammars*. A basic notion of systemic grammar (and, more generally, any phrase structure grammar) is that language can be organized into three kinds of units—the *clause,* the *group,* and the *word.* The *word* is the basic unit, and within this unit exist several major classes, often referred to as *parts of speech* or *lexical categories.* The major parts of speech in English include, of course, the noun (NOUN), adjective (ADJ), verb (V), determiner (DET), and preposition (PREP), all of which we shall become concerned with later.

The next level, the *group,* is constructed of words. There are several classes of groups, which Winograd (1972 a,b, p. 17–18) identifies as noun group (NG), verb group (VG), preposition group (PREPG), adjective group (ADJG). These groups are not only structural or syntactic units but also have a semantic function. In a simple declarative sentence, for example, the noun group describes the subject of the sentence while the verb group provides information concerning action, time, direction and object of action, and so on.

The top unit, the *clause,* is in turn constructed of groups. (In systemic grammar, a sentence is not considered to be a separate language unit, but rather consists of one or more clauses.) There are several kinds of clauses: a "question," a "declarative," or an "imperative." Also, clauses may be "active" or "passive." Semantically, the clause conveys information about relationships among objects and events or actions, times, places, and logical connections.

Syntactic Analysis: Parsing Trees and Replacement Rules

The nice feature about describing word strings in this hierarchical manner is that any given string of words (such as a sentence) can be separated or *parsed* into well-defined components, making it possible to evaluate the syntactic structure of the word string. A common way to represent an analysis of this sort is with a *parsing tree.* In constructing a parsing tree, each branch must follow one of only a limited set of structural rules. These rules, taken together, constitute a *grammar.* If the structural rules have been followed, then each branch will convey one of only a limited set of meanings. In this sense, then, syntactic analysis (parsing) can be a first step in the broader process of semantic analysis.

As an example of parsing, assume that the following simple declarative sentence is to be analyzed by a parser whose rules are taken from systemic grammar theory:

"The big blue ball is on the table."

A representation of this sentence (clause) in a parsing tree (some call it a *phrase structure diagram*) is shown in Figure 12–1. Analyzing a word string in this graphic manner helps in deciding if it follows grammatical rules; or, put in other words, it helps to determine whether or not the string is syntactically correct.

But what *are* these grammatical rules? And how can they be specified? Anyone who knows English will quickly recognize that the number of rules needed to account for all of the possible types of words and groups and clauses in the language is enormous. Winograd (1972a,b) describes in detail many (but not all) of these rules, and he indicates how he has specified them within his computer model. We need not examine here the lengthy

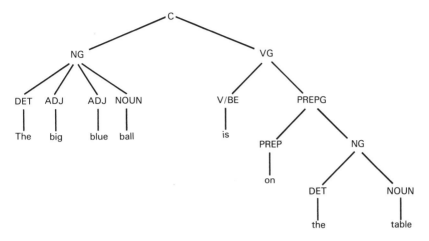

FIGURE 12–1   A parsing tree for the sentence "The big blue ball is on the table."

and complex grammar he used for his model. Rather, some of the flavor of Winograd's way of handling syntax can be captured if we examine for a moment a very simple grammar and the structure of a parsing program that uses it.

The best way to write a grammar for use in a computer program is to make a list of what are called *replacement rules,* or *rewrite rules.* These rules specify what lower-rank units (right side of the arrows below) can legitimately form some higher-rank unit (left side of arrows). For example, the sample sentence given above is a well-formed clause for the following grammar:

```
C                → NG + VG
NG               → DET + N | DET + (ADJ...) + N |
                   DET + (ADJ...) + N + PREPG
VG               → V/INTRANSITIVE | V/TRANSITIVE NG |
                   V/BE + PREPG | V/BE + ADJ
PREPG            → PREP + NG
PREP             → in | on | of | at | ...
DET              → the | a
N                → block | square | table | pyramid |
                   box | ball
ADJ              → big | little | red | blue | tall |
                   short
V/INTRANSITIVE   → runs | sleeps
V/TRANSITIVE     → eats | supports
V/BE             → is | was | were
```

The top line of this grammar says that a clause (C) must be made up of a

NG *and* (+) a VG, in that order. A NG, in turn, is defined as consisting of *either* a DET + N *or* (as signified by |) a DET + (*any number of* ADJ...) + N, *or* a DET + (ADJ...) + N + PREPG. The remaining lines give definitions to the various groups and classes of words in this simple example. Limited as this grammar is, if it is given a bigger dictionary of words (more determiners, adjectives, prepositions, nouns, and verbs) it can be used to parse a large number of simple declarative sentences.

Arranging for a computer to parse sentences according to replacement rules of this sort is not an elementary programming task; on the other hand, it is not impossible. Figure 12–2 shows a partial top-level flow diagram for a parser that follows the replacement rules in the grammar presented above. (Winograd's final system is much more complex, of course.) Worthy of note in Figure 12–2 is the heavy use of conditionals to make Yes-No tests on verbal data structures. LISP, with its capabilities for handling verbal lists as data structures, for processing predicate functions in COND statements, and for recursive programming, meets the programming requirements nicely.

Knowledge and Semantics in Winograd's Model

Parsing, which is the *syntax-handling* part of Winograd's system, is supported by two other major and interrelated components—*knowledge* and *semantics*. In the knowledge component, the robot's "model of the world" is stored—that is, its present representation of objects, properties, and relations in the miniature world of toy blocks. This database of knowledge is akin to what we humans store in long-term memory on the basis of our experiences with language and the physical world. It consists of information that may be quite simple, like "a ball is round and will roll"; or it can be more complex, like "pyramids are pointed, and points will not support other objects." Winograd makes provision for his robot to build this knowledge base as a result of its experience with its miniature world.

Finally, the *semantic* component of the system attempts to bridge the gap between the syntax and the knowledge components. It takes the output from the parser and tries to match it with the existing knowledge base. If successful, it in effect has obtained the "meaning" of the original input— that is, the input is consistent with present world knowledge. If there is no match, then either (1) the information is totally new and has no previous referent, in which case questions must be asked and some addition made to the knowledge database; or (2) the parse was wrong, in which case another parse of the input should be made.

This brief summary of just one complex programming system will suffice to point out the multiple components—and problems—that must make up a complete language processor. Obviously, not all of them can be

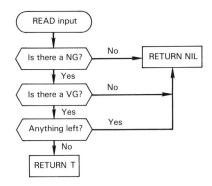

Noun Group Parser

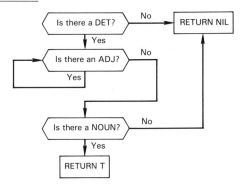

Verb Group Parser

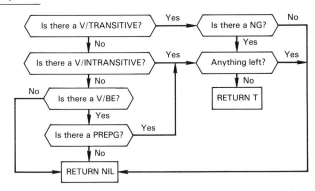

FIGURE 12–2 A partial flow diagram of a parser.
(Adapted from Winograd, 1972a,b, p. 83).

examined in depth here. In the remainder of this chapter we shall investigate just one of the many components by building a small parser that might serve as a prototype for more sophisticated programs.

BUILDING A SIMPLE PARSER

To keep things as basic as possible, consider a child robot, similar to Winograd's but possessing only the following simple grammar:

1.	C	→	NG + VG
2.	NG	→	DET + N | DET + (ADJ ...) + N
3.	VG	→	VB + PREPG
4.	PREPG	→	PREP + NG
5.	DET	→	A | THE
6.	N	→	BOX | BALL | WATER | BLOCK | RATTLE |
			FLOOR | TABLE
7.	PREP	→	IN | ON | OVER | UNDER
8.	ADJ	→	BIG | LITTLE | BLUE | RED | DIRTY |
			NICE
9.	VB	→	IS | WAS

Obviously, the child has a lot to learn. It doesn't yet know any rules for imperative or question clauses, and even its understanding of declaratives is limited to statements about single noun and verb groups such as "the blue ball is on the table." Even so, with a reasonable vocabulary of nouns, adjectives, and prepositions, it could identify correctly the syntax of a large number of sentences. And it is easy to see that a few additional rules would increase its domain immensely. For example, how many new sentences might become admissible as a result of these changes?

C   → NG + VG \| VB + NG + PREPG \| WHV + VB + NG
WHV → WHICH \| WHERE \| WHAT

These latter features will not be included when constructing the example model, but the serious psychologist-programmer may be able to add them independently later.

Given the replacement rules for this basic grammar, let us write a LISP program that will

1. read a string of words;
2. analyze it to determine if it follows the syntactic rules;
3. output the NG and VG parts of the sentence to show how it has been parsed into groups and words; and
4. for both the NG and VG, output *T* if the group follows the replacement rules or NIL if it does not.

The first task is to choose a data structure for storing the input string (a potential clause or sentence) in preparation for analysis. Since LISP is the choice of language, the input can be represented best as a *list*. Using a list as the data structure, one could write a user function PARSE that accepts one argument—a list containing the word string to be parsed. The function would be executed like this:

```
*(PARSE '(THE BLUE BALL IS ON THE TABLE))
    .
    .
    .
```

Using the same approach that has helped us to write other LISP programs, let us construct a PROG main function PARSE that will accept such a list as argument, pass the string (or parts of it) to various analyzers, and output the results of the analyses. The analyzers will be other LISP functions that will perform such specialized tasks as finding a NG, or a PREPG, or specific kinds of words required by the grammatical rules.

We begin writing PARSE by getting it to try to find and print a NG—the first kind of word group that must be found if the input is to satisfy the grammatical rules we are using. The first several lines of code might look like this:

```
(DEFUN PARSE (SENTENCE)    (PROG (S NG VG)
    (SETQ S SENTENCE)
    (SETQ NG (*NGROUP S))
    (PRINT NG)
    .
    .
    .
```

where S, NG, and VG are local PROG variables whose values will become lists containing, respectively, the original word string, the noun group, and the verb group.

The third line of this program segment is a bit complex. It first passes the list *S* as an argument to a *user-defined function* *NGROUP. This function, which we shall construct later, must locate the group of words that have the position in a sentence where, according to our grammar (see Replacement Rule 1 on page 254), a noun group must be found. Having located such a group, it must then return a *list* containing that word group to the main program so that the SETQ function can assign that list as the value of the variable NG. So when execution of Line 3 is complete, NG will contain a list of words that *may constitute* a noun group, athough the parser will still need to check it to see if it satisfies the rules for a noun group (see Replacement Rule 2).

The specific tasks to be accomplished by the *NGROUP function, then, are to (1) start at the beginning of the word string S and, for each word in the string, find out what part of speech it is; and (2) stop this word-by-word analysis when the end of a possible noun group has been reached.

As usual, there are several ways to program such tasks. Let us look at a method that will eventually produce the following type of list as the NG representation for our sample sentence:

((DET THE) (ADJ BLUE) (NOUN BALL))

The list as a whole is the parser's representation of a possible noun group. The elements of the list are sublists containing, in the order of the original sentence, each word and its part of speech.

In examining this list to be constructed by *NGROUP the first obvious question is, where does the function find the parts of speech for the words in its vocabulary? Clearly, some sort of *dictionary* for syntactic categories—a portion of the model's world knowledge that contains the part of speech for each word in the grammar—must be available. To see how such a dictionary may be constructed, we must digress for a moment and learn a new feature of the LISP language.

Property Lists

The capability of storing information about various and multiple *properties* of an event or object is important in a number of computing applications. One example in psychology, and education as well, is the need to store certain facts about people—be they psychotherapy patients, persons participating in an experiment, or students in a class. For instance, stored along with a person's name one might want such information as age, sex, IQ, parents' names, and other important items. Regarding language, for any given word stored in memory it would be advantageous to store with it such information as its part-of-speech, a description of its meaning, and perhaps even other information such as its associates, the context in which it usually occurs, and so on. LISP permits storage, addition, retrieval, and/or elimination of such "properties" of an event or object by providing a special kind of data structure called a *property list*.

The structure of LISP property lists can be conceptualized as shown in Figure 12–3. In Figure 12–3a, a person's last name has been stored as a variable (technically, it is a *literal atom*), and a pointer associated with that atom points to a list of alternating *property names* and *property values*. Thus for the literal atom JONES in Figure 12–3a, the property list shows that the property AGE has a value 25, SEX has a value MALE, NAME1 has a value GEORGE, and so on. Figure 12–3b, more specifically related to our present needs, not only shows how dictionary information may be stored on such property lists but also that the object-word "ball" is defined by the property S-PART (standing for "part of speech"), whose value is NOUN. Other properties, including in this example the shape and possible colors of a ball, may also be stored with the object-word. The general rules of structure for such property lists are easily understood:

Stored
Atom   Stored Properties

a) JONES ────► (AGE 25 SEX MALE NAME1 GEORGE PARENT (JOE MARY))

b) BALL ────► (S-PART NOUN SHAPE ROUND COLOR (BLUE RED GREEN))

FIGURE 12–3 Illustrations of property lists.

1. In a property list every other element, starting with the first, is a property name;
2. the property name must be an atom;
3. for each property name, the element following it (either an atom or a list) gives the value of that property.

There are three major LISP functions that allow the programmer to handle property lists: PUTPROP (which writes and adds property names and their values), GET (which retrieves property values), and REMPROP (which removes property names and their values from the property list). By learning how to use each of these functions, we can build the lexical dictionary needed by the parser. The syntax of the PUTPROP function is

```
(PUTPROP obj val prop)
```

When evaluated, PUTPROP puts the property name designated by the argument *prop* on the property list of the literal atom *obj,* and gives that property the value *val.* So, for example, to define the property list for the word (literal atom) "the" and store the part of speech DET as the value of its property S-PART we could enter

```
* (PUTPROP 'THE 'DET 'S-PART)
    DET
*         .
          .
          .
```

and the function would store on the LISP interpreter's *object list** the object THE, which would have a property list that looks like (S-PART DET). PUTPROP evaluates to the value of the property, as shown in this example by the fact that DET is printed as output when execution finishes.

---

*The *object list* is a list of all atoms that have been defined for the LISP interpreter, and a pointer for each to the location where the definition is stored. Objects on this list include all argument names and function names, as well as atoms defined by the PUTPROP function.

The function GET has the syntax

```
(GET obj prop)
```

It searches the property list of the literal atom *obj* for the property *prop*. If *prop* is found, the *value of that property* is returned; but if that *prop* is not found on the property list, the value returned for GET is NIL. Using the property list established in the example for PUTPROP above, we might use GET as follows:

```
* (GET 'THE 'S-PART)
        DET
* (GET 'THE 'AGE)
        NIL
*           .
            .
            .
```

Finally, the function

```
(REMPROP obj prop)
```

will remove both the property *prop* and its value from the property l ist of the literal atom *obj*.

A Dictionary for the Parser

Using the property list feature and the function PUTPROP, we can now build a *dictionary* for our model that would (1) place the words of the grammar on the *object list,* and (2) create for each of them a *property list* containing S-PART as a property name and one of the parts of speech (DET, N, PREP, ADJ, VB in our simple grammar) as a value. One way to accomplish the chore would be to write a separate PUTPROP command for every word in the dictionary, using the technique illustrated above for the word "the." Clearly, however, this would be a tedious process because of the substantial number of words that would need to be defined for even the simplest of dictionaries (for instance, there are 21 words to be defined even for the very simple grammar defined as an example).

To reduce the amount of time and tedium in dictionary building, it would be helpful to write a LISP function that would construct a property list simultaneously for *all of the words having some given part of speech.* One easily understood function that will accomplish the task is:

```
(DEFUN DICT (PROPERTY VALUE LIST)
    (COND ((NULL LIST) PROPERTY)
         (T  (PROG2 (PUTPROP (CAR LIST) VALUE PROPERTY)
                    (DICT PROPERTY VALUE (CDR LIST))))))
```

We can now, as an example, use this function DICT to establish a dictionary of prepositions for the sample grammar listed back on page 254 (see Replacement Rule 7) by the command:

```
* (DICT 'S-PART 'PREP ' (IN ON OVER UNDER))
     S-PART
*
```

This command will, of course, put the words "in," "on," "over," and "under" on the *object list,* and store for each one the property list (S-PART PREP). Similar commands can add the nouns, verbs, and determiners defined by the sample grammar to the set of words "known" by the language comprehender. (Note that, from a psychological standpoint, this strategy makes the *object list* a long-term memory storage area containing some of the knowledge required by the model.)

THE *NGROUP FUNCTION

Assuming that our model has the words of the grammar stored in a long-term memory dictionary (that is, stored on the *object list*), and each has a property list containing the word's value for S-PART, we can now construct the function *NGROUP to establish a list such as

```
( (DET THE)  (ADJ BLUE)  (NOUN BALL ) )
```

Recall now that *NGROUP has two major tasks—isolating the words that form the noun group, and finding and printing the part of speech for each of those words. In simple declarative sentences, isolating the noun group is easy; it will consist of all the words from the beginning of the word string up to (but not including) the verb. Thus a reasonable algorithm to accomplish the two tasks together is

Starting at the beginning of the word string SENT

1. Is the next word in SENT a verb? If so, print all previously collected words in the noun-group list, and stop; otherwise continue at 2.
2. Get the S-PART of the current word, add the word and its S-PART to the noun-group list, and continue at 1.

A LISP function implementing this algorithm will look like this:

```
(DEFUN *NGROUP (SENT)
   (COND    ( (EQUAL (GET (CAR SENT) 'S-PART) 'VB) NIL)
            (T (CONS
                  (CONS (GET (CAR SENT) 'S-PART) (LIST (CAR SENT)))
                  (*NGROUP (CDR SENT))))))
```

Line 2 of this recursive function is straightforward, simply testing to see if the next word in the sentence SENT is a verb (VB); and, if so, evaluating to NIL and ending execution. Lines 3, 4, and 5, which really form one large (p e) COND clause, are trickier. The initial *T* in the *p* position indicates that this clause must *always* go to the double CONS function on the *e* side. Let us rewrite this *e* segment in isolation to make it easier to see how it works.

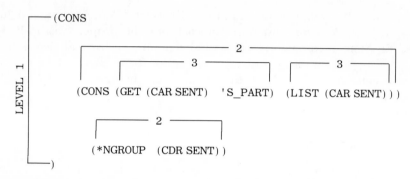

The initial CONS (Level 1) has two arguments (each at Level 2), as required. The first of these Level 2 arguments is another CONS, which in turn has its own required two arguments (Level 3). The first of these Level-3 arguments finds the part of speech for the word being processed, using the GET function. This part of speech is now CONSed with the word being processed (the second Level 3). The built-in function LIST used in this second Level-3 argument simply takes the *word* or *atom* that is currently the CAR of SENT and puts parentheses around it so it *becomes a list*. This step is necessary because the CONS function must always have a list as its second argument. So, using our example sentence, since the first word in the sentence SENT is "the," the Level 2 CONS will evaluate to

(DET THE) .

This sublist, in turn, is the *first argument in the Level 1* CONS. Following the rules for the CONS function, it gets placed as the CAR of the second (Level 2) argument, which is a recursive call to *NGROUP to start the process over using as an argument the list (CDR SENT)—which, in turn, is the rest of the sentence with the word "the" eliminated. Using the example sentence, this recursive call will result in a second sublist

(ADJ BLUE)

which in turn will then be CONSed with the result of the next recursion,

(NOUN BALL) .

On the next, and last, recursion, (CAR SENT) is a verb. When Line 2 of the function finds the verb, it returns NIL (the empty list) as the value of this last recursive call. This value causes the various sublists (stored until now temporarily on the stack) to be CONSed. The resulting evaluation will, of course, appear as

```
((DET THE) (ADJ BLUE) (NOUN BALL)).
```

The NGCHK and NGCHK1 Functions

Having isolated and identified the word group located before the verb, the parser must now check it to determine if it follows the rules of the grammar. Stating this operation verbally, the check must look for *just one* determiner, followed by *either* (1) *just one* noun *or* (2) *any number* of adjectives followed by *just one* noun; and in all cases the noun must be the last word in the list. The following pair of "helper" functions—interacting recursive predicate functions—will do the chore nicely, returning a value of *T* to the main function if the argument list NG satisfies any of the grammatical options and NIL if it does not:

```
(DEFUN NGCHK (NGP)
      (COND ((NOT (EQUAL (CAAR NGP) 'DET)) NIL)
            ((NGCHK1 (CDR NGP)) T)
            (T NIL)))

(DEFUN NGCHK1 NGP)
      (COND ((NULL NGP) NIL)
            ((EQUAL (CAAR NGP) 'NOUN)
                   (COND ((NULL (CDR NGP)) T)
                         (T NIL)))
            ((EQUAL (CAAR NGP) 'ADJ) (NGCHK1 (CDR NGP)))
            (T NIL)))
```

When the NG list—((DET THE) (ADJ BLUE) (NOUN BALL))) in our example—is passed as an argument to NGCHK, that function checks for a DET in the first-word position. This test is accomplished in Line 2 of NGCHK, using the built-in function NOT in conjunction with EQUAL. Recall that NOT changes *T* to NIL and NIL to *T*; so if the first word *is* a DET then the *p* condition of this (p e) COND clause evaluates to NIL and therefore execution proceeds to Line 3. Line 3 sends all of the NG list except the first word as an argument to the function NGCHK1.

The NGCHK1 function performs several tasks. Its second line returns NIL to the first function if the word list becomes empty before a noun is located. If NGP is *not* empty, control passes to Line 3. This line uses an interesting LISP tactic. If a noun is found in the *p* side of this (p e) COND clause, a COND statement is executed *in the e position*. This "COND-within-a-COND" tests to see if any word follows the noun just found, returning *T* if the noun is in fact the last word in the word group and NIL otherwise.

Line 4 of NGCHK1 contains a recursive call if an adjective is found. This recursion permits the function to find any number of adjectives, returning NIL if the last adjective is not followed by a noun (Line 2), and *T* if the last one is followed by a noun and no other word (Line 3). Finally, Line 5 returns NIL if on any execution of the function a word is found that has a part of speech *other than* ADJ *or* NOUN.

Analysis of the Verb Group

The rest of the parser can be written without difficulty by following the strategies already illustrated. A function called by some clever name such as *VGROUP, designed to isolate the string of words from the verb through the end of the sentence, could be written in a manner similar to *NGROUP. Then a syntax-checking function for the verb group (call it VGCHK) would need to be written to determine if it is well formed, and the program would be complete. The entire main PROG function for the model, including these additional verb group functions, would look like this:

```
(DEFUN PARSE (SENTENCE)  (PROG (S NG VG)
   (SETQ S SENTENCE)
   (SETQ NG (*NGROUP S))
   (PRINT NG)
   (PRINT (NGCHK NG))
   (SETQ VG (*VGROUP S))
   (PRINT VG)
   (PRINT (VGCHK (CDR VG)))
   (RETURN 'END-OF-PARSE)))
```

Construction of the *VGROUP and VGCHK functions are so similar to the ones just described for processing noun groups that they are left as an exercise for the reader, with encouragement to try writing them independently.

When the program PARSE is executed, a typical sample run with a well-formed sentence should look like this:

```
*  (PARSE '(THE BLUE BALL IS ON THE TABLE))
   ((DET THE)  (ADJ BLUE)  (NOUN BALL))
   T
   ((VB IS)  (PREP ON)  (DET THE)  (NOUN TABLE))
   T
   END-OF-PARSE
*
```

.

.

.

Note that PARSE has returned both the noun phrase and the verb phrase, with a *T* after each to indicate that both are well formed. An incorrectly structured sentence, however, would return the following:

```
*  (PARSE  '(THE BALL BLUE IS TABLE ON THE))
   ((DET THE) (NOUN BALL) (ADJ BLUE))
   NIL
   ((VB IS) (NOUN TABLE) (PREP ON) (DET THE))
   NIL
   END-OF-PARSE
*

                    .
                    .
                    .
```

While writing and testing this simple parsing model, you will un-doubtedly discover alternative ways to construct the necessary LISP func-tions, and will probably think of ways that it can be extended to parse more complex sentences. It's a long way from here to Winograd's robot; but the pursuit of such personal discoveries, hunches, and thoughts about ex-tending this sample exercise will offer the psychologist-programmer who is interested in how people learn, understand, and use language a useful start toward that goal.

CONCLUSION

In this chapter we learned how psychologists can use computing, and an extremely powerful programming language, to approach and study what is perhaps psychology's most complex and recalcitrant topic. No one yet knows all of the details concerning natural-language capability, of course; and in fact psychologists and linguists and AI researchers are just begin-ning to understand how people learn and comprehend language. Indeed, there are some who argue that we *never will* know much about this complex human process. But for those who are interested in pursuing such goals it is increasingly evident that computer modeling is a useful and valuable technique. By providing that nice combination of expressive rigor, formal testability, and the intellectual challenge of analyzing and resynthesizing complex processes, it has revitalized the interests and intellectual efforts of psychologists in an area that was once nearly unapproachable in a formal scientific sense.

SUGGESTED READINGS

For the reader who wishes to investigate language models in greater depth than the introductory level presented here, several good sources are available. Lachman, Lachman, and Butterfield (1979, Chapter 12) give excellent general descriptions of four important language models recently proposed by psychologists, including Anderson and Bower's (1973) HAM, Anderson's (1976, 1983) ACT, and Kintsch's (1974) theory. The first three of these have been implemented in computer programs, and their details can be found in the primary sources. A fifth model of considerable importance, called CDT (Conceptual Dependency Theory), has been developed by Schank, a computer scientist, and his colleagues (see Schank & Abelson, 1977; Schank & Riesbeck, 1981). Winograd's (1983) definitive text, entitled *Language as a Cognitive Process. Volume 1: Syntax,* is a must for the serious student of models of language comprehension. The book covers such topics as context-free grammars, transformational grammar, augmented transition network (ATN) grammars, and computer systems for parsing. If you want to see how advanced parsers can be constructed, Winston and Horn (1981, Chapters 19–21) describe LISP techniques and programs that perform syntactic analyses using ATNs.

EXERCISES

1. Use of a "miniature world," such as Winograd's blocks world, is a fairly common strategy in computer modeling and simulation. Why? Name some other miniature worlds we have encountered in this and previous chapters. What are their advantages and disadvantages?

2. The dictionary described in this chapter contained only the part of speech for each word.

    A. What other kinds of information would be useful in the dictionary if you were to build a computer model that would treat not only the syntax but also the semantics of word strings?

    B. Write a LISP program that will construct for any given word a property list containing the S-PART and at least one other type of information for the word. Have the program (1) ask the user for the word and the values of the properties you choose to enter in your dictionary, then (2) construct a property list for the word. A sample dictionary entry might be

        BALL ---> (S-PART NOUN SHAPE ROUND . . .)

    Arrange for the program to allow the user to construct property lists for any number of words before exiting from the program. (Note: You will need to use the built-in function (READ). Find its definition in Appendix E. The expression (SETQ XXX (READ)) will read input from the keyboard and assign it to XXX.)

    C. What are some of the difficulties, and decisions that will have to be made, when writing the kind of program described in 2B above?

3. Property lists may be used for storage and retrieval of many kinds of information in addition to dictionary knowledge. Write a LISP program that illustrates the construction and use of property lists in some area of psychology other than language processing.

4. Construct the parser described for the simple grammar presented on page 254. Test it with various sentences that are syntactically correct and incorrect to be sure that it handles all of the kinds of word strings the grammar allows.

5. Write a grammar that is more elaborate than the grammar on page 254; for example, one that includes questions as well as simple declarative sentences or handles different kinds of verbs. Write a LISP parser for your grammar.

13

Computer Modeling and Simulation of Human Problem Solving

A BRIEF HISTORICAL PERSPECTIVE

Problem solving occurs in situations where a person has a goal but no clear, known way to achieve it. Historically, experimental psychologists have studied human problem solving by asking people to solve some kind of puzzle or problem that is presented under controlled laboratory conditions that permit observation and measurement of their solutions. Information collected in such situations has led psychologists to describe the human problem-solving process as one in which the person develops, selects, and tests different approaches or *strategies* for solving the problem, trying each of these strategies in turn until the approach either leads to a solution or comes to a dead end. Often, after several false starts, a correct strategy suddenly becomes apparent, and the previously puzzled person is able to perform operations that he or she now "knows" will lead to problem solution. This is the famous "aha" experience of sudden insight about how a problem can be solved; it is a phenomenon that Gestalt psychologists have described as a change in *mental set,* which takes place when the problem and/or the tools necessary for its solution are perceived in a new way that makes the path to solution obvious.

The general facts about problem-solving behavior that have been discovered in the laboratory are of interest, but they raise in turn a number of questions that are particularly hard for the psychologist to investigate. The reason for this difficulty is, of course, that processes such as "developing solution strategies" or "changing mental set" are really *hypothesized mental operations* that, because they are not directly observable, are very difficult to examine. Thus important psychological questions about the way people solve problems remain unanswered. How does a person faced with a problem go about selecting the strategy he or she will take to try to solve it? Where, indeed, do such possible strategies come from? At what point should a given strategy be dropped and a new one formulated and tried? What processes result in the "aha" experience?

Although mental processing (cognitive) questions such as these have been difficult to answer in the psychology laboratory, interesting insights and possibilities have been generated using computer modeling and simulation techniques. In the 1950s a group of psychologists, stimulated mainly by the work of Herbert Simon and Allen Newell at Carnegie-Mellon University, began studying problem solving by writing computer programs that simulate the way humans presumably solve problems. They were among the early workers in artificial intelligence who focused upon designing programs to play complex games such as checkers and chess; and their views concerning problem solving were strongly influenced by that work, as well as by the developments in modern formal logic and cybernetics that were taking place at that time. From these influences, Newell and Simon constructed a theory of human thought and functioning in problem-solving situations that they called, prosaically, the *Information Processing System* (IPS). (You may recall that this theory was discussed briefly in Chapter 1.) In their challenging book, entitled *Human Problem Solving*, Newell and Simon (1972) describe in considerable detail the model and its applications to this psychological phenomenon.

In this chapter we will first examine briefly the major constructs and hypotheses upon which this information-processing model is based and then build a small LISP computer program that illustrates both Newell and Simon's theory and the strategy they use to study problem-solving processes. Before continuing, it is recommended that you go back to Chapter 1 and refresh your memory about the general structure of IPS.

NEWELL AND SIMON'S IPS

The Task Environment and the Problem Space

Having reviewed what was said in Chapter 1 about Newell and Simon's theory, we need to elaborate it a bit further. We know that IPS is based upon the general assumption that humans are *representable* as *information-processing systems.* With respect to problem solving, Newell and Simon make several additional pretheoretical assumptions:

(a)   the information processing representation (IPS) can be described in great detail for any given person and task;

(b)   substantial differences exist among *people* in the strategies or programs that detail how they solve problems—differences in program structure, method, and content;

(c)   substantial differences also exist among *tasks*, necessitating differences in the structure and content of the programs that operate upon them;

(d)   the task environment, plus the intelligence of the problem solver, determines to a large extent the problem-solver's behavior.
(Paraphrased from Newell & Simon, 1972, p. 788.)

From these assumptions, the two authors build a theory of human problem solving that is reflected in the following four propositions:

1.   A few, and only a few, gross characteristics of the human IPS are invariant over task and problem solver.

2.   These characteristics are sufficient to determine that a *task environment* is represented (in the IPS) as a *problem space,* and that problem solving takes place in a problem space.

3.   The structure of the task environment determines the possible structures of the problem space.

4.   The structure of the problem space determines the possible *programs* that can be used for problem solving.
(Newell & Simon, 1972, 788–789; italics added)

The terms *task environment, problem space,* and *programs* are important for their theory and thus need clarification.

The *task environment* in a problem-solving situation is the set of conditions *external* to the problem-solver, including the physical objects available, the goal or statement of the goal, and other instructions and information presented to the psychological subject. Figure 13–1 illustrates a typical task environment for a problem-solving situation—the person on the right is confronted with a board game (checkers or chess), an opponent, the rules of the game and other external stimuli. Historically, in this type of situation experimental psychologists have paid relatively little attention to the details of the external environment, probably because psychology is fundamentally concerned with the acting and reacting organism rather than the situation in which it acts or reacts. Newell and Simon claim that this is a mistake. They argue that in problem-solving situations an understanding of the task environment is critical because what the environment is, and the way it is presented, constrain the possible ways in which the subject can act or react.

This unusual emphasis upon the external environment explains why (unlike most psychological theorists) Newell and Simon's work is directed

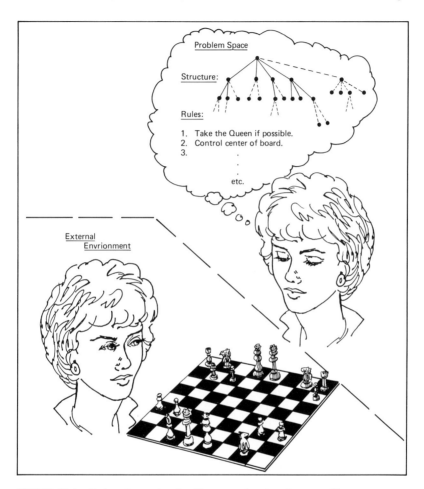

FIGURE 13–1.   Task environment and problem space for a board-game problem.

in large part at analyzing and evaluating in detail the tasks that are presented to their psychological subjects. The kinds of problems they have used in their own investigations are complex puzzles and games such as *number scrabble, cryptarithmetic, logic puzzles,* and *chess;* and substantial parts of their 1972 book are, in fact, devoted to task analyses of these problems. The use of such tasks, and the emphasis upon their structural and other characteristics, are considered by many to be insightful and valuable additions to the methodologies used traditionally by psychologists in the study of problem solving.

The task environment influences in turn the *problem space* of the problem-solver. This latter term is used when referring to the *internal* representation of the problem—that whole psychological arena in which problem-solving activity takes place (see Fig. 13–1). The problem space is a major construct of Newell and Simon's theory. Like most good constructs, it is an abstraction designed to help the theorists describe and analyze the psychological phenomenon in which they are interested. Newell and Simon define it formally by saying that it is the internal representation consisting of:

1. A *set of elements,* U, which are symbol structures, each representing a state of knowledge about the task.
2. A *set of operators,* Q, which are information processes, each producing new states of knowledge from existing states of knowledge.
3. An *initial state of knowledge,* u, which is the knowledge about the task that the problem solver has at the start of problem solving.
4. A *problem,* which is posed by specifying a set of final, desired states, G, to be reached by applying operators from Q.
5. The *total knowledge available* to the problem solver when he is in a given knowledge state, which includes (ordered from most transient to most stable):
   (a) *Temporary dynamic information* created and used exclusively within a single knowledge state.
   (b) The *knowledge state* itself—the dynamic information about the task.
   (c) *Access information* to the additional symbol structures held in LTM or EM (the *extended knowledge state*).
   (d) *Path information* about how a given knowledge state was arrived at and what other actions were taken in this state if it has already been visited on prior occasions.
   (e) *Access information to other knowledge states* that have been reached previously and are now held in LTM or EM.
   (f) *Reference information* that is constant over the course of problem solving, available in LTM or EM.
   Newell & Simon, 1972, (p. 810)

An Example

To get some feel for Newell and Simon's theoretical structure, let us look at what they say about their simplest "problem"—the game of Number Scrabble. In the process we shall see how the structure of the problem space determines the *programs* used for solving the problem. This is a two-person game with the following rules:

A set of nine cardboard squares (pieces), like those used in the game of Scrabble, is placed, face-up, between the two players. Each piece bears a different integer, from 1 to 9, so that all nine digits are represented. The players draw pieces alternately from the set. The first player who holds any subset of exactly three pieces, from among those he has drawn, with digits summing to 15, wins. If all the pieces are drawn from the set without either player obtaining three whose digits sum to 15, the game is a draw. Thus, if the alternate draws are 2,7; 5,8; 4,6; 9, the first player wins, since $2 + 4 + 9 = 15$. If the alternate draws are 5,2; 8,6; 7,3; 1,9; 4, neither player wins, since no combination of three digits selected from the set (5, 8, 7, 1, 4) sums to 15, nor does any combination of three selected from the set (2, 6, 3, 9). (From Newell & Simon, 1972, pp. 59–60)

To complete the description of the *task environment* for this problem, we add that each player (problem-solver) is told that the goal is to play for either a win or a draw.

And what are the ways in which a problem-solver might solve this problem? To answer this question, the psychologist can analyze the problem itself (the task environment), or study the various strategies people follow as they actually play the game (and thus infer possible problem spaces), or combine these methods in some fashion.

If we look first at the task, there are at least two major ways in which the game can be represented formally in the *problem space*. One is by using a *game-tree*, as shown in Figure 13–2. Starting at the root of this tree, where the game begins, all of the possible plays in the game can be traced by following the various paths from the root to each end branch. Obviously, there will be many end branches (Newell and Simon calculate there are 9! = 352,880 of them). It is clear also that only some of the various branches will result in wins, whereas others will lead to draws or losses. But the structure defines the game perfectly in a formal and objective sense; so the psychologist raises the question of whether this *external* representation might also be a useful *internal* representation that intelligent problem-solvers might include as part of their problem space when they develop and follow a strategy for solving the problem.

The answer to this psychological question, when we consider both empirical evidence and the IPS theoretical model, is—probably not. It is inefficient, because much of the information is unnecessary to goal solution. And, because human memory is rather constrained, the tree appears to be too large for the system (IPS) to handle it all effectively.

A second representation offered by Newell and Simon (1972, pp. 59–71) seems more fruitful psychologically. In looking at the game-tree, they recognize that it represents not only Number Scrabble but also the familiar game of tic-tac-toe. In tic-tac-toe there are also nine elements in the game, the players alternately choose elements one at a time, and the goal is to either play for a draw or to pick one of only a few winning combinations of three of the objects. Moreover, most people know how to play this game and have probably developed strategies for playing. Is it possible that there can be positive transfer from solution of one problem-game to solution of the other?

Looking at the external task itself, the answer to this question is clearly yes. First, a *task analysis* shows that the tic-tac-toe problem can be represented concisely by the "magic square" displayed in Figure 13–3. Representing the game in this manner, it can be seen that for any winning tic-

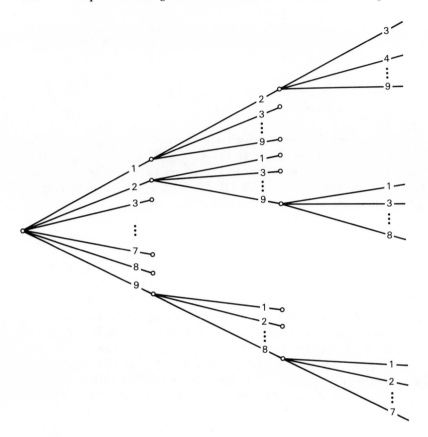

FIGURE 13–2. A game-tree representation of Number Scrabble.
(Reproduced from Newell & Simon, 1972, p. 61; with permission.)

tac-toe move the values of the three squares producing the win will sum to 15. This solution is, of course, identical conceptually to the goal in Number Scrabble, even though the task environments of these two problems differ dramatically. This representation, then, provides all of the information required to solve the Number Scrabble problem. Clearly it is more compact and efficient than the game-tree in Figure 13–2.

And is this formal representation a feasible internal representation for the problem-solver? Is it a good contender for that portion of the subjects' problem space, which—along with other components (see the list on page 268)—will describe how the subject represents and operates upon the problem psychologically? Most of us would agree that the magic square could be stored and accessed quite easily in human memory, and thus is a considerably more feasible structural alternative than the game-tree.

But remember that this efficient internal representation would still be only *part* of the problem space—the part that is covered by Items 1, 3, and 4

2	7	6
9	5	1
4	3	8

FIGURE 13–3. A "magic square" representation of tic-tac-toe and Number Scrabble.

in Newell and Simon's definition of the problem space (p. 270). Another critical aspect of the problem space is Item 2 in the list—the set of *operators* that can be performed on the internal representation and would guide the actual moves of the game. Even within this rather precise and efficient magic-square representation, there are a number of potential operations— which, when combined in certain sequences, become solution strategies— that a person might use to solve the problem. Some of these will be better than others, of course; and there is probably some ideal strategy—used, perhaps, by master Number Scrabble players—that will best solve the problem most of the time. Newell and Simon look upon these various potential strategies as internal *programs* that people might use for problem solving. Thus the fourth and final proposition upon which their problem-solving theory is based (p. 268) states that the way the person structures the problem (game-tree, magic square, or otherwise) influences the choice of strategies or *programs* available to the problem-solver.

Newell and Simon's use of the word "program" as a synonym for strategy is not at all fortuitous, for in fact they rely heavily upon computing and computer concepts when studying problem-solving strategies. From a *theoretical* standpoint, we know that they view the person in the problem-solving situation as an IPS. It seems quite consistent, then, to say that the sequence of behaviors that the person goes through to solve the problem is a "program" that processes the information in certain well-defined ways. From a computer *applications* standpoint, on the other hand, construction of a program that is a computer model of a problem-solving strategy serves the same two major purposes that we have encountered in other situations: (1) computer models help to define and clarify the theoretical ideas (including their shortcomings and inconsistencies); and (2) when executed as simulations, they provide tests of the theory.

A COMPUTER MODEL THAT PLAYS NUMBER SCRABBLE

Having become acquainted with the theory, let us look at how a LISP computer model of an internal *program*, determined by the "magic square" representation in the *problem space*, may be constructed so that it will simulate the solution to the relatively simple task of Number Scrabble. To do so, we must first review a new programming technique.

Production Systems

One of the discoveries that Newell and Simon have made in their empirical investigations of problem solving is that the kinds of programs people tend to use when solving problems can be characterized conveniently by what are called *production systems*. A production system is a particular way that a program is organized. Basically, a production system is organized as a set of *condition-action pairs*. The conditions and actions follow these general rules:

1. The instructions of the program are a set of "if-then" rules, each consisting of a *condition* to be tested and an *action* to be taken if the condition is present— that is, *if* a condition exists, *then perform* a specified set of operations;
2. these conditional instructions (each one called a *production*) are *ordered*, so that the condition of the most important production is tested first, then the next most important, and so on;
3. when the actions associated with any production have been executed, program control does not proceed serially to the next production in the series, but *returns to the top of the production system and begins* again.

These condition-action rules can be used to describe a large number of human skills and operations in many contexts, including problem solving. The descriptions may be either verbal or graphic, and can define in considerable detail the strategies people use to reach desired goals. To illustrate, consider what seems on the surface to be the simple task of starting a car that has an automatic transmission. Figure 13–4 represents graphically the strategy for solving this problem. The strategy can also be illustrated in a verbal flowchart:

STARTING A CAR:

P1: is engine running? → activate DRIVE production system, stop;

P2: is hand twisting key in ignition and starter inactive? → is car in gear? → put in neutral, continue;
T → call mechanic, stop;

P3: is hand twisting key in ignition and starter active? → continue;
P4: is key in ignition? → twist key;
P5: is key in hand? → insert key in ignition;
P6: is key in pocket? → grasp key in hand;
P7: T → activate GETKEY production system, stop.

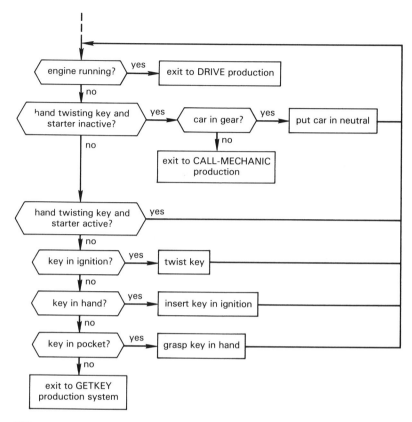

FIGURE 13–4. Flow diagram of production system for starting a car.

This production system consists of seven productions, each one holding a specific place in the serial order. The conditions on the left side of each production are expressed in predicate form; that is, to use our LISP terminology, the condition will evaluate to either *T* or NIL. The actions to be taken are found on the right side of the arrows in the verbal flowchart, and are only executed if the condition on the left side evaluates to *T*. Note that an *action* may be very simple (for example, continue or stop), it may branch to other production systems (DRIVE, GET-MECHANIC, GETKEY), or it may really be a set of actions that themselves are organized as a production system (see the second production in the example above). Likewise, a *condition* may be either very simple (the *T* in the last production above), or consist of a single test, or of two or more tests in conjunction (see the second and third productions above).

Obviously, systems having this much flexibility can themselves become quite complex and can describe quite complex strategies. Yet, despite the overall complexity, each test or action is relatively simple. This translation of a complex situation into an ordered set of simple perceptions and motor activities is of considerable interest psychologically. When used as models of human problem-solving strategies, production systems imply that, in spite of the overall complexity, at any given moment there is relatively little load placed upon such human psychological capacities (and frailties) as short-term memory, attention, visual scanning and detection, or motor performance.

Possible Strategies

With the organization and potential value of production systems defined, let us try to design and write a production system that models the problem-solving strategy needed to play the game of Number Scrabble. It is immediately apparent, however, that there are actually a number of potential strategies. For example, a very basic strategy—one that a child or novice player might use when first learning to play the game—is to simply pick a number each time one's turn comes around and, after the first two are picked, pick a winning number if one is left on the board. Simple (and simple-minded) as this strategy is, it already involves several productions; for example:

SIMPLE-SCRABBLE:

P1: are all pieces gone from the board?   → say "It's a draw," stop;
P2: did opponent just yell "I win!"?   → grimace, stop;
P3: are there fewer than 2
      pieces in my hand?   → pick a piece at random from board;
P4: is 15 minus the sum of any two pieces
      in my hand still on the board?   → pick that piece, holler "I win!", grin,
                                            stop;
P5: T   → pick a piece at random from board.

Obviously, this strategy will yield few wins or draws after even the first few games with a novice as opponent.

To discover other strategies, or at least other productions that could be grouped together to form reasonable strategy systems, we must analyze the problem in further detail, looking for those tests and actions that are essential or desirable in order to achieve the goal of a win or draw. The ideal strategy, even for this relatively simple game, is a rather complex process; and Newell and Simon take more than 10 pages to describe and discuss it. We can understand the general structure of a winning, although perhaps not ideal, strategy more briefly here by studying the following top-level design of a production system for the game:

WIN-SCRABBLE:

P1: are all pieces gone from board?   → declare a draw, stop;
P2: is 15 minus the sum of any 2
     pieces in my hand still on board?   → pick that piece to win, stop;
P3: is 15 minus the sum of any 2
     pieces in opponent's hand on board? → pick that piece;
P4: is the 5-piece on the board?   → pick the 5-piece;
P5: does opponent have an
     even-numbered
     piece X such that 10-X is on board   → pick 10-X;
P6: do I have an even-numbered piece Y
     such that 10Y is on board?   → pick 10-Y;
P7: is there an even-numbered piece on
     board?   → pick that piece;
P8: T   → pick any piece.

In this strategy, production P1 should indeed come first because its condition necessarily stops the game. P2 will also stop the game with a win. If neither P1 nor P2 results in actions, then in P3 the strategy defends against a next-move win by the opponent. Note, however, that the P3 condition requires either a good short-term memory or an algorithm that will reconstruct the opponent's pieces* and then test all combinations of two of them in search of a winning move. Either alternative is a formidable psychological task for many people when they are caught up in a tense game situation, and it is possible that for the typical player this production is either not present or works only part of the time.

The P4 strategy is a good one because the 5-piece, like the center position of tic-tac-toe (see Fig. 13–3), is the most versatile piece in the game. Putting this action relatively high in the production priorities assures that the player will pick it up on the first move if the opponent hasn't already taken it.

The P5, P6, and P7 productions are all associated with what tic-tac-toe experts call a *forking move*—a strategy that sets up the game for a possible win in the future. The magic square shown in Figure 13–3 reveals the rationale for the forking move. Any player who does *not* have the 5-piece but can get any three of the four corners (even numbers) will have two winning possibilities. Any player *having* the 5-piece will have a multiple-win possibility by possessing only two of the four corners (even numbers). In either case, the opponent can defend against only one of the possibilities on the next draw, and so the player with a successful forking move will win.

Alternatively, the best defense against a forking move is to try to gain

---

*If Number Scrabble is played like word Scrabble, then players cannot see each other's pieces.

possession of the opposite corner whenever the opponent picks an even number. The magic square shows that given any even number, the opposite corner contains the *tens complement* of that number; that is, the number that, when added to the given number, will yield the sum of 10. Calculation of the tens complement for any number X is simply $10 - X$.

With these fascinating bits of knowledge about forking moves now clearly in mind, we can see that productions P5, P6, and P7, placed in proper order, constitute good offensive *or* defensive moves, depending upon the state of the game. Also, note that P5, like P3, requires a good short-term memory and/or a substantial number-manipulation algorithm, making it susceptible to difficulties in human performance under tension. Naturally, P8 follows, but only because other possibilities have been exhausted.

The Program

And now, at last, we have sufficient psychological and computing background to write a reasonable LISP model of a strategy for solving the Number Scrabble program. To keep the task manageable, we shall construct only a limited subset of the winning strategy just described and leave the full strategy as an advanced exercise for the serious psychologist-programmer. Specifically, let us assume that the person (the IPS) we are modeling is a new player who understands the forking move but that he or she has a poor short-term memory and has either not discovered, or is incapable of operating, an algorithm that permits review of the opponent's pieces. This makes him or her a good offensive player but a poor defensive player—with serious consequences at times. The production system characterizing such a player's strategy might look like this:

NO-DEFENSE-STRATEGY:

P1:	is board empty?	→ declare draw, stop;
P2:	is 15 minus sum of any 2 pieces in my hand on board?	→ pick that piece, declare win, stop;
P3:	is tens complement of opponent's last move on board?	→ pick that piece;
P4:	is the 5-piece on board?	→ pick that piece;
P5:	is the tens complement of any of my even pieces on board?	→ pick that piece;
P6:	is an even piece on board?	→ pick that piece;
P7:	T	→ pick any piece.

For the sake of simplicity, we follow the procedure used in previous examples of LISP and write a PROG function as a main program that calls other types of LISP functions as needed. If the name of the main function is SCRABBLE, and it has as a single argument a list of the pieces that make up the board when play begins, then we can call the function with the statement:

```
*  (SCRABBLE '(1 2 3 4 5 6 7 8 9))
   .
   .
   .
```

and play will continue from there.

As is usually the case for any program, there are bound to be at least a few "housekeeping" chores that must be taken care of before the main portion of the program is executed. Figure 13–5, a top-level design for the main program, shows that in order to play Number Scrabble provision must be made to (1) establish data structures to contain the board pieces, the opponent's pieces, the player's pieces; (2) establish who will make the first move; and (3) provide for a human opponent to interact with the model by inputting moves and reading the current state of the game after each move is made. The following segment, which carries the program to the point where the production system begins, shows one way to accomplish these chores.

```
(DEFUN SCRABBLE (BOARD)     (PROG (BD PLYR OPP A)
      (SETQ BD BOARD)
      (SETQ PLYR '())
      (SETQ OPP '())
      (SETQ A 1)
    (PRINC "WILL YOU START?<TYPE YES OR NO.")  (TERPRI)
    (COND ((EQUAL (READ) 'NO) (GO PLAYER)))
  TOP
    (TERPRI)
    (OUTPT PLYR OPP BD)
    (COND ((NULL BD) (RETURN 'IT*IS*A*DRAW)))
    (PRINC "YOUR PLAY--PICK FROM BOARD")  (TERPRI)
    (SETQ A (READ))
    (COND ((OPPWIN A OPP) (RETURN 'YOU*WIN!)))
    (SETQ OPP (CONS A OPP))
    (SETQ BD (REMOVE A BD))
  PLAYER
      .
      .
      .
```

In this segment the local variables within PROG are

```
BD     = list of current pieces on board
PLYR   = list of current pieces in the hand of
         the player being modeled
```

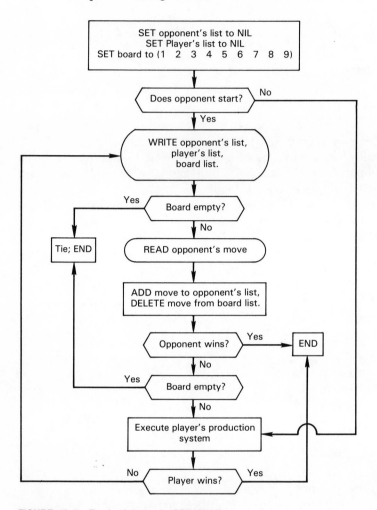

FIGURE 13–5. Top-level design for SCRABBLE.

OPP = list of current pieces in opponent's hand

A = a multipurpose temporary variable used in various places in the main function

You should examine carefully the use of the built-in function READ in Lines 7 and 13 of the segment above. This function, which has no arguments, is the major input instruction in LISP. When evaluated it reads *a number, an atom, or a list* from the user's keyboard, and what is read becomes the value of the function. Thus when the human SCRABBLE player, in response to the message on Line 6, types YES or NO on the keyboard followed by a carriage return, the (READ) in Line 7 evaluates to that word (in this case, an atom). The atom then becomes the first argument for the EQUAL function in Line 7. In similar fashion, when the user picks a number from the board (Line 12), that number is read by (READ) in Line 13 and becomes the second argument to the SETQ function on that line.

The user functions OUTPT, OPPWIN, and REMOVE in the SCRABBLE segment above also deserve some description. OUTPT, with the lists PLYR, OPP, BD as arguments, is simply a function that will print and label these three lists—allowing the human player (the opponent, or the experimenter) to see the current states of the player's hand, the opponent's hand, and the board, respectively. It can be written like this:

```
(DEFUN OUTPT (P O B) (PROG ()
    (PRINC "PRESENT PLAYER, OPPONENT (BOARD STATES, ARE: ")
    (TERPRI)
    (PRINT P) (PRINT O) (PRINT B) (TERPRI) (RETURN)))
```

Note that even when PROG has no local variables it must have a variable list, so the null list () is provided.

OPPWIN is a predicate, recursive function that evaluates to *T* if the opponent's list contains three numbers adding to 15, otherwise NIL is returned. This test gets a bit complex, because as the number of pieces in the opponent's list grows the number of combinations of three numbers that must be tested increases and becomes cumbersome. For example, if the opponent picks the 9-piece and the current list OPP contains the numbers

(3 4 1 5)

the function must test the following combinations: $9+3+4$, $9+3+1$. $9+3+5$, $9+4+1$, $9+4+5$, before getting to $9+1+5=15$. Fortunately, however, LISP is recursive and thus the following two functions, working together, can perform the test effectively regardless of the size of the opponent's list:

```
(DEFUN OPPWIN (PICK LST)
    (COND ((NULL LST) NIL)
          ((WINA PICK (CAR LST) (CDR LST)) T)
          (T (OPPWIN PICK (CDR LST)))))

(DEFUN WINA (PICK NUM L)
    (COND ((NULL L) NIL)
          ((EQUAL (PLUS PICK (PLUS NUM (CAR L))) 15) T)
          (T (WINA PICK NUM (CDR L)))))
```

The arguments to OPPWIN are the piece picked by the opponent (PICK) and the list of pieces that the opponent currently possesses (LST). Use as an example PICK = 9 and LST = (3 4 1 5) to work through these functions and see how they cooperate with each other to return a correct value *T*.

REMOVE is not a predicate function, but is designed instead to remove a piece *A* from the board and then return the new board with *A* missing. This is a standard construction type of function in LISP, and in our program it can be used to remove from the board the pieces chosen by either the opponent or the simulated player. With PICK as the piece picked and LIST as the present board, it looks like this:

```
(DEFUN REMOVE  (PICK LIST)
    (COND  ((NULL LIST) NIL)
           ((NOT  (EQUAL PICK  (CAR LIST)))  (CONS  (CAR LIST)
                                   (REMOVE PICK  (CDR LIST))))
           (T  (REMOVE PICK  (CDR LIST))))))
```

Note that (1) this function uses CONS to build a new list that is eventually returned as the value of the function; (2) in Line 3, CONS is evaluated only if PICK and (CAR LIST) are *not* equal, and if they *are* equal control passes to (3) Line 4, which in effect "loses" the item in LIST that is equal to PICK.

With these housekeeping problems solved the player's strategy—that is, the production system—can be written. The remaining instructions needed in the main function are surprisingly mundane, because the best way to write a production system in LISP is to construct separate functions for all but the simplest conditions and actions. Matching the productions in the program to those in the verbal flowchart on page 278, we proceed as follows:

```
              .
              .
              .
PLAYER
  (COND
     ((NULL  BD)        (RETURN 'IT*IS*A*DRAW))
     ((P2  PLYR  BD)    (PROG2  (WIN  (P2 PLYR BD))
                        (OUTPT PLYR OPP BD) (RETURN 'I*WIN)))
     ((P3  A  BD)       (PROG2  (SETQ A  (P3 A BD)) (GO CONTINUE)))
     ((MEMBER  5  BD)   (PROG2  (SETQ A 5) (GO CONTINUE)))
     ((P5  PLYR  BD)    (PROG2  (SETQ A  (P5 PLYR BD)) (GO CONTINUE)))
     ((P6  BD)          (PROG2  (SETQ A  (P6 BD)) (GO CONTINUE))))
     (SETQ A  (CAR BD)))
  CONTINUE
     (SETQ PLYR  (CONS A PLYR))
     (SETQ BD  (REMOVE A BD))
     (GO  TOP)))
```

You should pause a moment at this point to study carefully the arrangement that starts with COND below the line labeled PLAYER. Note that the six (p e) clauses in this COND statement correspond to the productions P1 through P6 of the strategy being modeled. In the *p* position is the *condition* for the production and, of course, the *action* occupies the *e* position. The productions P1 and P4 have such simple conditions that the built-in LISP functions NULL and MEMBER can be used, respectively, to make the necessary conditional tests. The production P7 really has no condition, so P7 is represented by the statement (SETQ A (CAR BD)) that follows the last conditional statement. The remaining productions have more complex test conditions. User-built functions—labeled P2, P3, P5, and P6 to correspond to the production labels in the verbal flowchart on page 278—must be written for each of them. These functions will be discussed in a moment.

On the *action* or *e* side of each of the conditional statements, several interesting programming features should be noted. First, the productions P1 and P2 contain RETURN statements in their actions, while all other actions end with (GO CONTINUE). Recall that in a PROG function a RETURN command evaluates the function *and* halts its execution. Because P1 and P2 result in either a draw or a win to end the game, the RETURN is used as an appropriate action to report the outcome and then halt the entire main PROG function SCRABBLE.

The (GO CONTINUE) command, on the other hand, is the programming equivalent to the production-system rule that, following the action of any production, control returns to the top of the system. Actually, in the program written here the CONTINUE label is *below* the production system; but control remains there only long enough to update the PLYR and BD lists (simply a housekeeping chore), then goes to the top of the sequence to resume play by asking the opponent to make a move.

The remaining task in the program analysis is to examine the user functions that are called in the production system written above. There are four of them on the conditional side (P2, P3, P5, and P6) and one on the action side (WIN). Of these, P2 and P3 are a bit complicated, so it is instructive to look at them in some detail. When their structure is understood, the others will be quite comprehensible at a glance.

Programming the P2 Production

The objective of the conditional part of the P2 production is to decide whether, given the player's current hand and the current board, a winning move is possible; and, if so, which piece should be taken from the board to accomplish the win. This set of decisions is complex enough to qualify as a subproblem within the main problem. As such, it calls for a strategy that will analyze the subproblem into a set of elementary steps that, when executed in a properly ordered program, will give a solution. So, looking at the

P2 production from the standpoint of either the psychologist-programmer or the typical human subject playing the game, we must develop an algorithm (a strategy) that will permit attainment of the subgoal.

The analysis of this subproblem is straightforward. A winning number on the board will be the *fifteens complement* of the sum of any pair of numbers in the player's hand. The practical strategy, then, is to (1) pick a pair of numbers from the player's hand; (2) find the fifteens complement of their sum; and (3) scan the board to determine if that number is present. If this strategy is continued for all possible pairs, it will eventually yield a predicate—that is, the last step (3) will be either a *T* at some point or else will give a NIL for all of the possible pairs.

Reviewing this analysis, the experienced LISP programmer will immediately recognize step 3 as the MEMBER function—that is, each time a fifteens complement of a pair of pieces is calculated, MEMBER can determine if that element (the first argument) is a member of the list BD.

Storing this easy solution (3) in mind for later use, we must develop plans for solving the other steps as well. Turning to step 2, we write the following LISP function to find the fifteens complement of any number. Will it do the job?

```
(DEFUN COMP-15 (N)
    (COND  ((GREATERP N 15)  0)
           (T (DIFFERENCE 15 N)))))
```

(Remember that GREATERP is a built-in predicate function that evaluates to *T* if the first of the two numerical arguments is greater than the second, otherwise it evaluates to NIL.)

The remaining task is to find a way of testing *all possible* pairs in the player's current hand. A good method is to pick the first number in the hand and pair it successively with all of the following numbers, then pick the second number in the hand and compare it with all of the following numbers *except* the one previously tested, and so on. For example, if the player's hand was

(1 3 5 8)

then the successive pairs chosen by this method would be: $1+3$, $1+5$, $1+8$, $3+5$, $3+8$, $5+7$. Translating this procedure into LISP, and combining it with the COMP-15 and MEMBER solutions described above, we can write P2 and a supporting function PAIR as follows:

```
(DEFUN P2 (PL B)
    (COND ((NULL PL) NIL)
          ((NULL (CDR PL)) NIL)
          ((PAIR (CAR PL)  (CDR PL) B) (PAIR (CAR PL) (CDR PL) B))
          (T (P2 (CDR PL) B)))))
```

```
(DEFUN PAIR (FIRST-NUM LST BRD)
   (COND ((NULL LST) NIL)
         ((MEMBER (COMP-15 (PLUS FIRST-NUM (CAR LST))) BRD)
                  (COMP-15 (PLUS FIRST-NUM (CAR LST))))
         (T (PAIR FIRST-NUM (CDR LST) BRD)))))
```

The two lists passed as arguments to P2 are PL = the player's current hand, and B = the current board.

Semi-Predicates

Both P2 and PAIR demonstrate an aspect of the recursive and COND functions that has not been encountered until now. Note first that both of them are predicate functions when a winner is *not* found, in that they both evaluate to NIL if the player's hand or the board is exhausted. However, looking at the third line in PAIR, notice that if MEMBER evaluates to *T* (that is, a winner is found on the board), the *e* part of the COND clause does not cause the function PAIR to evaluate to *T*, but rather to *the winning number.* So PAIR is not *purely* a predicate function, because one of its possible values is neither *T* nor NIL.

Could this cause a problem in the program? For example, PAIR is a *p* element in a COND clause in Line 4 of P2, and so the proper operation of P2 depends upon whether PAIR evaluates to *T* or NIL. Because PAIR clearly *can* evaluate to NIL but, being an "impure" predicate function, *cannot* evaluate to *T*, what happens?

The answer requires that we, and the LISP language, hedge a bit on the pure definition of a predicate. In LISP, a function can serve as a predicate for COND if it evaluates to NIL or to *any non-NIL value,* with the latter domain of values *all being interpreted as T.* Technically, predicate functions of this type should be called *semi-predicates* because they can evaluate to actual values such as numbers, other atoms, or lists, but still can be interpreted as predicates on the conditional or *p* side of a COND clause. Thus P2 and PAIR are examples of such semi-predicates.

The semi-predicate is useful because it can allow a function to serve a double purpose. It makes a true-false test, as needed in both production systems and LISP generally, but at the same time it can identify information if the test proves to be true. Thus, in the P2 and PAIR functions, if a winning number is found then both functions *evaluate to that number.*

Looking back now at the production system in the main function SCRABBLE (p. 282), we find that P2 is in fact used in a COND clause as *both* a predicate function (in the *p* position) *and* a numerical function (as part of *e*); specifically it is used like this:

```
((P2 PLYR BD) (PROG2 (WIN (P2 PLYR BD)) ....))))
```

The operation here is:

> if P2 evaluates to NIL go to the next COND clause;
>
> if P2 evaluates to a number, assume the value *T* for the *p* segment of this COND clause, and the numeric value of P2 as the argument to the function WIN, which labels and prints the winning board selection.

Programming the P3 Production

By comparison with P2, an analysis of P3 will be fairly easy to understand. In this production, the player must first recall the opponent's last pick (a minor short-term memory requirement) and determine if it was an even number, and, if so, to search the board for its tens complement. If the tens complement is on the board, the player will pick it. We know how to get the complement of a number, and how to search the board, so the LISP programming required to accomplish P3 is not difficult:

```
(DEFUN P3 (NUM BRD)
   (COND ((NOT (EQUAL (REMAINDER NUM 2) 0)) NIL)
         ((MEMBER (COMP-10 NUM) BRD) (COMP-10 NUM))
         (T NIL)))

(DEFUN COMP-10 (N)
   (COND ((GREATERP N 10) 0)
         (T (DIFFERENCE 10 N)))))
```

The only new technique, in Line 2 of P3, is the test for whether the numeric value for NUM is even. Using the built-in LISP function REMAINDER, we divide NUM by 2 and test whether the remainder from this division is 0. If it is, then of course NUM is an even number. Remember, however, that EQUAL is a predicate function, and so it will evaluate to *T* if the remainder equals 0. To make the test evaluate to NIL if NUM is even, and thus allow program execution to continue on the next COND clause, we simply make the value of EQUAL the argument for NOT. Because the built-in function NOT changes *T* to NIL and NIL to *T,* it is clear that the *p* segment of this COND clause will result in an evaluation of P3 to NIL if NUM is not even; otherwise it will result in execution of the next COND clause, which searches the board for the tens complement of NUM.

A number of other supporting functions must be written—P5, P6, WIN—before the main SCRABBLE function can become operative. By comparison with those just covered, however, they are neither conceptually abstract nor do they require LISP programming techniques beyond those already covered. The reader is invited to try to write them without further help or explanation.

CONCLUSION

In this chapter we learned how information-processing psychologists can use computing to test and demonstrate hypotheses about the ways that people solve problems. Because of the complexity of the topic, the program illustration was necessarily limited in several ways. Obviously the problem upon which it was based is not nearly as complex as those that many people encounter in real life. Also, it shows only a single solution strategy and provides no capability for improving its strategy on the basis of experience (learning), or generalizing its strategy to other similar problems or situations. Indeed, the model as written does not account for how it adopted its strategy in the first place.

These shortcomings are acceptable, probably desirable, when the primary objective is to gain some experience in reading and using the LISP language. They become more serious if the objective is to construct and test a comprehensive theory of problem solving. Unfortunately, however, the development of comprehensive theories of problem solving is still in its embryonic stage, and many critical theoretical questions have not been fully resolved. Few if any of the current theoretical efforts can address effectively the questions of how strategies are developed, or how they are selected for testing, or how they are refined by experience, or become generalizable to other similar problems. So there is still much work to be done before psychologists can begin to feel they really understand the problem-solving process. Even so, interesting research and theorizing are going on; and computer modeling and simulation are clearly contributing to the process.

SUGGESTED READINGS

Several of the recent texts in cognitive psychology (Anderson, 1980; Mayer, 1983; Reynolds & Flagg, 1983; Solso, 1979) contain very readable chapters describing in greater detail the historical psychological research in problem solving and how it has evolved to the information-processing and computer-modelling orientations described in this chapter. A brief history of the development of the first computer models of problem solving, and their impact upon both cognitive psychology and artificial intelligence, can be found in McCorduck's *Machines Who Think* (1979, Chapters 5–7). Newell and Simon (1972) summarize their theory and research in Chapter 14 of their text. Theoretical alternatives to Newell and Simon can be found in Wickelgren's (1974) book entitled *How to Solve Problems: Elements of a Theory of Problems and Problem Solving;* in a theory presented by Greeno (1973), which emphasizes the importance of memory; and in a structural/process approach proposed by Scandura (1977). A recent text by Hayes (1981) follows up the Newell-Simon theory, and in addition offers instruction in how to improve your own problem-solving ability. If you want to try solving a number of interesting problems that emphasize changes in mental set, you can find them in Martin Gardner's (1978) enjoyable book entitled *Aha! Insight.*

EXERCISES

1. Rewrite the first two lines of the SCRABBLE function (p. 279) so it can be called without giving an argument; for example:

   * (SCRABBLE)
           .
           .
           .

2. Complete the model described in this chapter by constructing LISP functions P5, P6, and WIN. (The WIN function simply labels and prints the winning board selection.)

3. Add memory to the SCRABBLE model as written, allowing it to remember all of the pieces in the opponent's hand. Then write a defensive production that uses this memory by having the model examine the board and, when appropriate, pick any piece that is the tens complement of an even-numbered piece held by the opponent. (See production P5 on p. 277.)

Appendix A

Programming in Pascal

This appendix is a quick review of Pascal. It is intended both for students who already know a programming language such as FORTRAN or BASIC and for students who may know Pascal but want to review it before going further. It is *not* an introduction to programming for students who have had no prior programming experience; so if you happen to be completely new at the programming game you should read an introductory Pascal text and/or get some outside help rather than trying to learn the language here.

Because many of the statements in Pascal are quite similar to those used in FORTRAN and BASIC, anyone who has even a rudimentary familiarity with those or similar languages can quickly transfer to using Pascal after a brief review of certain similarities and differences. One major difference is that Pascal is a highly *organized* language. Its basic program structure consists of three components, arranged as follows:

The 3 Components:

```
<program heading>
<declaration-part>
<statement-part>
```

A simple example*:

```
PROGRAM sum (input, output);

VAR num1, num2, result: integer;

BEGIN
        read (num1,num2);
        result := num1 + num2;
        writeln (result)
END.
```

As this example shows, every Pascal program must start with a <program heading>. The heading always begins with the reserved word PROGRAM, is followed by whatever *name* the programmer wants to give the program (in the example the name is *sum*), is then followed by a statement (in parentheses) of the input and output devices to be used in the program, and ends with a semicolon (as do virtually all command lines in Pascal). On most machines that support Pascal, the words *input* and *output* reserve the keyboard and the TV screen as the devices where information is read from or written to; but it is probably wise to check with your computer center for possible local exceptions to this rule, as well as other rules mentioned in this general review.

The other two sections—the <declaration-part> and the <statement-part>—each have several rules, and therefore will be discussed separately.

THE STATEMENT-PART OF A PASCAL PROGRAM

There are several basic kinds of statements, already familiar to anyone who knows another language, that will get you started immediately with Pascal. As shown in the example above, these statements can be arranged in any desirable sequence and executed together when they are put into an ordered group that starts with the reserved word BEGIN and ends with the reserved word END. In most cases, individual statements are ended with a semicolon. In the next several sections we shall review the Pascal syntax and usage of a number of statements that bear a distinct similarity to those used in other languages: the *assignment, input/output* (I/O), *if*, and *FOR .. DO* statements. Others will be introduced later.

Assignment statements.   These statements assign the value of any expression found on the right side of the symbol := to the variable name

---

*Note: Pascal receives commands in either upper or lower case. Upper case will be used here simply to emphasize certain features of any given example.

found on the left of the symbol. In general, they follow the same rules as similar statements in FORTRAN or BASIC, but you must use := in place of the = sign. Variable names can be of any size, but must start with a letter of the alphabet. Also, each variable name must have been previously defined in the <declaration-part> of the program, and the results of the expression must match the data type declared for the variable—for example, integer, real, and so on. We will investigate data types later in some detail, so don't worry about them for now. Typical examples of assignment statements are

```
pi: = 3.1416;                   (pi declared as real in
                                <declaration-part> of
                                program)
count: = count + 1;             (count declared as
                                integer)
var1: = (n * sq - sum**2) / n**2;  (where * is multiplication,
                                / is division, ** means
                                raising to a power, and
                                mathematical operations
                                occur by the usual math
                                priorities)
alph: = 'a';                    (alph declared as char)
list [10]: = 459;               (list declared as an array
                                of integers with at least
                                10 cells)
```

As in other languages, spaces between operators and variables are not required, but it is good practice to insert spaces liberally because they make the statement easier to read.

Input/Output Statements. We must distinguish two different kinds of input statements in Pascal. The standard statement is

```
READ (a, b, c, ...);
```

which will read as many data points as necessary from the input device and assign them, successively, to the variable names a, b, c, ... etc. The data assigned must be of the same type as the variable to which it is assigned, of course.

There is sometimes a problem with this READ statement because when it finishes reading it does not automatically advance to the next line of input. Thus the next READ statement will simply continue reading from the same line as the previous one until all data have been read—a situation that at times is desirable but at other times can be quite confusing. To overcome this problem, an alternative statement can be used that advances to a new line when it finishes execution.

The statement is

READLN (x, y, z) ;

which will read three data points into x, y, and z, then automatically go to the beginning of the next data line regardless of how much data still remains on the rest of the line it just read. Incidentally, this statement without parentheses, for example:

READLN;

will skip a line of input—a useful operation at times.

The two types of WRITE statements correspond in output function to the input statements just described. For example,

WRITE (outx, outy, outz) ;

will print the contents of the three named variables onto the output device, but *will not then advance to the next line.* If you want to print something and then advance to a new line in preparation for the next output, you must use

WRITELN (outx, outy, outz) ;

which will cause an advance to the next line automatically when printing is completed. And, of course, if you want to skip an output line (double spacing, for example) you can use

WRITELN;

If either of the WRITE statements shown above is used, the values of the three variables OUTX, OUTY, and OUTZ will be printed in three *fields* of a standard width as determined by the machine being used. This standard width is often large, so it is sometimes useful to be able to specify how many columns (what "field width") should be used when printing each variable. For example, if the three variables OUTX, OUTY, and OUTZ in the statement above are the integers 3, 4, and 5, the output might be spread out like this on the screen (or other output device):

          3   4   5

If we want to arrange the output so the integers are closer together when printed on the screen, we can pick a field width of some number of columns for each variable and write the statement like this:

```
WRITELN(outx:5,outy:5,outz:5)
```

This statement, when executed, will produce the following arrangement:

```
3    4    5
```

where each integer is now right-justified in a five-column field. The rule is, add :W to each variable name, where *W* is the number of columns you want to use for printing that variable.

This field-width rule holds for integers, characters, character strings, and real numbers alike. Real numbers pose an additional problem, however, because we need to specify not only the total field width of a decimal number but also the number of digits to the right of the decimal point that should be printed. This is easily done by adding :W:D to a real variable, where *W* specifies the total field width (including a space for the decimal point) and *D* specifies the number of digits to the right of the decimal. For example, if a real variable PI equals 3.14159 . . . , the statement

```
WRITELN('pi = ',pi:5:3);
```

will print

```
pi = 3.142
```

which shows the number in five columns, with three digits to the right of the decimal (automatically rounded off). Note in this last example that the way to write messages and labels corresponds closely to both FORTRAN and BASIC message operations; that is, simply enclose the message in single quotes.

The IF Statement. The short form of this statement, similar in both function and syntax to the IF in other languages, is

```
IF <boolean expression> THEN <statement>;
<next statement>;
            .
            .
            .
```

and executes as follows. The <boolean expression> is any expression whose value is either TRUE or FALSE. If this expression evaluates to FALSE, then execution of the program simply continues with the <next statement>. But if it evaluates to TRUE, then <statement> is first executed before going on to <next statement> and the rest of the program. Boolean expressions in Pascal use the symbols

<	less than
>	greater than
=	equal to
<=	less than or equal to
>=	greater than or equal to
<>	not equal to

;so
$$\left\{\begin{array}{l} 3<2 \\ 2>3 \\ 2=3 \\ 3<=2 \\ 2>=3 \\ 3<>3 \end{array}\right\}$$
are all FALSE

Pascal also permits use of the reserved words AND, OR, and NOT in boolean expressions. Their use allows for what are called *compound* boolean expressions; for example:

```
if (3>2) and (5<6) then . . .      evaluates to TRUE
if (8<=8) or (2>3) then . . .      evaluates to TRUE
if not (7<=9) then . . .           evaluates to FALSE
```

Note that when using AND, OR, and NOT, each simple boolean expression should be enclosed by parentheses.

The <statement> part of the IF statement differs from, and is more powerful than, the IF in some other languages because by using BEGIN . . . END it is possible to execute not just one but many statements. For example, consider the following:

```
READLN(answer);
IF answer <> 10 THEN
                BEGIN
                   writeln('your answer was wrong');
                   writeln(' 10 was correct');
                   err:= err + 1
                END;
<next statement>;
                .
                .
                .
```

where ANSWER had previously been declared as an integer variable. Note that by use of BEGIN . . . END we can execute three statements if the answer was not correct, and of course could have added as many others as necessary. This technique allows us, in essence, to execute a small program in between the reserved words BEGIN and END. Multiple statements of this sort, bounded by these two reserved words as shown, are called *compound statements*. Thus the <statement> following THEN may be either simple or compound.

The long form of the IF statement has the syntax

```
IF <boolean expression> THEN <statement1> ELSE <statement2>;
<next statement>;
          .
          .
          .
```

Here, as with the short form, if <boolean expression> is TRUE then <statement1> following THEN is executed before going to <next statement>; but if it is FALSE then <statement2> following the reserved word ELSE is executed before going to <next statement>. So this long form is designed to execute either <statement1> or <statement2> every time the IF is executed. (You already may have guessed that, since both <statement1> and <statement2> may be compound statements, a single IF may become quite complex—especially when any statement within a compound statement may itself be an IF!)

The FOR . . DO Statement.   The last statement you need to know about in order to transfer easily from other languages to Pascal is what BASIC and FORTRAN programmers call a "loop" statement and we shall refer to as a "repetitive" statement. Anyone who has used the "DO loop" in FORTRAN or the equivalent "FOR . . . NEXT loop" in BASIC will immediately recognize the near identity to the following Pascal statements:

Example 1

```
FOR i:= 1 TO 20 DO
        writeln(i);
```

Example 2

```
sum:= 0;
n:  = 30;
FOR x:= 1 TO n DO
        BEGIN
                sum:= sum + 1;
                array[x] := sum;
                writeln(sum:5)
        END;
```

The first example simply prints a column of integers ranging from 1 through 20. Note that the statement must contain the reserved words FOR, TO and DO in proper order and that the counting variable (*i* or *x* in the examples) must have been declared previously as an integer. The FOR . . DO statement ends with a semicolon, as do most Pascal statements.

The main difference between the first and second example is that the first example executes a *single* statement repetitively, whereas the second example repeats a *compound* statement, which, like all compound statements, begins with BEGIN and ends with END. Examine in particular the semicolon usage in the second example, and convince yourself that the FOR . . DO statement does in fact (1) contain a statement following the reserved word DO (in this case a compound statement); and (2) end with a semicolon after the statement it is supposed to execute repetitively (that is, the semicolon following the reserved word END). The second example also illustrates that the counting variable X may be used in any statement within the FOR . . DO range, including use as an integer subscript for an array.

As in other languages, the FOR . . DO statement may be nested; for example,

```
sum: =  0;
m: =  4;
n: =  5;
FOR  r: =  1  TO  m  DO
        FOR  s: =  1  TO  n  DO
                BEGIN
                        sum: =  sum  +  1;
                        mat [r, s] : =  sum
        END;
```

where, as expected, the inside FOR . . DO (using S as a counter) is exhausted before the outside FOR . . DO is incremented.

We shall examine several other types of Pascal statements later, but before doing so should become familiar with another required part of any Pascal program that is quite different from many other languages.

THE DECLARATION-PART OF A PASCAL PROGRAM

Unlike some otherwise similar languages, Pascal is quite specific about indicating what kind of data may be assigned to a given variable name. A variable may be assigned any one, and *only* one, of the following standard *data types:*

```
integer
real
char      (character)
boolean   (values of TRUE or FALSE)
```

Variable names, and their types, are designated for any program in the <declaration-part>, directly after the <program-heading>. Designation begins with the reserved word VAR, and proceeds as in the example

```
VAR      i, j, num, count: integer;
         x, dec: real;
         letters: char;
         trufals: boolean;
```

where each declaration normally includes a list of the variable names to be used in the program, each separated by commas, followed by a colon, followed by one of the reserved words indicating the data type for the preceding variable names, and ending with a semicolon. Thus this example says that in this program the variable name COUNT may be assigned only integer values, DEC will be an identifier for real (decimal) values, LETTERS will be a variable to which alphabetic characters or numerals or punctuation marks may be assigned, and TRUFALS will always be limited to the value "true" or "false."

Declaring an array is a simple extension of these rules; for example:

```
scores: ARRAY [1..20] OF integer;
mat: array [1..5,1..4] of real;
```

where the variable name for the array is followed by a colon, then by reserved words ARRAY [..] OF, then by the data type of each cell in the array, and ending with the usual semicolon. The pairs of numbers within the brackets are always separated by two periods and indicate the subscript range of the variable. So the one-dimensional array SCORES consists of 20 cells, numbered 1 through 20, with each cell containing an integer value. MAT is declared above as a two-dimensional array—a 5 x 4 matrix of real numbers, where the rows of MAT are numbered 1 through 5 and the columns are numbered 1 through 4. The number of dimensions possible may vary with the type of computer being used, so you will need to explore that limit for yourself. An array may be assigned any of the standard data types described earlier, and may also be assigned other type definitions using a technique that will be described in a later section.

A SIMPLE EXAMPLE

Before examining additional features of the Pascal language, let us as an exercise put together those covered thus far into a program that anyone who has not used Pascal but is familiar with either BASIC or FORTRAN can easily understand and write. The following program, entitled SCORES, is designed to read test scores of N< = 10 people, then calculate and print the mean and standard deviation for the group of scores.

```
PROGRAM scores (input, output);

(* Comment: This program calculates M and SD for
            N scores *)

VAR     i, n, score: integer;
        sum, sq, mean, sd: real;

(* --------------------------------------------------------- *)
              (* MAIN PROGRAM BEGINS HERE *)
(* --------------------------------------------------------- *)
BEGIN
  writeln('Enter number of cases');
  readln(n);
  sum:= 0;
  sq:= 0;
  writeln('Enter scores, 1 per line');
  for i:= 1 to n do
        BEGIN
                readln(score);
                sum:= sum + score;
                sq:= sq + score**2
        END;
  mean:= sum / n;
  sd:= sqrt((n * sq - sum**2) / (n * (n - 1)));
  writeln; writeln;
  writeln('mean = ', mean: 6: 2);
  writeln('sd = ', sd: 6: 2)
END.
```

If you are a BASIC or FORTRAN programmer who has never used Pascal, you should examine this example carefully, comparing it with the information in the preceding paragraphs, until you are sure you understand each Pascal instruction. Note that in Pascal a comment or documentation statement is enclosed by parentheses and asterisks; for example:

```
(* .. comment.. *).
```

(Comments may also be enclosed by braces—{..comment..}—if your keyboard has them.) SQRT is one of a set of *built-in functions* in Pascal, the rest of which are given in Table A–1. SQRT returns the square root of the real-

TABLE A–1   Built-In Functions in Standard Pascal

Arithmetic Functions

abs(x)	returns absolute value of x
sqr(x)	returns square of x
sqrt(x)	returns square root of x
ln(x)	returns natural log of x
exp(x)	returns e to the power x

Trigonometric Functions

sin(x)   cos(x)   arctan(x)

Transfer Functions

trunc(x)	returns "whole number" part of x as integer
round(x)	returns x rounded to nearest integer

*Ordinal Functions**

ord(char)	returns integer value (code) of char
chr(integer)	returns char value of integer
pred(char)	returns the predecessor of char (e.g., pred('Y') is 'X', pred('6') is '5')
succ(char)	returns the successor of char (e.g., succ('Y') is 'Z', succ('6') is '7')

Boolean Functions

odd(integer)	returns "true" if integer is odd, else "false"
eoln	returns "true" if next character to be read is the end-of-line character, else "false"
eof	returns "true" if next character to be read is the end-of-file character, else "false"

*Depending upon the computer being used, ordinal functions manipulate either ASCII or EBCDIC numerical codes for characters.

valued argument inside the parentheses. Other features to examine are punctuation rules; for example, the end of the program is signified by a period following the END statement for the main BEGIN..END block of program statements, and simple statements nearly always end with a semicolon. (An exception is the last simple statement before an END, which need not be terminated with a semicolon.) More than one statement may occur on a single line (as in WRITELN; WRITELN; above). With a little practice you will be able to program as easily in Pascal as in your "native" programming language.

ADDITIONAL FEATURES OF PASCAL

In addition to the statements described above, there are some others not found in most versions of languages such as FORTRAN and BASIC, which add considerably to Pascal's power. It is important to become acquainted with some of them here because they will be used in future examples, and also because they are critical to the techniques of *structured programming*, which is described in Chapter 2 and used in all of the Pascal programs in this text. The features that we need to examine are two types of repetitive statements (WHILE..DO and REPEAT..UNTIL), the CASE statement, and the construction rules for PROCEDUREs and FUNCTIONs. Let us look at these in turn.

The WHILE..DO statement.   Although the FOR..DO statement is useful and familiar, it is designed to repeat a group of instructions a certain number of times, and that number (and the accompanying ranges) must be specifiable at the beginning of the repetition. Sometimes specifying the exact number and range is awkward or not possible, and under these circumstances the WHILE..DO can be a useful alternative. The syntax for this statement is

```
WHILE <boolean expression> DO <statement>
```

and its operation is schematized in Figure A–1. As the figure shows, the <boolean expression> is always evaluated *before* the <statement> is repeated, and as soon as the evaluation is FALSE the repetition ends. The <statement> component may be either a simple or a compound statement. For example, the following program segment can replace the FOR..DO statement used in the SCORES program above, and makes it unnecessary to know the value of *N* in advance:

```
n: = 0;  sum: = 0;  sq: = 0;
readln(score);
WHILE score >= 0 DO
        BEGIN
                n: = n + 1;
                sum: = sum + score;
                sq: = sq + score**2;
                readln(score)
        END;
        .
        .
        .
```

In this segment, collection of sums and sums of squares continues until the user enters a negative number as the next SCORE. At that point the expression SCORE >= 0 evaluates to FALSE, so the compound statement following DO is no longer executed and program execution continues with the instruction following the WHILE..DO statement.

The REPEAT..UNTIL statement.   This statement is similar in purpose to

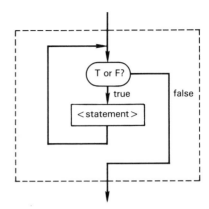

FIGURE A–1. Execution of a WHILE. .DO statement.

the WHILE..DO instruction, except that it executes the repetitive <statement> *first* and *then* decides whether or not to continue repeating. Its syntax is

```
REPEAT <statement sequence> UNTIL <boolean expression>
```

and its operation is illustrated in Figure A–2. Interestingly, the <statement sequence> in this instruction may be compound without the necessity of surrounding the several instructions in a BEGIN..END block. The following segment could replace either the FOR..DO or the DO..WHILE alternatives for the SCORES program:

```
n: = 0;
sum: = 0;
sq: = 0;
readln(score);
REPEAT
        n: = n + 1;
        sum: = sum + score;
        sq: = sq + score**2;
        readln(score)
UNTIL score < 0;
        .
        .
        .
```

This segment assumes, of course, that there will be at least one score given; that is, the first score should be nonnegative because the <statement sequence> will be executed the first time *automatically,* and before a decision is made about whether or not to repeat. As in the WHILE..DO example above, this segment allows the user to calculate sums and sums of squares without needing to know N in advance. The boolean expression SCORE <0 is evaluated *after* each repetition; if it is FALSE the sequence is repeated again, but if TRUE then program execution continues with the statement following the REPEAT..UNTIL block.

The CASE statement. This is a decision statement, like IF.. THEN..ELSE, except that instead of making a decision between just two alternatives it can decide among many. It is much like the "computed GO TO" statement found in both BASIC and FORTRAN. Look at the following example:

```
CASE point OF
   1: x:= 3;
   2: BEGIN   x:= 5;  y:= 6;  END;
   4: BEGIN   x:= 0;  y:= 4;  m:= x;  END;
   .
   .
   .
  25:  y:= 2
END;
<next instruction>
      .
      .
      .
```

The first line contains the reserved words CASE..OF with an integer variable (POINT) between them. Each of the following lines begins with an integer and is followed by a colon and any standard statement in Pascal. At execution the statement on the line with the integer value corresponding to

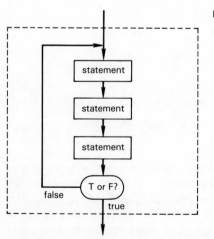

FIGURE A–2. Execution of a REPEAT. .UNTIL statement.

POINT will be executed, and then execution continues with the next instruction after the END of the entire CASE statement. Any number of lines, each of which represents a possible decision, may be defined. On any given execution, however, only one of them—the one to which POINT points—will be chosen and executed.

It is useful to note that more than one integer may be used on each line of a CASE statement. Consider the following program, which simply prints some silly messages and quits:

```
PROGRAM oddbird(input, output);

VAR    number: integer;

(* ------------------------------------------------ *)
            (* MAIN PROGRAM BEGINS HERE *)
(* ------------------------------------------------ *)

BEGIN
  writeln('Type any integer between 1 and 9');
  readln(number);
  CASE number OF
        1, 3, 5, 7, 9: writeln(number:2, ' is odd.');
        2, 4, 6, 8: writeln(number:2, 'is even')
  END;
  writeln('That''s all, folks!')
END.
```

(Notice in the last WRITELN statement that you can print an apostrophe within a message by inserting two single quotes.)

Procedures. Most programming languages have the capability of using *subprograms,* which are separate and largely self-contained sets of instructions that a main program can access and execute during the course of its own execution. In FORTRAN and BASIC, these subprograms are referred to as *subroutines* and *functions.* In Pascal, a rough equivalent of the subroutine is called a PROCEDURE. The structure of a PROCEDURE is identical to that for a main Pascal program except for the heading. It can be illustrated as

```
PROCEDURE name (parameter-list);
<declaration-part>
<statement-part>
```

where <declaration-part> and <statement-part> follow all the same rules as given in the preceding section for Pascal programs in general. Looking at the top line—the *procedure heading*—we see that the reserved word PRO-

CEDURE must be followed by a name that identifies the subprogram. The name, in turn, *may* be (but *need not* be, as we shall see) followed by a parameter-list enclosed in parentheses. The options available for such parameter lists are several, and they will be described below. First, however, let us look at a simple example that does not require a (parameter-list). The following version of the SCORES program will show you at a glance where PROCEDUREs are placed in a program, and how they are called and used:

```
PROGRAM scores (input, output);

VAR      n: integer;
         sum, sq, mean, sd:  real;

(*----------------------------------------------------------*)

PROCEDURE getsums;
VAR score: integer;
BEGIN
         n:= 0;  sum:= 0;  sq:= 0;
         writeln('Enter scores, 1 per line');
         writeln('After last score, type a negative number');
         readln(score);
         repeat
                 n:= n + 1;
                 sum:= sum + score;
                 sq:= sq + score**2;
                 readln(score)
         until score < 0
END;  (* Procedure GETSUMS Ends Here *)

(*----------------------------------------------------------*)
                (* MAIN PROGRAM STARTS HERE *)
(*----------------------------------------------------------*)

BEGIN
         getsums;
         mean:= sum / n;
         sd:= sqrt((n * sq - sum**2) / (n * (n - 1)));
         writeln('mean =', mean: 6: 2);
         writeln('sd =', sd: 6: 2)
END.
```

This example shows, first of all, that PROCEDUREs are located in the <declaration-part> of the main program, after the VAR declarations and just before the beginning of the <statement-part> of the main program. Second, look at the first statement in the main program and note that the way a procedure gets activated or called is to give its name as a statement. So the first statement in the main program says, in effect, "execute the procedure GETSUMS, then return here and continue with the main program." (The remainder of this sample program calculates and prints the mean and standard deviation of the data obtained in GETSUMS. These operations could have been put into other procedures, of course, at the discretion of the programmer.)

Examine now the PROCEDURE itself. In structure, it is like a small program. It begins with a VAR declaration, which identifies the integer variable SCORE. Because it was declared inside the procedure, SCORE is what we call a *local* variable; it is used only within the procedure, and disappears when control is transferred back to the calling program block. Any number of local variables may be declared within a procedure, using the declaration rules presented in the previous sections. Thus the procedure can act as an independent program block, having its own variables and statements, and need not interact at all with the program block that called it. As you may already have guessed, this means that other procedures may be declared within a procedure and can then be accessed from the procedure. Procedures that are declared within other procedures are said to be *nested*.

But procedures may also work with variables that have been declared in the calling program block. In our example, the variables N, SUM, and SQ were declared in the main program SCORES, and so are available for use—and change of value—within GETSUMS. In general, any variable previously declared in or for the calling program block is usable within a procedure. Such variables are said to be *global*, in contrast to *local*. The GETSUMS example, then, operates with both local and global variables. The local variable disappears when GETSUMS finishes execution; but the globals, with new values now assigned to them, are still available for use in the calling program block. There may be times, of course, when no local variables are needed in a procedure. In such cases, the <declaration-part> of the procedure may simply be omitted.

Elaborations on the basic structure of a procedure as illustrated by GETSUMS mainly concern the precise identification of the global variables, or *parameters*, that are to be used in the procedure. These identifications are made in the (parameter-list) portion of the procedure heading. Several types of parameters may be listed in this manner, but we need to look at only two types here—the "variable parameter" and the "value parameter." Designation of variable parameters is particularly useful when we have a procedure that may operate on a number of different globals at different times. Consider the following arbitrary example, which accepts two pairs of numbers as input, then reorders them by size and prints each pair with the large number first:

```
PROGRAM hilow (input,output);

VAR     a,b,c,d: integer;

(*----------------------------------------------*)

PROCEDURE reorder (VAR x,y: integer);
VAR     temp: integer;
BEGIN
        if x < y then
                BEGIN
                        temp:= y;  y:= x;  x:= temp
                END;
        writeln(x:4,' is larger than ',y:4)
END;    (* Reorder Ends Here *)

(*--------------------------------------------------*)
          (* MAIN PROGRAM STARTS HERE *)
(*--------------------------------------------------*)

BEGIN
        writeln('enter 2 pairs of numbers, 1 pair per
                line');
        readln(a,b);
        readln(c,d);
        reorder(a,b);
        reorder(c,d)
END.
```

Note first that in the main program the procedure **REORDER** is called twice, specifying different parameters on each occasion. Now look at the procedure heading for **REORDER** to see how these differing parameters may be handled by a single procedure. The (parameter-list) in the procedure heading indicates that the procedure will accept any two global variables, as long as they are integers, and make them equivalent within the procedure to the integer variables *X* and *Y*. The procedure then is executed, changing the values of *X* and *Y* as needed, *and correspondingly changing the values of the global variables assigned to X and Y*. So if, for example, the original assignments to variables *A* and *B* were 2 and 4, respectively, following the call REORDER(A,B) the values for *A* and *B* would have been switched. Can you rewrite the example above to prove that this change at the global level does indeed occur? Try it.

There may well be times when you would like changes in parameter values to be made locally (that is, within the procedure), but have the global parameters *keep their original values at the global level*. Considering again the example in which $A:=2$ and $B:=4$, you might want to print them out in reversed order as done in REORDER, but have *A* and *B* remain 2 and 4, respectively, back in the main program. This can be accomplished by passing *A* and *B* to REORDER as *value parameters,* rather than variable parameters. To do so, simply change the procedure heading to

```
PROCEDURE reorder (x,y:  integer);
```

where the only change is that VAR has been omitted from the (parameter-list). This omission gives *X* and *Y* the *values* of the global variables given as parameters in the calling statement, but those parameters are not assigned as *variables* to *X* and *Y,* and therefore will not change at the global level when *X* and *Y* change locally. The calling statement remains the same as shown in the example above. Try this simple change to convince yourself of the difference between "variable parameters" and "value parameters."

Functions.   Even though a number of built-in functions are available in Pascal (see Table A–1), there are times when it is useful to build one's own functions. The placement and syntax for programmer-defined functions is similar to that for procedures. Functions must appear in a program before the beginning of the <statement-part>. Syntactically, they consist of a <function heading>, a <declaration-part>, and a <statement-part>—the same structure as used in other program blocks in Pascal. The following example, which receives two real numbers as arguments and returns the smaller number, illustrates the structure:

```
FUNCTION small (x,y: real): real;
BEGIN
        if x < y then small:= x else small:= y
END;
```

Because no local variables were needed for this simple function, the <declaration-part> was omitted; but you should be aware that a VAR statement and declaration of variables in the usual manner is permissible within a function. Looking at the <function heading>, we see that it has a (parameter-list) written in the same manner as described for procedure headings. Following the (parameter-list), however, it is necessary to insert a colon and then declare the data-type that the function will return when execution is finished. In the example, the final value of SMALL will be a real number as designated at the end of the <function heading>. This value is, of course, calculated down in the <statement-part> of the function, where the statements SMALL: = X and SMALL: = Y assign one or the other of the two parameters as the value of SMALL, depending upon which is the smaller number.

To call a function defined as above, you would insert a calling statement in the same manner as used in calling built-in functions in Pascal and other languages; for example:

```
val:= small(a,b);
```

where A, B, and VAL have been declared as real variables. The function will return the value of either A or B, whichever is smaller, and that value will be assigned to VAL. Knowing these basic rules, it should be easy for you to write any type of function needed.

HANDLING STRINGS

We have covered all of the basic features of the Pascal language except one—handling groups of characters, such as words, names, and so on. This important type of data is customarily referred to as a *string* of characters. Unfortunately, Standard Pascal does not have a way to declare a string as a standard data type, so we must find out for ourselves how to build, store, and retrieve strings. This is a good exercise, however, because in doing so we will get a chance to use most of the techniques presented in this appendix.

The first step in becoming able to handle strings is to find out how Pascal allows the programmer to define new data types. The trick is performed by using the reserved word TYPE in the <declaration-part> of a program. A variety of TYPEs might be defined. Most are not of immediate importance to us, but one—the *packed array*—is necessary because it permits us to build strings. Let us approach the problem with an example. Suppose we want to declare an array that will store the names of N<=10 people, one name per cell. Each cell will have to be able to hold a string of characters—that is, each cell must itself be a small array of the data-type CHAR. To define such a cell, and then an array of 10 such cells, we must write

```
TYPE    personame = PACKED ARRAY [1..20] OF char;
VAR     names: ARRAY [1..10] OF personame;
```

The TYPE statement declares a new data-type called PERSONAME, which is a "string variable" consisting of 20 characters. The VAR statement then declares a standard 10-cell array NAMES in which each cell is of the newly defined data-type PERSONAME. Thus each cell of the array called NAMES is itself an array—a PACKED ARRAY—that, in this example, has room for 20 characters.

To see how such string-handling declarations can be used in actual programming, consider the following program LIST, which will read up to

10 names into an array called LIST, then skip two lines and output the names given, one name per line:

```
PROGRAM list (input, output);

(* Loads names in LIST until the user types an asterisk,
        then prints LIST. Each name may be up to 20
        characters long, and up to 10 names may be
        given. *)

TYPE personame = packed array [1..20] of char;

VAR    nom: personame;
       list: array [1..10] of personame;
       i: integer;
       nomore: boolean;

(* ------------------------------------------------- *)

PROCEDURE getname;
VAR    ch: char;
       lngth: integer;

BEGIN

       for lngth:= 1 to 20 do nom[lngth]:= ' ';
       repeat
       read(ch)
       until ((ch>='A') and (ch<='Z')) or (ch='*');
       if ch <> '*' then
       BEGIN

            lngth:= 1;
            repeat
              nom[lngth]:= ch;
              lngth:= lngth + 1;
              read(ch)
            until (ch<'A') or (ch>'Z') or (lngth>20);
            if lngth>20 then
               writeln('Error -- name too large')
       END
       else nomore:= true
END; (* End of Getname *)

(*---------------------------------------------------------*)

PROCEDURE printlist (i: integer);
VAR j: integer;
```

```
BEGIN
for j:= 1 to i do writeln(list[j])
END;  (* End of Printlist *)

(*---------------------------------------------------------*)
              (* MAIN PROGRAM STARTS HERE *)
(*---------------------------------------------------------*)

BEGIN
        nomore:= false;
        writeln('Enter up to 10 names, capitals only');
        writeln('and maximum of 20 letters.');
        writeln('Type an asterisk to end your list.');
        getname;
        i:= 0;
        while (i<10) and (nomore=false) do
              BEGIN
                        i:= i + 1;
                        list[i]:= nom;
                        getname
              END;
        printlist(i)
END.
```

The most important new feature to examine is the procedure GETNAME, which when called will load a string variable called NOM with the letters of the next name to be read. Note that NOM is a global variable of data-type PERSONAME, and thus is of the same type as each cell of the array LIST. Look carefully at the procedure and convince yourself that it (1) fills NOM with blank characters to start the process; (2) reads characters from the input device until it gets to a letter between A and Z, which will be the beginning of the next name; (3) reads that and successive (capital) letters into the character cells of NOM until it comes to a character that is not a letter or exceeds 20 letters; and (4) returns control to the calling program block. The one exception occurs if it reads an asterisk, which serves as a signal to (1) reset the global boolean variable NOMORE to TRUE, then (2) return to the calling program block.

Now look down at the main program, where GETNAME is called repeatedly within a WHILE..DO statement. Each time it is called, it returns either a new name in NOM, which can now be assigned to a cell in the string array LIST, or else returns with NOMORE:= TRUE, which will terminate the WHILE..DO statement and continue with the remainder of the program. The rest of the program is easily understood; it simply skips two output lines, then calls a second procedure that prints out the names previously stored in LIST.

CONCLUSION

The program LIST provides an example of how to declare variables of various types, including string and string-array variables; it also gives procedures that show how to read, store, and retrieve strings. In addition, it illustrates the basic structure of a typical Pascal program and uses most of the kinds of declarations and statements we shall need in the future. If you understand the program, you are ready to use the Pascal language to the level of sophistication required to understand the Pascal programs presented in the various chapters in this text.

EXERCISES

1. Write a small Pascal program that will (1) ask a question of the user; (2) read the user's answer; and (3) tell the user the answer was either correct or incorrect. Use an IF..THEN..ELSE statement, elaborating the example shown on page 295.
2. Revise the program SCORES (p. 304) so that the <statement part> of the main program consists of calls to three procedures, for example:

```
BEGIN
getsums;
calcstats;
printstats
END.
```

3. Write and execute the program HILOW (p. 306) in two ways: (A) using *variable* parameters for the procedure REORDER, as shown in the example; (B) using *value* parameters, as discussed on p. 307. Modify the program so it will show, in each case, the final values of the global variables A, B, C, and D.
4. For the program LIST (p. 309) to execute properly, is it necessary for the user to type each name on a new line, with only one name per line? Why, or why not?
5. If a name of more than 20 characters is given to the program LIST as it is written on page 309, what happens to the extra letters? How could you change the program to correct potential problems that might arise when the user types an oversized name?
6. (A) Why does the program LIST work only if names are spelled with capital letters? (B) Rewrite LIST so it will accept either lower-case or upper-case letters and blanks (spaces), permitting the program to store first and last names, for example:

```
Suzy Smith
Billy Budd
```

Appendix B

The Pandemonium Model

Listed below is the program PANDO, a computer model of Selfridge's pandemonium theory of perceptual feature analysis. A full explanation of the program is found in Chapter 3.

```
PROGRAM PANDO (input, output, features, letters);

var      alphafeat: array [1..26,1..7] of integer;
         labels: array [1..26] of char;
         features: text;
         letters: text;
         cog: array [1..26] of integer;
         image, feat: array [1..7] of integer;
         i, seed: integer;
         prattend: real;

(* ------------------------------------------------------ *)

   (* Define pseudo-random number function for your
      computer *)

FUNCTION mth$random (var seed: integer): real; extern;

(* ------------------------------------------------------ *
```

```
PROCEDURE loadfile(var features: text);

        (* loads ALPHAFEAT from FEATURES file *)

var     ii,jj:integer;

begin
reset(features);
for ii:= 1 to 26 do
        for jj:= 1 to 7 do
           read(features, alphafeat[ii,jj])
end;    (*end of loadfile *)

(* -------------------------------------------------- *)

PROCEDURE loadfile1(var letters: text);

        (* loads LABELS from LETTERS file *)

var     ii:integer;

begin
reset(letters);
for ii:= 1 to 26 do
        readln(letters,labels[ii])

end;    (* end of loadfile1 *)

(* -------------------------------------------------- *)

PROCEDURE stage1;

        (* ****BEGIN STAGE1**** *)

var     i: integer;

begin
for i:= 1 to 7 do
        read(image[i])
end;    (* end of stage1 *)

(* -------------------------------------------------- *)
PROCEDURE stage2;

        (* ****BEGIN STAGE2**** *)

var     i: integer;
        ran: real;
```

```
begin
for i:= 1 to 7 do
        begin
        ran:=mth$random(seed);
        if ran <= prattend
                then feat[i]:= image[i]
                else feat[i]:= 9
        end
end;    (* end of stage2 *)

(* ---------------------------------------------------- *)
PROCEDURE stage3;


        (* ****BEGIN STAGE3**** *)


var     p, q: integer;

begin
for p:= 1 to 26 do
        cog[p]:=0;
for p:= 1 to 7 do
        if feat[p] <> 9 then
            for q:= 1 to 26 do
                if feat[p] = alphafeat[q, p] then
                    cog[q]:= cog[q] + 1
end;    (* end of stage3 *)

(* -------------------------------------------------- *)
PROCEDURE stage4;


        (* ****BEGIN STAGE4**** *)


var     i, loud, numties, shout, guess: integer;
        ties: array [1..26] of integer;

begin
numties:= 0;
loud:= 0;
                (* find loudest shout(s) *)
for i:= 1 to 26 do
        if cog[i] > loud then
            begin
                numties:= 1;
                loud:= cog[i];
                ties[1]:= i
            end
```

```
        else if cog[i] = loud then
            begin
                numties:= numties + 1;
                ties[numties]:= i
            end;
writeln;            (* now print response *)

if numties = 0 then writeln('No match found')
else if numties = 1 then writeln('The letter is ',
                labels[ties[1]])
        else
            begin
            guess:= 1 + trunc(numties*mth$random(seed));
            writeln('My guess is ',labels[ties[guess]])
            end
end;      (* end of stage4 *)


(* -------------------------------------------------- *)
                (* MAIN PROGRAM *)
(* -------------------------------------------------- *)

begin
                            (* housekeeping *)
loadfile(features);
loadfile1(letters);
writeln('Enter seed, prattend');
readln(seed,prattend);
                            (* main loop *)
        stage1;
repeat
        stage2;
        stage3;
        stage4;
        stage1
until image[1] = 9
end.      (* end of main program *)
```

Appendix C

The Duplex Memory Model

Listed below is the program DUPLEX, a computer model of the duplex theory of memory. Complete documentation for the program is found in Chapter 4.

```
PROGRAM DUPLEX (input, output, memr);

TYPE    wd= packed array [1..6] of char;

VAR     stm: array [1..7,1..4] of wd;
        ltm: array [1..10,1..5] of wd;
        memr: text;
        item: wd;
        i,j,k,l,m,n,ix: integer;
        pr,r: real;

(* ---------------------------------------------------- *)

(*Define pseudo-random number function for your computer*)

FUNCTION mth$random(var seed:integer):real; extern;

(* ---------------------------------------------------- *)
```

```
PROCEDURE ldmem(var memr: text);

        (* loads LTM with words from MEMR file *)

var   ch: char;
      len: 1..7;

begin
  reset(memr);
  for i:= 1 to 10 do
  for j:= 1 to 5 do
  begin
    if not eof(memr) then
      repeat read(memr,ch)
      until ((ch>='A') and (ch<='Z')) or eof(memr);
    if not eof(memr) then
    begin
      len:= 1;
      item:= '       ';
      repeat
        item[len]:= ch;
        read(memr,ch);
        len:= len + 1
      until (ch<'A') or (ch>'Z') or (len=7)
    end
    else writeln('eof error in ldmem');
    ltm[i,j]:= item
  end
end;  (*ldmem*)


(* ------------------------------------------------------ *)


PROCEDURE blankstm;
                        (* loads STM with blanks *)
var      i, j: integer;
begin
  for i:= 1 to 7 do
    for j:= 1 to 4 do stm[i,j]:= '    '
end;     (* blank-stm *)

(* ------------------------------------------------------ *)


PROCEDURE getwd;

        (* reads new word into ITEM *)

var      ch: char;
         len: 1..7;
```

```
begin
  reset(input);
  if not eoln then
    repeat read(ch) until ((ch>='A') and (ch<='Z')) or eoln;
  if not eoln then
  begin
        len:= 1;
        item:= '       ';
        repeat
                item[len]:= ch;
                read(ch);
                len:= len + 1
        until (ch<'A') or (ch>'Z') or (len=7);
  end
  else writeln('eoln error in getwd')
end;  (*getwd*)


(* ------------------------------------------------------ *)


PROCEDURE bump;

        (* replaces old single item in STM with ITEM *)

var     randint, lr, lt, i, l:integer;
        lran:array[1..7] of integer;

begin
  for i:= 1 to 7 do lran[i]:= i;
  l:= 0;
  lt:= 7;
  while (lt > 0) and (l = 0) do
  begin
        lr:= 1 + trunc(lt*mth$random(ix));
        randint:= lran[lr];
        lran[lr]:= lran[lt];
        lt:= lt - 1;
        if stm[randint,2] = '       ' then
        begin
            stm[randint,1]:= item;
            l:= 1
        end
  end
end;  (*bump*)


(* ------------------------------------------------------ *)
```

```
PROCEDURE loadstm;

          (* puts ITEM just read into blank row of STM --
              if no blank rows, calls BUMP *)

var      m, k: integer;

begin
  k:= 1;
  m:= 0;
  repeat
        if stm[k,1] = '        ' then
        begin
          stm[k,1]:= item;
          m:= k
        end;
        k:= k + 1
  until (m <> 0) or (k > 7);
  if m = 0 then bump
end;      (* loadstm *)


(* ----------------------------------------------------- *)


PROCEDURE chunk(stmrow: integer);

          (* chunks a single item in STM *)

var      i, j, m, n: integer;

begin
                (* is stm[stmrow,1] in ltm? *)
  m:= 0;
  for i:= 1 to 10 do
  begin
    if m = 0 then
    for j:= 1 to 5 do
    begin
      if m = 0 then
        if ltm[i,j] = stm[stmrow,1] then m:= i
    end
  end;
          (* if stm[stmrow,1] is in ltm, is there another
              row of stm containing a word with which it
              can be chunked? *)
```

```
    n:= 0;
    if m <> 0 then
    for i:= 1 to 7 do
       if (n = 0) and (i <> stmrow) then
              for j:= 1 to 5 do
          if stm[i,1] = ltm[m,j] then n:= i;
             (* if there is a row in which stm[stmrow,1] can
                be chunked, then chunk it if that row has a
                blank cell *)
    if n <> 0 then
    begin
      j:= 2;
      repeat
          if stm[n,j] = '         ' then
             begin
                  stm[n,j]:= stm[stmrow,1];
                  n:= 100
             end;
            j:= j + 1
      until (j > 4) or (n = 100)
    end;
                       (* if chunked, blank out stm[stmrow,1] *)
    if n = 100 then stm[stmrow,1]:= '         '
end; (* chunk *)


(* ----------------------------------------------------- *)


PROCEDURE rehearsechunk;

              (* decides whether to rehearse and chunk
                   single items in STM *)

var    k: integer;
       r: real;

begin
  for k:= 1 to 7 do
          if (stm[k,1] <> '      ') and (stm[k,2] = '       ')
          then
          begin
            r:= mth$random(ix);
            if r < pr then chunk(k)
          end
end;     (* rehearsechunk *)

(* ----------------------------------------------------- *)
```

```
PROCEDURE skipout;

        (* skips lines and prints STM contents *)

var     i, j: integer;

begin
  writeln;
  writeln;
  writeln('   output');
  writeln;
  for i:= 1 to 7 do      (*output loop*)
    for j:= 1 to 4 do
      if stm[i,j] <> '      ' then writeln(stm[i,j])
end; (* skipout *)

(* --------------------------------------------------- *)
                   (* MAIN PROGRAM *)
(* --------------------------------------------------- *)

begin
                  (* housekeeping *)

  ldmem(memr);
  blankstm;
  writeln(' enter n, seed, and pr on 3 lines');
  readln(n); readln(ix); readln(pr);
                  (* main loop *)

  for 1:= 1 to n do
  begin
    writeln(' enter a word -- capitals only');
    getwd;
    loadstm;
    rehearsechunk
  end;
                  (* skip lines and print STM *)
  skipout
end.
```

Appendix D

A Pascal Model of ALDOUS

A general description of ALDOUS, Loehlin's computer model of personality, is given in Chapter 6. Details of a data structure and a Pascal program representing ALDOUS are presented here.

Data Structure

The three emotions of love, anger, and fear are the main constructs of Loehlin's model. As an aid in deciding upon data structures for these emotions, let us analyze in some detail what must occur for just one of them—the emotion of love—whenever Aldous is presented with a given person-object. Suppose for example that the blonde woman (object 312) alluded to in Chapter 6 becomes an object of Aldous's attention. If Aldous has met up with her before (familiarity index), he has stored for her in long-term memory some degree of love, the strength of which will be represented by a number ranging between 0.00 and 1.0. Now if the "love level" for this object is stored in cell number 312 of a 3-dimensional array similar to the one labeled LUV in Figure D–1, we will have provided Aldous with a way of accessing the degree of this emotion associated with this object. Moreover, the same structure can also store identifiable degrees of LUV for such objects as brown-haired boys (LUV[1,2,1]), red-haired old men (LUV[4,3,1]), and so on.

This structural plan suggests a $4 \times 3 \times 2$ array for each of the emotions. We must consider also, however, Loehlin's proposal regarding generalization from the specific object to its various conceptual components. This added complexity can be taken into account simply by increasing the array size by one on each dimension and using the extra integer to represent generalization. For instance, if LUV is dimensioned as a $5 \times 4 \times 3$ array, then when Aldous recognizes the blonde woman he can identify his affection for her as a specific object in LUV [3,1,2], and also for blonde adults in general in LUV[3,1,3], for blonde people in LUV[5,1,3,], and so on. This strategy may be used to represent the other emotions also, as portrayed in Figure D–1 by the arrays ANGER and FEAR. A similar

FIGURE D–1.   Data structure for ALDOUS.

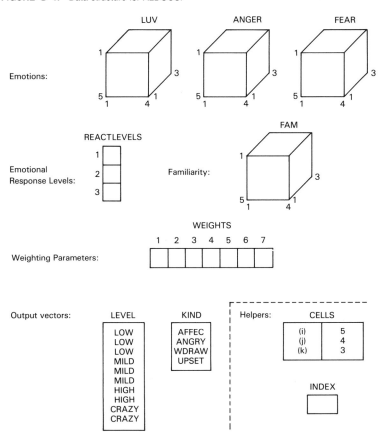

3-dimensional array FAM can be used to keep track of familiarity. This integer array will store the number of times each object, and each of its generalizations, has been encountered.

To understand the structures REACTLEVELS and WEIGHTS shown in Figure D–1, we need to consider the general strategy of the program. Recall from Chapter 6 that the purpose of Stage 2 in the model is to establish a current internal emotional response. In the program, this process can be accomplished by:

1. In STAGE1, finding out from the array FAM how familiar the current object, and all of its generalizations, are to ALDOUS;
2. in STAGE2, using this familiarity index, in conjunction with weighting parameters for the different levels of generalization, to calculate for each of the emotions a weighted reactivity level that takes into account the object itself and all of its generalizations;
3. storing these weighted reactivity levels for later use in STAGE3.

The calculation for weighting reactivity is a bit complex and will be discussed in detail later. Important for now is the fact that in order to calculate it, a vector WEIGHTS must be created to store the various weighting parameters for the different levels of generalization. These parameters are read into the vector WEIGHTS at the beginning of the program. Later, in STAGE2, they are used to calculate reactivity levels for each of the three emotions. The resulting current emotional levels for LUV, ANGER, and FEAR are stored in respective cells of the vector REACTLEVELS.

These are the major *theoretical* structures for the program. Obviously, as shown in Figure D–1, other "helper structures"—places to store information temporarily or to help complete some algorithmic process—will also be needed. These will be described below as they become necessary.

Program Construction

Figure 6–1 presented a top-level design for Aldous, which for convenience is copied here as Figure D–2. A nice advantage of a top-level diagram like this is that the various modules, being relatively independent of each other, may be analyzed in virtually any order. We shall utilize this advantage by leaving the rather straightforward analysis of the Housekeeping module until later, and look first at the REPEAT..UNTIL segment, which is really the major portion of the model. Let us begin by assuming that the statement part of the main program will look something like this:

```
(******  Main Program  ******)
begin
        (Put coding for Housekeeping here later)
          .
          .
```

```
again:= 'y';
repeat
  writeln('Enter ijk values for next person meeting
          Aldous');
  readln(i,j,k);
  stage1;
  stage2(luv,1);
  stage2(anger,2);
  stage2(fear,3);
  stage3;
  stage4;
  writeln('continue? [y/n]');
  readln(again)
until again = 'n';

              .
              .
```

where STAGE1, STAGE2, STAGE3, and STAGE4 are procedures, I,J,K are variables holding the three digits that define the person-object to be encountered by Aldous, and AGAIN is a character-variable that, when assigned the value 'n' (for "no"), will signal the end of the REPEAT..UNTIL loop. Because the heart of the program, and the theory, is embodied in the four procedures (stages), we shall look at them in order.

Stage1. This procedure has two major goals: to "recognize" the current person-object by getting an INDEX of its familiarity, and then to increase the appropriate FAM cells by one, to account for the present encounter with the current object and all of its generalizations. These objectives can be met by the following program block:

```
              .
              .

PROCEDURE STAGE1;
(***** Gets familiarity weighting, updates FAM *****)
VAR     a,b,c,d,e,f,g,p,q,r: integer;

begin
a:= fam[i,j,3];
b:= fam[i,4,k];  (* FAM cells are set to variables A-G. *)
c:= fam[5,j,k];  (* A-G are easier to use in statements
                    below. *)
d:= fam[i,4,3];
e:= fam[5,j,3];
f:= fam[5,4,k];
g:= fam[i,j,k];
```

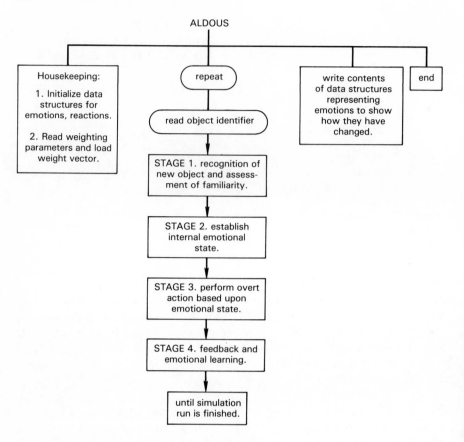

FIGURE D–2. A top-level structure diagram for ALDOUS.

```
          (* Routine to determine familiarity weightings
Set INDEX=8 to show no familiarity. Then adjust INDEX
to show (a) which single characteristic is familiar
(INDEX=5,6,7), or (b) which pairs of characteristics
are familiar (INDEX=2,3,4), or (c) if the ijk object
itself is familiar (INDEX=1). INDEX will be used in
STAGE2 to assess emotional levels. *)

index: = 8;
if  (d<>0) and (e=0) and (f=0) then index: = 5;
if  (e<>0) and (d=0) and (f=0) then index: = 6;
if  (f<>0) and (d=0) and (e=0) then index: = 7;
if  (a<>0) and (b=0) and (c=0) then index: = 2;
if  (b<>0) and (a=0) and (b=0) then index: = 3;
if  (c<>0) and (a=0) and (b=0) then index: = 4;
if g<>0 then index: = 1;
```

```
        (* Routine to increment familiarity of FAM[ijk]
and all generalization cells. This uses a global 3×2 array
CELLS to store various subscripts that will be used in the
triple-nested
FOR..DO loops. *)

    cells[1,2] := 5;
    cells[2,2] := 4;
    cells[3,2] := 3;
    cells[1,1] := i;
    cells[2,1] := j;
    cells[3,1] := k;
    for p:= 1 to 2 do
       for q:= 1 to 2 do
          for r:= 1 to 2 do
             fam[cells[1,p],cells[2,q],cells[3,r]] :=
                fam[cells[1,p],cells[2,q],cells[3,r]] + 1
    end;      (* end of stage1 *)
```

The local variables A–G are used to store the familiarity levels, that is, the integer counts of number of previous encounters, for the current object and all of its generalizations. These counts are then compared in a series of IF..THEN statements to establish an INDEX between 1 and 8. INDEX is a global variable that will be used later, in STAGE2, as a subscript pointing to the cell of WEIGHTS that will be stressed because of familiarity when calculating the strength of the various emotional reactions to the current object. Note that the INDEX values 5, 6, 7 indicate that only a single characteristic of the current object is familiar (has been encountered in the past); the values 2, 3, 4 signal that various combinations of just two of the various characteristics are familiar; a value of 1 indicates that the object itself is familiar; and 8 signals that neither the object nor any of its generalizations have been encountered previously. (Note also, for possible future elaboration of the program, that this is a very crude way of establishing an index of familiarity for emotional weightings, and that more elegant schemes could be contrived to replace it.)

The second task of the procedure, to increment the relevant FAM cells to account for the current encounter, poses the following problem: We need to add to the count in FAM[i,j,k], which is easy; but must also increment FAM[i,j,3], FAM[i,4,k], ..., etc., to indicate increased familiarity for all of the generalizations as well. In essence, to increment all of the appropriate cells we must use as subscripts all of the following triples: (i,j,k), (i,j,3), (i,4,k), (5,j,k), (i,4,3), (5,j,3), (5,4,k), and for good measure let us add (5,4,3). The strategy used to accomplish this chore is to employ a global

2-dimensional array CELLS, load it with the needed subscripts (as shown in Fig. D–1), and then use triple-nested FOR..DO loops to identify each integer stored in CELLS and use it as a subscript for accessing FAM. Convince yorself that this scheme will work. Can you design an alternative, perhaps easier or faster, strategy?

Stage2. The goal of this procedure is to calculate a weighted emotional strength for each of the three emotions and to store the result in the respective cells of the global array REACTLEVELS. (These strengths will then be used in the next stage to determine Aldous' reaction to the current object.) The general strategy employed here is to first pass the LUV, ANGER, and FEAR arrays, each in turn, as value parameters to the procedure; after that the procedure will use appropriate cells in the array, along with WEIGHTS and INDEX, to calculate an emotional strength EMOT and store it in REACTLEVELS. The other parameter passed in each procedure call is an integer (1, 2, or 3), which identifies the respective emotions and is used as a subscript when storing EMOT in REACTLEVELS. One way to write the procedure is like this:

```
PROCEDURE STAGE2 (x: box; y: integer);
   (* This procedure determines emotion level for each
   emotion, stores levels in vector ReactLevels cells
   1,2,3 *)

var      w: array [1..7] of real;
         emot,max: real;
         n: integer;

begin
max:= 0;
for n:= 1 to 7 do
   begin
   w[n]:= weights[n];
   max:= max + w[n]
   end;
if index<>8 then              (* Adjust weights for *)
                              (* familiarity of *)
            begin             (* current object *)
               w[index]:= w[index] + famil;
               max:= max + famil
            end;
emot:= w[1] * x[i,j,k] + w[2] * x[i,j,3] +
       w[3] * x[i,4,k] + w[4] * x[5,j,k] +
       w[5] * x[i,4,3] + w[6] *
```

```
        x[5,j,3]  + w[7]  *  x[5,4,k];

emot:= emot / max * 10 + 1;         (* Sets EMOT between
1.0 *)
                                    (* and 11.0 *)
ReactLevels[y]:= emot
end;       (* end of STAGE2 *)
```

.

Note first the two *value* parameters. The parameter *Y* is an integer, identifying which of the three emotions is being passed. The variable *X* is of the type BOX, and of course is the $5 \times 4 \times 3$ array representing the emotion. But what does BOX signify? As can be seen in the complete listing (p. 336), BOX is a special TYPE, defined at the beginning of the main program by the statement

```
TYPE    BOX = array [1..5,1..4,1..3] of real;
```

It is necessary to identify the 3-dimensional array in this manner because in standard PASCAL the use of ARRAY is not permitted when identifying parameters for procedures.

The first FOR..DO loop loads a local array W with the contents of the global array WEIGHTS, and calculates the value MAX, which is the sum of the weights on this run. (Note that this could be done in at least two other, more efficient, ways; one might pass WEIGHTS as another value parameter, or do the whole business once at the beginning of program execution. The technique shown here was chosen because it works, and it perhaps makes the variables within the procedure more comprehensible to anyone reading the program code.)

The IF..THEN statement uses INDEX, calculated in STAGE1, to first decide if the standard weights (now in W) should be adjusted for familiarity with the current object. Recall that an INDEX of 8 means no familiarity with the object or any of its generalizations, in which case no adjustment should be made. If INDEX is not 8, then an appropriate weight in W receives an added adjustment. This adjustment, FAMIL, may be a global constant or can be read in as part of the Housekeeping chores at the beginning of execution. In either case, it is the theory's way of taking familiarity into account when Aldous establishes his emotional reaction levels.

The emotion level itself (EMOT) is calculated by multiplying the current strength of the emotion assigned to the object, and each of its six generalizations, by their respective weights, and summing these products. What kind of number will be the result? Remember that strength varies between 0.00 and 1.00. If all seven *X* cells are 0.00, then EMOT will obviously equal 0.00 as a minimum value. Alternatively, if all $n = (1..7)$ cells in the equation are 1.00, then the sum of 1.00 times each weight W[n] will give EMOT a maximum value equal to the *sum of the weights*—which is the value MAX.

The last chore in the procedure is to store the EMOT value in the appropriate cell of REACTLEVELS. Here, however, another slight adjustment must be made. For reasons that will become apparent in STAGE3, we first transform EMOT from a value between 0.00 and MAX to a value between 1.0 and 11.0. Prove for yourself that the statement

```
emot := emot/max * 10.0 + 1.0
```

will perform this transformation.

Stage3. This stage must *decide* and *report* Aldous' reaction to the current object. The first of these two tasks is the easier one. Recall that if there is a tie between any two of the emotional strengths (now stored in ReactLevels) then Aldous will show some form and degree of *conflict*; but if there are no ties his behavior will reflect the strongest of the three emotions. The four IF..THEN statements at the beginning of the following procedure set an index P1 to 4 if there is conflict, and to 1, 2, or 3 if Aldous is to show *love*, *anger*, or *fear*, respectively. The strength of the behavior has already been calculated, of course; it is the real number between 1.0 and 11.0 in the appropriate cell of REACTLEVELS that was calculated back in STAGE2.

```
PROCEDURE STAGE3;
(***** Determines KIND and LEVEL of Aldous's reaction *****)

VAR      a,p1,p2: integer;          (* pointers to KIND and *)
                                    (* LEVEL of action *)

begin
p1:= 0;
if (ReactLevels[1]=ReactLevels[2]) or
       (ReactLevels[1]=ReactLevels[3]) or
       (ReactLevels[2]=ReactLevels[3]) then p1:= 4;
if (ReactLevels[1]>ReactLevels[2]) and
       (ReactLevels[1]>ReactLevels[3]) then p1:= 1;
if (ReactLevels[2]>ReactLevels[1]) and
       (ReactLevels[2]>ReactLevels[3]) then p1:= 2;
if (ReactLevels[3]>ReactLevels[1]) and
       (ReactLevels[3]>ReactLevels[2]) then p1:= 3;
writeln('level and kind of response made -- ');
```

```
if p1<>4 then
        begin
          p2:= trunc(ReactLevels[p1]);
          if p2<1 then p2:= 1;
          if p2>10 then p2:= 10;
          writeln(level[p2],kind[p1]);
        end

else    begin
          p2:= 0;
          for a:= 1 to 3 do
            if ReactLevels[a]>p2 then
            p2:= trunc(ReactLevels[a]);
          if p2<1 then p2:= 1;
          if p2>10 then p2:= 10;
          writeln(level[p2], kind[p1])
        end

end;    (* end of STAGE3 *)
```

.

.

Having isolated both type and degree of overt reaction, we must now work out some way of reporting it. The method chosen here uses two string vectors, KIND and LEVEL, which, as shown in Figure D–1, are loaded with words signifying that Aldous' reactive behavior is characterized by *affection, anger, fear,* or *confusion,* and the levels graduate in steps of two or three from *low* to *crazy.* (The string contents of these vectors can be loaded from a disk file when program execution begins; see the procedure LDMEM in the listing on p. 336.) We now see that the index value P1, calculated above and ranging between 1 and 4, can be used as a subscript to print KIND[P1] showing the type of behavior Aldous will display. But it is necessary also to calculate another index P2, which will range between 1 and 10 and be used to print the degree of emotion shown—for example, LEVEL[P2]. This calculation and the output are accomplished by the IF..THEN..ELSE statement that ends STAGE3.

Stage4. In this final stage, the user is requested to input to the program the type (satisfaction, aggression, injury, designated by the integers 1, 2, and 3, respectively) and power (low, medium, high, also designated by 1, 2, or 3, respectively) of response to Aldous' behavior. These type and power levels constitute feedback from the outside world, and they are used to *increment* or *decrement,* as appropriate, the strength levels stored in the LUV, ANGER, and FEAR arrays. The following procedure accomplishes these objectives:

```
PROCEDURE STAGE4;
(***** Gets TYPE and POWER of feedback, increments and
    decrements appropriate LUV, ANGER, FEAR cells *****)

VAR      typo: integer;
         power: real;

(* FEEDBACK is a procedure within stage4 *)

procedure FEEDBACK (var x: box);
var      a, b, c: integer;
         sign: real;

begin
sign:= 0. 0;
if power<0 then sign:= -1. 0;
for a:= 1 to 2 do
  for b:= 1 to 2 do
    for c:= 1 to 2 do
      x[cells[1, a], cells[2, b], cells[3, c]]:=
      x[cells[1, a], cells[2, b], cells[3, c]] + power *
      abs((1. 0 + sign) - x[cells[1, a], cells[2, b], cells
         [3, c]])
end;              (* end of feedback *)


begin
writeln('Give type [1, 2, 3] and power [1, 2, 3]
         of feedback');
readln(typo, power);
         (* make power = .2, .3, or .4 *)
power:= (power + 1) * 0. 1;
case typo of
1: begin
        feedback(luv);
        power:= power * (-1. 0);
        feedback(anger);
        feedback(fear)
   end;
2: begin
        feedback(anger);
        power:= power * (-1. 0);
        feedback(luv);
        feedback(fear)
   end;
```

```
3: begin
        feedback(fear);
        power:= power * (-1.0);
        feedback(luv);
        feedback(anger)
    end
end       (* end of case statement *)
end;      (* end of stage4 *)
```

.

.

In studying the STAGE4 procedure, note first that another procedure—named FEEDBACK—is embedded within it. This nested procedure is designed to take care of the second major task of this stage; namely, incrementing and decrementing the emotion arrays.

Before examining FEEDBACK, we should look at the sequence of statements that (1) prompts the user, (2) reads values for the two variables TYPO and POWER, and then (3) sends the appropriate arrays to FEEDBACK for incrementing or decrementing. Although both TYPO and POWER are entered as integers ranging between 1 and 3, it is necessary to convert POWER to a decimal value that may range between 0.00 and 1.00, and which in this example is made to range between 0.2 and 0.4. The CASE statement that follows this conversion contains three alternatives that are designed to make the following kinds of adjustments to the strength values stored in the emotion arrays:

When TYPO is:	then INCREMENT	and DECREMENT
1	LUV	ANGER, FEAR
2	ANGER	LUV, FEAR
3	FEAR	LUV, ANGER

These possibilities reflect an aspect of the psychological theory upon which the program is based; namely, that the type of feedback Aldous receives will increment the strength of a corresponding emotion, and at the same time weaken to some degree the other emotional tendencies, toward the current object. Thus the CASE statement uses TYPO to signal which increment-decrement pattern should be made and sends each of the three arrays off to the procedure FEEDBACK for appropriate change. The signal indicating whether to increment or decrement is the sign of POWER, where positive means increment and negative means decrement.

The remaining problem is to devise a technique for incrementing and decrementing appropriate cells of the emotion arrays. It is clear that the technique must not raise any strength above 1.00 or lower it below 0.00, so the equations for incrementing and decrementing must yield asymptotic curves. A good first approximation meeting these requirements is shown in Figure D–3. Psychologists will quickly recognize the negatively accelerated learning and forgetting curves so often obtained in studies of human learning. Because Aldous is really going through an emotional learning stage, these curves seem quite appropriate as starters, although it is possible that empirical research could yield data suggesting alternative shapes. So, using the incremental equation from Figure D–3 and translating it into a Pascal statement designed to increment the LUV emotion for the 312 object from previous examples, we get

$$LUV[3,1,2] := LUV[3,1,2] + POWER * (1.0 - LUV[3,1,2])$$

which would increment the contents of LUV[3,1,2] by an amount that is weighted by the POWER of the feedback received, and also gets smaller and smaller as the value of the cell approaches 1.0.

Taken by itself, this equation is easy enough to program. However, remember that in addition to the object itself all of its associated generalizations must also be incremented—making a total of seven equations. Moreover, according to the rules of the model, both ANGER[3,1,2] and

FIGURE D–3. Curves and functions for incrementing and decrementing emotional reactivity level (ERL), where P = power level between 0.01 and 0.99.

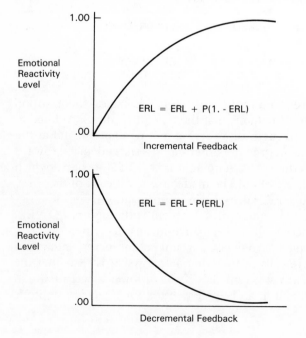

FEAR[3,1,2], and all of their associates, must be decremented. This latter task requires another 14 equations of the form

```
FEAR[3,1,2] := FEAR[3,1,2] - POWER * FEAR[3,1,2]
```

It would be worthwhile to find a way to reduce this sizable number of required equations if possible. The procedure FEEDBACK is designed for this purpose.

In analyzing this procedure, note first that X must be a *variable* parameter because we want any changes made in any of the 3-dimensional emotion arrays to be permanent—that is, to be changed at the global level rather than just within the procedure. Note also that a single statement accounts for both the incrementing and decrementing equations shown above and in Figure D–3. This is accomplished by a simple algebraic trick that can be readily understood using the variable names in Figure D–3. Examine the following equation

```
ERL = ERL + P * abs((1 + Z) - ERL)
```

where if P is positive then $Z=0$ but if P is negative then $Z=-1$, and *abs* yields an absolute result. Convince yourself that a positive P will make this equation yield results identical to the incremental equation, whereas a negative P will yield the result for the decremental equation. FEEDBACK uses a Pascal counterpart of this equation, along with the sign changes in the POWER variable back in the CASE statement, to either increment or decrement cells in an array, depending upon whether POWER is positive or negative. The subscripts for the cells use the array CELLS in the same manner it was used back in the STAGE1 procedure.

Program Listing

The procedures that have been described above in some detail may be inserted into the main program listed below to form a program that, when executed, will simulate a series of encounters by Aldous with various person-objects that are defined by the user. In this version, the beginning strength levels of LUV, ANGER, and FEAR are arbitrarily set at the beginning of execution to 0.2, 0.3, 0.4, respectively, thus weighting the initial model toward a mild fear disposition. Before terminating, the program prints the newly learned values of the LUV array to show how the original strengths have been changed by experience. Obviously the program could be elaborated to print changes and internal states of the other data structures as well. Moreover, this version uses a data file ALDO that contains the appropriate words to be loaded into the cells of the output vectors KIND and LEVEL, respectively, as shown in Figure D–1. The procedure LDMEM transfers the words from the disk file to the vectors.

```
                (* Loehlin's ALDOUS *)

PROGRAM ALDOUS (input,output,aldo);

TYPE    box = array [1..5,1..4,1..3] of real;
        string = packed array[1..6] of char;

VAR     i,j,k,index,m,famil: integer;
        again: char;
        fam: array[1..5,1..4,1..3] of integer;
        luv,anger,fear: box;
        weights: array [1..7] of real;
        cells: array [1..3,1..2] of integer;
        ReactLevels: array [1..3] of real;
        kind: array [1..4] of string;
        level: array [1..10] of string;
        spell: string;
        aldo: text;

PROCEDURE LDMEM(var mem: text);
(* Loads ALDO data file from disk into KIND, LEVEL *)

var     ch: char;
        len: 0..6;
        a: integer;

begin
reset(mem);
for a:= 1 to 14 do
  begin
  if not eof(mem) then
    repeat read(mem,ch)
    until ((ch>='A') and (ch<='Z')) or eof(mem);
  if not eof(mem) then
    begin
    len:= 0;
        repeat
          begin
          len:= len + 1; spell[len]:= ch; read(mem,ch)
          end;
        until (ch<'A') or (ch>'Z') or (len=7);
    for len:= len + 1 to 6 do spell[len]:= ' ';
    end;
  if a<=4 then kind[a]:= spell
    else level[a-4]:= spell
end
end;      (* end of ldmem *)
```

```
      .
      .
(**** Insert STAGE1 - STAGE4 procedures here ****)
      .
      .


(******** BEGIN STATEMENT PART OF MAIN PROGRAM ********)

begin
writeln('enter 7 weights, all on 1 line, spaces between');
for i:= 1 to 7 do
  read(weights[i]);
writeln('enter a familiarity factor');
readln(famil);
ldmem(aldo);

(* Set up emotional arrays with initial values *)

for i:= 1 to 5 do
  for j:= 1 to 4 do
    for k:= 1 to 3 do
      begin
        luv[i,j,k]:= 0.2;
        anger[i,j,k]:= 0.3;
        fear[i,j,k]:= 0.4
      end;

again:= 'y';

                    (* Start main REPEAT loop here *)

repeat
  writeln('enter ijk values signifying person meeting
          Aldous');
  readln(i,j,k);
  stage1;
  stage2(luv,1);
  stage2(anger,2);
  stage2(fear,3);
  writeln('emotional levels for luv, anger, fear = ');
  writeln(ReactLevels[1]:6:2,ReactLevels
          [2]:6:2,ReactLevels[3]:6:2);
  stage3;
  stage4;
  writeln('continue? [y/n]');
  readln(again)
until again='n';
```

```
         (* Print current contents of LUV *)

writeln('display of luv at end of run');
for k:= 1 to 3 do
  for i:= 1 to 5 do
writeln(luv[i,1,k]:6:2, luv[i,2,k]:6:2, luv[i,3,k]:6:2,
        luv [i,4,k]:6:2)
end.
```

Appendix E

Important LISP Functions

The following list identifies some of the built-in LISP functions commonly used in LISP programming. Some have been described in the text and will be referenced by page numbers. Others were not included in the text, but are useful enough to the LISP programmer that they are presented here. More complete lists can be found in more advanced and/or specialized LISP texts (see Charniak, Riesbeck, & McDermott, 1980; Winston & Horn, 1981; Wilensky, 1984).

For any given function described below, the function name is given in capital letters, followed by an indication of the kinds of arguments it will require or accept. Argument types have a dash at the beginning and end of the word describing them for example:

```
-atom-      indicates an atom is required as an argument
-number-    indicates a numeric argument
-list-      indicates that the argument must be a list
-exp-       indicates that any type of expression can
            be used
```

```
************************************
```

(ABS -number-)   returns absolute value of -number-.

(ADD1 -number-)   returns -number- + 1. (p. 244)

(AND -exps-)   returns the last -exp- if all -exps- evaluate to a non-nil value; otherwise returns nil. (p. 206)

(APPEND -lists-)   returns a single list formed by joining all of the -lists- together. (p. 208)

(ASSOC -exp- -alist-)   requires an -alist- (association list) that looks like this: ((JOE 15)(HARRY 12)(SUZY 13) ...). ASSOC looks successively at each associative pair in such a list, and returns the first pair whose first element is the same as -exp-.

(ATOM -exp-)   returns *T* if -exp- is a number or character or string of characters; otherwise nil. (p. 202)

(CAR -list-)   returns first element of -list-. (p. 193)

(CDR -list-)   returns all of -list- except the first element. (p. 193)

(C _____ R -list-)   a short notation for finding composite CARs and CDRs of a list. Depending upon the LISP interpreter being used, a number of combinations of A and D can be inserted in C _____ R. (p. 199–201)

(COND -(p1 e1)- -(p2 e2)- ...-(pn en)-)   an if-then function. For each -(p e)-, if *p* evaluates to non-nil then the value of *e* is returned as the value of COND; but if *p* returns nil then the next -(p e)- clause is tried. (p. 203–206)

(CONS -exp- -list-)   a list-construction function. Returns a list consisting of the original -list- argument with the -exp- argument inserted as its CAR. (p. 195)

(DEFUN -atom- (-args-) -exps-)   defines a user-built function. (p. 199)

(DIFFERENCE -numbers-)   returns the difference between the first -number- and the sum of the rest of the -numbers- used as arguments. (p. 186)

(EQ -exp1- -exp2-)   returns *T* if the two arguments are stored at the same place in memory; otherwise nil.

(EQUAL -exp1- -exp2-)   returns *T* if the two arguments are equal in form (they need not be stored in the same memory location); otherwise nil. (p. 202)

(EVAL -exp-)   evaluates -exp- and returns the result of the evaluation. EVAL is basic to the operation of LISP, being used to evaluate any expression. An example; (EVAL '(CONS 'a '(b))) --> (a b)

(EXPLODE -list-)   returns a list of the characters in -list-. For example; (EXPLODE '(hello)) --> (h e l l o)

(GET -atom1- -atom2-)   used to get values from a property list. -atom1- is the name of the object word and -atom2- is the property name. If property -atom2- is found, GET returns its value; otherwise it returns nil. (p. 258)

(GO -atom-)   branches program control to the statement following -atom-. Can be used only in a PROG function. (p. 223)

(GREATERP -number1- -number2-)   returns *T* if -number1- is larger than -number2-; otherwise nil. (p. 203)

(LENGTH -list-)   returns the number of elements in -list-. For example; (LENGTH '((a b) c (d e f))) --> 3

(LESSP -number1- -number2-)   returns *T* if -number1- is less than -number2-; otherwise nil. (p. 203)

(LIST -exps-)   returns a list of the -exps-. For example; (LIST 'a '(b c) 'd) --> (a (b c) d). (p. 259–260)

(MAPCAR -function- -list-)   applies -function- to each succeeding CAR of -list-, returning a list of the results. For example; (MAPCAR ADD1 '(2 3 4 5)) --> (3 4 5 6)

(MEMBER -exp- -list-)   returns *T* if -exp- is a member of -list-, otherwise nil. (p. 212)

(MINUS -number-)   returns the negative of -number-.

(NOT -exp-)   returns *T* if the value of -exp- is nil; otherwise returns nil. (p. 206)

(NULL -exp-)   same as NOT. Returns *T* if -exp- evaluates to nil; otherwise returns nil. (p. 202)

(NUMBERP -exp-)   returns *T* if -exp- is a number; otherwise nil. (p. 203)

(OR -exp1- -exp2- ... -expn-)   evaluates each argument in turn from left to right; if any one argument evaluates to non-nil, OR returns *T*; otherwise, OR returns nil.

(PLUS -numbers-)   adds all of the -numbers- listed as arguments and returns their sum. (p. 185)

(PRINC "-exp-")   prints -exp- without the delimiters (for example, quotation marks). (p. 226, 240)

(PRINT -exp-)   starts a new line, prints and returns -exp-. (p. 217–218)

(PROG2 -exps-)   may take two to five -exps- as arguments, depending upon the system being used. Evaluates the -exps- and returns the value of the second one. (p. 217–219)

(PUTPROP -atom1- -exp- -atom2-)   establishes a property list under the object word -atom1-. The property -atom2- is given the value -exp-. (p. 257)

(QUOTIENT -number1- -number2-)   returns the integer part of the result when -number1- is divided by -number2-. (p. 186)

(READ)   reads an expression (number, atom, list) from the keyboard. (p. 264, 280)

(READCH)   reads one character.

(REMAINDER -number1- -number2-)   returns the remainder part of the result when -number1- is divided by -number2-. (p. 286)

(REMPROP -atom1- -atom2-)   removes the property -atom2- and its value from the property list of the object word -atom1-. (p. 258)

(RETURN -exp-)   stops the evaluation of a PROG and returns the value of -exp-. (p. 223–224)

(REVERSE -list-)   returns a list in which the elements of -list- appear in reverse order.

(RPLACA -list- -exp-)   replaces the CAR of -list- with -exp- and returns the new -list-. For example, (RPLACA '((a b) c d e) 'x) --> (x c d e)

(RPLACD -list- -exp-)   replaces the CDR of -list- with -exp- and returns the new list. For example, (REPLACD '(a b) 'x) --> (a x)

(SET -atom- -exp-)   binds the value of -exp- to -atom-. For example, (SET 'r 'hello) gives r the value 'hello.

(SETQ -atom- -exp-)   binds the value of -exp- to -atom-, as in SET, but it is not necessary to quote the -atom-. (p. 189)

(SUB1 -number-)   returns -number- minus 1. (p. 216)

(TERPRI)   starts a new line. (p. 240)

(TIMES -number1- -number2- ... -numbern-)   returns the product of all of the numbers given as arguments. (p. 186)

(ZEROP -number-)   returns *T* if -number- is zero, otherwise nil. (p. 203)

References

Allen, J.R. (1978). *Anatomy of LISP*. New York: McGraw-Hill.

Angle, H.V. (1981). The interviewing computer: A technology for gathering comprehensive treatment information. *Behavior Research Methods and Instrumentation, 13,* 607–612.

Anderson, J. R. (1976). *Language memory, and thought.* Hillsdale, NJ: Erlbaum.

Anderson, J.R. (1983). *The architecture of cognition.* Cambridge, MA: Harvard University Press.

Anderson, J.R., (1985). *Cognitive psychology and its implications* (2nd ed.). San Francisco: W.H. Freeman & Company Publishers.

Anderson, J.R., & Bower, G.H. (1973). *Human associative memory.* New York: John Wiley.

Apter, M.J., & Westby, G. (Eds.) (1973). *The computer in psychology.* New York: John Wiley.

Atkinson, R.C., Bower, G.H., & Crothers, E.J. (1965). *Introduction to mathematical learning theory.* New York: John Wiley.

Atkinson, R.C., & Shiffrin, R.M. (1968). Human memory: A proposed system and its control processes. In K.W. Spence & J.T. Spence (Eds.), *The psychology of learning and motivation* (Vol. 2). New York: Academic Press.

Baddeley, A.D. (1976). *The psychology of memory.* New York: Basic Books.

Baddeley, A.D. (1978). The trouble with levels: A reexamination of Craik and Lockhart's framework for memory research. *Psychological Review, 85,* 139–152.

Barron, D.W. (1968). *Recursive techniques in programming.* London: Macdonald.

Bellack, A.S., & Hersen, M. (1980). *Introduction to clinical psychology.* New York: Oxford University Press.

Bird, R.J. (1981). *The computer in experimental psychology.* New York: Academic Press.

Bolles, K.L. (1977). *Problem solving using Pascal.* New York: Springer-Verlag.

Bourne, L.E., Dominowski, R.L., Loftus, E.F., & Healy, A.F. (1986). *Cognitive processes* (2nd ed.). Englewood Cliffs, NJ: Prentice-Hall.

Bower, G.H., & Hilgard, E.R. (1981). *Theories of learning* (5th ed.). Englewood Cliffs, NJ: Prentice-Hall.

Bremser, R.F., & Davidson, R.S. (1978). Microprocessor-assisted assessment in the clinical research laboratory. *Behavior Research Methods and Instrumentation, 10,* 582–584.

Bruner, J.S., Goodnow, J., & Austin, G. (1956). *A study of thinking.* New York: John Wiley.

Carbonell, J.G. (1981). POLITICS: An experiment in subjective understanding and integrated reasoning. In R.C. Schank & C.K. Riesbeck (Eds.), *Inside computer understanding: Five programs plus miniatures.* Hillsdale, NJ: Erlbaum.

Charniak, E., Riesbeck, C.K., & McDermott, D.V. (1980). *Artificial intelligence programming.* Hillsdale, NJ: Erlbaum.

Clippinger, J. (1977). *Meaning and discourse: A computer model of psychoanalytic speech and cognition.* Baltimore, MD: Johns Hopkins.

Colby, K.M. (1981). Modeling a paranoid mind. *The Behavioral and Brain Sciences, 4,* 515–560.

Colby, K.M., Weber, S., & Hilf, F.D. (1971). Artificial paranoia. *Artificial Intelligence, 2,* 1–25.

Colby, K.M., Hilf, F.D., Weber, S., & Kraemer, H.C. (1972). Turing-like indistinguishability tests for the validation of a computer simulation of paranoid processes. *Artificial Intelligence, 3,* 199–221.

Colby, K.M., & Hilf, F.D. (1974). Multidimensional evaluation of a simulation of paranoid thought processes. In L.W. Gregg (Ed.), *Knowledge and cognition* (pp. 287–293). Hillsdale, NJ: Erlbaum.

Coran, S., Porac, C., & Ward, L.M. (1984). *Sensation and perception (2nd ed.)* New York: Academic.

Cooper, D., & Clancy, M. (1982). *Oh! Pascal!* New York: Norton.

Craik, F.I.M., & Lockhart, R.S. (1972). Levels of processing: A framework for memory research. *Journal of Verbal Learning and Verbal Behavior, 11,* 671–684.

Cranton, P.A. (1976). Computer models for personality: Implications for measurement. *Journal of Personality Assessment, 40,* 454–463.

Dennett, D.C. (1978). *Brainstorms: Philosophical essays on mind and psychology.* Montgomery, VT: Bradford.

Dreyfus, H.L. (1972). *What computers can't do: A critique of artificial reason.* New York: Harper & Row.

Elwood, D.L. (1969). Automation of psychological testing. *American Psychologist, 24,* 287–289.

Feigenbaum, E.A. (1963). The simulation of verbal learning behavior. In E.A. Feigenbaum & J. Feldman (Eds.), *Computers and thought.* New York: McGraw-Hill.

Feigenbaum, E.A., & Simon, H.A. (1984). EPAM-like models of recognition and learning. *Cognitive Science, 8,* 305–336.

Frijda, N.H. (1972). Simulation of human memory. *Psychological Bulletin, 77,* 1–31.

Gardner, M. (1978). *Aha! Insight.* San Francisco: W.H. Freeman & Company Publishers.

Glanzer, M., & Cunitz, A.R. (1966). Two storage mechanisms in free recall. *Journal of Verbal Learning and Verbal Behavior, 5,* 351–360.

Golden, C.J. (1979). *Clinical interpretation of objective psychological tests.* New York: Grune & Stratton.

Greeno, J.G. (1973). The structure of memory and the process of solving problems. In R.L. Solso (Ed.), *Contemporary issues in cognitive psychology: The Loyola symposium.* Washington, DC: Winston.

Halliday, M.A.K. (1967). Notes on transivity and theme in English. *Journal of Linguistics, 3,* 37–81 (and 1968, *4,* 179–215).

Halliday, M.A.K. (1970). Functional diversity in languages seen from a consideration of modality and mood in English. *Foundations of Language, 6,* 322–361.

Hathaway, S.R., & McKinley, J.C. (1967). *Minnesota Multiphasic Personality Inventory: Manual.* New York: Psychological Corporation.

Haugeland, J. (Ed.) (1981). *Mind design: Philosophy, psychology, artificial intelligence.* Cambridge, MA: MIT Press.

Hayes, J.R. (1981). *The complete problem solver.* Philadelphia, PA: Franklin Institute.

Hintzman, D.L. (1968). Explorations with a discrimination net model for paired-associate learning. *Journal of Mathematical Psychology, 5,* 123–162.

Hunt, E.B., Marin, J., & Stone, P.J. (1966). *Experiments in induction.* New York: Academic Press.

Johnson, J.H., & Williams, T.A. (1975). The use of on-line computer technology in a mental health admitting system. *American Psychologist, 30,* 388–390.

Kinney, G.C., Marsetta, M., & Showman, D.J. (1966). *Studies in display symbol legibility, part XII. The legibility of alphanumeric symbols for digitalized television.* Bedford, MA. The Mitre Corporation, ESD–TR–66–117.

Kintsch, W. (1974). *The representation of meaning in memory.* Hillsdale, NJ: Earlbaum.

Kleinmuntz, B. (1963). MMPI decision rules for the identification of college maladjustment: A digital computer approach. *Psychological Monographs, 77* (Whole No. 577).

Kleinmuntz, B. (1969). *Clinical information processing by computer: An essay and selected readings.* New York: Holt, Rinehart & Winston.

Kleinmuntz, B. (1975). The computer as clinician. *American Psychologist, 30,* 379–387.

Knuth, D.E. (1973). *The art of computer programming: Vol. 1 fundamental algorithms* (2d ed.). Reading, MA: Addison-Wesley.

Kuhn, T.S. (1970). *The structure of scientific revolutions (2nd. ed.)* Chicago: University of Chicago Press.

Lachman, R., Lachman, J.L., & Butterfield, E.C. (1979). *Cognitive psychology and information processing: An introduction.* Hillsdale, NJ: Erlbaum.

Lehman, R.S. (1977). *Computer simulation and modeling: An introduction.* Hillsdale, NJ: Erlbaum.

Lindsay, P.H., & Norman, D.A. (1977). *Human information processing: An introducation to psychology* (2nd ed.). New York: Academic Press.

Loehlin, J.C. (1968). *Computer models of personality.* New York: Random House.

Marx, M.H. Formal theories. In M.H. Marx & F.S. Goodson (Eds.) *Theories in contemporary psychology (2nd ed.).* NY: Macmillan.

Mayer, R.E. (1983). *Thinking, problem solving, cognition.* San Francisco: W.H. Freeman & Company Publishers.

McCorduck, P. (1979). *Machines who think.* San Francisco: W.H. Freeman & Company Publishers.

Medin, D.L., & Smith, E.E. (1984). Concepts and concept formation. *Annual Review of Psychology, 35,* 113–138.

Mezzich, J.E., Dow, J.T., & Coffman, G.A. (1981). Developing an efficient clinical information system for a psychiatric institute: I. Principles, design, and organization. *Behavior Research Methods and Instrumentation, 13,* 454–458.

Miller, G.A. (1956). The magical number seven plus or minus two: Some limits on our capacity for processing information. *Psychological Review, 63,* 81–97.

Miller, G.A., Galanter, E., & Pribram, K.H. (1960). *Plans and the structure of behavior.* New York: Holt, Rinehart and Winston.

Minsky, M.L. (1967). *Computation: finite and infinite machines.* Englewood Cliffs, NJ: Prentice-Hall.

Neisser, U. (1967). *Cognitive psychology.* New York: Appleton–Century–Crofts.

Newell, A., & Simon, H.A. (1972). *Human problem solving.* Englewood Cliffs, NJ: Prentice-Hall.

Norman, D.A. (Ed.). (1970). *Models of human memory.* New York: Academic Press.

Norman, D.A. (Ed.). (1981). *Perspectives on cognitive science.* Hillsdale, NJ: Erlbaum.

Peterson, L.R., & Peterson, M.J. (1959). Short-term retention of individual verbal items. *Journal of Experimental Psychology, 58,* 193–198.

Reilly, K.D., Freese, M.R., & Rowe, P. B., Jr. (1984). Computer simulation modeling of abnormal behavior: A program approach. *Behavioral Science, 29,* 186–211.

Reitman, W.R. (1965). *Cognition and thought: An information processing approach.* New York: John Wiley.

Reynolds, A.G., & Flagg, P.W. (1983). *Cognitive psychology* (2d ed.). Boston, MA: Little, Brown.

Rich, E. (1983). *Artificial intelligence.* New York: McGraw-Hill.

Ringle, M. (Ed.) (1979). *Philosophical perspectives in artificial intelligence.* Atlantic Highlands, NJ: Humanities Press.

Rogers, C.R. (1951). *Client-centered therapy: Its current practice, implications, and theory.* Boston, MA: Houghton Mifflin.

Rumelhart, D.E., & Norman, D.A. (1975). The computer implementation. In D.A. Norman, D.E. Rumelhart, & the LNR Research Group, *Explorations in cognition* (pp. 159-178). San Francisco: W.H. Freeman & Company, Publishers.

Scandura, J.M. (1977). *Problem solving: A structural/process approach with instructional implications.* New York: Academic Press.

Schank, R.C. (1972). Conceptual dependency: A theory of natural language understanding. *Cognitive Psychology, 3,* 552–631.

Schank, R.C. (1975). *Conceptual information processing.* Amsterdam: North Holland.

Schank, R.C., & Abelson, R.P. (1977). *Scripts, plans, goals, and understanding.* Hillsdale, NJ: Erlbaum.

Schank, R.C., & Riesbeck, C.K. (1981). *Inside computer understanding: Five programs plus miniatures.* Hillsdale, NJ: Erlbaum.

Selfridge, O., & Neisser, U. (1971, August). Pattern recognition by machine. *Scientific American, 203,* 69–80.

Sidowski, J.B., Johnson, J.H., & Williams, T.A. (Eds.) (1980). *Technology in mental health care delivery systems.* Norwood, NJ: Ablex.

Simon, H.A. (1974). How big is a chunk? *Science, 183,* 482–488.

Smith, E.E., & Medin, D.L. (1981). *Categories and concepts.* Cambridge, MA: Harvard University Press.

Solso, R.L. (1979). *Cognitive psychology.* New York: Harcourt Brace Jovanovich.

Space, L.G. (1981). The computer as psychometrician. *Behavior Research Methods and Instrumentation, 13,* 595–606.

Stout, R.L. (1981). New approaches to the design of computerized interviewing and testing systems. *Behavior Research Methods and Instrumentation, 13,* 436–442.

Tenenbaum, A.M., & Augenstein, M.J. (1981). *Data structures using Pascal.* Englewood Cliffs, NJ: Prentice-Hall.

Tomkins, S.S., & Messick, S. (Eds.). (1963). *Computer simulation of personality.* New York: John Wiley.

Touretsky, D.S. (1984). *LISP: A gentle introduction to symbolic computation.* New York: Harper & Row.

Tulving, E. (1972). Episodic and semantic memory. In E. Tulving & W. Donaldson (Eds.), *Organization of memory.* New York: Academic Press.

Tulving, E. (1985). How many memory systems are there? *American Psychologist, 40,* 385–398.

Turing, A.M. (1950). Computing machinery and intelligence. *Mind, 59,* 433–460.

Van Tassel, D. (1978). *Program style, design, efficiency, debugging, and testing* (2d ed.). Englewood Cliffs, NJ: Prentice-Hall.

Waugh, N.C., & Norman, D.A. (1965). Primary memory. *Psychological Review, 72,* 89–104.

Weiss, B. (Ed.) (1973). *Digital computers in the behavioral laboratory.* New York: Appleton–Century–Crofts.

Weizenbaum, J. (1966). ELIZA—A computer program for the study of natural language communication between man and machine. *Communications of the ACM, 9,* 36–45.

Weizenbaum, J. (1976). *Computer power and human reason.* San Francisco: W.H. Freeman & Company Publishers.

Wickelgren, W.A. (1974). *How to solve problems: Elements of a theory of problems and problem solving.* San Francisco: W.H. Freeman & Company Publishers.

Wilensky, R. (1984). *LISPcraft.* New York: Norton.

Winograd, T. (1972a). Understanding natural language. *Cognitive Psychology, 3,* 1–91.

Winograd, T. (1972b). *Understanding natural language.* New York: Academic Press.

Winograd, T. (1983). *Language as a cognitive process. Volume 1: Syntax.* Reading, MA: Addison-Wesley.

Winston, P.H. (1984). *Artificial intelligence* (2d ed.). Reading, MA: Addison-Wesley.

Winston, P.H., & Horn, B.K.P. (1981). *LISP.* Reading, MA: Addison-Wesley.

Wirth, N. (1976). *Algorithms + data structures = programs.* Englewood Cliffs, NJ: Prentice-Hall.

Yourdon, E. (1976). *Techniques of program structure and design.* Englewood Cliffs, NJ: Prentice-Hall.

Subject Index

Author Index

DATE DUE

		DISCARDED	
GAYLORD			PRINTED IN U.S.A.